A Textbook in Classical Tibet

A Textbook in Classical Tibetan is the first comprehensive course book in the Classical Tibetan language written in English. The textbook describes the grammar of pre-16th-century Classical Tibetan works for beginners and students of intermediate level. It is intended to cover the most essential topics that can be mastered within two semesters of an academic class. Classical Tibetan is a written Middle Tibetan language that has been in use in Tibet since the 9th century. Until the early 20th century it served all purposes, from administrative, to medical, to religious. Nowadays Classical Tibetan remains an important part of religious identity and services for communities also outside of cultural Tibet, foremost in India, Nepal, and Bhutan, but also elsewhere, most importantly in Europe, North America, and Australia.

The main body of the textbook consists of an introduction to the Tibetan script, eighteen lessons, and a reading section. Each lesson elucidates several grammatical topics which are followed by an exercise and a word list. The chapter Readings contains four supplementary readings. In addition to the main parts of the textbook, a brief introduction to Tibetic languages provides linguistic context for the language taught in the textbook, whereas the chapter Translations of Exercises and Readings contains translations and explanatory notes to the exercises provided at the end of each lesson, as well as to the readings.

A Textbook in Classical Tibetan is essential reading for both undergraduate and graduate students without any knowledge of Classical Tibetan, but also for those who would like to deepen their experience of the language by reading annotated excerpts from well-known pieces of Tibetan literature.

Joanna Bialek is a research associate in the Department of Asian and African Studies, Humboldt-Universität Berlin, Germany.

A Textbook in Classical Tibetan

Joanna Bialek

Routledge
Taylor & Francis Group
LONDON AND NEW YORK

Cover image: © Mareike Wulff

First published 2022
by Routledge
2 Park Square, Milton Park, Abingdon, Oxon OX14 4RN

and by Routledge
605 Third Avenue, New York, NY 10158

Routledge is an imprint of the Taylor & Francis Group, an informa business

British Library Cataloguing-in-Publication Data
A catalogue record for this book is available from the British Library

Library of Congress Cataloging-in-Publication Data
A catalog record for this book has been requested

ISBN: 978-1-032-12357-8 (hbk)
ISBN: 978-1-032-12356-1 (pbk)
ISBN: 978-1-003-22419-8 (ebk)

DOI: 10.4324/9781003224198

Typeset in Times New Roman
by Apex CoVantage, LLC

Contents

Figures & Tables

Figures

Tables

Acknowledgements

I owe a great debt of gratitude to many people that supported (sometimes maybe even unconsciously) the composition of this textbook. Moreover, the textbook could never have been written without the engagement of generations of scholars in clarifying the intricacies of Classical Tibetan grammar. I am well aware that a great number of grammatical phenomena still await elucidation, but with the progress made in the past two decades I optimistically look forward to the research coming in the near future.

The main part of the textbook was written for classes in Classical Tibetan taught by myself in Marburg (2009–2013) and in Berlin (2017–present). I would like to express my deepest gratitude to Prof. Dr. Jürgen Hanneder (Philipps University, Marburg) and Prof. Dr. Toni Huber (Humboldt University, Berlin) for providing me with this teaching opportunity. I wish to thank my students, especially Tom Heumann and Jakub Čejka, for their commitment but also patience with topics that only over the course of the years acquired a comprehensive treatment. Their interest, sometimes expressing itself in the most unexpected questions, was often the most genuine stimulus to further research, encouraging minute investigations of the problems until a satisfactory answer has been found. Furthermore, the textbook truly benefited from numerous comments, suggestions, and corrections provided by Maximilian Mehner (Philipps University, Marburg) who in the course of his own class in Classical Tibetan tested an earlier draft of the textbook. I likewise gratefully acknowledge academic exchange over the years with Michael Balk, Mitsuyo Demoto, Nathan Hill, Toni Huber, and Johannes Schneider. Lastly, I would like to thank Mareike Wulff for graciously providing the cover photo.

Finally, I would like to thank the team at Routledge, especially Andrea Hartill, for their expert care and patience in seeing this work through the press.

Introduction

Those who know the textbook of Michael Hahn, *Lehrbuch der klassischen tibetischen Schriftsprache* (1996), will certainly notice how much the present textbook owes to the first textbook of Classical Tibetan written in a Western language. This is neither an accident nor an intended outcome, but rather the natural course of learning processes we all undergo. I learnt Classical Tibetan with Hahn's *Lehrbuch* and also prepared its translation into Polish (Hahn 2009). It was exactly the latter undertaking that forced me to look more critically at some parts of the *Lehrbuch* and compare its contents with the most recent works on Tibetic languages. At that point I had already been teaching Classical Tibetan at the Philipps University in Marburg (Germany), working in my classes partly with the *Lehrbuch* and partly with my own lecture notes. As the years passed, the latter became the germ of this textbook.

The textbook is intended for both academic classes in Classical Tibetan and for self-study. However, it is not the aim of the textbook to provide a comprehensive description of the grammar of Classical Tibetan. On the contrary, it was my deliberate decision to break with the tradition of combining a textbook for beginners with a grammar. Firstly, our understanding of the Classical Tibetan grammar is still not satisfactory enough, and many topics cannot be given comprehensive and adequate explanations. Secondly, not all topics need to be discussed at the beginner's level. The reader will therefore notice the lack of some subjects on morphology (foremost, the verb morphology) or etymology that were treated in previous textbooks.[1] Information that can be acquired from dictionaries (including detailed semantic definitions or word formation) was likewise intentionally omitted. Instead, more attention was paid to issues related to syntax and discourse, which are being discussed for the first time in a textbook. Grammatical explanations are primarily based on the five texts prepared for reading exercises: *How Sems-čan-čhen-po offered his body to a tigress* (Lessons 12–18); *Householder Dbyig-pa-čan* (Reading I); *The descent of Tibetan people from a monkey and a rock-ogress* (Reading II); *The death of Mi-la Ras-pa's father* (Reading III); and *Investigation of wise ones* (Reading IV). The readings (forming a roughly homogeneous and

DOI: 10.4324/9781003224198-1

representative collection) have supplied the basic grammatical framework of the textbook since the primary objective was to provide a textbook that would explain the grammar necessary to independently read texts at the level of those included here. Not only the level but also the time of composition of the chosen works played a role: the textbook is intended to describe the grammar of pre-16th-century classical works.

Every book is linear. In the case of a textbook this is particularly evident when a subject has to be introduced that requires other topics that might not have been covered yet. For instance, in order to explain various verb classes of Tibetan, the student should be familiar with the notion of case. At the same time, however, in order to present the grammatical category of case, some exemplary verbs have to be introduced. Since one has to start somewhere, I decided to tackle this issue in two ways. Firstly, when a topic is introduced that presupposes basic understanding of other elements, a cross-reference is given to the respective part in the textbook. Secondly, if a more complex structure is involved, I discuss it with English examples and introduce Tibetan equivalents first when the topic is fully covered.

When explaining Classical Tibetan grammar, I make use of concepts developed in Western linguistics instead of introducing native Tibetan concepts. In the latter case students would have to learn not only completely foreign grammatical terms but also confront themselves with grammatical concepts unknown in Western linguistics. To begin to learn Classical Tibetan with Tibetan concepts does not seem didactically practicable for Western students. Certainly, those interested in the indigenous grammatical tradition will have to learn the respective terms and concepts at some point, but this can be postponed until a student has competence to independently analyse works of Tibetan grammarians. Another reason for avoiding Tibetan terminology is the lack of native terms for many of the topics discussed, foremost those related to the syntax of complex clauses and discourse. Thus, not every topic covered by the textbook could have been given a native name, not to mention that the understanding of single terms (even if they seem interchangeable) in Western and Tibetan grammatical traditions usually differ considerably. Instead, the textbook introduces and makes use of modern linguistic terminology that at the beginning might seem peculiar and unfamiliar to most students. This is certainly not intended to make the learning process more difficult but, as strange as it sounds, to facilitate it – one needs a term to name the phenomenon one is talking about, otherwise no communication is possible. The terms used in the textbook are widely applied in linguistics and usually serve to describe very similar phenomena in various languages of the world. Their rudimentary definitions are supplied in the Linguistic Glossary at the end of the textbook. The advantage of using Western terminology is that the words can also be looked up either in linguistic dictionaries or on the internet.

Another feature that distinguishes this textbook from all previous general works on Classical Tibetan is that I have refrained from providing modern pronunciation for written Tibetan forms. The reasons behind this decision are explained in the chapter Tibetan Script (p. 15). However, it should be stressed that at least a rough knowledge of Standard Tibetan (a modern dialect of Central Tibet) is of great advantage when reading classical texts. The latter frequently contain orthographic errors that can be understood and corrected only with the knowledge of contemporary dialectal pronunciation. Here I would also add that there are excellent textbooks and grammars available for several modern Tibetan dialects (see References).

It is not the aim of a textbook to lead a scholarly discussion with either previous textbooks or other specialised works. Accordingly, I refrain from any comments or critical notes on parallel approaches. Likewise, references to existing literature were reduced to an absolute minimum, so as not to confound any students who just started to learn Classical Tibetan. Instead, at the end of the textbook I have provided a list of selected references on distinct grammatical topics that would be appropriate for the beginner's and intermediate level.

The textbook uses Tibetan དབུ་ཅན་ *dbu čan* script. In addition, a transliteration is introduced in the chapter Tibetan Script and is applied in the first three lessons to support the reading of the Tibetan script. For the transliteration, italic type is consequently used. In several cases modern pronunciation of single terms was provided in square brackets following the convention of the International Phonetic Alphabet (IPA). English translations of Tibetan passages are enclosed in quotation marks. Tibetan syllables enclosed in slashes indicate morphemes with changing forms. For example, /སྟེ་/ means that སྟེ་ is one of a few forms of the morpheme called gerundial (see Lesson 9).

Structure of the textbook

The main body of the textbook consists of an introduction to the Tibetan དབུ་ཅན་ *dbu čan* script (Tibetan Script chapter), eighteen lessons and a reading section (Readings I–IV). In general, the order of subjects treated in the textbook proceeds from simple units to the more complicated – and so the textbook begins with the introduction of the script and syllable structure in written Tibetan. These topics are followed by the discussion of word classes and phrases. Thereafter clauses are introduced, starting with the simplest ones and proceeding towards complex sentences that consist of several simple clauses.

In addition to the main parts of the textbook, a brief introduction to Tibetic languages provides linguistic context for the language taught in the textbook (chapter Language History). Seven appendices summarise and diagram the most important script-related and grammatical information presented in the lessons. Their main purpose is to provide a brief overview of the topics and thus in an easily accessible, graphic outline to which the student can refer, for instance, when studying the texts provided in the Readings chapter. Since many students of Classical Tibetan do not have access to academic classes but nevertheless would like to learn the language, the chapter Translations of Exercises and Readings shall support them in their efforts. It contains translations and explanatory notes to the exercises provided at the end of each lesson, as well as to the readings. For didactic reasons, all translations are made literal rather than literary. The complete Tibetan vocabulary of the textbook can be found in the Glossary, ordered according to the order of the Tibetan alphabet. The Linguistic Glossary explains technical terms that are used in the textbook. Finally, the Subject Index should help in navigating the grammatical topics discussed in the textbook.

Structure of the lessons

The lessons all have the same basic structure: each lesson elucidates several grammatical topics which are followed by an exercise and a word list. I have striven to introduce the simpler topics in the first place, with each lesson adding more complexity to the already discussed issues.

The grammatical explanations are illustrated with examples which generally come from the readings provided in the textbook. When necessary, examples have been quoted from other sources, usually other published grammars or textbooks of Classical Tibetan. For more complex examples, like phrases and clauses, the source is always provided so that the student can check their textual context. The examples are original. However, due to the specificity of the language it has been extremely difficult to collect examples of simple clauses – therefore, many of the examples have been shortened but their elements retain the original grammatical markings. The only change that had to be made was the replacement of converbal particles (see Lesson 8) by the final particle (see Lesson 3). This procedure has been applied to examples in Lessons 1–11. From Lesson 12 onward examples are quoted in original forms.

Exercises at the end of each lesson address grammatical topics discussed in the respective lesson or in any of the preceding lessons. The clauses have been excerpted from the readings. For ease of reference the examples are enumerated with Tibetan numbers. Beginning with Lesson 12, students read the story *How Sems-čan-čhen-po offered his body to a tigress*. The complete story is divided between Lessons 12 to 18, but it is quoted without any editorial changes in the text. Translations to all the exercises are provided in the chapter Translations of Exercises and Readings.

Lessons 1–11 end with word lists that include all new lexemes as they occur in the exercise of the respective lesson. The word lists do not contain vocabulary from the lessons; this has to be looked up after in the Glossary at the end of the textbook. The Glossary should also be consulted for the reading exercises of Lessons 12–18.

Reading exercises

Readings I–IV provide four further pieces of Tibetan literature that can be studied after the main course in Classical Tibetan grammar has been completed. These are (I) *Householder Dbyig-pa-čan* from the canonical collection of མཛངས་བླུན།; (II) the seventh chapter of རྒྱལ་རབས་གསལ་བའི་མེ་ལོང་། on the descent of Tibetan people from a monkey and a rock-ogress; (III) the second chapter of Mi-la Ras-pa's biography (རྣམ་ཐར།) that concerns difficulties Mi-la Ras-pa faced after the death of his father; and (IV) the first chapter of Sa-skya Paṇḍita's work ལེགས་པར་བཤད་པ་རིན་པོ་ཆེའི་གཏེར།. Whereas the first reading is an example of Indian literature translated early into Tibetan, the remaining readings represent indigenous Tibetan literature. The difficulty is that they are all examples of Buddhist literature and therefore require at least some basic knowledge of Buddhist concepts. Hence, whenever possible, a short explanation is provided for a technical term, either in a footnote to the respective passage or in the Glossary.

The texts as well as their translations (see Translations of Exercises and Readings) are richly annotated in order to facilitate the reading. The versions presented to the students are collated on the basis of the available copies, specified at the beginning of the respective text. It was my utmost wish to present a selection of texts of significant cultural value for which at least some text-critical work has already been done. The selection unfortunately ended up biased, representing only the Buddhist culture of Tibet and India. I would have gladly added at least one text of the Bon tradition, but unfortunately the textual studies in this field are not as advanced as Buddhist studies, and to the best of my knowledge not even one critically edited Bon text has been published thus far.

Because this publication is not a text-critical edition of a work, not all variant spellings have been noted. The latter have been included or discussed only in cases of utmost relevance to the interpretation of a particular passage.

The readings are arranged in order of increasing difficulty, and it is advisable that they are studied in this order. The level of the first two readings corresponds to the knowledge the student should have acquired in the course of studying the textbook. Readings III and IV are more advanced, but the experience gained from the first readings (and the notes added to the Tibetan texts and their translations) should facilitate their perusal. The story *Householder Dbyig-pa-čan*, even though not a piece of indigenous literature, has been included due to its uncomplicated language and a storyline that can be followed without difficulty even by beginners. The remaining readings are more demanding and therefore the experience the student gains by studying the stories *How Sems-čan-čhen-po offered his body to a tigress* (Lessons 12–18) and *Householder Dbyig-pa-čan* (Reading I) is of benefit for further readings.

Before reading an original Tibetan text, students are advised to consult Sommerschuh (2008) in order to learn about the internal structure of Tibetan works. Reading IV of the textbook gives a first impression on how a Tibetan work may begin. It includes the title, invocation, and introductory verses – all three elements are regularly encountered at the beginning of indigenous Tibetan Buddhist works. Another work worth consulting is Cabezón and Jackson (1996), which provides a sound overview of the genres of literary Tibetan. The detailed reference work of Schwieger (2006) should become the main resource for consulting new grammatical topics encountered during the study of further Classical Tibetan texts.

In recent years two anthologies of short Buddhist texts in Classical Tibetan have been published to support students in their study of the language. These are Bentor (2013) and Hackett (2019). With these and this textbook at hand students of Classical Tibetan are now well equipped with supplementary material that hopefully encourages study of the language.

Note

1 Apart from a brief overview of the morphology of transitive and intransitive verbs in Lesson 15, I deliberately resigned from the description of Tibetan verb morphology. Verb inflection was not productive anymore in the period of Classical Tibetan so that its elucidation would necessitate numerous references to Old Tibetan verb morphology (for the description of the latter, see Bialek 2020a).

Language history

Tibetic languages and their genetic affiliation

All historically attested Tibetan languages and dialects together form the Tibetic group of languages.[1] Tibetic languages are regarded as belonging to the Bodish subgroup within the Bodic branch of the Trans-Himalayan macrofamily. The latter is also referred to as the Sino-Tibetan or Tibeto-Burman language family.[2] Recent studies in historical linguistics reckon Tibetic and Tshangla-East Bodish languages among the members of the Bodish subgroup. Though this is a generally acknowledged position, no research has been carried out thus far to substantiate the hypothesis on the relationship of Tibetic languages to their assumed closest relatives within either the Bodic branch or the Bodish subgroup. The hypothesised genetic affiliation of Tibetic languages can be sketched as follows:

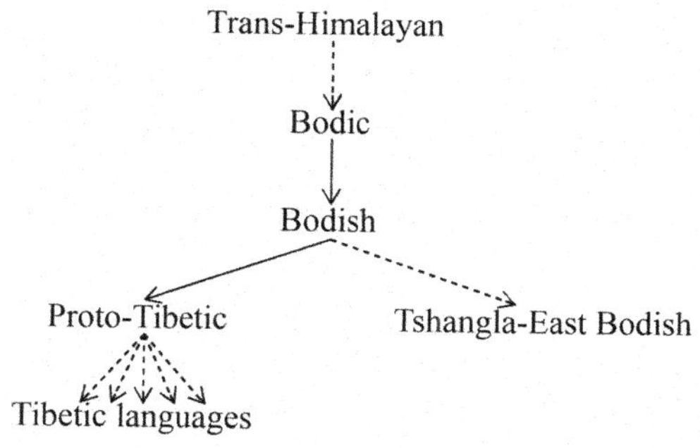

Figure II.1 Trans-Himalayan language family

Tibetic languages can be reconstructed to a common ancestor language that can be called 'Proto-Tibetic', in accordance with modern linguistic nomenclature. Proto-Tibetic is not a historically attested language and can be approached only through reconstruction based on historically attested Tibetic languages. The oldest historically attested Tibetic language is the Old Tibetan.

DOI: 10.4324/9781003224198-2

Geographic distribution of Tibetic languages

The socio-political centre of the Tibetan Empire (ca. 630s–840s) was located in the valleys of the Skyi-čhu (now: Skyid-čhu) river and its upper tributaries. In the first half of the 7th century, the Tibetan polity – already controlling regions that came to be known as Central Tibet (so-called Three Horns) – started its expansion and conquest of the neighbouring polities. Until the 660s Źaṅ-źuṅ, Sum-pa, and Ɣa-źa peoples were conquered and incorporated into the rapidly growing Tibetan Empire. Within the next two centuries Tibetan emperors – called བཙན་པོ་ *bcan po* in Old Tibetan – subdued the whole Tibetan Plateau, twice occupied Tarim Basim, and spread their military control as far as Gilgit (in present-day Pakistan).

The present-day geographic distribution of Tibetic languages and dialects results from the military expansion of the Tibetan Empire in the 7th–9th centuries.[3] Modern Tibetic languages are spoken in north-eastern Pakistan (Baltistan), northern India (Ladakh, Himachal Pradesh, Uttarakhand, Sikkim, Arunachal Pradesh), Nepal (along the whole border with China), Bhutan, Myanmar (Kachin), and China (Yunnan, Sichuan, Gansu, Qinghai).[4] However, not all communities that speak a genetically Tibetic language consider themselves Tibetans. On the other hand, there are likewise communities (located primarily on the eastern marches of the Tibetic-speaking area) that speak a non-Tibetic language but identify themselves as ethnic Tibetans. One should be aware of these facts and avoid automatically equating linguistic affiliation with ethnicity.

Characterisation of Tibetic languages

All Tibetic languages share the following linguistic features:

- SOV word order in a clause (see Lessons 2 and 5)
- Word order in an NP: Noun – Adjective – Numeral – Determiner (see Lesson 1)
- Group inflection of NPs (see Lesson 1)
- Nominal agglutination (see Lesson 1)
- Morphological ergativity (see Lesson 5)
- Postpositions (see Lesson 10)
- Palatalisation of alveolars (**tj-*, **dj-*, **nj-*, **zj-*, **sj-*) and **lj-*
- Negations *ma* and *m(y)i* (see Lesson 6)
- Numeral *bdun* "seven"

The last three features are exclusive to Tibetic languages and allow us to distinguish them from other Trans-Himalayan languages of the region.[5]

Tibetic languages in diachrony

Old Tibetan

Old Tibetan is the oldest historically attested language among Tibetic languages. Its phase started with the introduction of Tibetan script in the 630s or 640s and lasted until the rise of phonemically distinctive tones and analytical verb constructions at the beginning of the 9th century.[6] Within the period of roughly two hundred years, the language underwent several major changes and therefore can be divided into Early, Middle, and Late Old Tibetan. The changes not only allow for the subdivision of Old Tibetan, but also hint at the early dialect formation with important consequences for the outreach and distribution of modern Tibetan dialects. Namely, all modern Tibetan dialects derive from Early Old Tibetan.[7] Figure II.2 presents the *Stammbaum* of Old Tibetan and its descendants.

Two groups of modern Tibetan dialects derived directly from Old Tibetan: Western Archaic Tibetan (WAT) dialects derived from Early Old Tibetan; whereas Amdo Tibetan (AT) dialects derived from Middle Old Tibetan. Late Old Tibetan developed into Early Middle Tibetan that was characterised by phonemically distinctive tones and analytical verb constructions. Whether some modern dialects or dialect groups derived directly from Late Old Tibetan or whether all dialects (besides WAT and AT) are descendants of Early Middle Tibetan has not yet been settled.

Middle Tibetan

It is assumed that no later than at the beginning of the 9th century Middle Tibetan started with the rise of phonemically distinctive tones and the introduction of analytical verb constructions.[8] Classical Tibetan is the most renowned Middle Tibetan language. It is a standardised form of Old Literary Tibetan that assimilated some of the later developments of Middle Tibetan languages, like the analytical verb constructions and evidentiality, among others.[9] Parallel to Classical Tibetan,

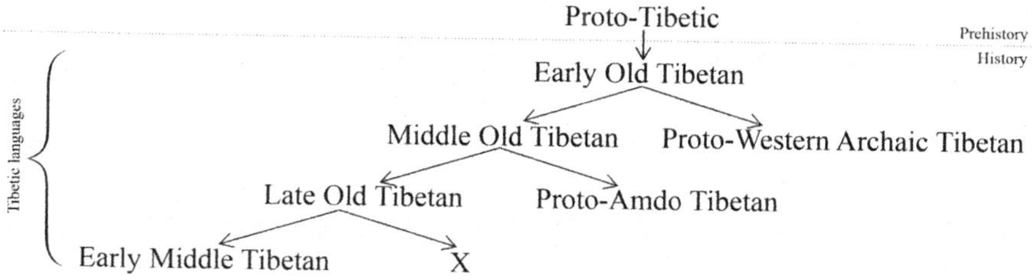

Figure II.2 Stammbaum of Tibetic languages

which is a written language, spoken varieties of Middle Tibetan thrived. The latter were either a direct outcome of Late Old Tibetan or evolved from Early Middle Tibetan.

Modern Tibetan

All modern Tibetan dialects and dialect groups go back to one or another form of Old Tibetan. As they were developing independently from each other, sometimes for over 1300 years, there are significant differences between single dialects. The vast majority of modern spoken varieties of Tibetic languages still await a thorough description, although detailed grammars of some dialects already exist. Tournadre estimates the overall number of spoken varieties to over 200 (2014: 118). Some of them can certainly be classed together as dialect groups, but we still lack consistent and reliable linguistic criteria for their subgrouping. Mutual interactions of neighbouring dialects, influences from prestigious dialects, and intense contacts with other non-Tibetic languages (especially in border areas) all constitute serious obstacles to a clear-cut subgrouping.

Side by side with spoken dialects is Modern Literary Tibetan, which can be classed as a modern continuation of Classical Tibetan but enriched by persistent influences from Standard Tibetan – an interregional *koiné* based on Central Tibetan dialects, mainly the Lhasa dialect.

Written vs spoken Tibetic languages

Throughout their history one can distinguish between spoken and written Tibetic languages. Old Literary Tibetan, Classical Tibetan, and Modern Literary Tibetan represent written Tibetic languages. Classical Tibetan is a standardised version of Old Literary Tibetan that acquired some influence from historical spoken varieties as time passed. Modern Literary Tibetan has evolved from Classical Tibetan under the strong influence of modern media, and modern culture, in general. In the past few decades attempts have been made to develop written language for other spoken varieties as well. This mainly concerns Ladakhi in India and Dzongkha in Bhutan. Accordingly, the term 'written Tibetic' encompasses all forms of written languages attested in the history of Tibetic languages.

Old Literary Tibetan orthography rather faithfully reflects the pronunciation of a historical Central Tibetan dialect at the time of the script invention. However, since written forms tend to conservatism, soon after the script invention the spoken language started diverging from the newly introduced written language; dialect formation began as early as in the 7th century. It was the spoken language that accumulated changes at the highest ratio, triggering the diversification between local varieties. Basically, from the second half of the 7th century, spoken and written languages developed parallel to each other, although the former continued to influence the latter.

Systematic documentation of spoken Tibetic languages started in the 19th century, but earlier works of Tibetan authors contain traits of contemporary dialects that give us insight into the state of a particular vernacular at a particular time in history. For instance, the biography and songs of Mi-la Ras-pa are famous for their lively language that reflects a spoken variety of 15th-century Central Tibet.

Classical Tibetan

What then do we learn when we learn 'Classical Tibetan'? Classical Tibetan is a written Middle Tibetan language that has been in use in Tibet since approximately the first half of the 9th century. Until the early 20th century it served all purposes, from administrative, to medical, to religious. With the development of Modern Literary Tibetan the scope of its application reduced primarily to the sphere of religion.

Tibetan culture exerted its influence far beyond the borders of Tibet even prior to Chinese occupation and the exile of thousands of Tibetans since the 1950s. The cultural area of Tibetan influence (termed 'Tibetosphere' by Tournadre)[10] traditionally spread as far as southern Russia (Kalmykia, Tuva, Buryatia), Mongolia, western China, northern India, Bhutan, Sikkim, Nepal, Ladakh, and, to a certain degree, northern Pakistan. Some of the regions had periods in their history of political dependence on Tibet, some adapted elements of Tibetan culture through other channels. What they share until today (apart from Pakistan) is the lasting impact of Classical Tibetan in their religious and cultural life.[11] Even if the language of everyday affairs is not Tibetan, Classical Tibetan remains an important part of religious identity or services for communities that do not belong to any of the major religions of Tibet, like Buddhism or Bon.

The most basic division one can make to structure works written in Classical Tibetan is to distinguish between indigenous Tibetan works and translational literature.

Indigenous Tibetan literature

Indigenous Tibetan literature may be very broadly defined as comprising any work, written or oral, originally composed in a Tibetic language. Written literature has played an immense role in Tibetan culture ever since the introduction of the script in the 7th century. This did not prevent the simultaneous development of oral literature, not only due to the fact that literacy was never universal in pre-modern times in Tibet but also because of the paramount significance of oral transmission of religious teachings practised in all branches of Tibetan religious traditions. However, literacy is the key to the past, and so only words that have been written down had the chance to survive through historical turbulence. This of course may provide a biased picture of the cultural heritage when judged from a modern perspective.

Whatever its external form, written or oral, since the later period of the Tibetan Empire indigenous Tibetan literature seems to have been preponderantly concerned with religious matters. Certainly secular genres did exist, including primarily administrative or personal writings, but their overall share was rather insignificant compared to the religiously inspired literature. This is understandably related to the influence religious institutions exerted on Tibetan politics.

Translational literature

The core of the literary works translated into Classical Tibetan is organised into two collections known as བཀའ་འགྱུར། *bkaɣ ɣgyur* (sometimes transcribed as Kanjur) and བསྟན་འགྱུར། *bstan ɣgyur* (sometimes transcribed as Tanjur). Each of the collections has been preserved in at least several editions and multiple copies (although sometimes only partially). When compared with each other, single editions may differ to a considerable extent in the organisation of the collections but also on the texts included. In addition, རྙིང་མའི་རྒྱུད་འབུམ། *rñiṅ maɣi rgyud ɣbum*, a collection of the Rñiṅ-ma school extant in several editions, likewise contains texts translated from Sanskrit.

The first texts were translated not later than in the 8th century before translational activity came under the aegis of the state by the end of the century. At the beginning of the 9th century rules were officially issued, stipulating the standards for all new translations and restricting the source language of the works translated to Sanskrit. Old translations were revised and brought into line with the new rules. New translations were still made as late as in the 17th and 18th centuries and added to the already existing collections.[12]

In general, the language of works translated into Classical Tibetan from Chinese or (preponderantly) Sanskrit differs from the language of works composed by Tibetans. It frequently contains lexical but also syntactic calques which are difficult to understand without a good comprehension of the source language. Many of the works were originally composed in verses, and their rendering into Classical Tibetan encountered serious problems due to the differences in metrical rules of Sanskrit and Classical Tibetan. Furthermore, the texts were translated by variably skilled persons, and some can be made intelligible only when re-translated back to Sanskrit.

Notes

1 The term 'Tibetic' has been used with differing meanings in recent studies (cf. Tournadre 2014: 105ff.). In the textbook it has collective meaning, denoting the group of *all* historically attested Tibetan languages. That is, 'Tibetic' is a more general term than 'Tibetan'. The latter is used only to refer to a concrete historical language such as Old Tibetan, Lhasa Tibetan, and Balti Tibetan.

2 The terms 'Tibeto-Burman', 'Sino-Tibetan', and 'Trans-Himalayan' are not interchangeable but represent distinct paradigmatic and methodological approaches to the genetic classification of languages presumably belonging to the family.

3 Bialek (2018b), (Forthcoming).

4 Map 7 in Ryavec (2015: 26–7) gives a good overview of the approximate distribution of modern Tibetic languages and dialects; see also Tournadre (2014: 117f.).

5 Some of the features are discussed in more detail in Tournadre (2014: 109ff.).

6 Takeuchi (2012), Bialek (2018b).

7 Bialek (2018b).

8 Takeuchi (2012), Bialek (2018b).

9 See Lesson 16.

10 Tournadre (2014: 108).

11 In Pakistan, among Balti speakers, Classical Tibetan remained in use until approximately the 16th century when the region converted to Islam.

12 Harrison (1996).

Tibetan script

History

According to the indigenous Tibetan tradition, Tibetan script was invented by Thonmi Sambhoṭa during the lifetime of the *bcan po* Khri Sroṅ-rcan (?–649).[1] Whereas the identity of the script inventor (if there was indeed only one person) remains uncertain, it is beyond doubt that the Tibetan script was invented between the 630s and 648. According to Chinese sources, in 648 Tibetans sent a mission to the Chinese court asking for ink and paper manufacturing technology. From this we can infer that by 648 Tibetans already possessed a script. The first mention of a written text (ཡི་གེ་ *yi ge*) in Tibetan sources stems from an Old Tibetan text popularly known as the *Old Tibetan Annals*. In the annual entry of the year 655/6 we read:

> བློན་ཆེ་སྟོང་རྩན་གྱྀས། འགོར་ཏྀར། བཀའ། གྲྀམས་གྱྀ་ཡི་གེ་བྲྀས། (PT 1288: 29–30)[2]
> *blon čhe stoṅ rcan gyīs/ ɣgor tīr/ bkaɣ/ grīms gyī yi ge brīs/*
> "At Ɣgor-ti grand councillor [Mgar] Stoṅ-rcan [Yul-zuṅ] wrote down the text of the sovereign laws."

After its primary invention the script underwent a few minor modifications before it reached its final form around the mid-8th century – the form that is still in use today.

The script

The Tibetan script introduced and used throughout the textbook is called དབུ་ཅན་ *dbu čan*, lit. "having the head". The "head" (དབུ་ *dbu*) referred to in the name is the upper horizontal bar characteristic of this script, which is clearly seen above most of the letters of the alphabet, cf.:

ཀ	ད	ཙ
k	*d*	*c*

DOI: 10.4324/9781003224198-3

Like all the other Tibetan scripts, དབུ་ཅན་ *dbu čan* is written from left to right. It is the script traditionally used in woodblock prints and modern printing. It should be learnt as the first Tibetan script because the remaining scripts are either based on it or can be more easily approached with the knowledge of དབུ་ཅན་ *dbu čan.*[3]

Letters versus sounds

At the time of its invention the Tibetan script was phonetic. That means one letter corresponded to one particular sound of the spoken language.[4] As a consequence, learning Tibetan script is almost synonymous with learning the phonetics of the Tibetan language of the 630s. This of course raises the question of how to pronounce the letters when reading a Classical Tibetan text. Basically two options are at hand: (1) to read the text as it is written, pronouncing each sound to which a letter is ascribed; or (2) to read the text according to the pronunciation of one of the modern Tibetan dialects. Certainly, for somebody who has just started learning Classical Tibetan and for whom Classical Tibetan is the first Tibetic language learned, the first option would be the easier one. The pronunciation of most of the modern Tibetan dialects has diverged considerably from the written forms of the words. This situation can be compared with French *l'eau* "water", which is currently pronounced as [lo], i.e. four letters represent only two sounds, or Eng. *plough* [plaʊ] – six letters for four sounds. Consequently, the level of difficulty in learning Classical Tibetan with modern pronunciation is much higher for a beginner. Another advantage of the first method is that by learning the classical language in a pronunciation distinct from modern ones, students may avoid confusing two (or more) Tibetic languages, in case they should simultaneously study, for example, Classical Tibetan and Lhasa Tibetan.[5] The problematic part of this method of reading texts is that by the period of Classical Tibetan (roughly 9th–19th century; see the chapter Language History) the pronunciation had already deviated from the original, and therefore ascribing Old Tibetan sound values to Classical Tibetan texts might seem anachronistic. However, the second option for reading Classical Tibetan texts (i.e. according to a modern pronunciation) seems even more problematic. Firstly, it is likewise anachronistic because a modern pronunciation is projected on texts written several centuries earlier. Secondly, the pronunciation is arbitrarily chosen and depends on the dialect the teacher herself knows best – usually it is one of the so-called Central Tibetan dialects (Lhasa or the Standard Tibetan), but it may well be any of the modern dialects. Thirdly, classical orthography allowed for consonant clusters that are disallowed in modern written Tibetan (e.g. the onsets སྨྲ- *smr-* or སྩ- *sc-*); thus the problem arises how to pronounce these. Lastly and most importantly, from a didactic point of view, for students who simultaneously learn Classical Tibetan and a modern Tibetan dialect this option often results in much confusion.

The most typical situation is when a Classical Tibetan word is attributed a meaning from a modern language because in the Classical Tibetan class and in the modern Tibetan class the word is pronounced in exactly the same manner.

Since the main purpose of the textbook is to present the basic grammatical notions of Classical Tibetan in a written form in order to prepare students for *reading* texts, I will restrict the explanations of the script to discussing the letters and the sound values represented by them at the time of the script invention. The most obvious consequence of this approach is the equation:

Tibetan script	= Transliteration	= Phonetic transcription (= pronunciation)
བོད་ཡིག་ "written Tibetan"	*bod yig*	[bodjig]

The textbook abstains from introducing modern pronunciation. This approach leaves it to the teacher whether she would like to teach any modern pronunciation to her students, and if so, which of the modern dialects is preferred. The textbook does not impose any dialect and so is more easily accessible to all teachers of Classical Tibetan, disregarding their skills in modern Tibetic languages.[6]

Alphabet and transliteration

The Tibetan alphabet is called ཀ་ཁ་ *ka kha* in Tibetan. The name consists of the first two letters of the alphabet: ཀ *k* and ཁ *kh*. This can be compared with the Eng. *alphabet* that was borrowed from Latin *alphabetum*, ultimately derived from Greek αλφάβητος *alphábētos* that likewise names the first two letters of the Greek alphabet: *alpha* and *bēta*.

The Classical Tibetan alphabet consists of thirty letters:[7]

ཀ	ཁ	ག	ང
ཅ	ཆ	ཇ	ཉ
ཏ	ཐ	ད	ན
པ	ཕ	བ	མ
ཙ	ཚ	ཛ	ཝ
ཞ	ཟ	འ	
ཡ	ར	ལ	
ཤ	ས	ཧ	ཨ

and four additional signs to mark vowels:

◌ི ◌ུ ◌ེ ◌ོ

As the Tibetan alphabet was based on Gupta alphabets, the arrangement of its letters follows (to some extent) the arrangement of the letters in Indian alphabets. The first four rows contain letters that at the time of the script invention represented velar, alveolo-palatal, alveolar, and labial consonants, respectively. The letters within the columns of the first four rows are arranged according to their manner of articulation. The first column contains voiceless unaspirated, the second voiceless aspirated, the third voiced, and the fourth nasal consonants of the respective group. For instance, letter ད *d* belongs to the third, alveolar row, and is the third letter in this row – that means it represented a voiced alveolar consonant. Beginning with the fifth row, the rules of the arrangement change slightly. They will be explained together with the pronunciation of the letters in the following sections.

Pronunciation of the letters

As mentioned, the letters of the Tibetan alphabet have been systematically arranged according to the original place and manner of articulation of their corresponding sounds.[8]

Latin letters written beside Tibetan letters in Table III.1 form the transliteration system used in the textbook.[9] This system has been adapted from the system used earlier by Jacques Bacot. Its methodological foundations are explained in Bialek (2020b). In the meantime, many scholars and publishing houses around the world have shifted to the so-called Wylie system, which is currently the most frequently applied transliteration system for Classical Tibetan.[10] However, due to the serious limitations of Wylie's transliteration in textual and linguistic studies, the new transliteration will be used throughout the textbook instead.

Consonants

Table III.1 provides the phonetic values (in square brackets) of the corresponding Tibetan letters, as well as the transliteration of the latter (in italics).

Table III.1 Consonantal letters

	Voiceless/ unaspirated		Voiceless/ aspirated		Voiced		Nasal	
Velar	ཀ	*k* [k]	ཁ	*kh* [k^h]	ག	*g* [g]	ང	*ṅ* [ŋ]
Alveolo-palatal	ཅ	*č* [tɕ]	ཆ	*čh* [tɕ^h]	ཇ	*ǰ* [dʑ]	ཉ	*ñ* [ɲ]
Alveolar	ཏ	*t* [t]	ཐ	*th* [t^h]	ད	*d* [d]	ན	*n* [n]

(Continued)

Table III.1 (Continued)

	Voiceless/ unaspirated		Voiceless/ aspirated		Voiced		Nasal	
Labial	པ	*p* [p]	ཕ	*ph* [p^h]	བ	*b* [b]	མ	*m* [m]
Alveolar	ཙ	*c* [ʦ]	ཚ	*ch* [ʦ^h]	ཛ	*j* [ʣ]	ཝ	*w* [w]
Fricative (voiced)	ཞ	*ź* [ʑ]	ཟ	*z* [z]	འ	*ɣ* [ɣ]		
Approximants	ཡ	*y* [j]	ར	*r* [r]	ལ	*l* [l]		
Fricative (voiceless)	ཤ	*ś* [ɕ]	ས	*s* [s]	ཧ	*h* [h]	ཨ	*q* [Ø]

The letters of the first row all represent velar consonants:

ཀ voiceless unaspirated [k], like in Eng. *scan* [skan]
ཁ voiceless aspirated [k^h], similar to ཀ but with a strong aspiration
ག voiced [g], like in Eng. *go* [gəʊ]
ང nasal [ŋ], like in Eng. *sing* [sɪŋ] or Ger. *lang* [laŋ] "long"

The letters of the second row represent alveolo-palatal consonants:

ཅ voiceless unaspirated affricate [ʨ], like in Pol. *ćma* [ʨma] "moth"
ཆ voiceless aspirated affricate [ʨ^h], similar to ཅ but with a strong aspiration
ཇ voiced affricate [ʥ], like in Pol. *dźwięk* [ʥvjɛ̃k] "sound"
ཉ nasal [ɲ], like in French *agneau* [aɲo] "lamb" or Pol. *koń* [kɔɲ] "horse"

The letters of the third row represent alveolar consonants:

ཏ voiceless unaspirated [t], like in Eng. *star* [stɑ:]
ཐ voiceless aspirated [t^h], similar to ཏ but with a strong aspiration
ད voiced [d], like in Eng. *doll* [dɒl]
ན nasal [n], like in Eng. *note* [nəʊt]

The letters of the fourth row represent labial consonants:

པ voiceless unaspirated [p], like in Eng. *spear* [spɪə]
ཕ voiceless aspirated [p^h], similar to པ but with a strong aspiration
བ voiced [b], like in Eng. *ball* [bɔ:l]
མ nasal, like in Eng. *moth* [mɒθ]

The first three letters of the fifth row follow the pattern of the preceding rows:

ཙ voiceless unaspirated alveolar affricate [ʦ], like in Eng. *tsar* [ʦaː] or Ger. *Zeit* [ʦaɪt] "time"
ཚ voiceless aspirated alveolar affricate [ʦʰ], similar to ཙ but with a strong aspiration
ཛ voiced alveolar affricate [ʣ], like in Pol. *dzwon* [ʣvɔn] "bell" or It. *zero* [ʣɛːɾo] "zero"

With the following letter the pattern is broken:

ཝ voiced labio-velar approximant [w], like in Eng. *weep* [wiːp]

The sixth row contains letters that represent voiced fricative consonants:

ཞ voiced alveolo-palatal fricative [ʑ], like in Pol. *źle* [ʑlɛ] "badly"
ཟ voiced alveolar fricative [z], like in Eng. *zero* [zɪərəʊ]
འ voiced velar fricative [ɣ], like in Sp. *amigo* [amiɣo] "friend"

The seventh row gathers together approximants and a rhotic, which are all voiced.

ཡ palatal approximant [j], like in Eng. *you* [juː]
ར alveolar trill [r], like Eng. *role* [rəʊl]
ལ alveolar lateral approximant [l], like in Eng. *late* [leɪt]

The first three letters of the last row are voiceless fricatives, with the first two being counterparts of the first two voiced fricatives of the sixth row:

ཤ voiceless alveolo-palatal fricative [ɕ], like in Pol. *śliwa* [ɕliva] "plum"
ས voiceless alveolar fricative [s], like in Eng. *sleep* [sliːp]
ཧ voiceless glottal fricative [h], like in Eng. *help* [hɛlp]

The last letter of the alphabet, ཨ, was a placeholder for a vowel in an initial position of a syllable. The letter itself did not represent any sound and so must not be pronounced when reading a text. However, the indigenous Tibetan tradition treats the letter on par with other consonantal letters.

Vowels

At the time of the script invention, Tibetan had five vowels: *a* [a], *i* [i], *u* [u], *e* [ɜ], and *o* [ɔ]. In the Tibetan script, vowels do not have separate letters ascribed to them but are represented by additional graphemes below or above the 'consonantal' letter they follow. Vowel *a* constitutes an exception because it is never marked (see the next section Syllable). This system of writing vowels was likewise overtaken from Indian scripts. Table III.2 presents the 'vowel' graphemes and their Latin transliterations. The circle is a placeholder for any 'consonantal' letter.

Table III.2 Vowel signs

◌	*a* [a]	◌ི	*i* [i]	◌ུ	*u* [u]	◌ེ	*e* [ɜ]	◌ོ	*o* [ɔ]

Graphemes representing vowels *i*, *e*, and *o* are written above the 'consonantal' letter, and that of vowel *u*, below it. Tibetan grammatical tradition devised special names for each vowel sign: *i* = གི་གུ་ *gi gu*, *u* = ཞབས་ཀྱུ་ *źabs kyu*, *e* = འགྲེང་བུ་ *ɣgreṅ bu*, *o* = ན་རོ་ *na ro*.

Syllable

དབུ་ཅན་ *dbu čan* is a syllabic script.[11] This means that the end of every syllable is clearly marked in the script. On the other hand, words are not marked in any way. One can illustrate this with the English phrase *big mountain* which would be written *big moun tain* according to Tibetan orthography. A syllable in དབུ་ཅན་ *dbu čan* is a sequence of letters ending with the grapheme called ཚེག་ *cheg*: < ་ >. This sign marks the end of a syllable and must not be omitted.[12] In the transliteration system used in the textbook, the ཚེག་ *cheg* is not ascribed any particular sign but is transliterated as a space instead.

The majority of lexical words in Classical Tibetan consist of two syllables, although a considerable group of words exist that are formed from one syllable only. In the following sections, the syllable structure of Classical Tibetan will be illustrated with one-syllable words.

Simple syllable

In དབུ་ཅན་ *dbu čan* the simplest syllable consists of a single letter, the so-called base letter.[13] Such a syllable lacks a vowel sign and therefore is to be read as containing the inherent vowel *a*:[14]

ཕ་	*pha*	"father"	མ་	*ma*	"mother"
ས་	*sa*	"earth, place"	བ་	*ba*	"cow"

Such a syllable may be extended by adding a vowel sign, above or below the base letter:

མི་	*mi*	"man, human being"	བུ་	*bu*	"child, son"
མེ་	*me*	"fire"	ལོ་	*lo*	"year"

Any letter of the alphabet can take the position of the base letter in a simple syllable. By definition, all simple syllables are open, i.e. they end with a vowel. In general, any vowel sign can be attached to any base letter.

Complex syllable

In Classical Tibetan simple syllables can be extended in several ways. The base letter can be preceded or followed by another consonantal letter or even letters.[15] In the following sections, all possible extensions of a simple syllable will be discussed and illustrated with examples.

Postscripts

Postscript is a letter written to the right of the base letter. It changes an open syllable (ending with a vowel) into a closed syllable with a consonantal final. Only ten letters may take the place of a postscript:

-ག	-ང	-ད	-ན	-བ	-མ	-འ	-ར	-ལ	-ས
-g	*-ṅ*	*-d*	*-n*	*-b*	*-m*	*-ɣ*	*-r*	*-l*	*-s*

A syllable with a postscript consists of a base letter, a postscript, and (optionally) a vowel sign:

ཁབ་	*khab*	"residence"	མིང་	*miṅ*	"name"
གུར་	*gur*	"tent"	ལེན་	*len*	"to obtain"

If a syllable has only two letters and no vowel sign, the first letter is always the base letter, and the second the postscript (see ཁབ་ earlier).

The previous examples demonstrate simple postscripts that consist of only one letter. Complex postscripts also exist in which two letters stand to the right of the base letter. Only two letters are allowed to take the position of the second postscript: -ད *-d* and -ས *-s*. They have complementary distribution attaching to the following simple postscripts:

Second postscript -ད:

-ནད -རད -ལད
-nd *-rd* *-ld*

Second postscript -ས:

-གས -ངས -བས -མས
-gs *-ṅs* *-bs* *-ms*

Second postscript -ད *-d* (the so-called ད་དྲག་ *da drag*, widely attested in Old Tibetan documents) is not used in the Classical Tibetan orthography anymore; it has been abandoned as a consequence of a script reform in the 9th century. However, its previous presence has left traces in the forms of some morphemes that change when following a word that used to have the second postscript -ད *-d* in the old orthography.[16] For this reason it is important to be aware of the previous existence of -ད *-d* when reading Classical Tibetan texts.

ལིངས་ *liṅs* "hunting" ཞུགས་ *źugs* "fire"
OT ཀུནད་ *kund*/CT ཀུན་ *kun* "all"

Double onset

To the base letter may also be added an additional consonantal letter that will change a simple onset[17] with one consonant into a double-consonant onset. There are three ways in which a base letter can be extended: through a superscript, a subscript, or a prescript. Apart from the base letters ཝ *w*, འ *ɣ*, and ཨ *q*, all the other base letters can have additional letters added.

Superscripts

Superscript is written over the base letter, i.e. it is *super*scribed to the base letter. Only ར *r*, ལ *l*, and ས *s* are allowed as superscripts. In this position ལ and ས retain their shape but are written with smaller signs than when they take the position of the base letter. When functioning as a superscript, letter ར is replaced by the sign ཪ. Only in the combination 'superscript ཪ *r* + base letter ཉ *ñ*' does ར retain its original shape (see later). The following combinations 'superscript + base letter' are allowed:

SUPERSCRIPT ར-

When used as a superscript, letter ར occurs in the following combinations:

རྐ-	རྒ-	རྔ-	རྗ-	རྙ-	རྟ-	རྡ-	རྣ-	རྦ-	རྨ-	རྩ-	རྫ-
rk-	*rg-*	*rṅ-*	*rǰ-*	*rñ-*	*rt-*	*rd-*	*rn-*	*rb-*	*rm-*	*rc-*	*rj-*

SUPERSCRIPT ལ-

When used as a superscript, letter ལ occurs in the following combinations:

ལྐ-	ལྒ-	ལྔ-	ལྕ-	ལྗ-	ལྟ-	ལྡ-	ལྤ-	ལྦ-	ལྷ-
lk-	*lg-*	*lṅ-*	*lč-*	*lǰ-*	*lt-*	*ld-*	*lp-*	*lb-*	*lh-*

The graphical combination of ལ *l* and ཧ *h* – although counted by Tibetan grammarians among double onsets with the superscript ལ – represented a single sound (voiceless alveolar lateral approximant [l̥][18]) and not two sounds as did the remaining combinations with the superscript ལ.

SUPERSCRIPT ས-

When used as a superscript, letter ས occurs in the following combinations:

སྐ-	སྒ-	སྔ-	སྙ-	སྟ-	སྡ-	སྣ-	སྤ-	སྦ-	སྨ-	སྩ-
sk-	*sg-*	*sṅ-*	*sñ-*	*st-*	*sd-*	*sn-*	*sp-*	*sb-*	*sm-*	*sc-*

Here are a few sample words with a superscript:

རྔ་	*rṅa*	"drum"	རྒོད་	*rgod*	"vulture"	ལྔ་	*lṅa*	"five"
ལྡོག་	*ldog*	"to come back"	སྨིན་	*smin*	"ripe"	སྐུ་	*sku*	"body"

Subscripts

Four letters can be written below the base letter, that is, they can be *sub*scribed to the base letter. These are:

ཡ	ར	ལ	ཝ
-y-	*-r-*	*-l-*	*-w-*

Except for ལ, the remaining letters change their shape when used as subscripts. Instead of the previous signs, the following ones are used:

◌ྱ	◌ྲ	◌ྭ
-y-	*-r-*	*-w-*

Letter ལ does not change its shape but is written slightly smaller: ◌ླ.

The subscripts are not used randomly but can occur only in particular sets. All possible combinations of 'base letter + subscript' are listed as follows.

SUBSCRIPT -◌ྱ-

When used as a subscript, letter ཡ occurs in the following combinations:

ཀྱ-	ཁྱ-	གྱ-	པྱ-	ཕྱ-	བྱ-	མྱ-
ky-	*khy-*	*gy-*	*py-*[19]	*phy-*	*by-*	*my-*

SUBSCRIPT -◌ྲ-

When used as a subscript, letter ར occurs in the following combinations:

ཀྲ-	ཁྲ-	གྲ-	ཏྲ-	ཐྲ-	དྲ-	ནྲ-	པྲ-	ཕྲ-	བྲ-	མྲ-	ཤྲ-	སྲ-	ཧྲ-
kr-	*khr-*	*gr-*	*tr-*	*thr-*	*dr-*	*nr-*	*pr-*	*phr-*	*br-*	*mr-*	*śr-*	*sr-*	*hr-*

Not all combinations with the subscript ◌ྲ are equally common. Some of them occur only in loanwords, and some in onomatopoeic syllables.[20] The combination ཧྲ- *hr-*, although treated by native grammarians as consisting of two letters, represented one sound – voiceless alveolar trill [r̥], i.e. the voiceless counterpart of the voiced trill ར *r* [r].

SUBSCRIPT -◌ླ-

When used as a subscript, letter ལ occurs in the following combinations:

ཀླ-	གླ-	བླ-	ཟླ-	རླ-	སླ-
kl-	*gl-*	*bl-*	*zl-*	*rl-*	*sl-*

Subscript ལ differs from the remaining subscripts in terms of its history. Although it is counted as a subscript, in fact it represented the root consonant in the combinations. The distinct historical origin of the syllables written with the subscript ལ is still reflected in their pronunciation in all modern dialects.[21]

SUBSCRIPT -ྭ

ཀྭ-	ཁྭ-	གྭ-	ཅྭ-	ཉྭ-	ཏྭ-	དྭ-	ཙྭ-	ཚྭ-	ཞྭ-	ཟྭ-	རྭ-	ལྭ-	ཤྭ-	སྭ-	ཧྭ-
kw-	*khw-*	*gw-*	*čw-*	*ñw-*	*tw-*	*dw-*	*cw-*	*chw-*	*źw-*	*zw-*	*rw-*	*lw-*	*św-*	*sw-*	*hw-*

Subscript ྭ has its own name: ཝ་ཟུར་ *wa zur*. Combinations with the subscribed ྭ are not very frequent; it is used only in loanwords or to disambiguate words that would otherwise be homographs, cf.: དྭགས་ *dwags* vs དགས་ *dgas*. As the function of ཝ་ཟུར་ is mainly graphical, it does not have to be pronounced when reading texts. Here are a few sample words with the subscripts:

བྱེད་	*byed*	"to do"	སྲས་	*sras*	"son"
བློ་	*blo*	"mind"	རྭ་	*rwa*	"horn"

In Classical Tibetan there is one special case in which two subscripts are added to a base letter. This case concerns the word གྲྭ་ *grwa* "[1]corner; [2]school"; ག is the base letter, ྲ the first subscript, and ྭ the second subscript. In addition, the word ཕྱྭ་ *phya* "lot" has two alternating spellings: ཕྱ་ and ཕྱྭ་. In the latter case the subscripts ྱ and ྭ are attached to the base letter ཕ.

In the beginning students are usually confused by the complex onsets and hesitate when asked to analyse the syllable and determine which of the letters is the base letter. This issue can be easily settled by checking which of the letters is allowed as a superscript/subscript. For instance, the syllable སྐུ་ *sku* has two consonantal letters: ས and ཀ. Thus, we look whether ས can be a superscript. Yes, it can. Next, we have to check whether the combination 'superscript ས + base letter ཀ' is allowed or not. It is allowed. The last step is to determine whether ཀ can be a subscript. No, it cannot; the only allowed subscripts are ཡ *y*, ར *r*, ལ *l*, and ཝ *w*. Therefore, ས is the superscript and ཀ the base letter.

Prescripts

Five letters can be written to the left of the base letter, i.e. they can be *pre*scribed. These are:

ག-	ད-	བ-	མ-	འ-
g-	*d-*	*b-*	*m-*	*ɣ-*

Each prescript occurs with a limited number of base letters:

PRESCRIPT ག-

གཅ-	གཉ-	གཏ-	གད-	གན-	གཙ-	གཞ-	གཟ-	གཡ-	གཤ-	གས-
gč-	*gñ-*	*gt-*	*gd-*	*gn-*	*gc-*	*gź-*	*gz-*	*g.y-*	*gś-*	*gs-*

When transliterating the onset གཡ- *g.y-* one sets a dot (full stop) between the prescript ག and the base letter ཡ. This exceptional transliteration is necessitated by the existence of the combination 'base letter ག + subscript ◌ྱ'. The latter combination གྱ- is transliterated as *gy-*. Compare the two syllables:

གཡང་ *g.yaṅ* "prosperity" གྱང་ *gyaṅ* "pisé"

PRESCRIPT ད-

དཀ-	དག-	དང-	དཔ-	དབ-	དམ-
dk-	*dg-*	*dṅ-*	*dp-*	*db-*	*dm-*

PRESCRIPT བ-

བཀ-	བག-	བཅ-	བཏ-	བད-	བཙ-	བཞ-	བཟ-	བཤ-	བས-
bk-	*bg-*	*bč-*	*bt-*	*bd-*	*bc-*	*bź-*	*bz-*	*bś-*	*bs-*

PRESCRIPT མ-

མཁ-	མག-	མང-	མཆ-	མཇ-	མཉ-	མཐ-	མད-	མན-	མཚ-	མཛ-
mkh-	*mg-*	*mṅ-*	*mčh-*	*mǰ-*	*mñ-*	*mth-*	*md-*	*mn-*	*mch-*	*mȷ-*

PRESCRIPT འ-

འཁ-	འག-	འཆ-	འཇ-	འཐ-	འད-	འཕ-	འབ-	འཚ-	འཛ-
ɣkh-	*ɣg-*	*ɣčh-*	*ɣǰ-*	*ɣth-*	*ɣd-*	*ɣph-*	*ɣb-*	*ɣch-*	*ɣȷ-*

In Old Tibetan, prescript འ- marked prenasalisation of the following consonant and therefore the previous clusters should be pronounced as: [^{n}k^{h}-], [^{n}g-], [^{n}tɕ^{h}-], [^{n}dʑ-], [^{n}t^{h}-], [^{n}d-], [^{n}p^{h}-], [^{n}b-], [^{n}ʦ^{h}-], [^{n}ʣ-].

Sample words:

གཉིས་	*gñis*	"two"	མདའ་	*mdaɣ*	"arrow"	དགུང་	*dguṅ*	"sky"
འཚོལ་	*ɣchol*	"to obtain"	བཞི་	*bźi*	"four"			

Since the vowel sign is always attached to the base letter (above or below it) – in cases when such an additional sign is provided – there is no danger of misinterpreting the syllable structure and falsely identifying the base letter. However, some doubts may arise if a syllable consists of three consonantal letters and has the inherent vowel *a*, which is not marked in the script. For instance, in རབས་, is it the first grapheme (ར) that is the base letter, or is it the second one (བ)?[22] These kinds of question are absolutely justified when learning the Tibetan script. Of course, the more reading experience a student gathers, the more easily will she recognise the base letter. Luckily, gaining experience (in itself a fairly long process) can be facilitated with a few simple rules:

1 Check whether the first letter of a sequence is allowed as a prescript. In the example རབས་, the first letter (ར) is not allowed as a prescript. Therefore it has to be the base letter, with བ being the first postscript and ས the second postscript. The correct transliteration of the syllable is *rabs*. What about the syllable དགར་? Its first letter (ད) is allowed as a prescript.

2 If the first letter of a sequence is allowed as a prescript, check whether the last letter of a sequence is allowed as the second postscript. In དགར་ this is not the case. The only possible second postscript in Classical Tibetan is ས. If ར is the first postscript, it has to stand to the right of the base letter. Thus, the syllable consists of the prescript ད, the base letter ག, and the postscript ར. Its correct transliteration is *dgar*. But how to read དགས་?

3 If the first letter of a sequence of three letters is allowed as a prescript and the last one as a second postscript – like in དགས་ (with two potential readings: *dags* and *dgas*) – it is the second letter that represents the base letter by default. In order to differentiate between the readings *dags* and *dgas*, Tibetans have introduced the sign ◌ྭ (ཝ་ཟུར་ *wa zur*) to the Classical Tibetan orthography. This sign is added to the first letter if the first two letters cannot be unanimously identified by either of the aforementioned rules:

དྭགས་ *dwags* "bright" དགས་ *dgas* "to be cracked"[23]

In གངས་ no ཝ་ཟུར་ is attached to the first letter because the function of ག as the base letter is clear; ག cannot occur as a prescript of ང (see the prior list of possible combinations of the prescript ག), therefore it has to be the base letter of the syllable.

4 If a syllable consists of four consonantal letters and has no vowel sign, it is *always* the second letter in the sequence that is the base letter. Cf.:

མདངས་ *mdaṅs* "brightness" མཛངས་ *mjaṅs* "wise"

As can be inferred from the transliterations, in the first example ད is the base letter, and in the second it is ཛོ.

Complex onset

Until now only onsets formed with two elements (base letter + -script) have been discussed. It is also possible to combine more than one -script with a base letter. Four combinations are allowed:

- Prescript + superscript + base letter: བརྙ་ *brña* "to borrow" (བ = prescript, ར = superscript, ཉ = base letter)
- Prescript + subscript + base letter: དགྲ་ *dgra* "enemy" (ད = prescript, ག = base letter, ◌ྲ = subscript)
- Superscript + subscript + base letter: སྒྲ་ *sgra* "voice" (ས = superscript, ག = base letter, ◌ྲ = subscript)
- Prescript + superscript + subscript + base letter: བརྒྱ་ *brgya* "hundred" (བ = prescript, ར = superscript, ག = base letter, ◌ྱ = subscript)

A syllable can have only one element from a particular group of -scripts, i.e. no syllables are allowed with two prescripts or two superscripts, etc. The only exceptions concern the aforementioned syllables གྲྭ་ *grwa* and ཕྱྭ་ *phywa* that have two subscripts. All possible combinations of base letters with -scripts are presented in Appendix C.

Syllable structure. A summary

Table III.3 presents the structure of a maximal syllable that can be written in དབུ་ཅན་ *dbu čan* script, whereas Table III.4 illustrates two complex syllables with their single elements related to the elements sketched in Table III.3.

Table III.3 Maximal syllable

	(5) (Vowel sign)		
	(2) Superscript		
(1) Prescript	**(3) Base letter**	(6) 1st Postscript	(7) 2nd Postscript
	(4) Subscript		
	(5) (Vowel sign)		

The referential point for identifying the single elements of a syllable is always the base letter (3), marked bold in Tables III.3 and III.4.[24] The location of the remaining graphical elements is described with reference to the base letter; only

Table III.4 Maximal syllables *bsgrubs* and *brgyad*

		བསྒྲུབས་		བརྒྱད་	
		bsgrubs		*brgyad*	
(1)	prescript	བ	*b*	བ	*b*
(2)	superscript	ས	*s*	ར	*r*
(3)	**base letter**	ག	*g*	ག	*g*
(4)	subscript	◌ྲ	*r*	◌ྱ	*y*
(5)	vowel	◌ུ	*u*		*a*
(6)	1st postscript	བ	*b*	ད	*d*
(7)	2nd postscript	ས	*s*		

the base letter can take an additional vowel sign or -script(s). The numbers ascribed to each element in Table III.3 mark the order in which the elements are pronounced and transliterated:

- A prescript (1) is a letter preceding the base letter and thus located before it (*pre*script)
- A superscript (2) is a letter written over the base letter (*super*script)
- A base letter (3) is the graphic centre of each syllable
- A subscript (4) is a letter written below the base letter (*sub*script)
- A vowel sign (5) (if present) is written either below (◌ུ) or above (◌ི, ◌ེ, ◌ོ) the base letter. Irrespective of the position of the vowel sign towards the base letter, in the transliteration the vowel letter always comes directly after the base letter or after the subscript (if there is one)
- A postscript (6) is written to the right of, and thus after, the base letter (*post*script)
- A second postscript (7) is written still farther to the right of the base letter and after the postscript (6)

There is no need to learn all the possible combinations of base letters and -scripts by heart. In the beginning, however, it can be helpful to have all the -scripts at hand, listed on a separate sheet of paper. Then one can easily determine whether a particular letter is allowed (for instance, as a prescript).

Numbers

In addition to the letters of the alphabet, Classical Tibetan also has its own numbers:

༡	༢	༣	༤	༥	༦	༧	༨	༩	༠
1	2	3	4	5	6	7	8	9	0

Tibetan numerals will be introduced in Lesson 17. However, starting with Lesson 1 phrases and clauses in the exercise part of each lesson will be numbered with Tibetan numbers.

Punctuation marks

དབུ་ཅན་ *dbu čan* makes regular use of only a few punctuation marks. One of them has already been introduced: ཚེག་ *cheg*. A list of the popular and most important punctuation marks is provided next with a brief elucidation of their functions.[25]

ཚེག་

ཚེག་ *cheg* "dot" < ་ > marks the end of a syllable. It follows every syllable except for the one that stands directly before ཤད་ *śad* (see later). The ཚེག་ *cheg* before ཤད་ *śad* is omitted unless the syllable ends with the consonant -ང -*ṅ*, cf.:

བསད་དོ། *bsad do/* but ཡོང་ངོ་། *yoṅ ṅo/*[26]

In our transliteration system ཚེག་ *cheg* is transliterated as a space:

དབྱར་ཀ་ *dbyar ka*

In order to facilitate reading of Tibetan texts in translations, a hyphen '-' is introduced to connect syllables of Tibetan proper names, cf.:

དབྱིག་པ་ཅན་ Dbyig-pa-čan བོད་ཡུལ་ Bod-yul

In these cases, a hyphen transliterates a word-internal ཚེག་ *cheg*. Even though Tibetan scripts do not distinguish between upper and lower case of letters, it is a good practice to use upper case letters for the first letter of a proper name in translations. Using hyphens and uppercase letters is recommended only in translations or in more general works, but not in transliterations which should remain as faithful as possible to the original.

ཤད་

ཤད་ *śad* < ། >, more properly called ཚིག་ཤད་ *čhig śad* "a single *śad*", divides phrases within a clause or clauses within a sentence. Its usage is not strictly regulated. ཤད་

śad is transliterated as a slash: </>.[27] If the last letter in a clause or phrase is -ག -*g*, ཤད་ *śad* is omitted, cf.:

> ཡི་དགས་གྲོང་ཁྱེར་ལྟ་བུར་འདུག (GLR 23v2)
> *yi dags groṅ khyer lta bur ɣdug*

but not in

> སེམས་དགེ་བ་ཅིག་འདུག་གོ། (GLR 23r3–4)
> *sems dge ba čig ɣdug go/*

In the former case no ཚེག་ is put after the last letter ག and so the end of a text unit is clearly marked. In the latter example, the final particle གོ། *go* marks the end of the sentence (see Lesson 3).

(ག)ཉིས་ཤད་

(ག)ཉིས་ཤད་ (*g*)*ñis śad* "double *śad*" < །། > stands at the end of a sentence. It is also used in metrical texts to end a line of a stanza, in which case it does not have to be identical with the end of a sentence. No ཤད་ *śad* is used within the lines of a stanza. ཉིས་ཤད་ *ñis śad* is transliterated as a double slash: < // >.

བཞི་ཤད་

བཞི་ཤད་ *bźi śad* "quadruple *śad*" < །།   །། > is used to divide longer units of a text, e.g. chapters. བཞི་ཤད་ *bźi śad* is written so that a considerable space is left between the second and the third ཤད་ *śad*. That means བཞི་ཤད་ *bźi śad* is arranged in two groups of ཉིས་ཤད་ *ñis śad* and is respectively transliterated as < //   // >.

དབུ་

དབུ་ *dbu* "head" < ༄ > is written at the beginning of a text, chapter, or the front page (recto) of a leaf of traditional Tibetan དཔེ་ཆ་ *dpe čha* books.[28] It can also be written in a double (༄༅) or a triple form (༄༅༅). There is no generally acknowledged symbol for transliterating the དབུ་ *dbu* sign. As it begins a text unit, I propose transliterating དབུ་ *dbu* with the Latin section sign < § >. Repeated དབུ་ *dbu* can then be transliterated with the respective number of section signs, e.g. ༄༅༅ < §§§ >.

དབུ་ཅན་ *dbu čan* possesses a considerable number of ornamental marks that are ascribed special powers and are therefore applied frequently in religious texts. They do not have any relevant grammar or discourse functions.

Word order in dictionaries

Words in dictionaries of Classical Tibetan are ordered according to their base letters. The order of base letters and vowels corresponds to the order presented in Tables III.1 and III.2 (see pp. 17–8 and 20). The postscripts also occur alphabetically, e.g. དག་ *dag* precedes དང་ *daṅ*, because in the alphabet ག precedes ང. A simple postscript (consisting of one letter) precedes a double postscript, i.e. རབ་ *rab* before རབས་ *rabs*. Syllables with simple onsets (i.e. having only the base letter) are listed first, followed by complex onsets. The following juxtaposition summarises the order of complex onsets:

1 Base letter + subscript
2 Base letter + prescript
3 Base letter + prescript + subscript
4 Base letter + superscript
5 Base letter + superscript + subscript
6 Base letter + prescript + superscript
7 Base letter + prescript + superscript + subscript

All -scripts are ordered alphabetically. That means syllables with the superscript ལ are listed before syllables with the superscript ས, because ལ precedes ས in the alphabet. To illustrate, Table III.5 presents the order of onsets with the base letter ག:

Table III.5 Onset order in dictionaries

ག-	*ga-*	གླ-	*gla-*	མགྱ-	*mgya-*	སྒ-	*sga-*
གི-	*gi-*	དག-	*dga-*	མགྲ-	*mgra-*	སྒྱ-	*sgya-*
གུ-	*gu-*	དགྱ-	*dgya-*	འག-	*ɣga-*	སྒྲ-	*sgra-*
གེ-	*ge-*	དགྲ-	*dgra-*	འགྱ-	*ɣgya-*	བརྒ-	*brga-*
གོ-	*go-*	བག-	*bga-*	འགྲ-	*ɣgra-*	བརྒྱ-	*brgya-*
གྭ-	*gwa-*	བགྱ-	*bgya-*	རྒ-	*rga-*	བསྒ-	*bsga-*
གྱ-	*gya-*	བགྲ-	*bgra-*	རྒྱ-	*rgya-*	བསྒྲ-	*bsgra-*
གྲ-	*gra-*	མག-	*mga-*	ལྒ-	*lga-*		

There is no general agreement concerning the ordering of syllables that possess the subscript ◌ྭ *w*. Most frequently a syllable with the subscript ◌ྭ is listed directly following an analogously formed syllable without ◌ྭ. But this is only a rule of thumb. In the Glossary, the subscript ◌ྭ is ordered as the first subscript, following all respective syllables without a subscript. Thereafter, the subscripts ◌ྱ, ◌ྲ, and ◌ླ follow (cf. Table III.5). This order corresponds to the order of letters ཝ, ཡ, ར, and ལ in the alphabet.

Similarly, no strict rule governs the ordering of words with the postscript འ *y*. Even in the same dictionary they may sometimes occur before any other postscript, but sometimes they are listed according to the position of འ in the alphabet. In the Glossary, syllables with the postscript འ are consequently ordered according to the position of the letter in the alphabet.

Tibetan transliteration of Indian scripts

In order to enable transliteration of letters that represent sounds from Indic languages unknown to Tibetic languages, a set of special signs was designed. These should facilitate the transliteration of Indian scripts. In Tibetan texts, transliteration instead of translation is frequently applied with respect to loan-words, proper names or toponyms from Indic languages. Therefore knowledge of the additional letters is indispensable for more advanced reading courses. A complete set of letters used in transliterating Indian scripts in Tibetan and Latin alphabets is provided in Table III.6. The Indian script is represented by the Devanāgarī alphabet in the upper row followed below by the corresponding Tibetan letter.

Table III.6 Transliteration of Indian alphabets

Short vowels	अ ཨ	*a*	इ ཨི	*i*	उ ཨུ	*u*	ऋ རྀ	*ṛ*	ऌ ལྀ	*ḷ*
Long vowels	आ ཨཱ	*ā*	ई ཨཱི	*ī*	ऊ ཨཱུ	*ū*	ॠ རཱྀ	*ṝ*	ॡ ལཱྀ	*ḹ*
Diphthongs	ए ཨེ	*e*	ऐ ཨཻ	*ai*	ओ ཨོ	*o*	औ ཨཽ	*au*		
Velars	क ཀ	*k*	ख ཁ	*kh*	ग ག	*g*	घ གྷ	*gh*	ङ ང	*ṅ*
Palatals	च ཙ	*c* *c*	छ ཚ	*ch* *ch*	ज ཛ	*j* *j*	झ ཛྷ	*jh* *jh*	ञ ཉ	*ñ*
Retroflex	ट ཊ	*ṭ*	ठ ཋ	*ṭh*	ड ཌ	*ḍ*	ढ ཌྷ	*ḍh*	ण ཎ	*ṇ*
Dentals	त ཏ	*t*	थ ཐ	*th*	द ད	*d*	ध དྷ	*dh*	न ན	*n*

(Continued)

Table III.1 (Continued)

Labials	प པ *p*	फ ཕ *ph*	ब བ *b*	भ བྷ *bh*	म མ *m*
Semivowels	य ཡ *y*	र ར *r*	ल ལ *l*	व *v* བ/ཝ *b/w*	
Sibilants	श ཤ *ś*	ष ཥ *ṣ*	स ས *s*		
Glottal	ह ཧ *h*				
Anusvāra	◌ं ◌ཾ *ṃ*				
Visarga	◌ः ◌ཿ *ḥ*				
Anunāsika	◌ँ ◌ྃ ~				

The following Tibetan transliteration of the Sanskrit title of Sa-skya Paṇḍita's work (see Reading IV) illustrates the case:

Tibetan transliteration སུ་བྷཱ་ཥི་ཏ་ར་ཏྣ་ནི་དྷི་ནཱ་མ་ཤཱ་སྟྲ།

Latin transliteration *subhāṣitaratnanidhināmaśāstra*

Notes

1 བཙན་པོ་ *bcan po* was the native title held by Tibetan rulers of the Tibetan Empire (ca. 630–840s). In later sources Khri Sroṅ-rcan is more popularly known as Sroṅ-bcan Sgam-po.

2 Old Tibetan made use of additional marks and letters that were abandoned in later times. The quotation mirrors exactly the Old Tibetan orthography of the document.

3 Several other scripts (like cursive or ornamental) exist for writing down Tibetic languages. From among these, དབུ་ཅན་ *dbu čan* and དབུ་མེད་ *dbu med* (a cursive script) are the most frequently used ones. An informative overview can be found, for example, in Csoma (1834: 206ff.), Bacot (1912), and Scharlipp and Back (1996).

4 This is a simplified view which, however, is upheld here for didactic reasons.

5 My experience as a teacher is that the confusion in this case may concern not only pronunciation but in fact any aspect of the grammar in which the two Tibetic languages differ.

6 One should add that traditionally Classical Tibetan texts have been read according to a contemporary pronunciation of the reader's dialect or one of the prestigious dialects of the educational institutions.

7 Appendix A contains writing instructions for all letters.

8 In the following discussion of the pronunciation, the transcription system of the International Phonetic Alphabet (IPA) will be applied. The transcriptions of the sounds are provided in square brackets.

9 Transliteration is a conventionally established system of rewriting letters of one script with letters of another script, in which each letter of the original script acquires (ideally) one graphic equivalent in the target script. For instance, the aforementioned Greek word *αλφάβητος* can be transliterated with Latin letters as *alphábētos*. However, because Latin script has a limited number of letters, two strategies are followed in order to correlate the scripts: (1) one uses additional marks called diacritics, like the stroke above *s* in *ś*; and (2) one uses more than one Latin letter for one Tibetan letter, e.g. *kh* for ཁ. The latter strategy should be reduced to a minimum and applied only if absolutely indispensable.

10 A juxtaposition of the present transliteration with the Wylie system is provided in Appendix B.

11 Under this aspect it can be classified as an abugida script, that is, a writing system in which graphemes representing a consonant and a vowel are treated as one writing unit. In abugida scripts vowels do not have their own full representation as letters but are marked with additional signs on consonants.

12 One exception to this rule is discussed in the later section Punctuation Marks.

13 This letter is sometimes also called radical, root letter or root consonant. The term 'root' is misleading in this context and should be reserved for morphology.

14 Recall that the vowel *a* does not have any grapheme ascribed to it (see section Vowels).

15 These letters are usually called '-scripts' with modifying prefixes: *post*script, *super*script, *sub*script, and *pre*script. The prefixes 'locate' the particular -script with reference to the base letter. For instance, *pre*script is a -script (i.e. letter) written before (*pre*-) the base letter.

16 These changes will be presented in the respective lessons when discussing the morphemes.

17 Onset of a syllable in Classical Tibetan consists of all the elements that precede the vowel; every sign that stands before the vowel belongs to the onset.

18 This is the voiceless counterpart of ལ *l* [l].

19 In Classical Tibetan the combination པྱ- *py*- is not encountered in plain onset. Instead, it forms part of more complex combinations like དཔྱ- *dpy*- or སྤྱ- *spy*- (see later).

20 The plain combinations ནྲ- *nr*- and མྲ- *mr*- do not occur in Classical Tibetan. They are only encountered in the more complex onsets སྣྲ- *snr*- and སྨྲ- *smr*-, respectively.

21 Subscript ླ exemplifies the difficulties that arise when one uses the term 'root' with respect to the elements of the script. To wit, letter ལ is classified as a subscript in terms of orthography, but in terms of morphology it represents the *root* consonant, i.e. the consonant that etymologically belongs to the word stem. The letters that accompany ལ in these combinations (ཀ, ག, བ, ཟ, ར, ས), although termed 'base letters', were historically all prefixes. The same mismatch between the orthographic classification and etymology occurs with respect to combinations 'superscript ལ + base letters ཧ and ད', i.e. ལྷ- and ལྡ-. In both cases the superscript ལ represents the historical root consonant, whereas ཧ and ད used to be part of grammatical prefixes.

22 In the first case, the transliteration would be *rabs*, in the second, *!rbas*.

23 However, one has to admit that the application of ཝ་ཟུར་ *wa zur* is not always consistent within a text.

24 Determining the base letter of a syllable is crucial for two reasons. Firstly, it enables us to correctly locate the vowel of the syllable (if it is not marked by a special sign) and to read a sequence of letters as a syllable. Secondly, dictionaries of Classical Tibetan are arranged according to the base letters of words (see the section Word Order in Dictionaries). Therefore, it is necessary to determine the base letter of an unknown syllable in order to be able to check the meaning of the word in a dictionary. Furthermore, for those who simultaneously learn a modern Tibetan dialect, the correct identification of the base letter is required for proper pronunciation of a syllable.

25 No systematic study of Classical Tibetan punctuation has yet been undertaken. Thus, the functions described next should be understood as rough rules of thumb only.

26 According to Dotson and Helman-Ważny (2016: 83), "[i]n later Tibetan writing, *cheg* came to be inserted between the *ṅ* suffix and the *śad* so as to disambiguate it from a *g* suffix, and was often placed after an *y* suffix to disambiguate and (sic) *y* and *śad* from a *l* suffix." In the literature one can sometimes find another reason for inserting a ཚེག་ *cheg* between -ང -*ṅ* and ཤད་ *śad*, which is to distinguish between -ང -*ṅ* and -ད -*d* letters. Namely, it happens that the long vertical stroke of -ད -*d* is sometimes written shorter and so the letter then highly resembles -ང -*ṅ*. However, in woodblock printing (the traditional printing technique in Tibet) it is sometimes difficult to establish whether a ཚེག་ *cheg* precedes a ཤད་ *śad*.

27 In metrical passages or texts ཤད་ *śad* is frequently transliterated as a vertical bar < | > to mark the end of a verse (see Lesson 18).

28 In Tibetan this punctuation mark is sometimes also called ཡིག་མགོ་ *yig mgo* or དབུ་ཁྱུད་ *dbu khyud*.

Lesson 1

- Word
- Tibetan as an agglutinative language
- Particles
- Noun
- Adjective
- Demonstrative
- Indefinite particle
- Noun phrase
- Grammatical case

Word

Definition

In the textbook the term 'word' will be used interchangeably with 'lexical word'. Lexical word is a unit which has a meaning that can be defined independently of other words – this is the word one finds in a dictionary, isolated from the textual context, with clearly delimited meanings.[1] Words are not distinguished in Tibetan script. A syllable is distinguished from the following one by a ཚེག་ *cheg* < ་ > but there is no special sign to mark the end of a word. In Classical Tibetan words can have one or more syllables but the vast majority of them consist of two syllables. In the script each syllable of such a word is marked with a ཚེག་ *cheg* but the word as such does not acquire any additional mark. For instance, རྒྱལ་པོ་ *rgyal po* "king" is one word that consists of two syllables: རྒྱལ་ *rgyal* and པོ་ *po*. The end of each syllable is marked with a ཚེག་ *cheg* but no additional mark is added to the word itself, either in isolation or in a text flow. A sample sentence in Classical Tibetan looks like this:

> རྒྱལ་པོ་དེ་ལ་སྲས་གསུམ་མངའ་སྟེ། *rgyal po de la sras gsum mṅaŋ ste/* (MB D 139r2–3)
> "That king had three sons."

DOI: 10.4324/9781003224198-4

In this sentence we have the following words:

རྒྱལ་པོ་ = noun "king"	གསུམ་ = numeral "three"
དེ་ = demonstrative "that"	མངའ་ = verb "had"
སྲས་ = noun "son"	

In Classical Tibetan some lexical words may change their forms depending on the clause construction and their function within it. However, their 'basic form' (i.e. the form that can be found in a dictionary and that has been changed to meet the sentence requirements) can usually be easily identified.

Word classes

A word class, also called part of speech, is a category of words that exhibit similar grammatical characteristics. Words that belong to a particular word class behave alike or fulfil similar functions in comparable contexts. The following word classes can be distinguished in Classical Tibetan:[2]

- **Verb** (see Lesson 4): the only word class that can be inflected in Classical Tibetan; verbs can be modified (changed in their form) in order to express different grammatical categories. They follow all the other elements in a clause and can be negated.

  ཡིན་ *yin* "to be" བྱེད་ *byed* "to do"

- **Noun** (see Lesson 1): the only indispensable element of a noun phrase (NP). It can be modified by a preceding genitive phrase or by a following adjective, numeral or determiner. A noun can be followed by a case particle (see later).

  རྒྱལ་པོ་ *rgyal po* "king" རྟ་ *rta* "horse"

- **Adjective** (see Lesson 1): a constituent of a noun phrase that follows and modifies the noun. If all elements are present, adjectives stand between the noun and the numeral in a noun phrase.

  དཀར་པོ་ *dkar po* "white" ཆེན་པོ་ *čhen po* "big"

- **Numeral** (see Lesson 17): a constituent of a noun phrase, following the noun (and the adjective if present).

  གཉིས་ *gñis* "two" གཉིས་པ་ *gñis pa* "second"

- **Adverb** (see Lesson 8): modifies either an adjective or a verb. In this function it always precedes the word it modifies. When used independently (to express temporal or spatial relations) it usually stands at the beginning of a clause.

ཤིན་ཏུ་ *śin tu* "very"   ད་ *da* "now"

- **Pronoun** (see Lessons 1, 2, and 14): a word that can replace a noun phrase. Like nouns, pronouns can be followed by a case particle.

ང་ *ṅa* "I"   འདི་ *ɣdi* "this"

- **Relator noun** (see Lesson 10): a noun used in postpositional phrases. It follows a noun phrase to which it may be attached by genitive and may itself acquire another case particle. In contrast to normal nouns, relator nouns can be neither modified by adjectives or numerals nor replaced by a pronoun.

མདུན་ *mdun* "front"   མདུན་དུ་ *mdun du* "in front of, before"
ཕྱོགས་ *phyogs* "direction"   ཕྱོགས་སུ་ *phyogs su* "towards"

- **Postposition** (see Lesson 10): directly follows a noun or a noun phrase. It expresses relations that cannot be expressed by grammatical cases.

རྗེས་ *rǰes* "after, behind"   བཞིན་ *bźin* "according to; like"

- **Classifier** (see Lesson 8): precedes a word which it modifies. Classical Tibetan has only honorific (HON) classifiers that change a 'normal' word into an 'honorific' one.

classifier	'normal' word	honorific
དབུ་ *dbu* "(HON) head"	སྐྲ་ *skra* "hair"	དབུ་སྐྲ་ *dbu skra* "(HON) hair"
སྐུ་ *sku* "(HON) body"	ཚེ་ *che* "lifetime"	སྐུ་ཚེ་ *sku che* "(HON) lifetime"

- **Determiner** (see Lessons 1 and 17): follows a word or a noun phrase and modifies it, expressing the reference of a noun (definite, indefinite, quantity, distribution):

རེ་ *re* "each, every" (distributive determiner)

- **Interjection** (see Lesson 13): stands independently in a sentence, usually clause-initially:

ཀྱེ་མ་ *kye ma* "oh! alas!"   འོ་ན་ *ɣo na* "well; now then"

Tibetan as an agglutinative language

Concerning its morphology, Classical Tibetan is an agglutinative language.[3] This means the language makes use of additional morphemes in order to express various meanings or grammatical relations.[4] These morphemes, being mostly syllabic, are easily discernible in text and indicate one grammatical category each. Thus, the following equation is generally true:

> one morpheme = one syllable = one grammatical meaning

In the following sample clause, the particles have been emphasised:

> དེ་ནས་སྤྲེའུ་ཕྲུག་རྣམས་ཀྱིས་ལོ་ཐོག་ཟོས་པས་ཚིམ་པར་གྱུར་ཏོ། (GLR 23v4)
> *de **nas** spre**yu** phrug **rnams kyis** lo thog zos **pas** chim **par** gyur **to**/*
>
> "Then, because the monkey-children had eaten the crops, [they] became satisfied."

དེ་ = demonstrative "that"
ནས་ = (elative case) particle
སྤྲེའུ་ཕྲུག་ = noun "monkey-child"; -འུ་ = diminutive particle
རྣམས་ = plural particle
ཀྱིས་ = (ergative case) particle
ལོ་ཐོག་ = noun "crop"
ཟོས་ = verb "ate"
པས་ = nominal particle པ་ + (ergative case) particle **-ས**
ཚིམ་ = adjective "satisfied"
པར་ = nominal particle པ་ + (terminative case) particle **-ར**
གྱུར་ = verb "became"
ཏོ་ = final particle

Particles: An overview[5]

Generally speaking, particles in Classical Tibetan can be divided in two groups: (1) those that have a grammatical function in a clause (grammatical particles); and (2) those that serve to derive new words from existing ones (derivational particles). This juxtaposition gives an overview of the particles in each group:[6]

Grammatical particles	**Derivational particles**
indefinite (1)	nominal (7)
number (2)	diminutive (9)
case (3–6 & 12)	possessive (10)
sentence final (3, 6, 11)[7]	
negation (6)	
converbal (8–10 & 15)	
focus (9)	
quotative (13)	

Grammatical particles
comparative (15)
superlative (15)
auxiliary (16)
purposive (16)
numerical (17)
collective (17)

The particles are *not allowed* to stand alone in a clause. This feature distinguishes particles from all the other forms of the language. With the exception of the negation particle, they always *follow* the word to which they connect. Two or more particles can follow one word. Due to the pivotal role of these morphemes in Classical Tibetan grammar, a considerable part of its grammatical description is devoted to the elucidation of the functions and meanings of each of the particles.

Noun

Definition

A noun (N) is a word that names a thing, an idea, an emotion, and so on. One can define a noun in Classical Tibetan as the only indispensable element of a noun phrase (NP), which can function as a subject or an object in a clause. Nouns can be modified by preceding genitive phrases (Lesson 3) or by following adjectives or numerals. Tibetan nouns usually consist of one (ཁྱིམ་ *khyim* "house", རྟ་ *rta* "horse") or two syllables (བུད་མེད་ *bud med* "woman", ལག་པ་ *lag pa* "hand"), but longer nouns, first of all compounds,[8] are likewise encountered: རིན་པོ་ཆེ་ *rin po čhe* "jewel", བྱང་ཆུབ་སེམས་དཔའ་ *byaṅ čhub sems dpaɣ* = Skt. *bodhisattva*.[9]

Nominal grammatical categories[10]

Nouns in Classical Tibetan exhibit the following grammatical categories:

Category:	**[gender]**	**[number]**	**[definiteness]**	**case**	**[focus]**
Examples:	masculine	singular	definite	absolutive	
	feminine	plural	indefinite	dative, etc.	

Case is the only grammatical category that is obligatory for nouns in a clause. The remaining categories (bracketed in the table) are optional. Namely, Classical Tibetan possesses means to additionally express these (if needed or desired), but they are not required in a clause. All the 'optional' categories are expressed by means of particles. The order of categories, if applied to a noun, is also illustrated in the table: a category to the left precedes a category listed to its right. That is, a morpheme which marks gender (masculine or feminine) will always be placed before a morpheme that marks plurality, i.e. number. Cf.:

བཙུན་མོ་རྣམས་དེ་ལ་ *bcun mo rnams de la* "for the queens" (VC, D 3880, *dbu ma*, śa 250r7)
  བཙུན་མོ་ "queen"; མོ་ = feminine particle (gender; see Lesson 7)
  རྣམས་ = plural particle (number; see Lesson 2)
  དེ་ "the" = definite determiner (definiteness; see Lesson 1)
  ལ་ = dative (case; see Lesson 3)

བུ་མོ་འདི་རྣམས་ཀྱིས་ནི་ *bu mo ɣdi rnams kyis ni* "by these girls" (HJM, D 4152, *skyes rabs*, u 192v3–4)
  བུ་མོ་ "girl"; མོ་ = feminine particle (gender; see Lesson 7)
  འདི་ "this" = demonstrative (see Lesson 1)
  རྣམས་ = plural particle (number; see Lesson 2)
  ཀྱིས་ = ergative (case; see Lesson 5)
  ནི་ = focus (see Lesson 9)

Adjective

An adjective (A) is a word, the main role of which is to modify a noun or a noun phrase in a clause. In principle, adjectives function as attributes and are placed after the noun in Classical Tibetan:

བོད་ཁ་བ་ཅན་ *bod kha ba čan* "snowy Tibet" བོད་ (N) "Tibet"; ཁ་བ་ཅན་ (A) "snowy"
བྲག་རོག་པོ་ *brag rog po* "black rock" བྲག་ (N) "rock"; རོག་པོ་ (A) "black"

If more adjectives occur, they are placed one after another:

ནས་དཀར་མོ་མང་པོ་ *nas dkar mo maṅ po* "much white barley" ནས་ (N) "barley"
དཀར་མོ་ (A) "white"
མང་པོ་ (A) "many, much"

Demonstrative

The main demonstratives (DEM) in Classical Tibetan are:

དེ་ *de* "that" འདི་ *ɣdi* "this"

Demonstratives have a double function. On the one hand, they can substitute for a noun or a noun phrase (e.g. *Take* ***this*** *with you* instead of *Take* ***the bag*** *with you*) – this is the prototypical function of demonstrative pronouns.[11] On the other hand, demonstratives may behave like adjectives (e.g. *Take* ***this*** *bag with you* vs *Take* ***the blue*** *bag with you*). In the latter case one speaks of demonstrative adjectives. Both these functions can be fulfilled by demonstratives in Classical Tibetan.

Apart from a limited number of idiomatic expressions (see later), when acting as demonstrative adjectives, demonstratives follow the word or phrase which they modify (just as normal adjectives do):

སྤྲེའུ་དེ་ *spreɣu de* "that monkey"
རྒྱལ་ཁམས་འདི་ *rgyal khams ɣdi* "this kingdom"

The most commonly occurring exceptions are the idiomatic phrases:

དེ་སྐད་ *de skad* "those words"
འདི་སྐད་ *ɣdi skad* "these words"

འདི་སྐད་ introduces a quotation, whereas དེ་སྐད་ marks the end of a quotation (see Lesson 13).

Classical Tibetan does not have special forms for definite determiners like the English *the* or German *der/die/das*. The demonstrative དེ་ *de* is used instead as a determiner (see section Noun Phrase later). As a consequence, the phrase རྒྱལ་པོ་དེ་ *rgyal po de* can be translated either as "that king" or "the king".

Indefinite particle

Classical Tibetan has an indefinite particle (INDF) which can be used in one of three forms. The form is determined by the last letter of the preceding syllable:

ཅིག་ *čig*	after	-ག, -ད, -བ, *-ད་དྲག་[12]
ཞིག་ *źig*	after	-ང, -ན, -མ, -འ, -ར, -ལ, vowel
ཤིག་ *śig*	after	-ས

The indefinite particle follows the word to which it attaches:

རྒྱལ་པོ་ཞིག་ *rgyal po źig* "a king" རྒན་མོ་ཞིག་ *rgan mo źig* "an old woman"

It can also be used after numerals, in which case it has a collective function:

བུ་གཉིས་ཤིག་ *bu gñis śig* (MB D 138r7) "two sons"

The indefinite particle belongs to the so-called determiners (see next section) and therefore is the last element of a noun phrase directly preceding a case particle:

བུད་མེད་དག་ཅིག་ *bud med dag čig* (MB H 347, *mdo sde*, sa 346v4) "some women" (དག་ = plural particle)

Noun phrase

In Classical Tibetan a noun phrase (NP) consists of at least a noun as its head word, but it can also have other elements. These can include adjectives, numerals, and determiners, all of which follow the head element. If a noun phrase has more than one element, the first one is always a noun.

རྒྱལ་པོ་	*rgyal po*	"king"	N
རྒྱལ་པོ་ཆེན་པོ་	*rgyal po čhen po*	"great king"	N + A
རྒྱལ་པོ་གཉིས་	*rgyal po gñis*	"two kings"	N + NUM
རྒྱལ་པོ་དེ་	*rgyal po de*	"that king"	N + DEM
རྒྱལ་པོ་ཞིག་	*rgyal po źig*	"a king"	N + INDF

Word order in noun phrases

If a noun phrase consists of more than two words, the order of the words that may follow the noun is strictly determined:

Noun (N) – Adjective (A) – Numeral (NUM)[13] – Determiner (DET)[14]
མ་རྒན་མོ་དེ་ *ma rgan mo de* (MB D 138v5) "the/that old mother"

Depending on the context, དེ་ in this phrase can be interpreted as either a determiner ("the") or a determinative adjective ("that").

མི་འདི་གཉིས་ *mi ɣdi gñis* (MB D 140v5) "these two men"

In the latter example the demonstrative འདི་ functions as adjective (see earlier section Demonstrative) and therefore precedes the numeral གཉིས་.

སྲིན་པོ་ཆེན་པོ་ལྔ་ཞིག་ *srin po čhen po lṅa źig* (MB H 347, *mdo sde*, sa 264v2) "five great demons"

སྲིན་པོ་ *srin po* "demon"   ཆེན་པོ་ *čhen po* "great"
ལྔ་ *lṅa* "five"   ཞིག་ *źig* "(INDF) a"

The head element of the phrase, i.e. the one modified by additional elements (here: སྲིན་པོ་ *srin po* "demon"), comes first. The remaining elements of the phrase all modify the word སྲིན་པོ་. If an NP contains a numeral (like ལྔ་ *lṅa* "five" in the earlier example), དེ་ *de* "the" cannot follow it as determiner. The definite determiner དེ་ *de* "the" can only follow a plural particle (see Lesson 2).

Group inflection (Ger. Gruppenflexion)

Classical Tibetan displays yet another feature common to agglutinative languages: all grammatical particles are attached at the end of a **noun phrase**. That is, only the last element of a noun phrase acquires grammatical marking, whereas the preceding elements retain their basic form:

> རྒྱལ་བུ་ཐ་ཆུངས་ཀྱིས་ཕུ་བོ་གཉིས་ལ་སྨྲས་སོ། [*rgyal bu tha čhuṅs kyis*]$_{\text{ERG}}$ [*phu bo gñis la*]$_{\text{DAT}}$ *smras so/* (MB D 139r4–5)
> "The youngest prince said to [his] two elder brothers."

This clause contains two noun phrases:

- རྒྱལ་བུ་ཐ་ཆུངས་ཀྱིས་: རྒྱལ་བུ་ = noun "prince", ཐ་ཆུངས་ = adjective "youngest", ཀྱིས་ = ergative case particle (see Lesson 5). The ergative case particle has the whole noun phrase in its scope and therefore stands after all its elements. It marks རྒྱལ་བུ་ཐ་ཆུངས་ as an acting subject.
- ཕུ་བོ་གཉིས་ལ་: ཕུ་བོ་ = noun "elder brother", གཉིས་ = numeral "two", ལ་ = dative case particle (see Lesson 3). Here the same principle governs the application of the dative case particle, which is put only once at the end of the whole phrase.

Apart from gender, morphemes of all nominal grammatical categories (number, definiteness, case, focus) are attached only once: at the end of the whole noun phrase. Morphemes that mark gender are attached directly to the respective noun (see Lesson 7).

Grammatical case

Case is a grammatical category of nouns.[15] It reflects the grammatical function that a particular word or phrase has in a clause. In Classical Tibetan grammatical case is expressed by means of one of the so-called case particles. The following cases are distinguished:

• Absolutive		ABS	Lesson 2
• Locative	ན་	LOC	Lesson 3
• Dative	ལ་	DAT	Lesson 3
• Genitive	/ཀྱི་/	GEN	Lesson 3
• Terminative	/དུ་/	TERM	Lesson 4
• Ergative	/ཀྱིས་/	ERG	Lesson 5
• Comitative	དང་	COM	Lesson 5
• Elative	ནས་	EL	Lesson 6
• Delative	ལས་	DEL	Lesson 6

Case particles are the last element of a noun phrase in a clause;[16] they follow determiners and number particles.

Exercise

Transliterate and translate the following phrases. Determine the word classes of their elements.

	དཔེ་ཅན་	Transliteration	Translation
༠	བྲག་རོག་པོ་ཞིག་	*brag rog po źig*	"a (INDF) black (A) rock (N)"
༡	ཆོས་ཟབ་མོ་ (GLR 22r4)		
༢	རྟོག་འཛམ་པ་ (GLR 23v6)		
༣	ལོ་གསུམ་ (GLR 23r4)		
༤	རྒྱལ་པོ་དེ་ (MB D 273r4)		
༥	སྲས་ཐ་ཆུངས་དེ་ (MB D 139r3)		
༦	ཞག་དུ་མ་ (MB D 139r4)		
༧	ཤ་རྣོན་པ་ (MB D 139r6)		
༨	ཁྲག་དྲོན་མོ་ (MB D 139r6)		
༩	རྒྱལ་བུ་ཐ་ཆུངས་དེ་ (MB D 139r7)		
༡༠	ཡུན་རིང་པོ་ (MB D 140v5)		
༡༡	ཚལ་བ་རྟོན་པོ་ (MB D 139v3)		

༡༢ ཚིག་སྙན་པ་ (MB D 140r5)

༡༣ ཉེས་པ་ཆེན་པོ་ (MB D 138v6)

༡༤ ཕུག་རོན་གསུམ་ཞིག་ (MB D 139v5)

༡༥ བུ་མོ་ངན་པ་ (MB D 270v6)

Word list[17]

ཁྲག་ blood
རྒྱལ་པོ་ king
རྒྱལ་བུ་ prince
ངན་པ་ bad
ཆེན་པོ་ great
ཆོས་ Buddhist teaching
འཇམ་པ་ mild
ཉེས་པ་ evil
སྙན་པ་ well-sounding
ཐ་ཆུངས་ the youngest
དུ་མ་ many
དེ་ (DEM) that
དྲོན་མོ་ warm
རྣོན་པོ་ sharp
ཕུག་རོན་ dove
བུ་མོ་ daughter
བྲག་ rock
ཚལ་བ་ splinter
ཚིག་ word
ཞག་ day
ཟབ་མོ་ profound
ཡུན་ time
རིང་པོ་ long
རོག་པོ་ black
རློན་པ་ fresh
ལོ་ year
ཤ་ flesh, meat
སྲས་ son
གསུམ་ three

Notes

1 This 'definition' is based on common (or popular) understanding of what a 'word' is in a language. In linguistics, the status and definition of 'word' is much debated.
2 More exhaustive descriptions of the word classes are provided when a particular word class is discussed in more detail in the textbook.
3 Only verbs in Classical Tibetan inflect; for details, see Lesson 4.
4 Traditionally these morphemes are called 'particles' in Western grammars and textbooks on Classical Tibetan; they are introduced in the section Particles.
5 Linguistically the particles can be classed as either suffixes or clitics, albeit one particle can be a suffix in one and a clitic in another context (e.g. case particles are clitics after a noun phrase, but suffixes after a verb). I have retained the term 'particle' for it has a long-standing tradition in literature related to Tibetan languages and allows to refer to a group of morphemes that share some of their features. 'Particle' is a technical term in linguistics, albeit its interpretation differs depending on the language discussed. In

Tibetan linguistics the term 'particle' seems to have been adapted from ཕྲད་ *phrad* "particle" as used in native Tibetan grammatical tradition. For an overview of all particles in Classical Tibetan see Appendix D.

6 Numbers in brackets refer to lessons in which the particles are discussed.

7 These are the particles of affirmative (Lesson 3), imperative (Lesson 6), and interrogative clauses (Lesson 11).

8 See Lesson 13.

9 In Buddhism a *bodhisattva* is a person who has expressed the aspiration to attain enlightenment in order to help other sentient beings.

10 Grammatical category is a property of words, like tense, case, number, or gender. Distinct word classes exhibit different grammatical categories.

11 On grounds of their function in the clause, demonstrative pronouns belong to the word class of pronouns.

12 On the second postscript ད་དྲག་, see the chapter Tibetan Script. ད་དྲག་ was primarily a verbal suffix and only very few non-verbs ended with it. Therefore, in Old Tibetan no examples are attested of the indefinite particle following a ད་དྲག་.

13 Instead of a numeral, a quantifier ("many", "few", etc.) can stand here.

14 Demonstrative དེ་ *de* "that; the" or the indefinite particle /ཅིག/ *čig* "a" can function as a determiner. Classical Tibetan also has other determiners, which are discussed in Lesson 17.

15 Case particles that can follow a verb will be discussed separately in Lesson 12.

16 If there is a focus (Lesson 9) or a concessive particle (Lesson 10), these will follow the case particle. These are the only instances in which a case particle will not be the last element of a noun phrase.

17 Word lists at the end of Lessons 1–11 contain only new vocabulary from the Exercise section of the respective lesson but they do not include particles. The word lists are arranged according to the alphabetical order of Tibetan dictionaries (for its elucidation, see the section on word order in dictionaries in the chapter Tibetan Script).

Lesson 2

- Word order in a clause
- Absolutive
- Copula ཡིན་ and its negation མིན་
- Number
- Personal pronouns

Word order in a clause

In Classical Tibetan, the basic word order in a clause with a verb that requires an object (i.e. a transitive verb) is:

Subject (S) – Object (O) – Verb (V)[1]

སྤྲེའུ་ཕྲུག་རྣམས་ཀྱིས་ལོ་ཐོག་ཟོས་སོ། (GLR 23v4)
[*spreyu phrug rnams kyis*]$_{S}$ [*lo thog*]$_{O}$ [*zos so*]$_{V}$/
"The monkey-children ate the crops."

If a verb is intransitive (i.e. does not require an object) the word order is:

Subject – Verb

བྲག་སྲིན་མོ་ཞིག་འོངས་སོ། (GLR 22r5)
[*brag srin mo źig*]$_{S}$ [*yoṅs so*]$_{V}$/
"A rock-ogress came."

DOI: 10.4324/9781003224198-5

In general, a verb is the last element of a clause or a sentence. Each of the elements of a clause can be additionally modified. The position of the modifying elements (modifiers) depends on the word class of the element which they are supposed to modify. For instance, if the subject is a noun, it can be followed and modified by adjectives and/or numerals in accordance with the word order within a noun phrase (see Lesson 1).

Absolutive

The absolutive (ABS) case does not have a marker that would signal its presence in a clause; one could call it a 'marker-less' case. Words standing in absolutive have the same form as when cited in dictionaries. In this regard absolutive can be compared to the nominative of languages like German, Russian, or Polish.

Depending on the verb and the clause structure, words standing in absolutive can have one of the following functions:

1 **Subject** of intransitive verbs (like "to go", "to dance") and of copulas (e.g. "to be" or "to exist");
2 **Direct object** of transitive verbs (e.g. "to buy **a car**");
3 **Predicative** of identity copulas ("to be **sth.**"; see the next section)
4 **Adjunct**

A detailed discussion of the functions will be provided with the introduction of the respective types of verb. The following description should serve as a most general overview.

1 In Classical Tibetan absolutive is the case of the subject (S) in clauses with:

A copula verb:

ང་དགེ་བསྙེན་ཡིན། [*ṅa*]$_{\text{S-ABS}}$ [*dge bsñen*]$_{\text{ABS}}$ *yin/*[2] (GLR 22r5)
"**I** am a lay practitioner."

An intransitive verb:

བཅོམ་ལྡན་འདས་རྒྱང་མ་ནས་གཤེགས་སོ། [*bčom ldan ɣdas*]$_{\text{S-ABS}}$ [*rgyaṅ ma nas*]$_{\text{EL}}$ *gśegs so/*[3] (MB D 137r7)
"**The Victorious One** (an epithet of the Buddha) came from afar."

2 Absolutive is likewise the case of the direct object (O) of a transitive verb:

ཞང་པོས་ཡི་གེ་བཀླགས་སོ། [*źaṅ pos*]$_{\text{ERG}}$ [*yi ge*]$_{\text{O-ABS}}$ *bklags so/* (ML D 12r)[4]
"The maternal uncle read **the text**."

3 In a clause with an identity copula (see next section) absolutive also marks the predicative (P), i.e. the element of a sentence that expresses a property assigned to the subject of the sentence:

ང་དགེ་བསྙེན་ཡིན། [*ṅa*]$_{ABS}$ [*dge bsñen*]$_{P\text{-}ABS}$ *yin/* (GLR 22r5)
"I am a **lay practitioner**."

In this clause, ང་ is the subject and དགེ་བསྙེན་ the predicative.

4 If a sentence contains an expression that specifies the time of the event, this expression (the so-called temporal adjunct) will frequently stand in absolutive as well:

དེའི་ཚེ་བཅོམ་ལྡན་འདས་ [. . .] བསོད་སྙོམས་ལ་གཤེགས་སོ།། (MB D 138r6)
[*deɣi che*]$_{ABS}$ [*bčom ldan ɣdas*]$_{ABS}$ [*bsod sñoms la*]$_{DAT}$ *gśegs so//*[5]
"**At that time**, the Victorious One went for alms."

This sentence contains two elements in absolutive: the temporal adjunct དེའི་ཚེ་ and the subject བཅོམ་ལྡན་འདས་.

Apart from these main functions, absolutive is also used to mark vocative, i.e. a noun that usually identifies a person or an anthropomorphic being who is addressed directly by the speaker. In the clause "The best among the deities, think [about us] kindly!"[6] the phrase "the best among the deities" addresses a person (in this case the Buddha) and thus functions as vocative. The vocative phrase is usually placed at the beginning of a clause:[7]

བླ་མ་ལགས། *bla ma lags/* (ML D 10r) "Dear (or: Venerated) Lama!"

After addressing Mi-la Ras-pa with these words, the proper utterance follows.[8]

Copula ཡིན་ and its negation མིན་

Copula is a verb that links a subject to a property assigned to it. Classical Tibetan has two basic copulas: ཡིན་ *yin* "to be" and ཡོད་ *yod* "to be there; to exist".[9] The negated form of ཡིན་ is མིན་ *min* "not to be". There is also a longer form of the negated copula: མ་ཡིན་ *ma yin*, that can be used interchangeably with མིན་. ཡིན་ and མིན་ have only one form each, i.e. they never change their form irrespective, for instance, of whether they are used to speak of present or past situations. The tense either follows from the context or is indicated by various temporal adverbs, like *today*, *last year*, etc. ཡིན་ and མིན་ can be used with all persons, in singular as well as in plural. The basic structure of copula clauses with ཡིན་/མིན་ is:

S_{ABS} P_{ABS} ཡིན་ (/མིན་) "S is (not) P."[10]

Both non-verbal elements of such sentences (i.e. the subject and the predicative) stand in absolutive. The subject *always* comes first, followed by the predicative. Copula ཡིན་/མིན་ may be used in two basic kinds of clause:

1 **Equative** clauses ("to be something/somebody") express identity, name, profession, ethnicity, nationality, religion, etc. of the subject, e.g.:

ང་དགེ་བསྙེན་ཡིན། [*ṅa*]$_{ABS}$ [*dge bsñen*]$_{ABS}$ *yin/* (GLR 22r5)
"I am a lay practitioner." (identity)

ངའི་ཡབ་རྒྱལ་པོ་ཟས་གཙང་མ་ཡིན། [*ṅaɣi yab*]$_{ABS}$ [*rgyal po zas gcaṅ ma*]$_{ABS}$ *yin/*[11] (MB D 140v4)
"My father is the king Zas-gcaṅ-ma." (name)

2 **Attributive** clauses ("to be in some way") ascribe attributes (like colour, age, etc.) to the subject, e.g.:

སྐད་སྙན་པ་ཡིན། [*skad*]$_{ABS}$ [*sñan pa*]$_{ABS}$ *yin/* (MB D 273v5) "The voice is pleasant."
ངེད་རབ་ཡིན། [*ṅed*]$_{ABS}$ [*rab*]$_{ABS}$ *yin/* (ML D 12v) "We are the best."

Number

Classical Tibetan has a set of particles that mark grammatical plural. The singular is included in the basic form of a word and does not have to be additionally expressed. The plural can be (but does not have to be!) additionally expressed by means of one of the so-called number particles.[12] In consequence, a basic form of a word can be either singular or plural and the correct interpretation depends on the context. The following number particles are used:

རྣམས་

རྣམས་ *rnams* is the most frequently used number particle. It can be used with any noun.

རི་རྣམས་ *ri rnams* "mountains"   མི་འདི་རྣམས་ *mi ɣdi rnams* "these men"

དག་

དག་ *dag* is also a very common number particle and can likewise be used with any noun. In some contexts it may have collective meaning.

> དེ་དག་ *de dag* "those"   མག་པ་དག་ *mag pa dag* "sons-in-law"

In works translated from Sanskrit དག་ may also render dual.[13]

ཚོ་

ཚོ་ *cho* is primarily used with nouns denoting living beings, with pronouns and numerals. When following a numeral, it has a collective meaning.

> བ་ཚོ་ *ba cho* "cows"   འདི་ཚོ་ *ɣdi cho* "these"

ཅག་

ཅག་ *čag* is used only with several personal pronouns.

> བདག་ཅག་ *bdag čag* "we" cf. བདག་ *bdag* "I"
> ཁྱེ་ཅག་ *ɣu čag* "we"   ཁྱེ་བུ་ཅག་ *ɣu bu čag* "we"

Unlike བདག་ཅག་, ཁྱེ་ཅག་ and ཁྱེ་བུ་ཅག་ do not have equivalents in singular.

འོ་ཅོག་

འོ་ཅོག་ *ɣo čog* was originally a nominalising plural particle[14] attached to non-nouns in order to change them into plural nouns.

> གསུམ་མོ་ཅོག་ *gsum mo čog* "the three ones"   གསུམ་ *gsum* "three"
> ཡོད་དོ་ཅོག་ *yod do čog* "the ones that are there"   ཡོད་ *yod* "to be there"

འོ་ཅོག་ *ɣo čog* is attached to a word so that the last consonant of the preceding syllable is repeated (-མ *-m* and -ད *-d* in the examples) and replaces འ- *ɣ-* – the onset of འོ་ཅོག་.[15]

Number particles have a fixed position in a noun phrase; they follow the noun and the adjective but precede the definite determiner དེ་ *de* "the" and the case particle (see Lesson 1):

> མི་འདི་རྣམས་ *mi ɣdi rnams* "these men" (འདི་ = DEM; GLR 23v5)
> དེ་དག་ལ་ *de dag la* "for those" (ལ་ *la* = dative case particle; MB D 138v2)

Numerals གཉིས་ and གསུམ་ as collective markers

གཉིས་ *gñis* and གསུམ་ *gsum* are in fact the numerals "two" and "three", respectively. They are frequently used after an enumeration of two or three items that form a particular set, in which case གཉིས་ and གསུམ་ mark the set as a collective.

ཕ་མ་གཉིས་ *pha ma gñis* "both mother and father; parents"
མ་སྨད་གསུམ་ *ma smad gsum* "the three, mother and [her two] children"

Personal pronouns

Personal pronouns are pronouns associated with persons. Classical Tibetan differentiates between personal pronouns of the 1st, 2nd, and 3rd person, in singular as well as in plural.

Simple personal pronouns

Classical Tibetan has the following basic set of personal pronouns:

Table 2.1 Personal pronouns[16]

	Singular			Plural
Person		*Honorific*	*Humble*	
1st	ང་ *ṅa*		བདག་ *bdag*	ངེད་ *ṅed*
2nd	ཁྱོད་ *khyod*	ཁྱེད་ *khyed*		ཁྱེད་ *khyed*
3rd	ཁོ་ *kho* (M)/མོ་ *mo* (F)	ཁོང་ *khoṅ*		

The difference between honorific and humble forms will be discussed in more detail in Lesson 8. For now it suffices to know that honorific pronouns are used when a person of higher social status is addressed, whereas the humble pronoun for the first person བདག་ "I" is used when the speaker speaks of herself in the presence of a person of higher social status.

In addition, other words can function as personal pronouns as well:[17]

1st person:

SG	ཁོ་བོ་ *kho bo* (M)	ཁོ་མོ་ *kho mo* (F)	ངན་བུ་ *ṅan bu*	ཕྲན་ *phran*
	ངོས་ *ṅos*	དངོས་ *dṅos*	རང་ *raṅ*	གུས་པ་ *gus pa*
PL	ཡུ་ཅག་ *yu čag*	ཡུ་བུ་ཅག་ *yu bu čag*	ཡོ་སྐོལ་ *yo skol*	ཡོ་ཅག་ *yo čag*

Some of these forms (e.g. ངན་བུ་, ངོས་, དངོས་, ཕྲན་, and གུས་པ་) are derived from nouns and are mainly used in marked contexts to express a humble position of the speaker towards her interlocutor. They usually accompany a pronoun and are often used in epistolary genres.

3rd person:

ཁོ་པ་ *kho pa* (M) ཁོ་མ་ *kho ma* (F)

In addition to the listed pronouns of the 3rd person, the demonstrative དེ་ *de* can likewise be used as a 3rd person pronoun.

As the presented forms demonstrate, Classical Tibetan has special forms for the 1st and the 3rd person singular pronouns that additionally indicate gender: masculine (M) and feminine (F). The aforementioned personal pronouns can be labelled 'simple' in contrast to the so-called complex personal pronouns.

Complex personal pronouns

Complex personal pronouns are formed from simple pronouns by adding either ཉིད་ *ñid* or རང་ *raṅ*; both could be literally translated as "self", e.g.:

ཁོ་ *kho* "he" ཁོ་རང་ *kho raṅ* "he (himself)"

Complex personal pronouns might have originally had an emphatic function but this faded away as time passed:

ངེད་ *ṅed* "we" ངེད་རང་ *ṅed raṅ* "we"

Plural of personal pronouns

In addition to the previously listed forms (see Table 2.1), plural personal pronouns can be formed by adding one of the plural particles (རྣམས་ *rnams*, ཚོ་ *cho*, ཅག་ *čag*; and seldomly also དག་ *dag*) to the basic pronoun, cf.:

ང་ *ṅa* "I" > ང་ཚོ་ *ṅa cho* "we"
འོ་སྐོལ་ *ɣo skol* "we" > འོ་སྐོལ་རྣམས་ *ɣo skol rnams* "we"
ཁོ་རང་ *kho raṅ* "he" > ཁོ་རང་ཚོ་ *kho raṅ cho* "they" (M/F)

Exercise

Transliterate and translate the following phrases and clauses:

༡ རྒྱལ་བུ་སེམས་ཅན་ཆེན་པོ་དེ་ (MB D 140r2–3)
༢ སྡུག་མོ་ལྡོགས་པ་ (MB D 140r6)

༣ སེམས་ཅན་ཁྲི་ (GLR 22v2)
༤ སྲོག་ཆགས་སྟོང་ (GLR 22v2)
༥ བརྡ་མང་དུ་ (GLR 22r5)
༦ མགོན་པོ་ཐུགས་རྗེ་ཅན་ (GLR 22v4)
༧ སྤྲེའུ་ཕྲུག་ལྔ་བརྒྱ་ (GLR 23r4–5)
༨ ཁྱིམ་མཚེས་དྲག་པ་ཀུན་ (ML D 10v)
༩ ལྟོ་གོས་ངན་པ་ (ML D 11r)
༡༠ སྟོན་མོ་བཟང་པོ་ (ML D 12r)
༡༡ རྒྱལ་པོ་ཆེན་པོ་ (MB D 140r6)
༡༢ འཁོར་མང་པོ་རྣམས་ (MB D 140v3)
༡༣ བུ་མོ་དེ་དག་ (MB D 270v2)
༡༤ བདག་རྒྱལ་བུ་སེམས་ཅན་ཆེན་པོ་ཡིན། (MB D 140r6)
༡༥ ང་དགེ་བསྙེན་ཡིན། (GLR 22r5)

Word list

ཀུན་ (A) all
ཁྱིམ་མཚེས་ neighbour
ཁྲི་ ten thousand
འཁོར་ attendants
དགེ་བསྙེན་ lay practitioner
མགོན་པོ་ protector
ང་ (1SG) I
ལྔ་བརྒྱ་ five hundred
ལྟོ་གོས་ food and clothing
ལྟོགས་པ་ hungry
སྟག་མོ་ tigress
སྟོང་ thousand
སྟོན་མོ་ feast
ཐུགས་རྗེ་ཅན་ compassionate
དྲག་པ་ noble
བདག་ (1SG) I
བརྡ་ sign
སྤྲེའུ་ཕྲུག་ monkey-child
མང་དུ་ many
མང་པོ་ many
བཟང་པོ་ excellent
ཡིན་ to be
སེམས་ཅན་ living being
སེམས་ཅན་ཆེན་པོ་ (PN) Sems-čan-čhen-po
སྲོག་ཆགས་ animated being

Notes

1 In linguistic typology languages can be classified according to their word order in a clause. Classical Tibetan (as any other Tibetic language or dialect) is an SOV language, i.e. a language with the basic word order: subject – object – verb.
2 From now on, each time a new type of clause is introduced a schematic illustration of its structure, including the main elements and their cases, will be provided. Elements

included within the square brackets belong to one phrase. Abbreviations following the brackets and written in lower index stand for the respective case or function.

3 The elative case (EL) will be explained in Lesson 6.

4 For ergative (ERG) as the subject case, see Lesson 5.

5 The dative case (DAT) will be explained in Lesson 3.

6 For the quotation, see the Reading (MB D 138v1) in Lesson 13.

7 For the interjection ཀྱེ་ frequently used with vocative, see Lesson 13.

8 For the function of ལགས་, see Lesson 8: Speech Register.

9 Copula ཡོད་ will be discussed in Lesson 3.

10 S = subject; P = predicative.

11 ངའི་ *ṅaɣi* "my" is the genitive form of ང་ *ṅa* "I". For details, see Lesson 3.

12 'Number particles' are also called 'plural particles' in literature because the latter are the only number particles in Classical Tibetan – the singular is 'contained' in the basic form of a word by default.

13 For details, see Hahn (2003b).

14 It is a complex particle consisting of the old demonstrative འོ་ *ɣo* and the plural particle ཅག་ *čog*.

15 For a detailed description of the assimilation rules, see Lesson 3: Final Particle.

16 One should however be aware that differences exist between works with regard to the set of basic pronouns; depending on time of their composition, the impact of the spoken language, or the mother tongue of the composer. For instance, the biography of Mi-la Ras-pa uses the following pronouns in one of the chapters (Hill 2007):

	Singular	Plural
1st	ང་	རང་རེ་ (INCL)
	བདག་ (HML)	ངེད་ (EXCL)
2nd	ཁྱོད་	ཁྱེད་
3rd	ཁོ་	ཁོང་

The text uses yet another form for the 1st person plural: ཉུ་ཅག་. Furthermore, ཁྱེད་ is used for the 2nd person plural but also honorifically for the 2nd person singular (compare hereto Fr. *vous*).

17 These lists were presented for the first time by Francke and Simon (1929: 27–9) and then taken over by Hahn (1996: 111–13); see also Schwieger (2006: 45–6). However, they must not be accepted without objections. It is most probable that they are an assemblage of literary and colloquial forms from various dialects.

Lesson 3

- Locative
- Dative
- Copula ཡོད་ and its negation མེད་
- Genitive
- Possessive pronouns
- Final particle འོ་

Locative

In Classical Tibetan the locative (LOC) case is marked with the particle ན་ *na*. Locative can have one of the following meanings in a clause:

Location denotes a place at which an event takes place or in which something is located. It answers the question 'Where?':

གྲོང་ཁྱེར་དེ་ན་ *groṅ khyer de na* (MB D 138r7) "**in** the town"
མཉན་དུ་ཡོད་པ་ན་ *mñan du yod pa na* (MB D 138r5) "**in** Mñan-du-yod-pa" (Mñan-du-yod-pa was Indian town Śrāvasti)
འདི་ན་ *ɣdi na* "here", lit. "**in** this [place]"

Time provides information about when or at what time an event takes place. It answers the question 'When?':

ཚེ་ན་ *che na* "**at** the time"
སྔ་ན་ *sṅa na* "earlier", lit. "**at** an earlier time"
དུས་གཅིག་ན་ *dus gčig na* "one day", lit. "**at** one time"

Dative

In Classical Tibetan the dative (DAT) case is marked with the particle ལ་ *la*. Depending on the verb and the clause structure, the dative can mark one of the following syntactic constituents of a clause:

DOI: 10.4324/9781003224198-6

- **Predicative** in possessive clauses with a copula of existence (see later)
- **Indirect object** of ditransitive verbs like "to give", "to speak", e.g. *John gave* ***me*** *the book*
- **Direct object** of some verbs of thinking or feeling, e.g. "to think **about**"
- **Oblique** of some verbs or adjectives, e.g. "(to be) skilled **in**"
- **Adjunct**

The first four are obligatory arguments and must not be omitted from a clause if one of the respective verbs is used. The functions of the dative will be introduced together with the respective verb types. An adjunct is an optional part of a clause. If it is removed, the clause remains intact. For instance, in the clause "Yesterday, I watched a good movie" the word *yesterday* is an adjunct. If one removes it, the clause "I watched a good movie" is still correct.

Dative can have one of the following meanings in a clause:

Location denotes a place at which an event takes place or in which something is located. It answers the question 'Where?':

ས་ལ་ *sa la* (MB D 139v5) "**on** the ground"
ཡིད་ལ་ *yid la* (MB D 139r7) "**in** [one's] mind"

Time provides information about when or at what time, etc., an event takes place. It answers the question 'When?':

ཉིན་རེ་ལ་ *ñin re la* (GLR 22v1–2) "**on** each (རེ་) day"
སྐད་ཅིག་ལ་ *skad čig la* (GLR 23r6) "**in** one moment"

Beneficiary marks an object or a person for whose benefit the event takes place. It answers the question 'For whom?':

ཕ་མ་གཉིས་ལ་སྐྱེད་ *pha ma gñis la skyed* (MB D 140r5) "to generate **for** both of [my] parents"

Purpose indicates a reason for which an action occurs. It answers the question 'For what?':

བསོད་སྙོམས་ལ་གཤེགས་ *bsod sñoms la gśegs* (MB D 138r6) "to go **for** alms"

Experiencer marks a person who is sensorily or emotionally affected by the action:

ཐམས་ཅད་ལ་འདྲ་ *thams čad la ɣdra* (MB D 139r3) "to seem **to** all"

Recipient expresses a change in ownership:

ང་ལ་སྦྱིན་ *ṅa la sbyin* (ML D 11v) "to give **me**"

Stimulus is an entity that causes a sensory or emotional reaction:

ཁྱེད་ལ་ཞེན་ *khyed la źen* (GLR 22v1) "to long **for** you"
བདག་ལ་དགོངས་ *bdag la dgoṅs* (GLR 22v2) "to reflect **on** me"

Direction marks the location towards which the action is directed. It answers the question 'Whither?':

ནམ་མཁའ་ལ་ལྟ་ *nam mkhaɣ la lta* (MB D 140r5) "to look **at** the sky"
ཞབས་ལ་ཕྱག་འཚལ་ *źabs la phyag ɣchal* (MB D 138v3) "to bow **to** [his] feet"

Maleficiary marks the referent as harmed or negatively acted upon by something or someone. Usually this dative can be translated with "against":

མ་ལ་གཤེ་ *ma la gśe* (MB D 270v3) "to inveigh **against** the mother"

Topic introduces new information or marks the element of greatest relevance for the context. Usually this dative can be translated with "as for, concerning":

དེ་ལ་ (GLR 23v5) "**concerning** that"
རྒྱལ་པོ་ལ་ (GLR 24v3) "**as for** the king"

Copula ཡོད་ and its negation མེད་

In Classical Tibetan the basic copula of existence is ཡོད་ *yod* "to be; to exist". Its negated equivalent is མེད་ *med* "not to be; not to exist". ཡོད་ and མེད་ do not change their forms irrespective of the context in which they are used. The copulas ཡོད་ and མེད་ are primarily used in two kinds of clause: locative ("to be somewhere") and possessive ("to have").

Locative clauses

Locative clauses with the copulas ཡོད་ *yod* and མེད་ *med* have the basic structure:

P_{LOC} S_{ABS} ཡོད་ (/མེད་) "S is/exists (is not/does not exist) in P."

The subject (S) stands in absolutive, i.e. is not marked with any additional particle (see Lesson 2). The predicative (P) stands in locative (ན་ *na*). As the following examples demonstrate, the order of subject and predicative is flexible.

ངེད་འདི་ན་ཡོད། (ML D 13r) $[\textit{ṅed}]_{ABS}$ $[\textit{ɣdi na}]_{LOC}$ *yod/*
"We are here (lit. in this [place])."

འཛམ་བུ་གླིང་འདི་ན་རྒྱལ་པོ་ཤིང་རྟ་ཆེན་པོ་ཡོད། (MB D 139r2)
[ɣjam bu gliṅ ɣdi na]$_{\text{LOC}}$ *[rgyal po śiṅ rta čhen po]*$_{\text{ABS}}$ *yod/*
"In this continent there was a king Śiṅ-rta-čhen-po."

In the prior clauses locative marks the place of the event, whereas the following clause contains a phrase in locative that expresses the time of the event:

སྔ་རོལ་ན་རྒྱལ་པོ་ཤིང་རྟ་ཆེན་པོ་ཡོད། (MB D 139r2)
[sṅa rol na]$_{\text{LOC}}$ *[rgyal po śiṅ rta čhen po]*$_{\text{ABS}}$ *yod/*
"Earlier (or: in earlier times) there was a king Śiṅ-rta-čhen-po."

Possessive clauses

Possessive clauses with the copulas ཡོད་ *yod* and མེད་ *med* have the basic structure:

P$_{\text{DAT}}$ S$_{\text{ABS}}$ ཡོད་ (/མེད་) "P has/possesses (does not have/possess) S."

The subject (S) of the clause stands in absolutive (see Lesson 2), whereas the predicative (P) stands in dative (ལ་ *la*). The order of subject and predicative is flexible.

རྒན་མོ་ཞིག་ལ་བུ་གཉིས་ཞིག་ཡོད། *[rgan mo źig la]*$_{\text{DAT}}$ *[bu gñis śig]*$_{\text{ABS}}$ *yod/* (MB D 138r7)
"An old woman had two sons."

ཁྱེད་རང་ཚོ་ལ་ནོར་ཡོད། *[khyed raṅ cho la]*$_{\text{DAT}}$ *[nor]*$_{\text{ABS}}$ *yod/* (ML D 11v)
"You (PL; ཚོ་) have wealth."

དེ་ངེད་ལ་མེད། *[de]*$_{\text{ABS}}$ *[ṅed la]*$_{\text{DAT}}$ *med/* (ML D 13r)
"We (ངེད་) do not have it."

In the last clause དེ་ is the 3rd person singular pronoun "it" (see Lesson 2: Personal Pronouns).

Genitive

In Classical Tibetan the genitive (GEN) case particle mainly connects nouns or noun phrases with each other. This distinguishes it from other case particles that establish a particular relationship between the word they follow and the verb (or, in rare cases, the adjective).[1]

Forms

The genitive case particle changes its form depending on the last letter of the preceding syllable:

ཀྱི་ *kyi*	after -ད, -བ, -ས
གྱི་ *gyi*	after -ན, -མ, -ར, -ལ
གི་ *gi*	after -ག, -ང
-འི་ *ɣi*	after -འ, vowel
ཡི་ *yi*[2]	after -འ, vowel

Function and meaning

The main function of the genitive particle is to mark a noun or a noun phrase as modifying another noun. The genitive particle always comes after the modifying phrase, i.e. between it and the noun that is modified:

MODIFIER$_{\text{GEN}}$ HEAD
"HEAD of MODIFIER"

རྒྱལ་པོའི་སྲས་གསུམ་ *rgyal poɣi sras gsum* "king's three sons" (GLR 25r4)

སྲས་གསུམ་ is a complex head of the genitive phrase. It consists of the noun སྲས་ "son" and its modifier གསུམ་ "three". This noun phrase is then modified by the phrase in the genitive: རྒྱལ་པོའི་, lit. "of the king".

It is also possible that a genitive phrase itself acquires a modifier in the genitive:

ཡབ་ཀྱི་ཞལ་ཆེམས་ཀྱི་ཡི་གེ་ *yab kyi źal čhems kyi yi ge* (ML D 12r) "the text of father's testament"

The head noun of the whole phrase is ཡི་གེ་ "text" which is modified by the phrase ཞལ་ཆེམས་ཀྱི་ in genitive. In addition, ཞལ་ཆེམས་ "testament" itself functions as a head of the noun phrase ཡབ་ཀྱི་ཞལ་ཆེམས་ and is modified by ཡབ་ཀྱི་ "of the father".

The relationship established between the modifier (the phrase followed by the genitive particle) and the head of the phrase (i.e. the noun that is modified) can have various meanings. The most common ones are listed next accompanied by respective examples.

Possession: The referent of the head is possessed by the referent of the modifying phrase:

ངེད་རང་གི་ཁང་པ་ *ṅed raṅ gi khaṅ pa* (ML D 11v) "our house"
བདག་གི་ཕ་མ་ *bdag gi pha ma* (MB D 140r4) "my parents"

Substance: The genitive marks material or substance from which the head is made:

ཤིང་གི་ཚལ་བ་ *śiṅ gi chal ba* (MB D 139v3) "wooden splinter", lit. "splinter **of** wood"
རིན་པོ་ཆེ་སྣ་བདུན་གྱི་སྒྲོམ་ *rin po čhe sna bdun gyi sgrom* (MB D 140v2) "a chest [made] **of** seven kinds [of] jewel"

Source: The genitive marks the head of the phrase as coming from something or being its inseparable part:

ལུས་ཀྱི་ཤ་ *lus kyi śa* (MB D 139v3) "flesh **of** the body"

Origin: The genitive marks the head of the phrase as originating from a particular place:

དགའ་ལྡན་གྱི་ལྷ་ *dgaɣ ldan gyi lha* (MB D 140r6) "deity **from** the Dgaɣ-ldan (Skt. Tuṣita) heaven"

Partition: Partitive genitive marks a part from a whole:

ལྷའི་གཙོ་བོ་ *lhaɣi gco bo* (MB D 138v4) "the best **among** the deities"

Beneficiary: The genitive expresses for whom or to whose advantage something is meant. It can usually be translated with "for":

འབྲུའི་བང་མཛོད་ *ɣbruɣi baṅ mjod* (ML D 10v) "store-room **for** corn"
སེམས་ཅན་གྱི་དོན་ *sems čan gyi don* (MB D 271r3) "welfare **of** sentient beings"

Purpose: Indicates a reason for which an action occurs:

བསོད་སྙོམས་ཀྱི་དུས་ *bsod sñoms kyi dus* (MB D 138r6) "[proper] time **for** alms"

Description: The descriptive genitive is used in qualitative descriptions:

མྱ་ངན་ལས་འདས་པའི་བདེ་བ་ *mya ṅan las ɣdas paɣi bde ba* (MB D 138v7) "happiness of *nirvāṇa*", i.e. happiness that arises or results from *nirvāṇa*
བུ་ཕོའི་བླ་ *bu phoɣi bla* (MB D 139v6) "a symbol for a son", i.e. a symbol that represents one's son

Descriptive genitive is also used in similes:

མྱ་ངན་གྱི་རྒྱ་མཚོ་ *mya ṅan gyi rgya mcho* (MB D 140r7) "ocean of misery", i.e. misery which is as great as an ocean

བདེ་སྐྱིད་ཀྱི་ཉི་མ་ *bde skyid kyi ñi ma* (Guru 689; *apud* Schwieger 2006: 238) "the sun of the happiness", i.e. happiness that shines like the sun

The use of genitive in similes is most possibly a calque from Sanskrit.

Subject: Subjective genitive expresses the subject as a cause or initiator of the event referred to in the head:

འཇིག་རྟེན་པའི་གཏམ་དཔེ་ *yǰig rten payi gtam dpe* (ML D 11r) "folk's proverb", i.e. a proverb that a folk tells

བཅོམ་ལྡན་འདས་ཀྱི་བཀའ་དྲིན་ *bčom ldan ydas kyi bkay drin* (MB D 138v3) "kindness of the Victorious One", i.e. kindness that the Victorious One (i.e. the Buddha) showed to somebody

Object: Objective genitive expresses the object of the event referred to in the head noun:

བུ་འདིའི་སྐྱབས་ *bu ydiyi skyabs* (MB D 138v1) "protection of these sons", i.e. protection given to the sons

Compare hereto the verb phrase "to protect the sons" in which *sons* is the direct object of the verb *to protect*. This meaning of the genitive is seldomly encountered in texts.

Possessive pronouns

In Classical Tibetan there are no special words that would correspond to English possessive pronouns like *his* or *yours*. Instead, genitive forms of personal pronouns are used, cf.:

བདག་གི་བུ་ *bdag gi bu* (MB D 138v1) "my sons"	བདག་ "I"
ངེད་རང་གི་ཁང་པ་ *ṅed raṅ gi khaṅ pa* (ML D 11v) "our house"	ངེད་རང་ "we"
དེ་དག་གི་སྲོག་ *de dag gi srog* (MB D 138v2) "their lives"	དེ་དག་ "they"

In the following example དེ་ is used twice in two different functions:

དེའི་མ་རྒན་མོ་དེ་ *deyi ma rgan mo de* (MB D 138v5) "their old mother", lit. "the old mother of theirs"

དེ་ in དེའི་ is a 3rd person pronoun but the genitive འི་ turns it to a possessive pronoun "theirs".[3] The second དེ་ at the end of the phrase is the determiner "the" (see Lesson 1).

Final particle འོ་

The final particle འོ་ *ɣo* (FNL) marks the end of an indicative sentence.[4] The final particle is the last element of a sentence, coming directly after the verb. No other element is allowed to stand after the final particle. The final particle འོ་ *ɣo* changes its form depending on the last letter of the preceding syllable. In general, the last letter of the syllable is repeated at the onset of the particle and the grapheme འ is omitted. The particular assimilation rules are illustrated as follows.

- After words with a final consonant:

  སྨྲས་སོ་ *smras so* < **smras* + *ɣo* འཆར་རོ་ *ɣčhar ro* < **ɣčhar* + *ɣo*

- After an earlier second postscript -ད *-d* (the so-called ད་དྲག་ *da drag*):

  གྱུར་ཏོ་ *gyur to* < **gyurd* + *ɣo* བསྟན་ཏོ་ *bstan to* < **bstand* + *ɣo*

- After words with a final vowel:

  མཆིའོ་ *mčhiɣo* < **mčhi* + *ɣo* ལྟའོ་ *ltaɣo* < **lta* + *ɣo*

- After syllables that end with the letter -འ *-ɣ*:

  མངའོ་ *mṅaɣo* < **mṅaɣ* + *ɣo* དགའོ་ *dgaɣo* < **dgaɣ* + *ɣo*

The final particle འོ་ *ɣo* may have one of the following functions:

1 Copula: འོ་ may replace the copula ཡིན་ *yin*. In these cases the final particle is to be translated as copula "to be":[5]

ཕུག་རོན་བུ་ཕོའི་བླའོ། (MB D 139v6) = *ཕུག་རོན་བུ་ཕོའི་བླ་ཡིན།
phug ron bu phoɣi blaɣo/
"A dove is (འོ་) a sign for a son."

2 Final particle (proper): འོ་ ends the sentence, standing after a verb:

ཁྱོད་ཀྱི་སྐད་སྙན་པ་ཡིན་ནོ། (MB D 273v5)
khyod kyi skad sñan pa yin no//
"Your voice is pleasant."

If a sentence ends with a verb and the final particle, the final particle is not translated. The final particle འོ་ *yo* is frequently omitted after the copulas ཡིན་ *yin* and ཡོད་ *yod*, so that the last sentence would also be correct if formed as:

*ཁྱོད་ཀྱི་སྐད་སྙན་པ་ཡིན།

There is no difference in meaning between sentences with a copula and a final particle and those that end only with a copula. In Classical Tibetan a complete sentence must end either with a copula or with a final particle.

Exercise

Transliterate and translate the following phrases and clauses:

༡ སྤྲེའུའི་རྒྱལ་པོ་ཆེན་པོ་ (GLR 22r6)
༢ ཁ་བ་ཅན་གྱི་རྒྱལ་ཁམས་འདི་ (GLR 22v2)
༣ སྲིན་པོའི་ཕྲུ་གུ་དཔག་མེད་ (GLR 22v2)
༤ སྲིན་པོའི་གྲོང་ཁྱེར་དག་ (GLR 22v2)
༥ འགྲོ་བའི་མགོན་པོ་ (GLR 22v4)
༦ བུད་མེད་ཀྱི་ཆས་ (GLR 22r5)
༧ ངའི་སྡོམ་པ་ (GLR 22r6)
༨ རི་རབ་ཀྱི་ཁོང་སེང་ (GLR 23v3)
༩ བདག་ཅག་གི་ཚེ་སྲོག་ (MB D 138v3–4)
༡༠ འབྱུང་པོའི་བྱ་རྣམས་ (SSP 3d)
༡༡ བྲམ་ཟེ་དེའི་ཆུང་མ་དེ་ (MB D 270v2)
༡༢ གྲོང་ཁྱེར་དེ་ན་རྒན་མོ་ཞིག་ལ་བུ་གཉིས་ཞིག་ཡོད། (MB D 138r7)
༡༣ ང་སྤྱན་རས་གཟིགས་ཀྱི་དགེ་བསྙེན་ཡིན། (GLR 22r5)
༡༤ ཨ་ཁུ་ལ་བུ་མང་པོ་ཡོད། (ML D 12r–v)
༡༥ རྒྱ་མཚོ་ཆེན་པོ་ཆུ་ཡི་གཏེར་ཡིན། (SSP 1c–d)
༡༦ དེའི་ཚེ་ཡུལ་དེ་ན་བྲམ་ཟེ་སྦྱིན་ཏེ་ལོ་ཤུ་ཤ་ཡོད་དོ། (MB D 270v1)
༡༧ ཁྱོད་ཀྱི་སྐད་སྙན་པ་ཡིན་ནོ།། (MB D 273v5)

Word list

སྐད་	voice	ཁྱོད་	(2 SG) you
ཁ་བ་ཅན་	Tibet	གྲོང་ཁྱེར་	village
ཁོང་སེང་	inner cavern	འགྲོ་བ་	a being

རྒན་མོ་ old woman

རྒྱ་མཚོ་ ocean

རྒྱལ་ཁམས་ kingdom

ཆས་ garment

ཆུ་ water

ཆུང་མ་ wife

གཏེར་ treasury

བདག་ཅག་ (1PL) we

སྡོམ་པ་ vow

དཔག་མེད་ countless

སྤྱན་རས་གཟིགས་ (PN) Spyan-ras-gzigs

སྤྲེའུ་ monkey

ཕྱིན་ཏེ་ལོ་ཤུ་ཤ་ (PN) Phyin-te-lo-śu-śa

ཕྲུ་གུ་ child

བུ་ son

བུད་མེད་ woman

བྱ་ bird

བྲམ་ཟེ་ Brahmin

འབྱུང་པོ་ demon

ཚེ་ time

ཚེ་སྲོག་ life

ཡུལ་ region, country

ཡོད་ to exist; to have

རི་རབ་ (PN) Ri-rab, a mountain in Indian cosmology (Skt. Sumeru)

སྲིན་པོ་ demon

ཨ་ཁུ་ paternal uncle

Notes

1 Even though the modifying function is the most important function of the genitive in Classical Tibetan, the genitive is a syntactic case equal to other cases. This can be inferred from a small group of verbs that require the genitive particle for one of their arguments; e.g. རིགས་ "[1]to have the way, manner, to be suitable; [2]must": འདི་ལྟར་བྱ་བའི་རིགས་སམ། *ydi ltar bya bayi rigs sam/* (MB D 140v2) "Was it suitable (རིགས་) to act this way?"; དེ་ནི། རི་སེར་པོ་ཞིག་སྣང་བའི་རིགས། *da ni/ ri ser po źig snaṅ bayi rigs/* (MB H 347, *mdo sde*, sa 389r4) "Now, a yellow mountain must appear."

2 The form ཡི་ is a syllabic equivalent of the form -འི་. It is used mainly in metrical passages if an additional syllable is needed to fill a line of a stanza.

3 The plural number is not explicitly stated here but can be inferred from the context of the story.

4 Final particles of imperative and interrogative sentences are discussed in Lesson 6 and Lesson 11, respectively.

5 In very special cases the final particle འོ་ *yo* may also replace an action verb. For examples, see Schwieger (2006: 307).

Lesson 4

- Tibetan verbs
- Intransitive verbs
- Terminative

Tibetan verbs: An overview

Verbs are the most complicated and diverse word class in every language. In Classical Tibetan one distinguishes between the following types of verb:

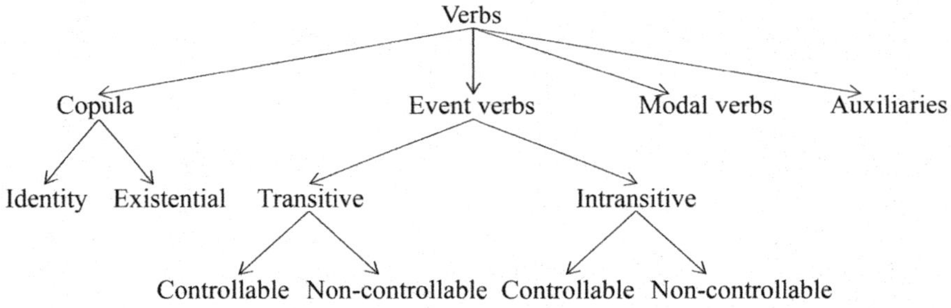

Figure 4.1 Types of Tibetan verb

Each type of verb is bound to a particular sentence construction and also differs from other verb types in terms of its semantic contribution to the overall meaning of the sentence.

The two most important copula verbs in Classical Tibetan, ཡིན་ "to be" and ཡོད་ "to exist", have already been discussed (see Lessons 2 and 3). In this and the next lesson, larger sections will be devoted to the most numerous type of verbs – the event verbs. Modal verbs will be discussed in Lesson 13 and auxiliaries in Lesson 16.

DOI: 10.4324/9781003224198-7

Tibetan event verbs

'Event verb' is a type of verb that expresses an action, an occurrence, or a state.[1] In contrast to the remaining types of verb (copulas, modal verbs, auxiliaries) which have special grammatical functions, event verbs first of all name the event itself, i.e. provide the semantic content of the event. In Classical Tibetan event verbs are the only verbs that can be modified by adverbs. There are also grammatical particles that can only follow an event verb, e.g. the imperative particle (see Lesson 6), coordinative particle (see Lesson 8), or auxiliary particle (see Lesson 16). In Classical Tibetan every event verb can be ascribed two properties: transitivity and controllability.

Transitivity

Transitivity as a grammatical category refers to the ability of a verb to take a direct object. Depending on the occurrence of a direct object with a verb, one distinguishes between intransitive verbs (INTR; no direct object) and transitive verbs (TR; one direct object). Within the group of transitive verbs one can further discern a relatively small subgroup of ditransitive verbs (DITR) that require two objects: one direct and one indirect object. All these types of verb (intransitive, transitive, and ditransitive) are attested in Classical Tibetan.

Controllability

Controllability is a special grammatical category of Tibetan verbs that determines whether a particular event expressed by the verb can be controlled by the subject of the verb. Accordingly, in Classical Tibetan one distinguishes between controllable (C) and non-controllable (NC) verbs. Controllability is not only a matter of semantics, but also may have impact on the sentence structure.

Four classes of event verbs

Since in Classical Tibetan every event verb is either transitive or intransitive and either controllable or non-controllable, four classes of verbs (I–IV) can be discerned:

Table 4.1 Verb classes

	I	II	III	IV
Transitivity	TR	TR	INTR	INTR
Controllability	C	NC	C	NC
Syntax[2]	S_{ERG} O_{ABS} V	S_{ABS} O_{ABS} V	S_{ABS} V / S_{ERG} V	S_{ABS} V

I. Transitive and controllable verbs require a direct object and express actions that can be fully controlled by the subject. The examples of such verbs are:

འདེབས་ "to throw" བྱེད་ "to do"
གསོད་ "to kill" འཆིང་ "to bind"

The subject of these verbs stands in ergative (see Lesson 5) and the object usually in absolutive. The sentence structure of transitive and controllable verbs will be discussed in detail in Lesson 5.

II. Transitive and non-controllable verbs require a direct object but express an action that cannot be fully controlled by the subject (see Lesson 8). As examples one can cite:

འཆོར་ "to shed (tears)" དྲན་ "to remember"

Their subject stands in absolutive. They also differ from the verbs of the first class in their 'reduced' morphology (see the following section Verb Forms). In addition, they take partly different auxiliaries than transitive controllable verbs (see Lesson 16). Class II is much less numerous than class I.

III. Intransitive and controllable verbs do not take a direct object but express actions that can be controlled by the subject. To this class belong, among others:

འགྲོ་ "to go" འདུ་ "to come together"
སྡོད་ "to wait" བཞུགས་ "to stay"

Depending on the context, the subject of such verbs can stand either in ergative or in absolutive. The ergative case is a marked choice and emphasises the fact that the accomplishment of the event is fully controlled by the subject (see Lesson 5).

IV. Intransitive and non-controllable verbs do not take a direct object and express actions that cannot be controlled by their subject. The examples of such verbs are:

སྐྱེ་ "to be born" ན་ "to be ill"
འཆི་ "to die" འབབ་ "to fall"

The subject of these verbs always stands in absolutive.

There is a small group of verbs that can belong to more than one class. These verbs have more than one meaning and depending on the meaning required in a particular sentence they might be applied as belonging to either one or the other verb class.

Verb forms

In Classical Tibetan, verbs are the only word class that can be inflected. Depending on the class to which a verb belongs, verbs in Classical Tibetan may have up to four inflected forms (also called 'stems'). In the textbook the forms ('stems') are numbered and referred to as v1, v2, v3, and v4, respectively. These forms are traditionally called present (ད་ལྟ་བའི་ཚིག་ or བྱེད་ཚིག་), past (འདས་ཚིག་), future (མ་འོངས་པའི་ཚིག་ or བྱ་ཚིག་), and imperative (བསྐུལ་ཚིག་) by Tibetan grammarians.

Table 4.2 Verb inflection

				Inflected forms			
Verb	Meaning	Verb class		v1	v2	v3	v4
འདེབས་	"to throw"	I	TR/C	འདེབས་	བཏབ་	གདབ་	ཐོབ་
བྱེད་	"to do"	I	TR/C	བྱེད་	བྱས་	བྱ་	བྱོས་
སྟོན་	"to show"	I	TR/C	སྟོན་	བསྟན་	བསྟན་	སྟོན་
འཚོར་	"to shed"	II	TR/NC	འཚོར་	ཤོར་		
དྲན་	"to remember"	II	TR/NC	དྲན་			
འགྲོ་	"to go"	III	INTR/C	འགྲོ་	སོང་		(སོང་)
འདུ་	"to gather"	III	INTR/C	འདུ་	འདུས་		(འདུས་)
སྐྱེ་	"to be born"	IV	INTR/NC	སྐྱེ་	སྐྱེས་		
ན་	"to be ill"	IV	INTR/NC	ན་			

In the following discussion I will call a cell a 'slot' in columns v1, v2, v3, and v4 of Table 4.2. That is, for every verb, four slots are shown in the table but we see that not every slot is filled. 'Inflected form' (briefly: 'form') of a verb is a concrete form of a particular verb that fills a slot in column v1, v2, v3, or v4.

The first inflected form (column v1) corresponds to the form of a verb under which the particular verb can usually be found in dictionaries – this is the lemma. For transitive and controllable verbs, i.e. verbs of the first class (I), every inflectional slot in the Table 4.2 (i.e. in columns v1, v2, v3, and v4) must be filled – only these verbs can have four inflected forms. However, we observe that one and the same form may fill two slots (e.g. བསྟན་ in columns v2 and v3 of the verb སྟོན་).[3] Verbs of the other classes (II, III, IV) fill up to three slots, and they only have up to two distinct inflected forms. Only verbs of class I can fill slot v3. Only controllable verbs (i.e. verbs of classes I and III) can have a fourth form, i.e. can fill a slot in the fourth column (v4). With one exception, verbs of class III use in their fourth slot (v4) the forms of the second slot (v2); that is why the forms are bracketed in the Table 4.2. The exception concerns the honorific intransitive verb གཤེགས་ "to come; to go" with a special v4-form ཤོག་.[4] Table 4.3 summarises these findings.[5]

Table 4.3 Verb classes and verb inflection

Verb class		Inflected forms			
		v1	v2	v3	v4
I	TR/C	+	+	+	+
II	TR/NC	+	+		
III	INTR/C	+	+		(+)
IV	INTR/NC	+	+		

As may be expected, the inflected forms differ in their grammatical categories and thus also meanings. This will be the topic of the next section.

Grammatical categories of verbs: Voice, aspect, mood

As has been explained in the previous sections, in Classical Tibetan every event verb has the property of transitivity (transitive vs intransitive) and controllability (controllable vs non-controllable). However, Classical Tibetan verbs may also represent other grammatical categories which are then expressed by means of a particular inflected form. Unfortunately for students of Classical Tibetan, so far no agreement has been reached among scholars concerning the grammatical categories that are expressed by some of the inflected forms. In general, scholars agree that v1 and v2 express active voice and indicative mood, whereas v4 expresses imperative mood. The interpretation of the differences between v1 and v2, as well as of v3, has been a serious bone of contention. In this textbook the position is followed that v1 indicates imperfective and v2 perfective aspect. Imperfective aspect is used for events that are seen as ongoing and not complete in any temporal frame, past, present, or future. Perfective aspect is used for events perceived as complete and bounded, i.e. without internal duration. However, the exact meaning of an inflected form may vary depending on the meaning of the verb. Finally, v3 expresses passive voice. Thus, the particular inflected forms may be ascribed the following meanings:

Table 4.4 Grammatical categories

	V1	V2	V3	V4
Mood	INDICATIVE			IMPERATIVE
Voice	ACTIVE		PASSIVE	
Aspect	IMPERFECTIVE	PERFECTIVE		

As an illustration, the conjugation of the verb བྱེད་ is provided with exemplary translations:

v1 བྱེད། "[He] does [it]." or "[He] is/was/will be doing [it]."
v2 བྱས། "[He] did [it]."
v3 བྱ། "[It] was/will be done."
v4 བྱོས། "Do [it]!"

Intransitive verbs of classes III and IV do not have v3-forms because these express passive; by definition, intransitive verbs cannot form passive. Neither do transitive verbs of class II (TR/NC) have v3-forms. These are non-controllable verbs; that means the agent that undertakes the action expressed by such a verb does not control its course. This fact makes verbs of class II less prototypically transitive than the verbs of class I. In consequence, verbs of class II were blocked from inflecting for a v3-form.[6]

Intransitive verbs

Intransitive verbs are those that do not acquire a direct object. The subject (S) of intransitive verbs typically stands in absolutive. The basic structure of a sentence with an intransitive verb is:

S_{ABS} V_{INTR}-*ɣo*$_{\text{FNL}}$ "S does V."

བུ་གུམ་མོ།། [*bu*]$_{\text{ABS}}$ *gum mo*// (MB D 272v7)
"The child died."

བཅོམ་ལྡན་འདས་གཤེགས་སོ། [*bčom ldan ɣdas*]$_{\text{ABS}}$ *gśegs so*/ (MB D 138r7)
"The Victorious One came."

If the verb requires an additional element, this will typically be placed between the subject and the verb, cf.:

བཅོམ་ལྡན་འདས་མཉན་དུ་ཡོད་པ་ན་བཞུགས་སོ། (MB D 138r5–6)
"The Victorious One was abiding in Mñan-du-yod-pa (Skt. Śrāvasti, an Indian town)."

If there are other elements which neither depend on nor modify the verb (e.g. information on the time of the event), these will usually be placed at the very beginning of the sentence, cf.:

> དུས་གཅིག་ན། བཅོམ་ལྡན་འདས་མཉན་དུ་ཡོད་པ་ན་བཞུགས་སོ། (MB D 138r5–6)
> "One day the Victorious One was abiding in Mñan-du-yod-pa."
>
> དེའི་ཚེ་བཅོམ་ལྡན་འདས་བསོད་སྙོམས་ལ་གཤེགས་སོ།། (MB D 138r6)
> "At that time (དེའི་ཚེ་), the Victorious One went for alms."

Information on the time of event (e.g. in the last example དེའི་ཚེ་ "at that time") is frequently stated in absolutive.[7]

Terminative

The terminative (TERM) case is another grammatical case in Classical Tibetan with a primarily locative meaning.[8]

Forms

The form of the terminative particle depends on the final letter of the preceding syllable:

དུ་	after -ང, -ད, -ན, -མ, -ར, -ལ
ཏུ་	after -ག, -བ, *-ད་དྲག་
སུ་	after -ས
-ར	after -འ, vowel
རུ་[9]	after -འ, vowel

Syntactic function

In rare instances the terminative case can be used to mark the **direct object** of a transitive verb or the **indirect object** of a ditransitive verb. In these functions it merely replaces the dative (see Lesson 3).

Meaning

Terminative can express one of the following meanings:

Direction towards which the action proceeds; it answers the question 'Whither?':

གནས་སུ་ཁྲིད་ (MB D 138r7) "to lead **to** a place"
ཕྱི་རོལ་དུ་འཆག་ (MB D 139r4) "to go outside"

Location where the action takes place; it answers the question 'Where?':

ལྷའི་གནས་སུ་ (MB D 140r3) "**in** a deities' place"
གནས་གཞན་ཞིག་ཏུ་ (MB D 272r4) "**at** another place"

Time at which the action takes place; it answers the question 'When?':

སྔར་ "earlier", lit. "**at** an earlier time"
ཡུན་རིང་པོར་ "during a long period of time", lit. "during a long time"

Beneficiary denotes an object or a person for whose benefit the event takes place:[10]

སྐྱེ་བ་ཕྱི་མར་འཆོལ་ (SSP 7c) "to entrust [wealth] to [one's] later life."

Manner expresses the way in which the action is carried out:

རྒྱུན་དུ་ (SSP 10c) "continually"
སོ་སོར་ (MB D 270v2) "individually"

Result is the outcome of an action:

ཕྱེད་མར་བགོད་ (ML D 11r) "to divide **in** half"
དུམ་བུར་འཆད་ (MB D 140v1) "to be cut **to** pieces"

Function denotes the function or character that someone or something has or acquires. Terminative expressing function can usually be translated with "as":

ཟས་སུ་ཟ་ (MB D 139r6) "to eat **as** food"
བག་མར་གཏོང་ (MB D 270v2) "to give in marriage", lit. "to give **as** wife"

In rare situations the terminative particle can replace the comitative particle (see Lesson 5: Comitative). The terminative particle plays an important role in postpositions (see Lesson 10). Likewise of great significance is the terminative particle in forming adverbs; they will be introduced in Lesson 8.

Exercise

Translate the clauses and determine the meanings of the case particles used therein:

༡ རྫུས་བུ་ཚལ་ན་འདུག་གོ། (MB D 140r3)
༢ དེ་ནས་བྲག་སྲིན་མོ་ལངས་སོ། (GLR 22r6)
༣ སྲིན་པོའི་ཕྲུ་གུ་དཔག་མེད་སྐྱེས་སོ། (GLR 22v2)
༤ སྤྲེའུ་ཕྲུག་རྣམས་སྐྱེས་སོ། (GLR 23r1–2)
༥ དེ་ནས་ཞིང་ཐོག་རྣམས་ཟད་དོ། (GLR 23r5)
༦ འཕགས་པ་ཡར་བཞེངས་སོ། (GLR 23v3)
༧ བདག་སྲིན་མོའི་རིགས་སུ་སྐྱེས་སོ།། (GLR 22v1)
༨ ཡབ་མེས་རྣམས་ལ་ནོར་བྱུང་ངོ་། (ML D 11v)
༩ མི་དེ་ལ་བུ་ཕོ་མེད། (MB D 270v2)
༡༠ ཕྱིས་དམག་པ་དག་འདུས་སོ། (MB D 270v2)
༡༡ གོས་ངུར་སྨྲིག་ཏུ་གྱུར་ཏོ། (MB D 138v4–5)
༡༢ རྒྱལ་བུ་གཉིས་འོངས་སོ། (MB D 139v7)
༡༣ རྒྱལ་བུ་སེམས་ཅན་ཆེན་པོ་དེ་དེར་ཚེ་འཕོས་སོ། (MB D 140r2–3)
༡༤ ལྷ་ཕྱིར་གནས་སུ་སོང་ངོ་། (MB D 140v3)
༡༥ དེ་གཉིས་དོང་ངོ་། (MB D 271v3)
༡༦ དེ་དག་དེར་སོང་ངོ་། (MB D 271v4)

Word list[11]

སྐྱེ་ v2 སྐྱེས་ (INTR) to be born
སྐྱེས་ see སྐྱེ་
གང་བ་ full
གོས་ clothes
གྱུར་ see འགྱུར་
འགྱུར་ v2 གྱུར་ (INTR) to become
འགྲོ་ v2/v4 སོང་ (INTR) to go
ངུར་སྨྲིག་ yellowish red
གཉིས་ two
དེ་ནས་ thereafter
དེར་ there
དོང་ see འདོང་
འདུག་ (INTR) to lie
འདོང་ v2/v4 དོང་ (INTR) to go
ནོར་ wealth, goods
གནས་ place
ཕྱིར་ (Adv) back
འཕགས་པ་ the Noble One
བུ་ཕོ་ son
བྱུང་ see འབྱུང་

བྲག་སྲིན་མོ་ rock-ogress

འབྱུང་ v2 བྱུང་ (INTR) to occur

མི་ man

མེད་ not to have

ཚལ་ forest

ཚེ་འཕོ་ v2/v4 འཕོས་ (INTR) to die

ཚེ་འཕོས་ see ཚེ་འཕོ་

འཛད་ v2 ཟད་ (INTR) to be consumed

བཞེངས་ (INTR) to rise, get up

ཟད་ see འཛད་

འོང་ v2 འོངས་ (INTR) to come

འོངས་ see འོང་

ཡབ་མེས་ ancestors

ཡར་ up, upward

རིགས་ family, race

རུས་བུ་ small bone

ལང་ v2 ལངས་ (INTR) to rise

ལངས་ see ལང་

ལོ་ཏོག་ harvest, crop

ཤིང་ཏོག་ fruit (of trees)

སོང་ see འགྲོ་

སྲིན་མོ་ demoness

ལྷ་ deity

Notes

1 Event verbs can also be called 'main verbs' but I reserve the latter term for verbs that are used with auxiliaries.

2 The schematic representation of the sentence structures shall demonstrate the differences between the four verb classes. The syntax of the respective classes will be discussed separately for each class of verb in the following lessons.

3 The identity of different forms usually resulted from historical developments. For instance, the original forms of the verb སྟོན་ were v1 སྟོན་, v2 བསྟནད་, v3 བསྟན་, and v4 *སྟོནད་. v2 became identical with v3 and v4 with v1 after the second postscript -ད had been dropped in Old Tibetan.

4 It is feasible that the verb was originally transitive and its inflected forms were v1 གཞིགས་, v2 *བཞག་, v3 *གཞག་, and v4 ཞོག་.

5 At some point, one started compiling lists of verbs and their inflected forms, i.e. creating conjugation lists. However, by that time the original patterns of verb inflection were not productive anymore; that is, the prefixes and suffixes had lost their meanings and the semi-independent status of morphemes that could have been attached to a particular verb in order to express a particular grammatical category. The loss of productivity of the morphemes has led to the development of artificial conjugations with controllable verbs having four, non-controllable verbs three slots always filled. That is, for each controllable verb one felt forced to always list four, and for non-controllable verb three forms. The newly created forms were coined by analogy with well-established controllable and non-controllable conjugations respectively. In this way, a distorted picture of the verb morphology has been created that does not correspond to any stage in the language history. A characteristic representative of this approach is the modern dictionary བོད་རྒྱ་ཚིག་མཛོད་ཆེན་མོ། (BTC) with its conjugation table provided in the Appendix – one that must not be used when reading Classical Tibetan texts.

6 In the following lessons, all examples will only include imperfective v1- or perfective v2-forms. Clauses with imperative v4-forms will be introduced in Lesson 6, and those with passive v3-forms in Lesson 14.

7 See Lesson 2: Absolutive.

8 According to the native grammatical tradition the three cases, locative (ན་), dative (ལ་), and terminative, have to a large extent the same meaning. Therefore, they are frequently treated together under the label ལ་དོན་, lit. "[having] the meaning of the ལ་-particle". However, as can be inferred from their presentation in the textbook, the cases actually differ considerably in their meanings and functions in Classical Tibetan.

9 རུ་ is a syllabic equivalent of the form -ར. It is used mainly in metrical passages whenever an additional syllable is needed in a line.

10 This meaning was originally reserved for the dative, which is used much more frequently to mark beneficiary.

11 Starting with Lesson 4, all event verbs are marked as either transitive (TR) or intransitive (INTR) in word lists. In addition, if a verb has more than one form, these are likewise provided; e.g. the lemma "འོང་ v2 འོངས་ (INTR) to come" should be read as: the verb "to come" is intransitive (INTR) and it has the v1-form འོང་ and v2-form འོངས་.

Lesson 5

- Transitive verbs
- Tibetan as an ergative language
- Ergative
- Comitative
- Translation of clauses

Transitive verbs

A transitive verb is a verb that requires one or two objects in addition to a subject. For Classical Tibetan the basic clause structure with a transitive verb and one object argument can be sketched as:

$$S_{ERG}\ O_{ABS}\ V_{TR}\text{-}yo_{FNL}$$

"S does O."

Every element of the sentence can be further modified according to the rules of the word class to which it belongs. If the verb is ditransitive, i.e. requires two object arguments (direct and indirect object), the clause takes the following structure:

$$S_{ERG}\ O_{2/DAT}\ O_{1/ABS}\ V_{TR}\text{-}yo_{FNL}$$

"S does O_1 to O_2."

The direct object (O_1) stands in absolutive, as in the standard construction with one object. The second (indirect) object (O_2) takes the dative particle ལ་. Typical ditransitive verbs are verbs of giving, receiving, or speaking.

DOI: 10.4324/9781003224198-8

As sentences with transitive verbs demand a special case for the subject – the so-called ergative – examples of such sentences will be provided in the section Ergative.

Tibetan as an ergative language

In linguistic typology one distinguishes between so-called accusative and ergative languages depending on the pattern a language uses to mark the subject of transitive verbs. The difference is illustrated next with, on the one hand, accusative languages English and German and, on the other hand, Classical Tibetan (an ergative language).

Accusative languages (English, German)

INTR:	$S_{NOM}\ V_{INTR}$	She is dancing.	Sie tanzt.
TR:	$S_{NOM}\ V_{TR}\ O_{ACC}$	She saw him.	Sie hat ihn gesehen.

In accusative languages, subjects of transitive and intransitive verbs take the nominative case (INTR: *she*, *sie*; TR: *she*, *sie*), whereas direct objects of transitive verbs need the accusative case (*him*, *ihn*).

Ergative languages (Classical Tibetan)

INTR:	$S_{ABS}\ V_{INTR}$	བཅོམ་ལྡན་འདས་གཤེགས་སོ། [*bčom ldan ɣdas*]$_{ABS}$ *gśegs so*/ (MB D 138r7) "The Victorious One came."
TR:	$S_{ERG}\ O_{ABS}\ V_{TR}$	རྒྱལ་པོས་དེ་དག་བཏང་ངོ། [*rgyal pos*]$_{ERG}$ [*de dag*]$_{ABS}$ *btaṅ ṅo*/ (MB D 138v2) "The king set them free."

In ergative languages subjects of intransitive verbs stand in the same case as objects of transitive verbs (བཅོམ་ལྡན་འདས་, དེ་དག་), whereas subjects of transitive verbs (རྒྱལ་པོས་) have a distinct marking – they stand in the so-called ergative (ERG) case. In the last example, the consonant -ས in རྒྱལ་པོས་ (རྒྱལ་པོ་ = ABS) is the ergative particle (see the next section). Thus, the main difference between accusative and ergative languages concerns the issue of which argument of a transitive verb the subject of an intransitive verb shares its marking with; with the object in ergative languages and with the subject in accusative languages:

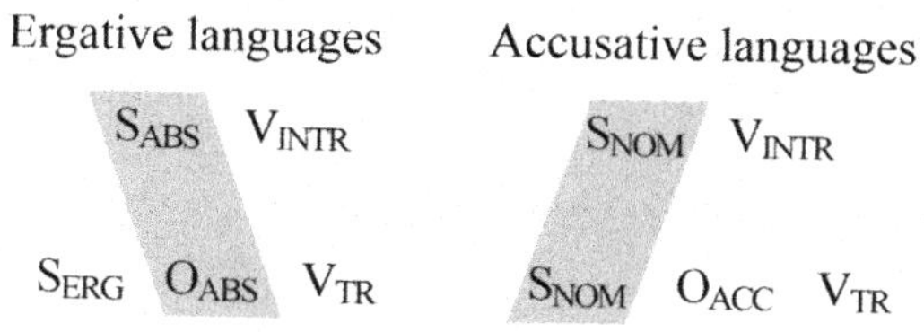

Figure 5.1 Ergative and accusative languages

Ergative

Forms

The particle of the ergative case (ERG) changes its form depending on the last letter of the preceding syllable:

ཀྱིས་	after -ད, -བ, -ས, *-ད་དྲག་
གྱིས་[1]	after -ན, -མ, -ར, -ལ
གིས་	after -ག, -ང
-ས	after -འ་, vowel
ཡིས་[2]	after -འ་, vowel

It is conspicuous that the ergative case particle has the same forms as the genitive particle extended by the final -ས. As in many dialects the pronunciation of the two particles used to be (and sometimes still is) identical or almost identical, it happens that the particles are confused in manuscripts or woodblocks. Therefore, when reading Classical Tibetan texts one should pay special attention to the clause structure because that is usually the only help in deciding whether a particle should be interpreted as genitive or ergative.

Syntactic functions

In Classical Tibetan ergative is the **subject** case of transitive controllable verbs. This is its only syntactic function in the sentence.

ཞང་པོས་ཡི་གེ་བཀླགས་སོ། (ML D 12r)
"The maternal uncle read the text."

This is the simplest clause with a transitive verb and two obligatory arguments: the subject ཞང་པོས་ in ergative and the direct object ཡི་གེ་ in absolutive.

> དེ་ནས་སྤྲེའུ་ཕྲུག་རྣམས་ཀྱིས་ལོ་ཐོག་ཟོས་སོ། (GLR 23v4)
> "Then, the monkey-children ate the crops."

The following sentence contains the ditransitive verb བྱིན་, a v2 of སྦྱིན་:

> ང་ལ་མཛེས་སེའི་ཕ་མས་གོས་ལྷམ་བྱིན་ནོ། (ML D 11v)
> "Mjes-se's parents gave me shoes and clothes."

As mentioned at the beginning of this lesson, ditransitive verbs require an indirect object which stands in dative. In the last example the indirect object is ང་ལ་, lit. "to me". གོས་ལྷམ་ in absolutive is the direct object, whereas ཕ་མས་ is the subject in ergative. The subject is additionally modified by the genitive phrase མཛེས་སེའི་ "of Mjes-se".

In particular cases, the subject of an intransitive verb may also stand in ergative. This happens when the verb is controllable (i.e. of class III) and the author of the text wishes to emphasise that the subject fully controls the action which was also initiated by her:

> ཕུ་བོ་གཉིས་ཀྱིས་བསྡད་དོ། (MB D 139v3)
> "Two elder brothers waited."

The ergative attached to the subject ཕུ་བོ་གཉིས་ emphasises that the brothers were waiting intentionally for the third brother, who had promised to join them shortly. If one wishes to reflect the Tibetan grammar in translation one can render the clause as "Two elder brothers waited (intentionally)."

Meaning

Ergative case is used in Classical Tibetan to express the following meanings:

Agent is a being that deliberately performs the action:[3]

> དབྱིག་པ་ཅན་གྱིས་བདག་གི་བུ་བསད་དོ། (MB D 272v6–7)
> "Dbyig-pa-čan killed my child."

> རྒྱལ་པོས་དེ་དག་བཏང་ངོ། (MB D 138v2)
> "The king set them free."

Instrument denotes an object that is used to carry out the action:

> བདག་གིས་ལུས་ཀྱིས་སྟག་མོ་ལྟོགས་པ་བསྐྱོད་དོ། (MB D 140r6)
> "I fed a hungry tigress **with** [my] body."

This clause contains two ergatives. The first one (བདག་གིས་) expresses the agent, the second one the instrument (ལུས་ཀྱིས་) with which the action is carried out.

Cause expresses the reason for which the action takes place:

བཅོམ་ལྡན་འདས་ཀྱི་བཀའ་དྲིན་ཆེན་པོས་ (MB D 138v3) "**due to** the great kindness of the Victorious One"
ལས་ཀྱིས་ (GLR 22r5) "**due to** [her] previous actions."

Manner denotes the way in which the action is carried out:

ཐུགས་རྗེས་ (GLR 22v3) "[Embrace me] **with** compassion!"
རིམ་གྱིས་ "successively, in a row"[4]

Comitative

In the most general sense, comitative denotes accompaniment. In English it can be rendered with prepositions "with", "together with", or "in company with". In Classical Tibetan the comitative (COM) particle is དང་. It has two basic functions within a clause. First of all, it is the particle of the comitative case. In addition, the particle དང་ also functions as a coordinating conjunction "and". These two basic functions of དང་ will be discussed in turn in the following sections.[5]

Comitative case

A group of verbs, the majority of which express similarity, association, or separation (dissociation), require a complement in comitative case.[6] For instance:

སྲིན་པོ་ཞིག་དང་འགྲོགས་ (GLR 22v1) "to come together **with** an ogre"
དཔེ་འདི་དང་འདྲ་ (ML D 11v) "to be like this proverb", lit. "to be similar **with** this proverb"
ཡབ་དང་འབྲལ་ (ML D 10r) "to be without the father", lit. "to be separated from the father"

In Classical Tibetan one can differentiate between the following basic meanings of the comitative case:

Simile expresses an entity to which sth. is similar:

བུ་གཅིག་པ་དང་འདྲའོ། (MB D 139r3) "[He] was **like** the only son." lit. "[He] was similar **with** the only son."

Companion expresses an entity with which sth. or sb. connects:

བཅོམ་ལྡན་འདས་ཀུན་དགའ་བོ་དང་བསོད་སྙོམས་ལ་གཤེགས་སོ། (MB D 138r6)
"The Victorious One went for alms **with** Kun-dgaɣ-bo."

བཅོམ་ལྡན་འདས་དང་ཕྲད་དོ། (MB D 138v6)
Lit. "[They] met **with** the Victorious One."

Separation expresses an entity from which sth. or sb. separates:

ཁྱེའུ་དེ་སྲོག་དང་བྲལ་ལོ།། (MB D 272r1)
"The boy died." Lit. "The boy was separated **from** [his] life."

Conjunction

The salient function of དང་ as the conjunction "and" is the coordination of two nouns or noun phrases:

སྨན་པ་དང་མོ་མ་རྣམས་ (ML D 10r) "doctors and diviners"
ཤ་རློན་པ་དང་ཁྲག་དྲོན་མོ་ (MB D 139r6) "fresh flesh and warm blood"

If an enumeration consists of several items, དང་ can be omitted after some of them. The omission usually concerns དང་ between the last two elements of the enumeration:

ཀྭ་དང་ལྷ་རོང་ "Kwa, Lha, and Roṅ" (Nel 16r7) instead of *ཀྭ་དང་ལྷ་དང་རོང་[7]
ཀ་ཆིགས་ཆེན་མོ་དང་། བཀའ་ཆེམས་ཀ་ཁོལ་མ། རྒྱལ་རབས་དཔག་བསམ་ལྗོན་ཤིང་རྣམས་ (GLR 28r2)
"*Ka chigs čhen mo*, *Bkaɣ čhems ka khol ma*, [and] *Rgyal rabs dpag bsam ljon śiṅ*"[8]

Sometimes an enumeration does not contain any comitative:

ནས། གྲོ། སྲན་མ། བྲ་བོ། སོ་བ་རྣམས་ (GLR 23v3)
"barley, wheat, beans, buckwheat, [and] unhusked barley"

As in this example, the elements of the enumeration are then usually separated by < । >. If the comitative particle is placed between repeated words it expresses distribution:

ཡུལ་དང་ཡུལ་ "region after region, each region" (Tār 37, 16; *apud* Schneider 2017: 431)
ཞག་དང་ཞག་ "every day, always" (J: 471b, s.v. ཞག་)

In rare cases such a repetition may serve to intensify the meaning:

ན་ (metrically for ན་བ་) དང་ན་ "more and more ill" (Padm 307v5; *apud* Schneider 2017: 432)

Terminative for comitative

The terminative case can replace the comitative case in two instances:

- *Metri causa*; in metrical passages in order to spare a syllable:
  སྦྲང་རྩིར་ལྡན་ instead of *སྦྲང་རྩི་དང་ལྡན་ (*apud* Schneider 2017: 443) "to be provided with honey"
- If more than one comitative particle is used in a phrase or a clause:
  ལས་དང་སྐལ་བར་ལྡན་པ་ instead of *ལས་དང་སྐལ་བ་དང་ལྡན་པ་ (Tār 14, 6; *apud* Schneider 2017: 443) "one with a [good] karma and [good] fortune"
  བྱམས་པ་དང་སྙིང་རྗེར་ལྡན་ (MB D 139r3) instead of *བྱམས་པ་དང་སྙིང་རྗེ་དང་ལྡན་ "to be possessed of (or: provided with) love and compassion"

The conjunction དང་ cannot be replaced by any other particle.

Translation of clauses

As the reader has certainly already realised, Classical Tibetan has a clause structure that differs considerably from clause structures of most European languages. At the beginning this might pose some problems. Nonetheless several simple rules can facilitate the analysis of a Tibetan clause:

- Start always from the end of a clause and identify its predicate.
- Determine whether the predicate is a copula or an event verb.
- If the verb is a copula, check the structure of the clauses with the respective copula verb in Lessons 2 (ཡིན་) or 3 (ཡོད་) in order to identify the obligatory elements of these clauses.
- If the verb is an event verb, use the word lists or Glossary to determine whether it is a transitive or an intransitive verb.
- If the verb is transitive, identify the subject (in ergative) and object (in absolutive).
- If the verb is intransitive, identify the subject in absolutive (ergative subject is rare, see the section Ergative).

- If the subject and (if present) the object have been identified, isolate and identify the remaining elements of the clause.

At the beginning it might also be helpful to mark the most important elements of a clause with different colours.

དེ་ནས་སྤྲེའུ་ཕྲུག་རྣམས་ཀྱིས་ལོ་ཐོག་ཟོས་སོ།

In this example, first the predicate is identified (here followed by the final particle སོ་). As it is a transitive verb (v2 < ཟ་ "to eat") one needs to identify its subject in ergative (སྤྲེའུ་ཕྲུག་རྣམས་ཀྱིས་) and its object in absolutive (ལོ་ཐོག་). In this way the major elements are identified and one clearly sees what remains to be explained: དེ་ནས་.

Exercise

༡ སྐྲ་དང་ཁ་སྤུ་རང་བྱིའོ། (MB D 138v4)
༢ དེ་ནས་རྒྱལ་བུ་ཐ་ཆུངས་དེས་ཡིད་ལ་འདི་སྙམ་དུ་བསམས་སོ། (MB D 139r7)
༣ དེའི་ཚེ་རྒྱལ་བུས་ཤིང་གི་ཚལ་བ་རྣོན་པོས་ལུས་ལ་ཁྲག་ཕྱུང་ངོ། (MB D 139v3)
༤ ཕ་མ་གཉིས་ཀྱིས་ནམ་མཁའ་ལ་བལྟས་སོ། (MB D 140r5)
༥ སྐྱེ་བ་དང་འཇིག་པ་ཀུན་ལ་སྲིད་དོ། (MB D 140r7)
༦ བུ་ཚས་འཁོར་བའི་འདམ་དུ་བདག་ཚུད་དོ།། (GLR 23r6–23v1)
༧ ང་བུ་གཅིག་པོར་སོང་ངོ། (ML D 12r)
༨ ཨ་ནེ་དང་ཨ་ཁུ་གཉིས་གཅིག་ཏུ་དྲིལ་ལོ། (ML D 12v)
༩ དོ་སྣད་ཚོ་ཕྱིར་སོང་ངོ། (ML D 12v)
༡༠ ཞང་པོ་དང་མཛེས་སེའི་ཕ་མིང་བསྡད་དོ། (ML D 13r)
༡༡ གླང་སྒོ་གཞན་དུ་སོང་ངོ། (MB D 271v1)
༡༢ རྐང་པ་ཆག་གོ། (MB D 271v3)
༡༣ ཁྱོད་ཀྱིས་ངའི་ཁྱོ་བསད་དོ། (MB D 271v5)
༡༤ བཅོམ་ལྡན་འདས་ཀྱིས་ཆོས་བསྟན་ཏོ། (MB D 138v5)
༡༥ དེའི་ཚེ་ན་ཕྱིན་ཏེ་ལོ་ཤུ་ཤས་འདི་སྙམ་དུ་བསམས་སོ།། (MB D 270v4)
༡༦ ཆུང་མས་རྟག་ཏུ་སྤྱོའོ། (MB D 270v4)
༡༧ བཅོམ་ལྡན་འདས་ཀྱིས་དེའི་བསམ་པ་ཐུགས་ཀྱིས་མཁྱེན་ནོ། (MB D 270v6–7)
༡༨ ཁྱོད་ཀྱིས་ངའི་རྟ་བསད་དོ། (MB D 271v4)
༡༩ ཐ་ག་པའི་ཆུང་མས་དབྱིག་པ་ཅན་དེ་བཟུང་ངོ། (MB D 271v5)

Word list

ཀུན་ (N) all

རྐང་པ་ leg

སྐྱེ་བ་ birth

སྐྲ་ hair

ཁ་སྤུ་ beard

ཁྱོ་ husband

མཁྱེན་ (TR) to recognise

འཁོར་བ་ cycle of existence

གླང་ ox

སྒོ་ door

གཅིག་ one

གཅིག་པོ་ (A) only

བཅོམ་ལྡན་འདས་ Victorious One, an epithet of the Buddha

ཆག་ see འཆག་

ཆོས་ Buddhist teaching

འཆག་ v2 ཆག་ (INTR) to break

འཇིག་པ་ decay

སྙམ་ thought

རྟ་ horse

རྟག་ཏུ་ always

ལྟ་ v2 བལྟས་ v3 བལྟ་ v4 ལྟོས་ (TR) to look (at + DAT)

སྟོན་ v2/v3 བསྟན་ v4 སྟོན་ (TR) to teach

བལྟས་ see ལྟ་

བསྟན་ see སྟོན་

ཐ་ག་པ་ weaver

ཐུགས་ mind

དོ་སྣད་ consort and [her] children

དྲིལ་ see འདྲིལ་

འདམ་ swamp

འདྲིལ་ v2 དྲིལ་ གཅིག་ཏུ་འདྲིལ་ to unite

སྡོད་ v2 བསྡད་ v4 སྡོད་ (INTR) to stay

བསྟད་ see སྟོད་

ནམ་མཁའ་ sky

སྐྱོ་ v2 སྐྱོས་ (INTR) to scold

ཕ་མ་ parents; father and mother

ཕ་མིང་ father and brother(s)

ཕྱིར་ out, outside

ཕྱུང་ see འབྱིན་

བུ་ཚ་ offspring

བྱི་ see འབྱི་

དབྱིག་པ་ཅན་ (PN) Dbyig-pa-čan

འབྱི་ v2 བྱི་ (INTR) to fall off

འབྱིན་ v2/v4 ཕྱུང་ v3 དབྱུང་ (TR) to cause to come forth, to take out

ཚུད་ see འཚུད་

འཚུད་ v2 ཚུད་ (INTR) to enter

མཇེས་སེ་ (PN) Mȷes-se

འཛིན་ v2 བཟུང་ v3 གཟུང་ v4 ཟུངས་ (TR) to seize

ཞང་པོ་ maternal uncle

གཞན་ other

བཟུང་ see འཛིན་

ཡིད་ mind

རང་ itself

ལུས་ body

ཤིང་ wood

སེམས་ v2 བསམས་ v3 བསམ་ v4 སོམས་ (TR) to think; སྙམ་དུ་སེམས་ to think

སྲིད་ (COP) to exist

གསོད་ v2 བསད་ v3 གསད་ v4 སོད་ (TR) to kill

བསད་ see གསོད་

བསམ་པ་ thought

བསམས་ see སེམས་

ཨ་ནེ་ aunt

Notes

1 There exists a homonym of the form གྱིས་; v4 of བགྱིད་ “to do” is likewise གྱིས་.

2 ཡིས་ is a syllabic equivalent of the form -ས. It is used mainly in metrical passages if an additional syllable is needed in a line.

3 This role is reserved for the subject of a transitive verb (or, in special cases, for the subject of an intransitive verb).

4 Manner ergative is mainly used to derive adverbs from nouns (see Lesson 8).

5 A thorough description of the comitative particle based on an extensive corpus of Classical Tibetan texts can be found in Schneider (2017).

6 A complete list of verbs that require the comitative case can be found in Schneider (2017: 437–41).

7 Kwa, Lha, and Roṅ are the first syllables of the proper names Kwa Ɣod-mčhog Grags-pa, Lha-luṅ Rab-ɣbyor-dbyaṅs, and Roṅ-ston Seṅ-ge-grags (Nel: 125).

8 These are the titles of three Tibetan historiographical works.

Lesson 6

- Elative
- Delative
- Negation
- Imperative
- Prohibitive

Elative

The elative (EL) particle is ནས་; it only has this one form.[1] Originally, the elative used to be another locative case with the basic meaning "out of" – it marked the initial point (spatial or temporal) from which an action started.

In Classical Tibetan one can differentiate between the following meanings of the elative case:

Source expresses a place from which an action begins:

བཅོམ་ལྡན་འདས་རྒྱང་མ་ནས་གཤེགས་སོ། (MB D 138r7) "The Victorious One came **from** afar."
ནམ་མཁའ་ནས་ (GLR 22v5) "**from** the sky"

Time expresses the point in time from which an action begins:

ཆུང་ངུ་ནས་ (MB D 139r3) "**since** [his] childhood"
དེ་ནས་ "then", lit. "**from** that [moment on]"

Substance expresses material from which an object is made:

པ་གུ་ནས་ "**from** bricks" (*apud* Hahn 1996: 110)

Cause expresses the reason for which an action occurs:

སྐོམ་ནས་ "[to die] **from** thirst" (*apud* Hahn 1996: 111)

DOI: 10.4324/9781003224198-9

Manner expresses the way in which the action is carried out:

སོ་སོ་ནས་ (MB 273r3) "individually"
རེ་རེ་ནས་ "individually"

The elative particle ནས་ can be used instead of the ergative particle to mark an agent of several verbs. This happens frequently in direct speech when the speaker is a respectful person. For examples see Lesson 13: Direct Speech. The role of the elative particle in adverbs will be discussed in Lesson 8.

Delative

The delative (DEL) particle is ལས་; it only has this one form.[2] Originally, delative used to be another locative case with the basic meaning "off the surface (of sth.)". Later it came to express a more general concept of origin.

Syntactic function

In Classical Tibetan there is a group of verbs that require delative in their argument structure. Those verbs have some semantic traits in common: they express separation or release from something (e.g. ཐར་, འགྲོལ་), victory over something (རྒྱལ་), passing over (འདའ་), rescue (སྒྲོལ་) or guarding from (སྐྱོབ་).

Meaning

In Classical Tibetan one can differentiate between the following meanings of the delative case:

Source expresses a place from which an action begins:

ནམ་མཁའ་ལས་བབས་སོ། (MB D 140r5) "[He] came down **from** the sky."

Origin expresses where an object or a person originated:

ཕ་སྤྲེའུ་དང་། མ་བྲག་སྲིན་མོ་གཉིས་ལས་ (GLR 23v5) "[to be begotten] from both a father-monkey and a mother rock-ogress"
བཀའ་ཆེམས་ཀ་ཁོལ་མ་ལས་ (GLR 24r4–5) "[the following quotation comes] from *Bkaɣ čhems ka khol ma*"

In the last example, the delative particle is used to mark a textual source from which something is quoted.

Separation expresses an entity from which sth. or sb. separates:

ཉེས་པ་ཆེན་པོ་ལས་ཐར་ (MB D 138v6) "to become free **from** great moral faults"
ཆུ་ལས་འོ་མ་འབྱེད་ (SSP 20d) "to separate milk **from** water"

Comparison/Difference expresses an entity that serves as a point of departure for a comparison:

ཀུན་ལས་རྒྱལ་ (GLR 25v3) "to be victorious over all", lit. "to be [more] victorious than all"

The comparative function of delative is discussed in more detail in Lesson 15.

Native grammarians treat elative and delative together. The younger a Classical Tibetan text, the greater the probability that the particles of elative and delative have the same functions or even that elative replaces delative throughout.[3]

Negation

Classical Tibetan has two negation (NEG) particles: མི་ and མ་.[4] They have a fixed position in a clause: they always precede the predicate.

བདག་གི་ཕ་མ་མི་དགའོ། (MB D 140r4) "My parents are not happy."

However, མི་ and མ་ have distinct distribution depending on what kind of word they negate. And so, མི་ typically stands before verb stems v1 (imperfective) and v3 (passive), whereas མ་ negates v2 (perfective):

མ་སྨད་ངེད་ཀྱིས་སྡུག་ཏུ་མི་འཇུག་གོ། (ML D 11r)
"We will not lead the mother and her children into misery."

བལ་པོས་སེ་འུ་མ་ཟོས་སོ།། (SSP 22c)
"A Nepalese did not eat the pomegranate."

The copula ཡིན་ is always negated with མ་, whereas the copula འདུག་ with མི་. The negated form of the copula ཡོད་ is མེད་.[5]

In addition, deverbal nouns are negated with མ་ and deverbal adjectives with མི་. The negation immediately precedes the deverbal:

Deverbal noun: མ་རིག་པ་ "ignorance"
Deverbal adjective: མི་མཐོང་བ་ (MB 270v2) "blind; not-seeing"

Negation མ་ put between two nouns indicates that neither of the two is meant, as in the well-known Tibetan proverb ར་མ་ལུག་, lit. "neither goat nor sheep", which is used to refer to something as a hybrid, a mixture of two things varied in character.[6]

Imperative

Imperative (IMP) mood is usually used to express a command or request. Classical Tibetan has a special final particle to mark an end of an imperative clause. This particle is called 'imperative particle'. Imperative particle is identical in its form with the indefinite particle (see Lesson 1) and undergoes the same assimilation changes depending on the final consonant of the preceding syllable:

ཅིག་	after -ག, -ད, -བ, *-ད་དྲག་
ཞིག་	after -ང, -ན, -མ, -འ, -ར, -ལ, vowel
ཤིག་	after -ས

Because imperative mood presumes that the addressed person is capable of consciously undertaking the action, only controllable verbs can form imperative clauses. If the verb has a distinct imperative stem (v4; see Lesson 4), the imperative particle follows on the v4-stem of the verb:

བདག་ལ་སྨྲོས་ཤིག (MB D 140r5) "Tell us!"
བརྩོན་འགྲུས་མཛོད་ཅིག (MB D 140r7) "Strain [yourself]!" Lit. "Make efforts!"

Sometimes, if a verb has a distinct v4-stem, the imperative particle can be left out:

ཐུགས་རྗེས་ཟུངས། (GLR 22v3) "Embrace [me] with compassion!"
ཚུར་ཤོག (MB D 271v4) "Come here!"

Prohibitive

Prohibitive (PROH) is the negative imperative mood used most commonly to express prohibition, i.e. that something must not be done. In Classical Tibetan prohibitive is formed from the imperfective stem (v1) negated with མ་:[7]

ད་མ་ངུ། (ML D 13r) "Now, don't cry!"

The sequence 'མ་ + v1-stem' can also be followed by the imperative particle:

> གཞན་དུ་མ་སེམས་ཤིག (MB D 140v5) "Don't think any differently (གཞན་དུ)!"
> སྡུག་ཏུ་མ་འཛུག་ཅིག (ML D 10v) "Do not lead [them] into misery!"

In pre-classical language prohibitive was formed with a negated (མ་) perfective stem (v2) of a verb:

> རྒོད་མ་མ་བཏང་། (MB D 271v3) "Don't let the mare escape!"

This form of prohibitive can still be found in Buddhist canonical texts that were translated earlier (during the སྔ་དར་ "earlier propagation [of Buddhism]") and not consistently edited in later centuries.[8]

Exercise

༡ རྡུལ་དང་དྲི་མ་ཟད་དོ། (MB D 138v5)
༢ བདག་ཡུན་རིང་པོ་ནས་འཁོར་བ་ན་འཁོར་རོ། (MB D 139r7)
༣ གླང་གླར་བྱིན་ཅིག (MB D 271v2)
༤ ད་ཟློ། (GLR 23v4)
༥ ཡན་ལག་རྣམས་སེར་གར་སོང་ངོ་། (ML D 11r)
༦ ཨ་མས་གྲལ་གྱི་དབུས་སུ་ལངས་སོ། (ML D 12r)
༧ ཞང་པོས་ཡབ་ཀྱི་ཞལ་ཆེམས་ཀྱི་ཡི་གེ་བཀླགས་སོ། (ML D 12r)
༨ མཛེས་སེའི་ཕ་མས་མི་ཤིང་བསྐུར་ཏོ། (ML D 13v)
༩ འབྱུང་པོའི་བུ་རྣམས་ལོང་བར་འགྱུར་རོ།། (SSP 3d)
༡༠ བཅོམ་ལྡན་འདས་བསམ་གྱིས་མི་ཁྱབ་བོ། (MB D 271r3)
༡༡ དེས་ཁྱིམ་བདག་ཅིག་ལས་གླང་ཞིག་བརྙས་སོ། (MB D 271r7)
༡༢ ལམ་གྱི་བར་དེ་ན་ཆུ་བོ་ཞིག་ཡོད། (MB D 271v6)
༡༣ སྙེའུ་ཆུར་ལྷུང་ངོ་། (MB D 271v7)
༡༤ དེའི་ཚེ་ཀུན་དགའ་བོས་དེ་ལྟ་བུའི་དངོས་པོ་དག་མཐོང་ངོ་། (MB D 138v5–6)
༡༥ བྲམ་ཟེ་དེའི་ཆུང་མ་དེ་མི་སྡུག་གོ། (MB D 270v2)

Word list

ཀུན་དགའ་བོ་ (PN) Kun-dgaɣ-bo
ཀློག་ v2 བཀླགས་ v3 བཀླག་ v4 ཀློགས་ (TR) to read
བཀླགས་ see ཀློག་

སྐུར་ v2/v3 བསྐུར་ v4 སྐུར་ (TR) to send
བསྐུར་ see སྐུར་
ཁྱབ་ (INTR) to be comprised (by + ERG)
ཁྱིམ་བདག་ householder
འཁོར་ (INTR) to turn round, to roam
གྲལ་ row
འགྲོ་ v2/v4 སོང་ (INTR) to become (+ TERM)
དངོས་པོ་ thing
ཆུ་ river
ཆུ་བོ་ river
བརྙ་ v2 བརྙས་ (TR) to borrow
བརྙས་ see བརྙ་
ལྷུང་ v2 ལྷུང་ (INTR) to fall
སྟེའུ་ axe
མཐོང་ (TR) to see
ད་ now
དེ་ལྟ་བུ་ of that kind, such
དྲི་མ་ impurities
རྡུལ་ dust
སྡུག་ (to be) pretty, nice
བར་ (N) middle
བྱིན་ see སྦྱིན་
དབུས་ (N) middle
སྦྱིན་ v2/v4 བྱིན་ (TR) to give
མེ་ཤིང་ firewood
ཞལ་ཆེམས་ testament
ཟ་ v2 བཟས་/ཟོས་ v3 བཟའ་ v4 ཟོ(ས)་ (TR) to eat
ཟོ་ see ཟ་
ཡན་ལག་ limb
ཡབ་ father
ཡི་གེ་ (written) text
ལམ་ road, way
ལོང་བ་ blind

སེར་ག་ crack, fissure

སོང་ see འགྲོ་

སླར་ (Adv) back

ལྷུང་ see ལྷུང་

ཨ་མ་ mother

Notes

1 Students should be aware that the elative particle has a homonym: ནས་ "barley".

2 Students should be aware that the delative particle has a homonym: ལས་ "deed, action".

3 For instance, in the story *The descent of Tibetan people from a monkey and a rock-ogress* (see Reading II) the text once reads "X ལས་ཆད་" (GLR 23v5) and once "X ནས་ཆད་" (GLR 24r3). In both cases the meaning is the same: "descended from X".

4 Both forms of negation have homonyms: མི་ "man, human being"; མ་ "mother". In addition, the homonymic syllable མ་ is a nominal particle used to form new words; for details, see Lesson 7.

5 For details, see Lessons 2 and 3.

6 Schiefner (1859) provides further examples of this use of the negation particle.

7 Notice that v1-stems in indicative clauses are negated with the negation མི་.

8 The archaic character of this prohibitive formation is confirmed by the fact that Balti, Purik, and Kargil – modern Tibetan dialects that have preserved many archaic features – also form prohibitive from v2-stems (Zeisler 2004: 345). Therefore Hahn's statement that v2 is used to form prohibitive (1996: 70) should be understood as referring to the older language.

Lesson 7

- Nominal particles

Nominal particles

Nominal particles are simple syllables (consisting of a consonant and a vowel) that serve to nominalise a word, a phrase, or even a whole clause. Whatever the original form might have been, the outcome of adding a nominal particle is always a noun or an adjective. A nominal particle is always added after the word or phrase which it nominalises. Classical Tibetan has a set of such nominal particles that will be discussed in detail in the following sections.

པ་ ~ བ་ particle

པ་ ~ བ་ particle has two variant forms, the application of which depends on the final letter of the preceding syllable:

པ་	after -ག, -ད, -ན, -བ, -མ, -ས, *-ད་དྲག་
བ་	after -ང, -འ, -ར, -ལ, vowel

The result of adding the པ་ ~ བ་ particle may be either a noun or a verbal adjective (i.e. participle).

Noun

The པ་ ~ བ་ particle can form nouns from v1-stems of verbs:

གསོལ་ "to request" གསོལ་བ་ "request"
འཇིག་ "to decay" འཇིག་པ་ "decay"
སྐྱེ་ "to be born" སྐྱེ་བ་ "birth"

DOI: 10.4324/9781003224198-10

As any other noun, those derived from verbs by means of the པ་ ~ བ་ particle can form noun phrases in clauses:

> སྐྱེ་བ་དང་འཇིག་པ་ཀུན་ལ་སྲིད་དོ། (MB D 140r7)
> "Birth and decay are intrinsic to everything." Lit. "Birth and decay exist in everything."

The particle can also form nouns from other word classes:

> ཅེས་ "(QUOT) thus" ཅེས་པ་ (MB D 140v1) "the-thus-said"[1]
> གང་ན་ "where" གང་ན་བ་ "the where-place; whereabouts"
> བཅོམ་ལྡན་འདས་གང་ན་བ་དེར་སོང་ངོ་། (MB D 138v3)
> "[They] went to the place where the Victorious One [was staying]."

Participle (verbal adjective)

Participles can be formed either from v1- or v2-stems. Imperfective participles (= present participles) are derived from v1-stems:

> རྐུ་ "to steal" རྐུ་བ་ "stealing"
> གཤེགས་ "to come" གཤེགས་པ་ "coming"

Perfective participles (= past participles) are formed from v2-stems:

> ཐོས་ "to hear" ཐོས་པ་ "heard"
> སྨྲ་ "to say" སྨྲས་པ་ "said, uttered"

Being verbal adjectives, participles may be used as attributes to modify a noun:

> སངས་རྒྱས་གཤེགས་པ་ (MB D 138v1) "the coming Buddha"
> སྐ་རགས་བཅིངས་པ་ (ML D 11r) "a bound girdle"
> དེ་སྐད་སྨྲས་པ་ (MB D 139v7–140r1) "those uttered words"

These noun phrases do not differ from other noun phrases formed from a noun and an adjective or a numeral. They can likewise be embedded in a clause:

> ལྷ་མོ་དེས་དེ་སྐད་སྨྲས་པ་ཐོས་སོ། (MB D 139v7–140r1)
> "The queen heard those words uttered."

Here the noun phrase དེ་སྐད་སྨྲས་པ་ functions as the direct object of the verb ཐོས་.

Like many other adjectives in Classical Tibetan, participles can also be used as nouns:

གདུང་ "to long for" གདུང་བ་ "longing for; one longing for"

ཟས་ལ་གདུང་བ་ཞིག་ (GLR 23r2) "a one longing for food"

པ་ particle

The nominal particle པ་ has only one form and is used to express one of the following meanings:

Affiliation

The particle པ་ forms a word that denotes a person who is in a general way affiliated to the thing denoted by the base word:

རྟ་ "horse"	རྟ་པ་ "horseman", lit. "one affiliated to a horse"
བོད་ "Tibet"	བོད་པ་ "Tibetan", lit. "one affiliated to Tibet"
དགོན་པ་ "hermitage"	དགོན་པ་པ་ "hermit", lit. "one affiliated to a hermitage"

The last example demonstrates that the པ་ particle can be attached to a word even if it already has another nominal particle (in this case པ་). པ་ can likewise be attached to a noun phrase:

བོད་ཁ་བ་ཅན་པ་ (GLR 23v5) "inhabitants (པ་) of the snow-clad Tibet"

བོད་ཁ་བ་ཅན་ means "snow-clad Tibet" (བོད་ "Tibet"; ཁ་བ་ཅན་ "snow-clad") so that the particle པ་ turns the whole noun phrase into lit. "one affiliated to the snow-clad Tibet".

Possession

The particle པ་ can mark the possessor of a thing denoted by the base word:

སེམས་བརྟན་ "firm mind"	སེམས་བརྟན་པ་ (MB D 138v5) "one having firm mind"
རྐང་གཉིས་ "two legs"	རྐང་གཉིས་པ་ (*apud* Hahn 1996: 33) "sb. who has two legs"

Ordinal numerals

The particle པ་ also serves to derive ordinal numerals from cardinal numerals:

གཉིས་ "two"	གཉིས་པ་ "the second"[2]
གསུམ་ "three"	གསུམ་པ་ "the third"

An exception is the ordinal numeral "the first" which is not derived from གཅིག་ "one", but has a distinct form: དང་པོ་. Any other ordinal numeral is derived from its cardinal equivalent by means of the particle པ་.[3]

པོ་ ~ བོ་ particle

The nominal particle པོ་ ~ བོ་ has two forms, the use of which depends on the final letter of the preceding syllable. The assimilation rules are the same as for the པ་ ~ བ་ particle:

པོ་	after -ག, -ད, -ན, -བ, -མ, -ས, *-ད་དྲག་
བོ་	after -ང, -འ, -ར, -ལ, vowel

The main function of the particle པོ་ ~ བོ་ is to mark the masculine gender. It can be attached to either nouns or adjectives.

Noun

བོན་ "Bon religion" བོན་པོ་ "a male adherent to the Bon religion"
གྲོགས་ "friend" གྲོགས་པོ་ "a male friend"

Adjective

མཁས་ "skilled" མཁས་པོ་ "a skilled male person; a scholar"
རྒན་ "old" རྒན་པོ་ "an old man"

པོ་ particle

The particle པོ་ has only one form. Its basic function consists of forming masculine agent nouns from v1-stems of verbs, which means nouns that denote male persons who are performing the action expressed by the respective verb:

རྒྱལ་ "to be victorious" རྒྱལ་པོ་ "king", lit. "victorious one"
བྱེད་ "to make" བྱེད་པོ་ "maker"

In addition, the particle can form collective nouns from numerals, cf.:

གསུམ་ "three" གསུམ་པོ་ "a trio", i.e. a group that consists of three things
མ་སྨད་གསུམ་པོ་ (MB D 138v6) "the trio: the mother and [her] children"
སྤྲེའུ་ཕྲུག་དྲུག་པོ་འདི་ (GLR 23r4) lit. "this sextet of monkey-children"

མ་ particle

The nominal particle མ་ forms feminine equivalents of formations in པ་ ~ བ་ and in པ་ in the following meanings:

Participle (see section པ་ ~ བ་ particle)

མཐོང་ "to see" མཐོང་མ་ "seeing she"

Affiliation (see section པ་ particle)

ཆང་ཚོང་ "tavern" ཆང་ཚོང་མ་ "female beer-seller"

Possession (see section པ་ particle)

རྐང་གཉིས་ "two legs" རྐང་གཉིས་མ་ "a woman having two legs"

Ordinal numeral (see section པ་ particle)

གཉིས་ "two" གཉིས་མ་ "the second she"

In addition, མ་ occurs in a group of words the original meaning of which seems to have been adjectival. However, in many cases the words underwent further lexicalisation (and sometimes changes in form) and are used as nouns with derived meanings in Classical Tibetan.

བླ་ "what is above" བླ་མ་ "the higher (one)" > "lama, teacher"
འདར་ "to tremble" སྡར་མ་ "trembling" > "coward"
གཏོར་ "to scatter" གཏོར་མ་ "scattered" > "strewing-oblation"

A very special usage of མ་ concerns its occurrence in titles of works.[4] The particle is regularly added at the end of a title which may be formed from the first words of the work, the number of its chapters, its origin, the main trait of its narrative, etc.:

བཀའ་ཆེམས་ཀ་ཁོལ་མ་ *Bkaẏ čhems ka khol ma*, lit. "Pillar-hole (ཀ་ཁོལ་) Testament (བཀའ་ཆེམས་)", due to the assumed place of its discovery in a hole of a pillar of the Lha-sa J̌o-khaṅ temple.

མོ་ particle

The nominal particle མོ་ indicates gender; it forms feminine forms either from verbs (only from v1-stems) or from nouns:

Verb (see section པོ་ particle)

རྒྱལ་ "to be victorious" རྒྱལ་མོ་ "queen", lit. "victorious she"

Noun (see section པོ་ ~ བོ་ particle)

སྟག་ "tiger" སྟག་མོ་ "tigress"
ལྷ་ "deity" ལྷ་མོ་ "goddess"

but

བོད་པ་ "Tibetan (man)" བོད་མོ་ "Tibetan (woman)"

In addition, adjectives with the second syllable པོ་ may form their feminine equivalents with མོ་:

དམར་པོ་ "red" དམར་མོ་ "red"
ཆེན་པོ་ "big" ཆེན་མོ་ "big"

Frequently there is an agreement between the genus of the head noun and that of its attribute, to the extent that a feminine form of an adjective is added to a feminine noun. This however is not a strict rule and multiple exceptions can be found.

ཀ་ ~ ཁ་ ~ ག་ particle

The three forms of the nominal particle ཀ་ ~ ཁ་ ~ ག་ are used depending on the final consonant of the preceding syllable:

ཀ་	after -ག, -ད, -བ, -ས
ཁ་	after -ན, -ར, -ལ
ག་	after -ང, -མ, -འ, vowel

However, the assimilation rules are not always strictly followed and deviations from the pattern are not infrequent (e.g. འདམ་ཀ་ cited next).

The main function of the particle ཀ་ ~ ཁ་ ~ ག་ is to form nouns from other word classes, mainly verbs and numerals. Nouns formed from verbs have usually abstract meaning:

འདམ་ "to choose" འདམ་ཀ་ "choice"
གཉེར་ "to take care of" གཉེར་ཁ་ "attention, care"

When used with numerals the particle forms collective nouns:

གཉིས་ "two" གཉིས་ཀ་ "a pair"
གསུམ་ "three" གསུམ་ཀ་ "a trio"

In this function ཀ་ ~ ཁ་ ~ ག་ resembles the nominal particle པོ་ which can also be used to form collective nouns.

A distinct function of the particle ཀ་ ~ ཁ་ ~ ག་ adds emphasis to a pronoun:

> དེ་ཀ་གྱིས། (ML D 13r) "Do exactly that!"
> འདི་ཀ་ནས་བྱེད། (ML D 13r) "From now on [I] will do [it]."

In this function the particle can be used with demonstrative pronouns as well as with personal pronouns.

ཀོ་ particle

The nominal particle ཀོ་ has only one form. The particle is used exclusively with pronouns to add emphasis to the base word.

བདག་ "I"	བདག་ཀོ་ "me myself"
དེ་ "that"	དེ་ཀོ་ "exactly that one"

General remarks

Even though for each of the nominal particles specific functions can be identified and described, there are still numerous cases in which none of the known functions can be ascribed to a particle. To illustrate, the following list contains examples of lexemes with nominal particles, the exact function of which cannot be established.

ལག་པ་ "hand"	རྐང་པ་ "foot, leg"	དམར་པོ་ "red"
ཆེན་པོ་ "big"	རྩེ་མོ་ "summit"	དབྱར་ཀ་ "summer"

The derivational processes are only seldom transparent enough to secure the proper understanding without knowing the exact meaning of the lexeme.

Exercise

I. Using the word list, determine the function of the nominal particles in the following words and phrases:

འགྲོ་བ་ "a being"	བཙུན་མོ་ "lady"
ལྔ་པ་ "the fifth"	སྲིན་མོ་ "demoness"
ཇོ་མོ་ "lady"	གསོལ་བ་ "request"
སྨན་པ་ "physician"	བྱ་མོ་ "hen"
དྲུག་པོ་ "a group of six"	སྐྱེས་པ་ "male person"

II. Translate the sentences:

༡ བདག་ལས་ཀྱི་དབང་གིས་སྲིན་མོའི་རིགས་སུ་སྐྱེས་སོ།། (GLR 22v1)

༢ དེའི་ཚེ་ན་གྲོང་ཁྱེར་དེ་ན་རྒན་མོ་ཞིག་ལ་བུ་རྐུ་བ་གཉིས་ཤིག་ཡོད། (MB D 138r6–7)

༣ བཅོམ་ལྡན་འདས་གཤེགས་པ་རྒན་མོ་མ་སྐད་གསུམ་གྱིས་མཐོང་ངོ་། (MB D 138r7–v1)

༤ ཉི་མའི་འོད་ཟེར་ཤར་རོ།། (SSP 3c)

༥ ཁྱོད་ཀྱིས་ངའི་གླང་བོར་རོ། (MB D 271v2)

༦ ཁྱོད་ཀྱིས་ངའི་སྤྲེའུ་ཆུར་བསྐྱུར་རོ།། (MB D 271v7)

༧ འདི་དག་གིས་ང་ཁྲིད་དོ། (MB D 272r3)

༨ ཞིང་མཁན་གྱི་མདུན་སོ་གཉིས་ཆོག་ཅིག (MB D 272v5–6)

༩ ཡི་གེ་འདིའི་དོན་བགྲེས་པ་ཀུན་གྱི་ཐུགས་ལ་གསལ་ལོ། (ML D 12r)

༡༠ དེ་ནས་སྤྲེའུ་དེས་སྤྲེའུ་ཕྲུག་རྣམས་དེར་ཁྲིད་དོ། (GLR 23v3–4)

༡༡ ཤ་རློན་པ་དང་། ཁྲག་དྲོན་མོས་དེའི་ཡིད་ཚིམ་པར་འགྱུར་རོ། (MB D 139r6)

༡༢ ལྔ་མོ་དེས་དེ་སྐད་སྨྲས་པ་ཐོས་སོ། (MB D 139v7–40r1)

༡༣ མི་མཐོང་བ་དེ་ལ་བུ་ཕོ་མེད། (MB D 270v2)

Word list

རྐུ་ v2 བརྐུས་ v3 བརྐུ་ v4 རྐུས་ (TR) to steal

སྐྱེ་ v2 སྐྱེས་ (INTR) to be born

སྐྱེས་ see སྐྱེ་

ཁྲིད་ (TR) to lead

བགྲེས་པ་ elder man

འགྲོ་ v2/v4 སོང་ (INTR) to go

ལྔ་ five

གཅོག་ v2 བཅག་ v3 གཅག་ v4 ཆོག(ས)་ (TR) to knock out

ཆོག་ see གཅོག་

འཆར་ v2 ཤར་ (INTR) to rise

ཇོ་བོ་ lord, master

ཉི་མ་ sun

ཐོས་ (TR) to hear

དེ་སྐད་ those words
དོན་ meaning
དྲུག་ six
མདུན་སོ་ incisor (lit. front) tooth
བོར་ see འབོར་
བྱ་ bird
དབང་ power
འབོར་ v2/v4 བོར་ (TR) to lose
མ་སྨད་ mother and her children
སྨན་ medicine, herb
སྨྲ་ v2/v3 སྨྲས་ v4 སྨྲོས་ (TR) to speak
སྨྲས་ see སྨྲ་
བཙུན་པ་ respectable, noble
ཚིམ་པ་ satisfied
འོད་ཟེར་ ray
རིགས་ family
ལས་ (previous) action
ཤར་ see འཆར་
ཤིང་མཁན་ carpenter
གཤེགས་ v4 ཤོག་ (INTR) to come
སྲིན་མོ་ demoness
གསལ་ (to be) clear
གསོལ་ (TR) to request
ལྷ་མོ་ queen

Notes

1 For the quotative (QUOT) particle /ཅེས་/, see Lesson 13.
2 Depending on the context, the previously quoted phrase རྐང་གཉིས་པ་ could also be interpreted as "the second foot/leg".
3 See also Lesson 17: Numerals.
4 See Taube (1970).

Lesson 8

- Converbs
- Coordinative particle
- Non-controllable transitive verbs
- Speech register
- Adverbs

Converbs

Until now only simple sentences that consist of one clause have been discussed. Classical Tibetan has of course means to combine two or more simple clauses into a complex sentence. In such a case, each clause ends with a verb, but only the last verb of the sentence bears the final particle and is therefore the main verb. Verbs in the preceding clauses acquire special particles to mark that they are not the main verb but instead denote events that are perceived as subordinate to the event of the main verb. There are two classes of particles that can be attached to a non-final verb:

- Proper converbal particles
- Case particles

These particles will generally be called 'converbal'. Proper converbal particles include coordinative, gerundial, and concessive particles which are discussed in Lessons 8–10. Case particles are identical with the already-discussed case particles (dative, locative, genitive, terminative, ergative, comitative, elative, delative) but have special functions when following a verb. These will be treated separately in Lesson 12.[1]

A verb plus a converbal particle form a so-called converb (CONV). A complex sentence basically has the following structure:

$$[[\ldots \text{CONV}]_{\text{CLAUSE}}\ [\ldots \text{CONV}]_{\text{CLAUSE}}\ [\ldots \text{CONV}]_{\text{CLAUSE}} \ldots \text{V}{+}\gamma o_{\text{FNL}}]_{\text{SENTENCE}}$$

DOI: 10.4324/9781003224198-11

The number of clauses that end with a converb is unlimited so that Classical Tibetan sentences may be very long. The order of clauses within a sentence essentially reflects the order of events in the real world.

Although only a sentence that ends with a final particle can be conceived of as complete, it is not always possible to render one Tibetan sentence with one sentence in a European language. Thus a correct translation must consider not only the grammar of Classical Tibetan, but also the grammar and stylistics of the target language. When analysing and translating complex clauses one is advised to first identify all converbs and translate the single clauses before putting them together in one or more complex sentences.

Coordinative particle

Forms

The coordinative (COORD) particle changes its form depending on the last letter of the preceding syllable:

ཅིང་	after	-ག, -ད, -བ, *-ད་དྲག་
ཞིང་	after	-ང, -ན, -མ, -འ, -ར, -ལ, -vowel
ཤིང་	after	-ས

Functions

The coordinative particle follows immediately after a predicate and relates it to the next one. It indicates temporal overlap between the event expressed by the verb with the coordinative particle and the event of the following verb. In this case the particle can usually be translated with "while; during". In most cases it coordinates two predicates which have the same subject, such as:

> བདག་ཡུན་རིང་པོ་ནས་འཁོར་བ་ན་འཁོར་ཞིང་། ལུས་སྲོག་གྲངས་མེད་པ་ཞིག་ཆུད་གསན་ཏོ། (MB D 139r7)
> "While roaming in the cycle of existence for a long time, I have wasted innumerable lives and bodies."

In this example the particle ཞིང་ coordinates འཁོར་ and the complex verb ཆུད་གསན་; their shared subject is བདག་. But sometimes the predicates may have distinct subjects:

དེ་དག་བཅོམ་ལྡན་འདས་ཀྱི་བཀའ་དྲིན་དྲན་ཞིང་དགའ་བ་སྐྱེས་སོ། (MB D 138v2–3)
Lit. "While they (S = དེ་དག་) were remembering the favour of the Victorious One, happiness (S = དགའ་བ་) arose [in them]."

In the course of time the original temporal function was replaced by the mere coordinative function so that the particle can frequently be rendered with "and" in English:

ཕུག་རོན་གསུམ་ཞིག་ཀུན་ཏུ་འཕུར་ཞིང་རྩེའོ། (MB D 139v5)
"Three doves were flying and playing around."

This meaning change has brought about another peculiarity of the particle; it may connect two predicates with very similar or even synonymous meanings:

རྒྱལ་པོ་དེ་ཕྱི་རོལ་ཏུ་འཆག་ཅིང་དོང་ངོ་། (MB D 139r3–4)
"The king went outside for a walk." Lit. "The king took a walk outside and went."

The verbs འཆག་ and དོང་ may be considered near-synonyms. In a similar way the coordinative particle can coordinate two attributive predicates:

དབང་པོ་ཀུན་ཞི་ཞིང་བདེའོ། (MB D 270v5)
"All the senses are calm and peaceful."

Non-controllable transitive verbs

When discussing verbs it was said that every event verb is either controllable or non-controllable and that this has impact on the structure of the clause (see Lesson 4). Transitive and non-controllable verbs (class II) denote events that cannot be controlled by the acting entity and therefore the subject of such verbs does not acquire the ergative particle but stands in absolutive:

[དེ་དག་]$_{\text{ABS}}$ [བཅོམ་ལྡན་འདས་ཀྱི་བཀའ་དྲིན་]$_{\text{ABS}}$ དྲན་ཞིང་ $_{\text{COORD}}$ [དགའ་བ་]$_{\text{ABS}}$ སྐྱེས་སོ། (MB D 138v2–3)
Lit. "While they were remembering the favour of the Victorious One, happiness arose [in them]."

The verb དྲན་ "to remember" is non-controllable because under normal circumstances a human being cannot control her memory; some things are remembered, some not. The subject of the verb, དེ་དག་ "they", stands in absolutive and not in ergative in order to emphasise that the persons spoken of did not control the action.

མི་སེམས་ཆུང་ཀུན་མཆི་མ་འཆོར་རོ། (ML D 11r)
"All timid people were shedding tears."

In this tale Mi-la Ras-pa relates the difficulties that he and his family were facing after the death of his father. The story is set in the past. Notice that འཆོར་ is the v1 (imperfective) stem. It is used here because the event is presented as recurring; again and again the people who saw Mi-la Ras-pa and his family were shedding tears over their fate. Shedding tears is usually a spontaneous action over which humans do not have control.

Some of the transitive/non-controllable (TR/NC) verbs also have meanings in which events are conceived of as controllable. One such example is the verb དྲན་ from the first sentence: in the meaning "to remember" it is non-controllable, but in the meaning "to (deliberately) recall" it is controllable and therefore requires subject in ergative. Students should be aware of the fact that ergative signals that the subject has control over the event. On the other hand, the absence of ergative with a transitive verb marks the lack of control. It is also important not to judge Tibetan verbs by their equivalents provided in Western dictionaries. One should first of all rely on the correct analysis of Tibetan clauses.

Speech register

Speech register is a variety of language used in particular social circumstances. For instance, a situation in which a lay person addresses a religious person like a lama (CT བླ་མ་) necessitates use of a type of language that differs from the one that two friends use when talking to each other in an informal situation. In many languages distinct forms can be used to emphasise that a particular speech situation is distinct from a usual one. In German, for example, one uses the personal pronoun *Sie* – a polite form – when addressing a person in an official setting or whom one does not know. A similar function is seen in the French pronoun *vous*, Spanish forms of address *señor*/*señorita*, Polish *pan*/*pani*, etc.

Classical Tibetan also distinguishes between different speech registers depending on the particular social situation. However, the speech registers of Classical Tibetan are much more elaborate than those of the aforementioned European languages. Classical Tibetan differentiates between three speech registers which are usually called 'normal', 'humble' (HML), and 'honorific' (HON). When the referent of the subject of the action is a person of a higher social status, like for instance a religious teacher or a political leader, the honorific register is used. The honorific register is called ཞེ་ས་ in Tibetan. The humble register applies when a person of higher social status is not the subject of a clause but participates in it in a different role, e.g. as the direct or indirect object.

In Classical Tibetan the differences between these registers are generally lexical. This means that depending on a particular situation a distinct word might be required. Only words of the following word classes participate in marking the register:

- Verbs (but not modal verbs and only some auxiliary verbs)[2]
- Nouns
- Personal pronouns

Theoretically every verb and every noun related to the sphere of human life and social interactions has its honorific equivalent. There is only one term denoting animal that also has an honorific equivalent: ཆིབས་ (HON) "horse" for the usual རྟ་ 'id.' In addition, the 1st person pronoun and a few verbs and nouns also have humble equivalents. The following table lists some of the more common sets of words for the three registers:

Normal	Honorific	Humble	Meaning
པ་	ཡབ་		"father"
མ་	ཡུམ་		"mother"
བུ་	སྲས་		"son, child"
ལུས་	སྐུ་		"body"
མགོ་	དབུ་		"head"
ཡིད་	ཐུགས་		"mind"
མིག་	སྤྱན་		"eye"
ང་		བདག་	"I" (1SG)
ཁྱོད་	ཁྱེད་		"you" (2SG)
ཡིན་	ལགས་	ལགས་	"to be"
ཡོད་	མངའ་	མཆིས་	"to exist, to have"
འདུག་	བཞུགས་	གདའ་	"to remain, to sit"
བྱེད་	མཛད་	བགྱིད་	"to do, to make"
འོང་/འགྲོ་	གཤེགས་	མཆི་	"to come, to go"
སྟེར་	གནང་	འབུལ་	"to give"
ཟེར་/སྨྲ་	གསུང་	ཞུ་	"to speak"

In reality, only a relatively small group of lexemes has its honorific and/or humble equivalent. If a word should be used that has no honorific equivalent, a new complex word is formed. In the case of nouns, a noun from the honorific group is added to the 'normal' (i.e. base) word but without changing the meaning of the base word.

One can call the honorific word in this function an 'honorific classifier' because it only marks the speech register of the base word as honorific. The honorific classifier always stands before the base word. It is chosen so as to have a meaning related to the meaning of the base word or to be its hypernym; that is, a word with a meaning more general than the meaning of the base word. The following examples illustrate formation of honorifics from normal nouns:

Base noun	HON classifier	HON equivalent	Meaning
སྐྲ་	དབུ་	དབུ་སྐྲ་	"hair"
དམ་	ཐུགས་	ཐུགས་དམ་	"vow"

In these examples, དབུ་ and ཐུགས་ are honorific classifiers added to the base word in order to form its honorific equivalent. Generally, a concrete base word has one particular honorific classifier that can be used with it. For instance, སྐྲ་ is always used with དབུ་ and never with སྐུ་.

An analogous strategy is available for forming honorific equivalents of verbs. Usually an honorific noun is added before the verb. The noun changes neither the meaning of the verb nor its argument structure:

Basic verb	HON classifier	HON equivalent	Meaning
འཁྲུང་	སྐུ་	སྐུ་འཁྲུང་	"to be born"
བརྩེ་	ཐུགས་	ཐུགས་བརྩེ་	"to love"

Here སྐུ་ and ཐུགས་ are honorific classifiers with the basic meaning "body" and "heart; mind". They do not contribute in any way to the meaning of the complex verbs སྐུ་འཁྲུང་ and ཐུགས་བརྩེ་, apart from changing the speech register to the honorific one.

When addressing a person of higher social standing the syllable ལགས་ may also be added after the form of address:

བླ་མ་ལགས། (ML D 10r) "Dear (or: Venerated) Lama!"

ལགས་ is derived from the verb ལགས་, an honorific equivalent of the copula ཡིན་.

When reading Classical Tibetan texts one is advised to always identify the speech register of the words in a sentence. In certain situations, these might be the only hints that help identifying the person involved in a particular action. Most dictionaries of Classical Tibetan mark whether a word belongs to a humble or an honorific register. If no additional information is provided, the word belongs to the normal register. Beginning with this lesson, honorific and humble registers will be marked in the word lists.[3]

Adverbs

Adverb (Adv) is a word that modifies an adjective (*quite* loud), a verb (run *quickly*), or another adverb (*very* loudly). In this function an adverb always stands directly before the word it modifies in Classical Tibetan:

རྟག་ཏུ་རྐུ་ (MB D 138r7) "to always (རྟག་ཏུ་) steal"
རབ་ཏུ་དགའ་ (MB D 138v3) "to be very (རབ་ཏུ་) happy"

Another function of an adverb is to modify a clause. Here it mainly expresses time or location of a particular event and is usually placed at the very beginning of the clause:

ད་མ་ངུ། (ML D 13r) "Now, don't cry!"
ཕྱིས་དམག་པ་དག་འདུས་སོ། (MB D 270v1) "Later, the sons-in-law gathered."

Formation

In Classical Tibetan the vast majority of adverbs are derived from corresponding adjectives by means of a terminative particle:

ལེགས་པ་ "good"	ལེགས་པར་ "well"
རབ་ "utmost; eldest"	རབ་ཏུ་ "very"

But other word classes can also form adverbs by means of the terminative particle:

Nouns:

སྟེང་ "top"	སྟེང་དུ་ "up"
རྒྱུན་ "flow, stream"	རྒྱུན་དུ་ "continually"

Ordinal numerals:

དང་པོ་ "first"	དང་པོར་ "firstly"
གཉིས་པ་ "second"	གཉིས་པར་ "secondly"

Apart from terminative, the locative, dative, elative, and ergative particles can also form adverbs:

འདི་ "this"	འདི་ན་ "here"
སྐད་ཅིག་ "a moment"	སྐད་ཅིག་ལ་ "instantly"

རིམ་ "row"	རིམ་གྱིས་ "successively, in a row"
ཀུན་ "all"	ཀུན་ནས་ "everywhere"

There is also a group of adverbs that can no longer be analysed and have to be learnt as simple words:

ད་ "now"	ཤིན་ཏུ་ "very"
ད་ལྟར་ "now"	སླར་ "back"

Because adverbs can be derived from any nominal word, nominalised clauses (see Lesson 11) can also be turned into adverbs. One of the most commonly encountered 'adverbialised' clauses is མ་ལུས་, lit. "to have not remained". It can be nominalised as མ་ལུས་པ་ "not having remained" and the latter turned into an adverb: མ་ལུས་པར་ "completely", lit. "so that nothing has remained".

Meaning

In terms of their meanings, one can distinguish between temporal, locative, and modal adverbs. Temporal adverbs indicate the time at which an event happens. This group of adverbs is usually formed by means of the case particles ན་, ལ་, and ནས་, cf.:

དེ་ "(DEM) that"	དེ་ནས་ "thereafter, then"

but also with terminative:

མཐའ་ "the end"	མཐར་ "in the end; finally"

Locative adverbs indicate the place at which an event happens. They are usually formed by means of the case particles ན་, ལ་, and ནས་, cf.:

འདི་ "this"	འདི་ན་ "here"

but also with terminative:

འདི་ "this"	འདིར་ "here; hither"
ཀུན་ "all"	ཀུན་ཏུ་ "everywhere"

Modal adverbs indicate the manner in which an event is carried out, cf.:

སོ་སོ་ "distinct, separate"	སོ་སོ་ནས་ "individually"
དེ་ལྟ་བུ་ "of that kind"	དེ་ལྟ་བུར་ "so; like that"

Adverbs that are formed with case particles other than terminative can usually be easily analysed and traced back in their meanings to one of the meanings of the respective case particle.

Exercise

༡ གཞན་དུ་མ་སེམས་ཤིག (MB D 140v5)

༢ སངས་རྒྱས་ཀྱི་བསྟན་པ་དར་ཞིང་རྒྱས་སོ། (GLR 22v6)

༣ བྲམ་ཟེའི་བུ་གཅིག་ཕུས་དགྲ་བོའི་ཚོགས་ཀུན་བཅོམ་མོ།། (SSP 11c–d)

༤ མཁའ་ལྡིང་གོས་སེར་ཅན་གྱི་བཞོན་པར་གྱུར་ཏོ།། (SSP 17c–d)

༥ དེའི་ཚེ་ན་ཀུན་དགའ་བོ་དང་། འཁོར་མང་པོ་ཡི་རངས་སོ།། (MB D 140v6)

༦ བྲམ་ཟེ་དེས་འཁར་བ་ལ་སྐྲོམ་ཚུགས་བཅས་སོ། (MB D 270v5)

༧ དེས་ཨུ་བུ་ཅག་གི་ཞལ་ཆེ་གཅོད་དོ། (MB D 271v4)

༨ ཁོ་བོའི་ཕྲིན་ཞིག་རྒྱལ་པོ་ལ་སྤྲོས་ཤིག (MB D 272r3)

༩ དབྱིག་པ་ཅན་གྱིས་བདག་གི་རྟ་རྒོད་མ་བཀུམ་མོ། (MB D 272v2)

༡༠ དུས་གཅིག་ན། བཅོམ་ལྡན་འདས་མཉན་དུ་ཡོད་པ་ན་བཞུགས་སོ། (MB D 138r5–6)

༡༡ བྲག་སྲིན་མོ་ཞིག་དེར་འོངས་སོ། (GLR 22r5)

༡༢ ཕུག་རོན་གསུམ་ཞིག་ཀུན་ཏུ་འཕུར་ཞིང་རྩེའོ། (MB D 139v5)

༡༣ རྒྱལ་པོ་དང་འཁོར་མང་པོ་རྣམས་ཕྱིར་ཕོ་བྲང་དུ་སོང་ངོ་།། (MB D 140v3)

༡༤ ངའི་བུ་སྣད་གསུམ་གྱི་སྐྱིད་སྡུག་གཉེན་ཚན་ཀུན་ཤེས་སོ།། (ML D 10v)

༡༥ བདག་ད་ལྟར་ཁྱིམ་ལ་དུར་ཙམ་དུ་འཛིན་ཏོ། (MB D 271r1)

Word list

ཀུན་ཏུ་ all around

བཀུམ་ see འགུམས་

སྐྲོམ་ཚུགས་ chin

སྐྱིད་སྡུག་ happiness and misery

ཁོ་བོ་ (1SG M) I

ཁྱིམ་ house

མཁའ་ལྡིང་ *garuḍa*-bird

འཁར་བ་ staff

གོས་སེར་ཅན་ (PN) Gos-ser-čan, lit. dressed in yellow clothes, an epithet of Viṣṇu

དགྲ་བོ་ enemy

འགུམས་ v2 བཀུམ་ v3 དགུམ་ v4 ཁུམས་ (TR) to kill

རྒོད་མ་ mare

རྒྱས་ (INTR) to increase

གཅིག་པུ་ sole

གཅོད་ v2 བཅད་ v3 གཅད་ v4 ཆོད་ (TR) to decide; ཞལ་ཆེ་གཅོད་ to pass a judgement

བཅས་ see འཆའ་

བཅོམ་ see འཇོམས་

འཆའ་ v2 བཅས་ v3 བཅའ་ v4 ཆོས་ (TR) to place (on + DAT)

འཇོམས་ v2 བཅོམ་ v3 གཞོམ་ v4 ཆོམ་ (TR) to conquer

གཉེན་ཚན་ relatives

མཉན་དུ་ཡོད་པ་ (PN) Mñan-du-yod-pa, Indian town Śrāvasti

བསྟན་པ་ teaching

ད་ལྟར་ now

དར་ (INTR) to spread

དུར་ grave

ཕོ་བྲང་ palace

ཕྲིན་ message

འཕུར་ v2 ཕུར་ (INTR) to fly

བུ་སྨད་ children and [their] mother

བྱེད་ v2 བྱས་ v3 བྱ་ v4 བྱོས་ (TR) to say; ཕྲིན་བྱེད་ to deliver a message

བྱོས་ see བྱེད་

ཙམ་ mere

རྩེ་ v2/v4 རྩེས་ (INTR) to play

ཚོགས་ troop

འཛིན་ v2 བཟུང་ v3 གཟུང་ v4 ཟུངས་ (TR) to take sth. (DAT) as (TERM)

ཞལ་ཆེ་ judgement

གཞན་དུ་ differently

བཞུགས་ (HON for འདུག་; INTR) to stay, abide

བཞོན་པ་ riding-beast

ཝ་བུ་ཅག་ (1PL) we

ཡི་ mind

རང་ v2 རངས་ (INTR) to rejoice; ཡི་རང་ to rejoice

རངས་ see རང་

ཤེས་ (TR) to know, be aware of

སངས་རྒྱས་ Buddha

སེམས་ v2 བསམས་ v3 བསམ་ v4 སོམས་ (TR) to think

Notes

1 The meanings of all converbal particles are presented in a tabular form in Appendix E.
2 See Lessons 13 and 16.
3 For a more detailed description of the honorific speech register in Classical Tibetan illustrated by further examples, see Lyovin (1992) and Potapova (1997).

Lesson 9

- Gerundial particle
- Focus particle
- Diminutive particle
- Apposition

Gerundial particle

The gerundial (GER) particle is another converbal particle used to connect two clauses with each other (see Lesson 8).

Forms

The gerundial particle changes its form depending on the last letter of the preceding syllable:

ཏེ་	after -ན, -ར, -ལ, -ས, *-ད་དྲག་
སྟེ་	after -ག, -ང, -བ, -མ, -འ, -vowel
དེ་	after -ད

Functions

The gerundial particle can be attached to any word class but usually it follows a verb. In the following clause the gerundial particle replaces the copula verb ཡིན་ and it attaches directly to the preceding noun phrase:

> བྲམ་ཟེའི་ཆུང་མ་ཁྲོ་ཞིང་གཏུམ་མོ་ཞིག་སྟེ། (MB D 270v2–3)
> "The wife of the Brahmin was a wrathful and hot-tempered woman."

DOI: 10.4324/9781003224198-12

The gerundial particle has multiple functions in Classical Tibetan, the most important of which are the introductory and gerundial functions.

Introductory function

The gerundial particle in introductory function may follow any word or phrase. It introduces an object, a person, or an event which is then described more precisely in the subsequent clause.

> འཛམ་བུ་གླིང་འདི་ན་རྒྱལ་པོ་ཤིང་རྟ་ཆེན་པོ་ཞེས་བྱ་བ་ཞིག་ཡོད་དེ། རྒྱལ་ཕྲན་ལྔ་སྟོང་སྙེད་ལ་དབང་བྱེད་དོ།། (MB D 139r2)
> "There was a king called (ཞེས་བྱ་བ་) Śiṅ-rta-čhen-po in this continent; [he] was ruling over about five thousand vassals."

> དེར་སྤྲེའུ་དེས། བྲག་རོག་པོ་ཞིག་ལ་བསྒོམས་ཏེ། དེའང་བྱམས་སྙིང་རྗེ་བྱང་ཆུབ་ཀྱི་སེམས་བསྒོམས་སོ། (GLR 22r4)
> "There the monkey meditated on a black rock; namely (དེའང་), [it] contemplated benevolence, compassion, [and] the thought of enlightenment."

Gerundial function

The gerundial particle informs that the action modifies the way the action expressed by the following verb is carried out. The precondition is that both verbs have the same subject.

> དེ་ནས་བྲག་སྲིན་མོ་ལངས་ཏེ། སྤྲེའུ་ལ་འདི་སྐད་ཅེས་ཟེར་རོ།། (GLR 22r6)
> "Thereafter, having risen, the rock-ogress said the following words to the monkey."

> རྒྱལ་པོས་ལག་པ་ནས་བཟུང་སྟེ། ཆོ་ངེས་བཏབ་བོ། (MB D 140r2)
> "The king, having seized [his son's] hand, lamented."

The next example contains two clauses that end with a gerundial particle: བཞེངས་ཏེ། and བླངས་ཏེ།. When translating such constructions one has to consider the grammar and style of the target language. Here I decided to render the first gerundial particle with the English gerund "having risen", adding the conjunction "and" in order to connect it to the second gerund "having taken":

> འཕགས་པ་ཡར་བཞེངས་ཏེ། ནས། གྲོ། སྲན་མ། བྲ་བོ། སོ་བ་རྣམས་རི་རབ་ཀྱི་ཁོང་སེང་ནས་བླངས་ཏེ། ས་ལ་གཏོར་ཏོ། (GLR 23v3)

"The Noble One, having risen (བཞེངས་ཏེ།) and having taken (བླངས་ཏེ།) barley, wheat, beans, buckwheat, [and] unhusked barley from the inner caverns of Ri-rab (Skt. Sumeru), scattered [them] on the ground."

In clauses with two distinct subjects, the gerundial function fades away. However, the semantic relationship between the action marked with the gerundial particle and the following one remains close, so that the gerundial particle can be rendered with a semicolon or sometimes with the conjunction "and":

སྐྲ་དང་ཁ་སྤུ་རང་བྱི་སྟེ། གོས་ཀྱང་ངུར་སྨྲིག་ཏུ་གྱུར་ཏོ། (MB D 138v4–5)
"[Their] head hair and beard fell off by itself (རང་) [and their] clothes even (ཀྱང་) turned yellowish-red."

Idiomatic phrases

The gerundial particle occurs in a set of idiomatic phrases in which its particular function cannot be determined anymore, cf.:

གལ་ཏེ་ "if"   འོན་ཏེ་ "or if not, or else"
དེ་སྟེ་ "now"   འདི་ལྟ་སྟེ་ "in this way; namely"

These phrases are usually glossed in dictionaries and must be learnt by heart since they are not analysable.

Focus particle

Classical Tibetan has a special particle that allows one to place emphasis on a particular part of a clause. This is the focus (FOC) particle ནི་. It is attached to the word or phrase that shall be emphasised:

དེ་བཞིན་གཤེགས་པ་ནི་ཡོན་ཏན་མངའོ། (MB D 138v6)
"Regarding Tathāgata, [he] possesses excellent qualities."

བདག་ནི་རྒྱལ་བུ་སེམས་ཅན་ཆེན་པོ་ཡིན། (MB D 140r6)
"As for myself, [I] am the prince Sems-čan-čhen-po."

In these examples it is the first phrase of a clause that acquires the focus particle. However, other phrases can also receive emphasis:

དེའི་ཚེ་སྟག་མོས་རྒྱལ་བུའི་ཤ་ནི་ཟད་པར་ཟོས་སོ། (MB D 140r1)
"By that time the tigress has completely eaten the flesh of the prince['s body]."

This clause stresses that it was the flesh (ཤ་ནི་) that the tigress ate, because in the next clause of the story we learn that the bones were scattered around on the ground. In the next example the focus is on sons (བུ་པོ་ནི་), because in the story this information is contrasted with the fact that the same person had seven daughters.

མི་མཐོང་བ་དེ་ལ་བུ་པོ་ནི་མེད། (MB D 270v2)
"The blind one didn't have a son."

The focus particle can follow any case particle:

རྒྱལ་པོས་ནི་ལག་པ་ནས་བཟུང་སྟེ།   ཆོ་ངེས་བཏབ་བོ། (MB D 140r2)
"The king, having seized [his son's] hand, lamented."

However, sometimes the case particle that precedes the focus particle is left out. This happens most frequently in metrical passages, like this one:

བདག་ནི་དགེ་བསྙེན་སྡོམ་པ་སྲོག་བཞིན་བསྲུངས།། (GLR 22v4)
"As for me, [I] protected the vow [of] a lay practitioner like [my own] life."

In this clause the ergative particle after བདག་ (as well as the genitive particle after དགེ་བསྙེན་ and the final particle after བསྲུངས་) fell prey to the prosody of Classical Tibetan (see Lesson 18: Metrics).

A distinct function of ནི་ consists of introducing a unit of a text, like a chapter for instance. Compare hereto the phrase གཉིས་པ་ནི། at the beginning of Reading III *The Death of Mi-la Ras-pa's father*.

The focus particle ནི་ is the 'weakest' particle and always takes the last position in a noun phrase, following the indefinite particle, demonstrative pronoun, case or any other particle. In addition, the particle plays an important role in Tibetan poetry (see Lesson 18).

Diminutive particle[1]

Like some other morphemes, the diminutive (DIM) particle has also developed various forms (allomorphs) depending on the final letter of the preceding syllable. The two most common variants are:

བུ་ after any final consonant
འུ་ after vowels:

མི་ "man"	མིའུ་ "dwarf"	རྟ་ "horse"	རྟེའུ་ "foal"
བྱ་ "bird"	བྱིའུ་/བྱེའུ་ "nestling"	རྡོ་ "stone"	རྡེའུ་ "pebble"

If the original word ends with the vowels *a* or *o*, the vowel is changed:

- *a* > *i* or *e* (e.g. བྱ་ > བྱིའུ་ ~ བྱེའུ་)
- *o* > *e* (e.g. རྡོ་ > རྡེའུ་)

In some cases an even more advanced assimilation has occurred: the last consonant of the first syllable is repeated in the diminutive particle, but at the same time elided from the first syllable, cf.:

གཟེར་ "nail"	གཟེ་རུ་ "small nail" (but usually: གཟེར་བུ་)
དབྱུག་ "stick"	དབྱུ་གུ་ "small staff"
ལུག་ "sheep"	ལུ་གུ་ (or ལུག་གུ་) "lamb"[2]

but

ནལ་ "incest"	ནལ་ལུ་ "bastard child"

The diminutive forms formed with -གུ་, -ངུ་, -རུ་, -ལུ་ frequently acquire very concrete meanings that cannot be directly derived from the meaning of the main word.

If the main word has a nominal particle, this is omitted before the diminutive particle is added:

ཁང་པ་ "house"	but ཁང་བུ་ "[1]little house; [2]room"
རིལ་བ་ "round"	but རི་ལུ་ "globula, pill"

The diminutive particle བུ་ has developed from the word བུ་ "child". Accordingly, its primary function was to denote an object that is smaller (or younger, in the case of living beings) than the object denoted by the original word. In the course of time the particle has also developed other meanings:

1. Child or young of a living being:

གླང་ "ox"	གླང་བུ་ "calf"	རྟ་ "horse"	རྟེའུ་ "foal"

2. An object or living being that is smaller in size than the object denoted by the main word:

ཁྱོ་ "man"	ཁྱེའུ་ "boy"	རྡོ་ "stone"	རྡེའུ་ "pebble"

3. An object that bears some similarity to the main object:

ཁང་པ་ "house"	ཁང་བུ་ "room"	ནོར་ "wealth"	ནོར་བུ་ "jewel"
སྨྱུག་མ་ "reed"	སྨྱུ་གུ་ "reed-pen"	རྩེ་ "summit"	རྩེའུ་ "thorn"

There is also a group of words of which the second syllable seems to be historically identical with the diminutive particle, but their meaning cannot be easily derived from the meaning of the main word, e.g.:

སྐྱེས་བུ་ "living being" ~ སྐྱེས་པ་ "man, male person"
གཅིག་པུ་ "alone, single" ~ གཅིག་ "one"

Apposition

Apposition is a type of grammatical construction in which two words or phrases occur next to each other and one of them (the so-called appositive) identifies the other. The elements of an apposition have a common referent, that is, they refer to the same object or person in the world. In Classical Tibetan the appositive (the identifying phrase) follows the main word or phrase:

NP + Appositive "NP which is Appositive"

བཙུན་མོ་ཡུམ་ (MB D 139v5) "the queen, the mother"

བཙུན་མོ་ is the main word followed by the appositive ཡུམ་. Both refer to one person who is a queen and a mother.

དགའ་ལྡན་ལྷའི་གནས་ (MB D 140r3) "Dgaɣ-ldan, a deities' place"
མ་བྲག་སྲིན་མོ་ (GLR 23v6) "the mother, a rock-ogress"
རྟ་རྒོད་མ་ཞིག་ (MD B 271v3) "a horse, a mare"

Apposition is a common construction in Classical Tibetan to introduce persons by their titles, functions, and names, cf.:

རྒྱལ་བུ་རྒྱལ་བྱེད་ (MB D 138r6) "prince Rgyal-byed"
འཕགས་པ་སྤྱན་རས་གཟིགས་ (GLR 22r3) "the Noble One, Spyan-ras-gzigs"

Since apposition forms one noun phrase, any kind of particle that could be added to it (number, case, focus, etc.) is placed after the last element of the apposition. The first element of the apposition (the one that is identified) always stands in absolutive:

རྒྱལ་བུ་རྒྱལ་བྱེད་ཀྱི་ཚལ་མགོན་མེད་ཟས་སྦྱིན་གྱི་ཀུན་དགའ་ར་བ་ན་ (MB D 138r6)
"in (ན་) the 'Grove of the Prince Rgyal-byed', a copse founded by (lit. of) Mgon-med-zas-sbyin"

This apposition consists of two genitive phrases: རྒྱལ་བུ་རྒྱལ་བྱེད་ཀྱི་ཚལ་ "the Grove of the Prince Rgyal-byed" and མགོན་མེད་ཟས་སྦྱིན་གྱི་ཀུན་དགའ་ར་བ་ "a copse of Mgon-med-zas-sbyin". The first phrase is formally in absolutive but the locative ན་ at the end has the whole apposition in its scope. The example also demonstrates that elements that form an apposition can themselves be complex phrases. Here are two other examples:

དེའི་ཚེ་དེའི་དུས་ན་ (MB D 140v3) "then, at that time"
ཆོས་ཟབ་མོ་སྟོང་པ་ཉིད་ལ་ (GLR 22r4) "[to devote oneself] to the profound Buddhist teaching, the voidness"

Exercise

༡ ཕྱུགས་བ་ར་བོང་གསུམ་ (ML D 10v)

༢ རྒྱལ་བུ་གཉིས་ནི་འོངས་སོ། (MB D 139v7)

༣ བདག་ནི་རྒྱལ་བུ་སེམས་ཅན་ཆེན་པོ་ཡིན། (MB D 140r6)

༤ དེ་ནི་ད་ལྟར་ངའི་ཡབ་རྒྱལ་པོ་ཟས་གཙང་མ་ཡིན་ནོ། (MB D 140v3–4)

༥ དེའི་ཚེ་དེའི་དུས་ན་རྒྱལ་པོ་དེའི་བཙུན་མོ་དེ་ནི་ད་ལྟར་ངའི་ཡུམ་སྒྲུ་མ་ལྷ་མཛེས་ཡིན་ནོ། (MB D 140v4)

༦ དེར་སྤྲེའུ་ཕྲུག་དྲུག་པོ་དེ་ནི་ཕ་བྱང་ཆུབ་སེམས་དཔའ་སྤྲེའུས། ནགས་མ་བྱ་ཚོགས་བྱ་
བ། ཤིང་ཐོག་མེད་པ་ཞིག་ཏུ་བསྐྱལ་ཏོ། (GLR 23r4)

༧ བདག་གིས་ལུས་ཀྱིས་སྟག་མོ་ལྟོགས་པ་བསྐྱོད་དོ། (MB D 140r6)

༨ བདག་ད་ལྟར་ཁྱིམ་ལ་དུར་ཙམ་དུ་འཛིན་ཏེ། ཆུང་མ་དང་། བུ་མོ་ལ་དགྲ་ཙམ་དུ་སེམས་སོ། (MB D 271r1–2)

༩ དེས་རྡོ་ཞིག་བླངས་ཏེ་འཕངས་སོ། (MB D 271v3)

༡༠ གནས་གཞན་ཞིག་ན་ཤིང་ཤ་གོ་ཏ་ཀ་ལ་བྱ་རོག་གཅིག་འདུག་གོ། (MB D 272r2–3)

༡༡ ཁྱོད་ནི་སྙིང་རྗེ་ཆེན་པོས་སྟག་མོ་བསྐྱོད་དེ་ཐམས་ཅད་ལ་སྙིང་བརྩེ་བ་ཡིན་ནོ། (MB D 140v1)

༡༢ ཕུག་རོན་བུ་ཕོའི་བླ་སྣེ། ཕུག་རོན་ནང་གི་ཆུང་དུ་ཁྲམ་ཁྱེར་རོ། (MB D 139v6)

༡༣ དགེ་སློང་གཽ་ཏ་མ་ནི་རབ་ཏུ་བདེ་སྐྱིད་དོ།། (MB D 270v6)

༡༤ མི་གཞན་ཞིག་གི་རྟ་རྒོད་མ་ཞིག་བྲོས་སོ། (MB D 271v3)

Word list

སྐྱེལ་ v2/v3 བསྐྱལ་ v4 སྐྱོལ་ (TR) to bring

བསྐྱལ་ see སྐྱེལ་

ཁྱེར་ see འཁྱེར་

ཁྲ་ falcon

འཁྱེར་ v2 ཁྱེར་ (TR) to carry away

གཽ་ཏ་མ་ (PN) Skt. Gautama, the name of the Buddha

དགེ་སློང་ monk

དགྲ་ enemy

སྒྱུ་མ་ལྷ་མཛེས་ (PN) Sgyu-ma Lha-mjes

ཆུང་ངུ་ the youngest

སྙིང་རྗེ་ compassion

སྙིང་བརྩེ་བ་ loving, kind

སྙོད་ v2/v3 བསྙོད་ (TR) to feed

བསྙོད་ see སྙོད་

ཐམས་ཅད་ (N) all

དྲུག་པོ་ a group of six

བདེ་སྐྱིད་ (INTR) to be happy

འདུག་ (INTR) to sit

རྡོ་ stone

ནགས་མ་ forest

ནང་གི་ among

ཕ་ father

ཕྱུགས་ cattle

འཕངས་ see འཕེན་

འཕེན་ v2 འཕངས་ v3 འཕང་ v4 འཕོང་ (TR) to throw

བ་ར་བོང་ cow, goat, and ass

བྱ་བ་ so-called

བྱ་ཚོགས་ (PN) Bya-chogs, name of a forest

བྱ་རོག་ crow

བྱང་ཆུབ་སེམས་དཔའ་ Skt. *bodhisattva*

ཁྲོས་ see འཁྲོས་

བླ་ sign, symbol

བླངས་ see ལེན་

འབྲོས་ v2 བྲོས་ (INTR) to flee

མོད་ to be abundant

བཙུན་མོ་ queen

ཟས་གཙང་མ་ (PN) Zas-gcaṅ-ma

ཡུམ་ (HON for མ་) mother

རབ་ཏུ་ very

ལེན་ v2 བླངས་ v3 བླང་ v4 ལོང(ས)་ (TR) to take

ཤ་ཀོ་ཊ་ཀ་ a tree species (Skt. *śākhoṭaka*)

ཤིང་ tree

Notes

1 Uray (1952) remains the most comprehensive study of the diminutive particle in Classical Tibetan; see also more recently Bialek (2021b).

2 Frequently cited word གཞོན་ནུ་ "a youth" is not a diminutive form but a synonymic compound (< གཞོན་- "young" + ནུ་- "young"; on compounds see Lesson 13). Since this is the only example with -ནུ་, it follows that the diminutive particle བུ་ can assimilate only to -གུ་, -ངུ་, -རུ་, and -ལུ་.

Lesson 10

- Concessive particle
- Postpositions and postpositional phrases
- Possessive particle ཅན་
- Adjectives ལྡན་ and བཅས་

Concessive particle

Forms

Depending on the final letter of the preceding syllable, the concessive (CONC) particle can take one of the following forms:

ཀྱང་	after	-ག, -ད, -བ, -ས, *-ད་དྲག་
ཡང་	after	-ང, -ན, -མ, -ར, -ལ
འང་	after	-འ, -vowel[1]

The concessive particle can be added to nouns and verbs. The form ཡང་ should be distinguished from the adverb ཡང་ "again; more; further" which never changes its form and always precedes the word to which it refers, whereas the concessive particle always follows the NP or clause it modifies.

Concessive particle with nouns

The concessive particle attached to a noun has two basic functions: additive and emphatic. If added to a noun phrase with a case particle, the concessive particle always follows the case particle.

DOI: 10.4324/9781003224198-13

Additive

In this function the concessive particle can usually be translated with "also; too":

དེའི་མ་རྒན་མོ་དེ་ཡང་ཆོས་ཐོས་སོ། (MB D 138v5)
"Their old mother also heard the Buddhist teaching."

Repeated usage of the concessive particle after two nouns in adjacent phrases or clauses has the meaning "X as well as Y". The phrases/clauses have to have a parallel structure. If the verbs of the clauses are negated, then the translation is "neither X nor Y"; cf.:

སྤུ་ཡང་ཐུང་དུ་སོང་། མཇུག་མ་ཡང་ཐུང་དུ་སོང་ངོ། (GLR 23v4)
"[Their] hair as well as tails grew shorter."

ལྷ་ཡང་ཕྱིར་གནས་སུ་སོང་ངོ༎ རྒྱལ་པོ་དང་འཁོར་མང་པོ་རྣམས་ཀྱང་ཕྱིར་ཕོ་བྲང་དུ་སོང་ངོ༎ (MB D 140v2–3)
"The deity went back to [its] place. The king together with [his] many attendants also returned to [his] palace." Lit. "The deity went back to [its] place as well as the king together with [his] numerous retinue went back to [his] palace."[2]

In the additive function the concessive particle is sometimes added to a demonstrative pronoun that stands at the beginning of a clause (འདི་ཡང་/འདིའང་, དེ་ཡང་/དེའང་). This expression shows that the new clause adds further information to what has already been stated in the previous clause and thus can be translated as "moreover; namely; in this respect":

དེར་སྤྲེའུ་དེས། བྲག་ནག་པོ་ཞིག་ལ་བསྒོམས་ཏེ། དེའང་བྱམས་སྙིང་རྗེ་བྱང་ཆུབ་ཀྱི་སེམས་བསྒོམས་སོ། (GLR 22r4)
"There the monkey meditated on a black rock; namely (དེའང་), [it] contemplated benevolence, compassion, [and] the thought of enlightenment."

Emphatic

In this function the concessive particle serves to emphasise the word or phrase to which it is attached. Usually it can be translated as "even, likewise, still, yet":

གོས་ཀྱང་ངུར་སྨྲིག་ཏུ་གྱུར་ཏོ། (MB D 138v4–5)
"[Their] clothes even turned yellowish-red."

With a negated verb the translation is "not even":

ལན་འགའ་ཡང་མ་འཕྲད་ (MB D 139v1) lit. "not to meet even once"

Sometimes the concessive particle is synonymous with the focus particle ནི་ (see Lesson 9):

རྒྱལ་པོས་ཀྱང་ [. . .] དེ་དག་བཏང་ངོ་། (MB D 138v2)
"As for the king, he did set them free."

ཞིང་གི་སོ་ནམ་ཡང་འདི་ཀ་ནས་བྱེད་དོ། (ML D 13r)
"And as for the cultivation of fields, from now on [we] will do [it]."

Concessive particle with verbs

The concessive particle added to a verb is another converbal particle. It mainly expresses limitation, i.e. that the action does not constitute a sufficient condition for the action of the main verb to occur. In such cases the concessive particle can be translated as "although, even though; despite":

ཁྱོད་ལ་ཉེས་པ་མང་དུ་བྱུང་ཡང་ངས་བཏང་ངོ་།། (MB D 273v5–6)
"Even though many calamities happened to you, I set [you] free."

ལུས་བཏང་ཡང་བསོད་ནམས་ཀྱི་ཞིང་དང་། ལན་འགའ་ཡང་མ་ཕྲད་དོ། (MB D 139v1)
"Even though [I] abandoned [many] bodies, [this body of mine] has not even once met with the field of virtue."

Postpositions and postpositional phrases

Postpositions (Postp) are a class of words used to express spatial or temporal relations, as well as to mark meanings that cannot be expressed by way of grammatical case. They are placed after a noun or a noun phrase, as opposed to prepositions, such as Eng. *after*, *at*, *on*, etc., which are placed before a noun phrase (Eng. *after* dinner, *at* home, *on* the table).

In Classical Tibetan postpositions usually consist of one syllable which is attached directly to the noun phrase and does not need any case particle following it. However, true postpositions seldomly occur in prose. The most popular ones are རྗེས་ "after, behind" and བཞིན་ "according to; like".

སྲོག་བཞིན་ (GLR 22v4) "like [my own] life"
ཁ་ཆེམས་བཞིན་ (ML D 11r) "according to the testament"

More frequently Classical Tibetan makes use of complex postpositional phrases which involve so-called relator nouns. Relator nouns (RN; e.g. སྒོ་, མདུན་, ནང་, བཞིན་, and དྲུང་ in the following examples) form a distinct word class. Some of them might still have homonyms that may occur independently as nouns in a clause (e.g. སྒོ་ "door") but many relator nouns are restricted to one or the other postpositional phrase. Relator nouns can be neither modified nor quantified. The relator noun is usually attached to the NP by means of a genitive (or rarely comitative) particle (cf. 1). There is, however, a relatively small group of relator nouns that connect by absolutive (cf. 2). The last element of postpositional phrases is a case particle which may be ergative, dative, locative, elative, or terminative. For the ease of reference, the part of a postpositional phrase that follows the NP will be called 'relator phrase'. Relator phrases are usually glossed in dictionaries under the respective relator noun. Postpositional phrases with relator nouns can take one of two forms:

1 NP+GEN+RN+case particle[3]

ཚིག་སྙན་པའི་སྒོ་ནས་ (MB D 140v2) "with (lit. by means of) kind words"

ཚིག་སྙན་པ་ is the noun phrase that forms the base of the postpositional phrase. སྒོ་ is a relator noun that is connected with the noun phrase by means of the genitive particle -འི་. ནས་ is the elative particle.

ཞལ་ཆེ་པའི་མདུན་དུ་ (MB D 138r7) "to a judge" (ཞལ་ཆེ་པ་ = noun; མདུན་ = relator noun)

ལྷའི་ནང་ན་ (MB D 138v1) "among deities" (ལྷ་ = noun; ནང་ = relator noun)

2 NP_{ABS}+RN+case particle

བཀའ་བཞིན་དུ་ (MB D 138v2) "according to the order" (བཀའ་ = noun; བཞིན་ = relator noun)

ཤིང་དྲུང་ན། (MB D 270v5) "under a tree" (ཤིང་ = noun; དྲུང་ = relator noun)

This type is formed analogously to the preceding one with the exception of the genitive particle which is omitted here.

Next is a sample list of relator phrases and their meanings. The phrases are grouped according to the case particle they take to attach to the NP. The third column contains nouns that are still used as independent words in Classical Tibetan and are homonymous with the respective relator nouns.[4]

1 Genitive

རྐྱེན་གྱིས་	"due to, because of"	རྐྱེན་ "cause"
ཁ་ན་/ལ་/ཁར་	"on, upon; at"	ཁ་ "surface"
རྒྱབ་ཏུ་/ན་/ལ་	"behind; after"	རྒྱབ་ "the back of the body"

རྒྱབ་ནས་	"from behind"	
སྒོ་ནས་	"by means of, by"	སྒོ་ "door"
ཆེད་དུ་	"on account of"	
རྗེས་ལ་/སུ་	"after, behind"	རྗེས་ "trace"
སྟེང་དུ་	"above, on(to)"	སྟེང་ "top, surface"
སྟེང་ནས་	"down from"	
མཐར་	"after, behind"	མཐའ་ "end"
དོན་དུ་	"for the sake of"	དོན་ "purpose"
དྲུང་ན་/དུ་	"near to, near by"	
མདུན་ལ་/ན་/དུ་	"before, at"	མདུན་ "front"
ནང་ན་/དུ་	"in, into"	ནང་ "interior"
ནང་ནས་	"out of; from (among)"	
ཕྱིར་	"behind; on account of"	
བར་དུ་	"during"	བར་ "the middle"
འོག་ན་	"below"	འོག་ "nether sphere"

2 Comitative

ལྷན་ཅིག་ཏུ་	"together with"

3 Absolutive

ཐོག་ཏུ་	"on"	ཐོག་ "what is uppermost"
ཕྱོགས་སུ་	"towards"	ཕྱོགས་ "direction"
བར་ལ་	"between; in the meantime"	
བཞིན་དུ་	"according to; like"	བཞིན་ "face"

True postpositions listed earlier can likewise form relator phrases with the same meanings:

རྗེས་ "after, behind"	རྗེས་ལ་/སུ་ "id."
བཞིན་ "according to; like"	བཞིན་དུ་ "id."

Possessive particle ཅན་

The possessive particle ཅན་ forms adjectives that express possession of the object denoted by the main word, cf.:

ནོར་ "wealth"	ནོར་ཅན་ "wealthy", lit. "possessing wealth"

ཁ་བ་ "snow" ཁ་བ་ཅན་ "snowy, covered with snow"
ཐུགས་རྗེ་ "compassion" ཐུགས་རྗེ་ཅན་ "compassionate"

Like any adjective in Classical Tibetan, those formed with the particle ཅན་ can also be used as nouns:

ནོར་ཅན་ "(A) wealthy" or "(N) a wealthy one"
ཁ་བ་ཅན་ "(A) snowy" or "(N) Tibet"

Some words formed originally with the possessive particle ཅན་ have become lexicalised, cf.:

སེམས་ "mind" སེམས་ཅན་ "a sentient being", lit. "one having mind"
གངས་ "snow-mountain" གངས་ཅན་ "Tibet", lit. "possessing snow-mountains"

Sometimes a whole noun phrase can be turned into a possessive phrase by the particle ཅན་:

བུད་མེད་ཀྱི་གཟུགས་ "the body of a woman" བུད་མེད་ཀྱི་གཟུགས་ཅན་ "possessing the body of a woman" (KGBP 45r; *apud* Schwieger 2006: 254).

Adjectives ལྡན་ and བཅས་

The adjective ལྡན་ has a very similar meaning to the possessive particle ཅན་; it expresses possession, usually of abstract qualities:

ནོར་ "wealth" ནོར་ལྡན་ "wealthy"
བློ་ "mind" བློ་ལྡན་ "wise"
འབྱོར་པ་ "wealth, riches" འབྱོར་ལྡན་ "rich"

ལྡན་ developed from a verb, a fact which still manifests itself in the following phrases:

ཡོན་ཏན་གསུམ་དང་ལྡན་ཏེ། (GLR 22v6) "endowed with three excellent qualities"
བྱམས་པ་དང་སྙིང་རྗེར་ལྡན་ཏེ། (MB D 139r3) "possessing kindness and compassion"

Here the original argument structure of ལྡན་ as a verb is demonstrated by the use of the case particles དང་ and -ར.

Whereas ལྡན་ restricts to possession, བཅས་ mainly expresses accompaniment:

> རྒྱལ་པོ་དེ་བློན་པོ་དང་བཅས། བཙུན་མོ་དང་སྲས་སུ་བཅས་ཏེ། (MB D 139r3–4) "the king accompanied by [his] ministers, the queen, and [his] sons"

but sometimes also possession:

> སྲིད་པ་དང་བཅས་པ་ (MB D 140r6) "what is possessed of existence"

Originally ལྡན་ and བཅས་ were construed with the comitative particle དང་. In some of the previous examples, དང་ has been replaced by a terminative particle (-ར or སུ་) because another comitative particle is used earlier in these clauses (see Lesson 5: Comitative).

Exercise

༡ སྲས་ཐ་ཆུངས་དེ་ཆུང་ངུ་ནས་བྱམས་པ་དང་སྙིང་རྗེར་ལྡན་ཏེ། ཐམས་ཅད་ལ་བུ་གཅིག་པ་དང་འདྲའོ། (MB D 139r3)

༢ རྒྱལ་པོས་ཀྱང་བཅོམ་ལྡན་འདས་ཀྱི་བཀའ་བཞིན་དུ་དེ་དག་བཏང་ངོ་། (MB D 138v2)

༣ དེའི་དུས་ན་སྲས་རབ་སྣྲ་ཆེན་པོ་དེ་ནི་བྱམས་པ་ཡིན་ནོ། (MB D 140v4)

༤ སྤུ་ཡང་ཐུང་ངུ་སོང་། མཇུག་མ་ཡང་ཐུང་ངུ་སོང་ངོ་། (GLR 23v4)

༥ དེའི་ཕ་མ་ཡང་སྐྱོ་བ་ཅུང་ཟད་སྐྱེས་སོ། (MB D 140v2)

༦ བུ་མོ་དག་ཀྱང་ཕྱིར་མ་ལ་གཤེའོ། (MB D 270v3)

༧ བདག་གིས་སྔོན་ཉེས་པ་བྱས་སོ། (MB D 270v4)

༨ དེ་བཞིན་གཤེགས་པ་ཤིང་དྲུང་ན་བཞུགས་སོ། (MB D 270v5)

༩ དབྱིག་པ་ཅན་གྱིས་གླང་དེ་ཁྱིམ་གྱི་ནང་དུ་བཏང་ངོ་། (MB D 271v1)

༡༠ དེ་བར་ལ་ངའི་བུ་སྣད་གསུམ་གྱི་སྐྱིད་སྡུག་ཁྱེད་གཉེན་ཚན་ཀུན་ཤེས་སོ།། (ML D 10v)

༡༡ ངའི་ཞང་པོ་དང་མཛེས་སེའི་ཕ་མིང་གིས་ལོ་རྒྱུས་བྱས་སོ། (ML D 11r)

༡༢ དེ་ནས་སྤྲེའུ་བྱང་ཆུབ་སེམས་དཔའ་དེས་སྤྲེའུ་ཕྲུག་རྣམས་དེར་ཁྲིད་དེ། ལོ་ཐོག་ལ་གཏད་དོ། (GLR 23v4)

༡༣ བོད་ཁ་བ་ཅན་པ་མི་འདི་རྣམས་ཕ་སྤྲེའུ་དང་། མ་བྲག་སྲིན་མོ་གཉིས་ལས་ཆད་པ་ཡིན་ནོ། (GLR 23v5)

༡༤ ཆུ་ཐམས་ཅད་དེར་སོང་སྟེ། སྐྱོང་ཆུ་ལག་ཏུ་ཐིམ་མོ།། (GLR 24r2)

༡༥ རྗེ་གཉའ་ཁྲི་བཙན་པོ་བོད་ཀྱི་རྒྱལ་པོ་ལ་བྱོན་ཏོ། (GLR 24r2–3)

༡༦ བལ་པོས་སེ་འུ་མ་ཐོས་ཀྱང་།། ཁ་དོག་ཉིད་ལས་བྲོ་བ་ཤེས།། (SSP 22c–d)

Word list

བཀའ་ (HON) order

སྐོང་ཆུ་ལག་ arm(s) of the Skoṅ-čhu river

སྐྱེ་ v2 སྐྱེས་ (INTR) to grow

སྐྱེས་ see སྐྱེ་

ཁ་དོག་ colour

ཁ་བ་ཅན་ snowy, snow-clad

ཁྱེད་ (2SG/PL; HON) you

འགྲོ་ v2/v4 སོང་ (INTR) [1]to go; [2]to become (+ TERM)

སྒྲ་ཆེན་པོ་ (PN) Sgra-čhen-po

སྔོན་ earlier

ཅུང་ཟད་ a little

གཅིག་པ་ (A) only

ཆད་པ་ begotten/born (from + DEL)

ཆུང་དུ་ childhood

མཇུག་མ་ tail

རྗེ་ lord

ཉིད་ the very

ཉེས་པ་ bad deed

གཉའ་ཁྲི་བཙན་པོ་ (PN) Gñaɣ-khri Bcan-po

གཏད་ see གཏོད་

གཏོང་ v2 བཏང་ v3 གཏང་ v4 ཐོང་ (TR) [1]to let go; [2]to let

གཏོད་ v2/v3 གཏད་ v4 ཐོད་ (TR) to point (towards + DAT)

བཏང་ see གཏོང་

ཐམས་ཅད་ (N) all; (A) all

ཐིམ་ (INTR) to disappear

ཐུང་ (to be) short

དུས་ time

དེ་བཞིན་གཤེགས་པ་ Tathāgata

དྲུང་ན་ (Postp) under (+ ABS)

འདྲ་ (INTR) to be similar, to be like (+ COM)

ལྡན་ (to be) possessed of (+ COM)

ནང་དུ་ (Postp) into, in (+ GEN)
སྐྲ་ hair
སྤྲོ་བ་ joy
བར་ལ་ (Postp) in the meantime, until (+ ABS/GEN)
བལ་པོ་ Nepalese
བུ་ child
བོད་ (PN) Tibet
བྱམས་པ་ [1]kindness; [2](PN) Byams-pa
བྱས་ see བྱེད་
བྱེད་ v2 བྱས་ v3 བྱ་ v4 བྱོས་ (TR) to do, to make; to tell
བྱོན་ see འབྱོན་
བྲོ་བ་ taste
འབྱོན་ v2 བྱོན་ (INTR) to appear
མ་ mother
བཞིན་དུ་ (Postp) according to (+ ABS)
བཞུགས་ (HON for འདུག་; INTR) to sit
ཟ་ v2 བཟས་/ཟོས་ v3 བཟའ་ v4 ཟོ(ས)་ (TR) to eat
ཟོས་ see ཟ་
རབ་ eldest
ལོ་རྒྱུས་ account
གཤེ་ v2 གཤེས་ (INTR) to inveigh (against + DAT)
སེ་འུ་ pomegranate
སོང་ see འགྲོ་

Notes

1 Frequently the form ཡང་ is used instead of འང་.
2 For an example of the negative construction "neither X nor Y", see Reading I (MB D 270v6).
3 In rare cases the postpositional phrase may be formed with a case particle distinct from genitive (GEN), e.g. comitative.
4 A more extensive list of relator phrases can be found in Schwieger (2006: 329–31).

Lesson 11

- Questions
- Nominalisation
- Relative clauses

Questions

In Classical Tibetan questions can be formed in two ways:

1. With the so-called final particle of interrogative clauses: འམ་
2. With an interrogative pronoun or word corresponding to Eng. *who*, *where*, *why*, etc.

The word order in questions is the same as in affirmative clauses. There is no punctuation mark (like the question mark < ? >) that would additionally indicate that the said clause is a question clause. A question can stand on its own, terminating with a ཤད་, or it can be embedded in another clause as a direct quotation.[1] In the latter case there is usually no ཤད་ after the question.

Interrogative particle འམ་

The question/interrogative (INT) particle འམ་ assimilates to the final letter of the preceding syllable. Assimilation rules are identical with those of the final particle of affirmative clauses (འོ་; see Lesson 3):

Verb	FNL འོ་	INT འམ་	
མཆི་	མཆིའོ་	མཆིའམ་	after a final vowel
མངའ་	མངའོ་	མངའམ་	after the final -འ
སྨྲས་	སྨྲས་སོ་	སྨྲས་སམ་	after a final consonant
གྱུར་	གྱུར་ཏོ་	གྱུར་ཏམ་	after an earlier ད་དྲག་

DOI: 10.4324/9781003224198-14

The interrogative particle འམ་ is used mainly in questions in which no other interrogative words occur, but it can also co-occur with other interrogative words. By means of འམ་ two types of questions can be formed: polar questions and alternative questions.

Polar questions

Polar questions (also called 'yes-no questions') are questions which one can answer with a simple "yes" or "no". The particle འམ་ is attached to the verb and so becomes the last element in the question clause:

> ནུས་པ་ཡོད་དམ། (MB D 139r7)
> "Is there anybody suitable?"

Alternative questions

An alternative question provides two or more alternative answers ("this or that") from which the respondent should choose. In Classical Tibetan this kind of question is likewise formed with the question particle འམ་ which, however, is placed between the words or phrases that express the alternatives:

> བདེན་ནམ་མི་བདེན། (ML D 18v)
> "Is [it] true or false (lit. not true)?"
>
> སྒུགས་དམ་འདིས་འོང་ངམ་མི་འོང་ངམ། (KDDS 46; *apud* Schwieger 2006: 166)
> "Will [it] come through (lit. with) this meditation or not?"

The latter example demonstrates that the basic structure of alternative questions came into being through the elision of the question particle after the second element:

X_{INT} Y_{INT} "Is X? Is Y?" > X_{INT} Y "Is X or Y?"

What was originally a sequence of two polar questions has been joined into an alternative question.

If more than two elements of an alternative are used, འམ་ occurs after every element apart from the last one:

> ཁྱེད་རང་གི་ནོར་གསེར་སེ་གཅིག་གམ། ནས་ཕུལ་གང་ངམ། མར་ཉག་གཅིག་གམ། གོས་དར་རྐྱང་སྣ་གཅིག (ML D 12v)
> "Your wealth, is it one nugget of gold? Or a handful of barley? Or a lump of butter? Or one kind of a single silk cloth?"

This function of the question particle influenced the development of yet another use of it: as the disjunctive conjunction "or":

མི་ཆེན་པོའམ་ཆུང་ངུ་ཞིག (*apud* Hahn 1996: 46) "a big (i.e. tall) or a small man"

Interrogative words

Interrogative words are function words used to ask a question, like Eng. *who*, *where*, *why*, etc. In Classical Tibetan one can distinguish between the basic forms which are interrogative pronouns, cf.:

སུ་ "who?" (used only with human or anthropomorphic beings)
ཅི་/ཇི་ "what?" (used with inanimate objects)
གང་ "who?", "what?", "which?" (used with both animate and inanimate objects)[2]

and interrogative words which are usually derived from the interrogative pronouns. The following list presents a selection of interrogative words:

ཅིའི་ཕྱིར་	"why?"	གང་དུ་	"whither?"
ཅི་ཙམ་	"how much?"	གང་ནས་	"where from?"
ཇི་ལྟར་	"how?"	ག་རེ་	"where?"
ནམ་	"when"	གར་	"whither?"

ལྷ་ཁྱོད་སུ་ཞིག་ལགས། (MB D 140r5) "Oh, deity, who are you?"

བུ་ནང་གི་སྡུག་པ་ཅང་མ་ཉེས་སམ་ག་རེ། (MB D 139v7) "Is the dearest of [my] sons unhurt? Where is [he]?"

This utterance contains two independent questions: (1) བུ་ནང་གི་སྡུག་པ་ཅང་མ་ཉེས་སམ།; and (2) ག་རེ།.

Interrogative pronouns can take case particles if the syntax requires it:

ཁྱོད་ཅི་ལ་འོངས། (MB D 272r7) "Why did you come?" Lit. "What for did you come?"

ཁྱོད་ཀྱི་ཁ་ཆེམས་ཀྱི་ཡི་གེ་སུས་བྲིས། (ML D 12v) "Who wrote the text of your testament?"

Since བྲིས་ is a transitive verb and requires the subject in ergative, the interrogative pronoun སུ་ stands in ergative (སུས་).[3]

Nominalisation

In Classical Tibetan any word, phrase, or even clause can be nominalised, i.e. changed into a noun or a noun phrase. This happens by adding the nominal particle

པ་/བ་ (see Lesson 7) to the word, phrase, or clause. Thus nominalised constructions underlie the same processes as any other noun phrase; they can acquire a case particle (including the genitive particle), a number particle, a postposition, an attribute, etc. In the syntax they can take any function that any other NP can take. If a clause or a sentence is nominalised, the argument structure of the verb and the word order of the clause remain unaltered. Nominalisation of clauses is very frequently used in Classical Tibetan and needs to be properly understood.

Nominalisation of verb phrases

Verb phrases are nominalised by adding the nominal particle པ་/བ་ to the respective phrase:

ཕྱུགས་སྐྱོང་ "to protect cattle" ཕྱུགས་སྐྱོང་པ་ "the one (པ་) protecting cattle"

Formally, ཕྱུགས་ remains the object of the verb སྐྱོང་ even after nominalisation.

བུ་རྟག་ཏུ་རྐུ་བ་གཉིས་ཞིག་ (MB D 138r7) "two always stealing sons"

The verb phrase རྟག་ཏུ་རྐུ་ "to constantly steal" consists of the adverb རྟག་ཏུ་ and the verb རྐུ་. In the prior example it is nominalised with བ་ and then used as an attribute of བུ་.

དེ་དག་བཅོམ་ལྡན་འདས་ཀྱི་བཀའ་དྲིན་དྲན་ཞིང་རབ་ཏུ་དགའ་བ་སྐྱེས་སོ། (MB D 138v2–3)
Lit. "While they were remembering the favour of the Victorious One, happiness arose [in them]."

Here again a verb phrase consisting of an adverb and a verb is nominalised as རབ་ཏུ་དགའ་བ་, lit. "the-being-very-happy", and then applied in the second clause as the subject of the verb སྐྱེས་, lit. "the-being-very-happy arouse".

Nominalisation of clauses

In nominalisation of clauses a whole clause is nominalised. The phrase

ངེད་འདི་ན་ཡོད་པ་ (ML D 13r) "we who are here"

has been nominalised from the clause

*ངེད་འདི་ན་ཡོད། "We are here."

The nominalisation changes neither case particles nor the word order of the original clause; it just adds the nominal particle པ་/བ་ to the clause.

རྒྱལ་བུ་ཐ་ཆུངས་གིས་ཕུ་བོ་གཉིས་ལ་སྨྲས་པ་ (MB D 139r4–5) "what (པ་) the youngest prince said to [his] both elder brothers"

The original clause would have been:

*རྒྱལ་བུ་ཐ་ཆུངས་གིས་ཕུ་བོ་གཉིས་ལ་སྨྲས་སོ། "The youngest prince said to [his] both elder brothers."

རྒྱལ་བུ་ཐ་ཆུངས་ is the subject of the verb སྨྲས་ and therefore is marked with the ergative particle གིས་. Likewise ཕུ་བོ་གཉིས་ (marked with ལ་) is the indirect object indiscriminately whether the verb is final or nominalised.

In the next example the clause *བུ་ཟ་ལ་ཐུག "[The tigress] was about to eat [her] cubs," has been nominalised (པ་ཞིག་) and functions as a direct object of the verb མཐོང་:

བུ་ཟ་ལ་ཐུག་པ་ཞིག་མཐོང་ངོ། (MB D 139r4)
"[They] saw a one (i.e. a tigress) that was about to eat [her] cubs."

The next example firstly demonstrates the nominalisation of a verb phrase and then its inclusion in another clause as the object of a new verb:

*མྱ་ངན་གྱི་རྒྱ་མཚོར་ལྷུང་ "to fall into the ocean of affliction"

མྱ་ངན་གྱི་རྒྱ་མཚོར་ལྷུང་བ་ "the falling into the ocean of affliction"

མྱ་ངན་གྱི་རྒྱ་མཚོར་ལྷུང་བ་མི་ཚོར། (MB D 140r7) "not to perceive the falling into the ocean of affliction"

Since a nominalised phrase or clause functions like any other NP within a clause, it can also be used in a postpositional phrase:

དེ་དག་གི་སྲོག་བསྐྱབ་པའི་སླད་དུ་ (MB D 138v2) "in order to save their life"

ལྷས་ལུང་བསྟན་པ་བཞིན། (GLR 24r6) "in accordance with the prophecy taught by deities"

Relative clauses

A simple relative clause is formed in Classical Tibetan with a genitive particle added to a nominalised phrase or clause. In this way, the nominalised phrase or clause serves to modify the following noun or noun phrase. For example, the verb phrase ཕྱུགས་སྐྱོང་ "to protect cattle" can be nominalised as ཕྱུགས་སྐྱོང་པ་ "the one protecting cattle" and used to modify the noun རྫི་ཝུ་ "herdsman" as in:

ཕྱུགས་སྐྱོང་པའི་རྫི་ཝུ་རྣམས་ "herdsmen who protect cattle"

ཤིན་ཏུ་དད་པའི་སེམས་ (MB D 138v5) "utterly religious mind", lit. "mind that utterly believes"

རྫུ་འཕྲུལ་སྟོན་པའི་སྤྲེའུ་ཞིག་ (GLR 22r4) "a monkey that is displaying magic tricks"

Classical Tibetan also knows relative clauses that are introduced by means of relative pronouns (see Lesson 14).

Exercise

༡ ཆུང་ཟད་ཅིག་ངལ་བསོ་བའི་བར་དུ་སྲས་གསུམ་པོ་ཚལ་གྱི་ནང་དུ་དོང་ངོ་། (MB D 139r4)

༢ སྟག་མོ་འདིས་ཟས་སུ་ཅི་ཟ། (MB D 139r6)

༣ བདག་ཚེ་འཕོས་པའི་རུས་བུ་ཚལ་ན་འདུག་པ་ལ་ཕ་མས་བསྐོར་ཏོ། (MB D 140r3)

༤ ཅིའི་སླད་དུ་བདག་འབའ་ཞིག་གི་ཕྱིར་མྱ་ངན་གྱི་རྒྱ་མཚོར་ལྷུང་བ་མི་ཚོར་རམ། (MB D 140r7)

༥ ཁྱོད་ཀྱི་ཡིད་ལ་ཅི་སྙམ་དུ་སེམས། (MB D 140v3)

༦ དེའི་ཚེ་དེའི་དུས་ན་རྒྱལ་པོ་ཤིང་རྟ་ཆེན་པོ་དེ་སུ་ཡིན། (MB D 140v3)

༧ དེའི་ཚེ་ན་ཀུན་དགའ་བོ་དང་། འཁོར་མང་པོ་ཐམས་ཅད་བཅོམ་ལྡན་འདས་ཀྱིས་གསུངས་པ་ལ་ཡི་རངས་ཏེ་མངོན་པར་བསྟོད་དོ།། (MB D 140v6)

༨ འགྲོ་བ་རིགས་དྲུག་ནས་ཚེ་འཕོས་པའི་སྤྲེའུ་ཕྲུག་རྣམས་སྐྱེས་སོ། (GLR 23r1–2)

༩ སེམས་ཅན་ཆེན་པོས་སྟག་མོ་ལ་ལུས་བྱིན་པའི་ལེའུ་སྟེ་གཉིས་པའོ།། (MB D 140v6–7)

༡༠ བྲམ་ཟེས་བཅོམ་ལྡན་འདས་ལ་འདི་སྐད་ཅེས་གསོལ་ཏོ། (MB D 271r1)

༡༡ དེ་ནས་འཕགས་པ་སྤྱན་རས་གཟིགས་དེས། རྫུ་འཕྲུལ་སྟོན་པའི་སྤྲེའུ་ཞིག་ལ། དགེ་བསྙེན་གྱི་སྡོམ་པ་བྱིན་ནོ། (GLR 22r3–4)

༡༢ རབ་ཏུ་དབུལ་ཕོངས་པ། བཟའ་བ་དང་བགོ་བ་མེད་པ་ཞིག་གོ། (MB D 271r7)

༡༣ དེས་རྩིག་པ་ཞིག་གི་སྟེང་དུ་མཆོངས་སོ། (MB D 271v4–5)

༡༤ དེ་ལ་ཆུང་མས་སྤྱོ་བ་ཡང་མེད། (MB D 270v6)

༡༥ ཡབ་མི་ལ་ཤེས་རབ་རྒྱལ་མཚན་དེ་སྙུན་ཞིག་གིས་ཟིན་ནོ། (ML D 10r)

Word list

བསྐོར་ v2/v3 བསྐོར་ v4 སྐོར་ (TR) to surround (+ DAT)

བསྐོར་ see སྐོར་

བགོ་བ་ clothes

འགྲོ་བ་ existence

ངལ་ weariness

མངོན་པར་བསྟོད་ v2/v3 བསྟོད་ v4 སྟོད་ (TR) to praise

ཅི་ what?

ཅིའི་སླད་དུ་ (INT) why? on account of what?

མཆོང་(ས)་ (INTR) to jump

སྙུན་ illness

སྟེང་དུ་ (Postp) on(to) (+ GEN)

སྟོན་ v2/v3 བསྟན་ v4 སྟོན་ (TR) to show

བསྟན་ see སྟོན་

དྲུག་ six

འདི་སྐད་(ཅེས་) these words

ཕྱིར་ (Postp) on account of, because of (+ GEN)

བར་དུ་ (Postp) during (+ GEN)

དབུལ་ཕོངས་ (to be) poor

འབའ་ཞིག་ alone, mere

མི་ལ་ཤེས་རབ་རྒྱལ་མཚན་ (PN) Mi-la Śes-rab Rgyal-mchan, the father of Mi-la Ras-pa

མྱ་ངན་ affliction

རྩིག་པ་ wall

ཚེ་འཕོ་ v2 འཕོས་ (INTR) to die, to be reborn

ཚོར་ (TR) to perceive

རྫུ་འཕྲུལ་ magic tricks

ཟས་ food

ཟིན་ (INTR) to be seized (with + ERG)

བཟའ་བ་ food

རིགས་ family; state

རུས་པ་ bone

ལེའུ་ chapter

ཤིང་རྟ་ཆེན་པོ་ (PN) Śiṅ-rta-čhen-po

སུ་ who

གསུང་ v2 གསུངས་ (HON for ཟེར་/སྨྲ་; TR) to speak

གསུངས་ see གསུང་

གསུམ་པོ་ a group of three

གསོ་ v2 བསོས་ v3 བསོ་ v4 སོས་ (TR) to cure; ངལ་གསོ་ to rest, to take a rest

གསོལ་ (HML; TR) to speak

བསོ་ see གསོ་

Notes

1 For details on direct speech, see Lesson 13.

2 Sometimes the older form ག་ can be likewise encountered.

3 Interrogative pronouns and words are also used to form indefinite pronouns (see Lesson 14).

Lesson 12

- Case converbs
- Verb + case particle
- Verb + /པ་/ + case particle

Case converbs

Apart from the already-introduced coordinative (Lesson 8), gerundial (Lesson 9), and concessive particles (Lesson 10), Classical Tibetan makes extensive use of the case particles to connect clauses with each other. One can differentiate between two types of construction:

1 Verb + case particle
2 Verb + པ་/བ་ + case particle

These two types will be discussed separately. In some instances, one and the same case particle can be used in both types, but then the functions of the case particle in either construction are usually distinct.

Verb + case particle

The type 'verb + case particle' includes constructions with elative, locative, comitative, terminative, genitive, dative, and ergative particles.

Elative

The primary function of the elative particle after a verb is to mark that the action of the following clause results from the action that is expressed by the verb with the elative particle. Thus, the elative particle can be said to form resultative converbs.

DOI: 10.4324/9781003224198-15

In the following sentence the queen hears about the death of her beloved son and faints; fainting is a direct result of hearing the bad news.

> ལྷ་མོ་དེས་དེ་སྐད་སྨྲས་པ་ཐོས་ནས་ཁམས་ཏེ། (MB D 139v7–140r1)
> "When the queen had heard these words uttered, [she] fainted away."

In the next example the converb བཞུས་ནས་ can also be interpreted as resultative; pure metals resulted from melting ores.

> སོལ་བས་རྡོ་གསུམ་བཞུས་ནས། དངུལ་ཟངས་ལྕགས་གསུམ་བཏོན། (GLR 26r4–5)[1]
> "[One] melted three ores with the charcoal [and] thereby obtained silver, copper, [and] iron, the three."

The meaning of elative was early generalised to also encompass temporal relation of anteriority. The resultative and temporal functions are closely related to each other because an event that results in another event has to precede it in time.

> རྒྱལ་བུ་སེམས་ཅན་ཆེན་པོ་དེ་དེར་ཚེ་འཕོས་ནས། དགའ་ལྡན་ལྷའི་གནས་སུ་སྐྱེས་སོ། (MB D 140r2–3)
> "After prince Sems-čan-čhen-po had died there (དེར་), [he] was reborn in Dgaɣ-ldan, a deities' place."

> དེ་ནས་འཕགས་པ་སྤྱན་རས་གཟིགས་དེས། རྫུ་འཕྲུལ་སྟོན་པའི་སྤྲེའུ་ཞིག་ལ། དགེ་བསྙེན་གྱི་སྡོམ་པ་བྱིན་ནས། བོད་ཁ་བ་ཅན་གྱི་རྒྱལ་ཁམས་སུ་བཏང་ངོ། (GLR 22r3–4)
> "At that time, after the Noble One, Spyan-ras-gzigs, had conferred the vow of a lay practitioner upon a monkey that was displaying magic tricks, [he] sent it (i.e. the monkey) to the realm of the snow-clad Tibet."

> དེའི་ཚེ་བཅོམ་ལྡན་འདས་བསོད་སྙོམས་ཀྱི་དུས་ལ་བབ་ནས། ཤམ་ཐབས་དང་ཆོས་གོས་བགོས་ནས་ལྷུང་བཟེད་བསྣམས་ཏེ། ཀུན་དགའ་བོ་དང་བསོད་སྙོམས་ལ་གཤེགས་སོ། (MB D 138r6)
> "Then, when the time for alms came, the Victorious One put on a lower garment and a monk-robe and, having taken up [his] alms-bowl, [he] went for alms with Kun-dgaɣ-bo."

In the last example, the converbal elative ནས་ is used in two functions: resultative བབ་ནས་, lit. "as a result of the time having come", and temporal བགོས་ནས་, lit. "after [he] had put [his] clothes on".

Locative

Locative particle ན་ forms temporal ("when") and conditional ("if") converbs.

Temporal meaning

Translation of the locative particle ན་ in temporal meaning can differ depending on the temporal relationship between the actions expressed by the converb and the main verb. Sometimes it can be anteriority ("after"), sometimes simultaneity ("when").

> གཞན་གྱི་སྐྱོན་ཐོས་ན་དགའ་བ་ (GLR 24r1)
> Lit. "those (བ་) who rejoice when [they] hear of others' harm"

The temporal meaning is weakened if the preceding clause contains an interrogative pronoun:

> རྒན་མོ་མ་སྨད་གསུམ་པོ་འདིས་སྔོན་ལེགས་པ་ཅི་ཞིག་བགྱིས་ན། ད་ལྟར་བཅོམ་ལྡན་འདས་དང་ཕྲད་དེ། (MB D 138v6)
> "What (ཅི་) good deeds (ལེགས་པ་) did the three, the old woman, the mother and her sons, accomplish earlier, so that now, [they] have encountered the Victorious One."

The first clause could be literally rendered as "Once these three, the old woman, mother and [her] children, have done any good deeds [. . .]."

Conditional meaning

> ཁྱོད་ངའི་ཁྱོ་མི་བྱེད་ན་ང་ཆེའི་དུས་བྱེད་དོ། (GLR 22r6)
> "If you don't become my husband, I will die."

> སྐྱེ་བ་ཡོད་ན་ངེས་པར་འཇིག་གོ། (MB D 140r6–7)
> "If [something] has birth, [it] will certainly perish."

> སྡིག་པ་བྱས་ན་སེམས་ཅན་དམྱལ་བར་ལྟུང་། དགེ་བ་བྱས་ན་མཐོ་རིས་སུ་སྐྱེ་སྟེ། (MB D 140r7)
> "If [one] committed an offence, [he] will fall to hell. If [one] did good deeds, [he] will be reborn in heaven."

In order to disambiguate the meaning of the converb, the conjunctions གལ་ཏེ་ or (rarely) ཅི་སྟེ་ "if" may be used in conditional clauses. They usually stand at the beginning of the clause.

Complex particle ན་ཡང་ (also ནའང་)

After the locative particle ན་ the concessive particle ཡང་ adds an emphasis to it. Their union reinforces the conditional function of ན་ and can be translated with "even if".

ཆར་འདོད་བྱི་འུ་སྐོམ་ན་ཡང་། །ས་ལ་འབབ་པའི་ཆུ་མི་འཐུང་།། (SSP 13c–d)
"Even if a *cātaka*-nestling is thirsty, [it] does not drink water that falls on the ground."

བློ་གྲོས་ཆེན་པོ་རྒུད་ན་ཡང་། །ལྷག་པར་བློ་གྲོས་སྟོབས་ལྡན་འགྱུར།། (SSP 5a–b)
"Even if a man of great intellect grows weak, [his] intellect becomes even stronger."[2]

Comitative

Comitative particle དང་ is added at the end of an imperative clause in order to connect this clause with the following, indicative one. The imperative particle may be left out between the verb and the comitative particle.[3] When དང་ connects an imperative clause with another clause, it also signals that the next clause has a subject distinct from the imperative clause.

མཆེད་གཉིས་སྔར་གཤེགས་ཤིག་དང་། བདག་དོན་ཞིག་གཉེར་ཏེ། སླད་བཞིན་པར་མཆིའོ། (MB D 139v2)
"Oh, brothers, go on ahead! Having taken care of something, I will come after."

In the first clause, two brothers are prompted to go. With the second clause the subject changes to the first person (བདག).

Terminative

The terminative particle directly after the verb stem serves to mark a purposive (or infinitive) clause that expresses purpose of an action and usually begins in English with "to, in order to, so that" or "lest".

བདག་གི་བུ་དགུམ་པ་ལ་ཐུག་པ་འདིའི་སྐྱབས་མཛད་དུ་གསོལ། (MB D 138v1)
"[I] beg [you] to save these sons of mine who are about to be killed."

སྐྱབས་མཛད་, lit. "to make a protection", is formed from the noun སྐྱབས་ and the light verb མཛད་ (see Lesson 15). Since སྐྱབས་ is formally a noun, it can be modified by any noun phrase. In this case the modifying phrase consists of the main part བདག་གི་བུ་ "my son(s)" and another modifying phrase, the attributive དགུམ་པ་ལ་ཐུག་པ་, lit. "one (པ་) who is close to being killed". The nominalised v3-stem དགུམ་པ་ is required by the verb ཐུག་. The subject of the verb གསོལ་ has to be assumed from the possessive pronoun བདག་གི་ "my". The subject of the verb མཛད་ is the person who is begged. This is the Victorious One, who is not explicitly mentioned here.

> སྤྲེའུ་བྱང་ཆུབ་སེམས་དཔའ་བལྟར་ཕྱིན་པས། (GLR 23r4)
> "The *bodhisattva*-monkey went to inspect [them]."

བལྟ་ is v3-stem because the construction 'V + TERM + verb of going (here: ཕྱིན་)' requires the first verb (V) to be a v3-stem (if transitive; in later texts v1 is also used instead).

> བཅོམ་ལྡན་འདས་ཀྱིས་ཀུན་དགའ་བོ་ལ་བཀའ་སྩལ་ཏེ། རྒྱལ་པོ་ལ་གསོལ་བ་འདེབས་སུ་བཏང་བ་དང་། (MB D 138v2)
> "The Victorious One, having spoken to Kun-dgaɣ-bo, sent [him] to submit a request to the king."

གསོལ་བ་འདེབས་, lit. "to throw a request", means "to make a request, to request" (see Lesson 15: Light Verbs). The subject of the verb བཏང་ is the Victorious One, but the subject of འདེབས་ is Kun-dgaɣ-bo.

Genitive

The genitive particle attached directly to a verb usually marks an adversative relationship between this verb and the following one. An adversative converb expresses an opposition or antithesis to the action represented by the main verb.

> སྡིག་པ་བྱས་ན་སེམས་ཅན་དམྱལ་བར་ལྟུང་གི། དགེ་བ་བྱས་ན་མཐོ་རིས་སུ་སྐྱེ་སྟེ། (MB D 140r7)
> "If [one] committed an offence, [he] will fall to hell. Whereas (གི་), if [one] did good deeds, [he] will be reborn in heaven."

Due to the complex structure of the Tibetan sentence, it is not possible to connect all four clauses into one sentence in English.

If one of the verbs is negated, a concessive ("although") or contrasting ("but") rendering might be more appropriate:

> མི་མཐོང་བ་དེ་ལ་བུ་པོ་ནི་མེད་ཀྱི། བུ་མོ་བདུན་ཡོད་དེ། (MB D 270v2)
> "Although the blind one didn't have a son, [she] had seven daughters."

Dative

When the dative particle ལ་ is added to a verb, it has a coordinating function and is used in two contexts:

1 ལ་ coordinates two clauses. Usually the clauses contain intransitive or attributive verbs:

སྟག་མོ་འདི་ནི་ཉམ་ཆུང་ལ་རིད་པ་ (MB D 139r5)
"this tigress, that was weak and (ལ་) meagre"

Here the dative particle ལ་ coordinates ཉམ་ཆུང་ "(to be) weak" and རིད་ "(to be) meagre".

མ་འོངས་པའི་དུས་སུ་སངས་རྒྱས་ཀྱི་བསྟན་པ་དར་ཞིང་རྒྱས་ལ་ཡུན་རིང་དུ་གནས་པ་དང་། (GLR 22v6)
Lit. "In a future time the teachings of the Buddha, while spreading, will increase and (ལ་) last for a long time."

In rare cases the dative may also coordinate transitive verbs:

ཆང་ཚོང་མ་ཁྱོད་བུ་གོར་བསྙལ་ལ་གོས་ཀྱིས་གཡོགས་པས། (MB D 272v7–3r1)
"You beer-seller, [you] laid [your] child down (གོར་, lit. on a spot) and (ལ་) covered [it] with a cloth."

2 ལ་ coordinates two imperative clauses:

ནོར་རྫས་ཡོག་ལ་ཕ་ཤུལ་བུས་འཛིན་དུ་ཆུག་ཅིག (ML D 10v)
"Give back the wealth and (ལ་) let[4] my son take over the patrimony!"

དེ་ཀ་གྱིས་ལ་བུ་འདི་ཡོན་ཏན་ཅིག་སློབ་ཏུ་ཐོང་། (ML D 13r)
"Do exactly that and send [your] son to learn a good skill!"

A common characteristic of ལ་ in this function is that it coordinates clauses with the same subject. This distinguishes it from the comitative particle དང་ after an imperative clause. Another difference between ལ་ and དང་ is that the latter particle coordinates an imperative clause with a non-imperative clause whereas ལ་ can only be used to coordinate two imperative clauses. Compare the use of ལ་ and དང་ in the following example:

ཁྱོད་ཤིན་ཏུ་ལེགས་པར་ཉོན་ལ་ཡིད་ལ་ཟུངས་ཤིག་དང་། ཁྱོད་ལ་བསྟན་པར་བྱའོ།། (MB D 271r5–6)
"Listen very carefully (lit. well) and take [it] into [your] mind! [It] will be taught to you."

Here ལ་ coordinates two imperative clauses (ཁྱོད་ཤིན་ཏུ་ལེགས་པར་ཉོན་ and ཡིད་ལ་ཟུངས་), whereas དང་ coordinates a complex imperative clause (ཉོན་ལ་ཡིད་ལ་ཟུངས་ཤིག་) with an indicative one (ཁྱོད་ལ་བསྟན་པར་བྱའོ་).[5]

Ergative

The ergative particle forms causal clauses, i.e. it marks an event as the cause of the following action.

སྟག་མོ་འདི་ནི་ཤིན་ཏུ་སྡུག་བསྔལ་གྱིས་གཟིར་ཏེ། (MB D 139r5)
"Regarding this tigress, because [she] was very afflicted, [she] was pained."

ཁྱོད་ཀྱིས་ངའི་གླང་བོར་གྱིས། གླང་སླར་བྱིན་ཅིག (MB D 271v2)
"Because you lost my ox, give [me another] ox back!"

བདག་གི་ཕ་མ་འདི་ལྟར་མི་དགའ་བའི་རྐྱེན་གྱིས་གལ་ཏེ་ན་ལུས་དང་སྲོག་གི་བར་ཆད་དུ་འགྱུར་གྱིས། དེ་ལ་སྤྲོ་བ་བསྐྱེད་ཅིང་གཏམ་བྱར་འགྲོའོ། (MB D 140r4)
"Because (གྱིས་), on account (རྐྱེན་གྱིས་) of my parents' unhappiness, a threat might (གལ་ཏེ་ན་, lit. perhaps) occur to [their] bodies or lives, I will go to (-ར) please them[6] and to talk to them."

The ergative particle may also occur following direct speech. For this function see Lesson 15: Ergative in Quotations.

Verb + པ་/བ་ + case particle

A separate group of constructions is formed by adding a case particle to the nominalised form of a verb. The case particles are those of comitative, terminative, ergative, delative, locative, and dative.

Comitative

The comitative དང་ after a nominalised verb serves to coordinate two syntactically equal clauses with each other. It can be translated as "and".

ལོ་གསུམ་ལོན་པ་དང་། སྤྲེའུ་བྱང་ཆུབ་སེམས་དཔའ་བལྟར་ཕྱིན་པས། (GLR 23r4)
"Three years passed and (དང་) the *bodhisattva*-monkey went to inspect [them]."

བཅོམ་ལྡན་འདས་ཀྱིས་ཀུན་དགའ་བོ་ལ་བཀའ་སྩལ་ཏེ། རྒྱལ་པོ་ལ་གསོལ་བ་འདེབས་སུ་བཏང་བ་དང་། རྒྱལ་པོས་ཀྱང་བཅོམ་ལྡན་འདས་ཀྱི་བཀའ་བཞིན་དུ་དེ་དག་བཏང་ངོ་། (MB D 138v2)
"The Victorious One, having spoken to Kun-dgaɣ-bo, sent [him] to submit a request to the king and (དང་) indeed (ཀྱང་), the king did set them free according to the words of the Victorious One."

The temporal relationship between the two clauses (frequently addressed in various grammars) is not contained in the converb but in the nature of actions that usually follow each other.[7]

Terminative

Following a nominalised verb, the terminative particle always takes the form -ར: verb + པར་/བར་.[8] The construction serves to introduce complement or adverbial clauses.

Complement clause

In complement clauses the terminative particle can usually be translated with "that":

ལྷའི་གཙོ་བོ་དགོངས་ཏེ། བདག་ཅག་ཆོས་ལ་རབ་ཏུ་འབྱུང་བར་ཅི་གནང་། (MB D 138v4)
"[Oh] the most eminent among the deities, having thought [of us], would [you] allow us to join the religion of the Buddha?" Lit. "[. . .] would you allow that we go for the religion of the Buddha?"

ཕྱི་མ་དམྱལ་བར་སྐྱེ་བར་ཐེ་ཚོམ་མེད།། (GLR 23v2)
"There is no doubt, that later [they] will be reborn in hell."

Adverbial clause

An adverbial clause is a type of clause that functions as an adverb towards the following verb, adjective, or another adverb.

ལྷའི་གཙོ་བོ་ཐུགས་བརྩེ་བར་དགོངས་ཏེ། (MB D 138v4)
"[Oh] the most eminent among the deities, having thought kindly [of us], [. . .]."

ཁ་ཡང་ཕྱེ་ནས་ལུས་ཀྱི་ཤ་མ་ལུས་པར་ཟོས་སོ། (MB D 139v3)
"After [the tigress] had even opened the mouth [she] completely[9] ate the flesh of [his] body."

ནོར་རྣམས་ལྷག་ལུས་མེད་པར་ཕོག་ལ། (ML D 10v)
"Give back the wealth completely!"[10]

Ergative

The variant -ས of the ergative particle is attached to a nominalised verb in order to form a causal clause. In the classical language no difference can be observed between the usage of the ergative particle directly after a verb and after a nominalised verb.

> དེའི་མ་རྒན་མོ་དེ་ཡང་ཆོས་ཐོས་པས་ལན་ཅིག་ཕྱིར་མི་ལྡོག་པར་གྱུར་ཏོ། (MB D 138v5)
> "Because their old mother also heard the Buddhist teachings, [she] became an *anāgāmin*."[11]

> བདག་གིས་ལུས་ཀྱིས་སྟག་མོ་ལྟོགས་པ་བསྐྱོད་པས་དགའ་ལྡན་ལྷའི་གནས་སུ་སྐྱེས་སོ།། (MB D 140r6)
> "Because I had fed a hungry tigress with my body, [I] was born in Dgaɣ-ldan, a deities' place."

Delative

When attached to a nominalised verb, the delative ལས་ indicates that the action of the converb is anterior to the following action.

> ཁྱིམ་བདག་ཀྱང་གླང་འོངས་པར་མཐོང་བ་ལས་མ་བཏགས་པས་ན། མིག་ཕྱུང་ཞིག (MB D 272v1)
> "Because (པས་ན་)[12] the householder, upon (ལས་) seeing that the ox came in, did not bind [it], gouge out [his] eyes!"

> དེའི་ཚེ་བློན་པོ་ཞིག་ཕ་རོལ་ནས་ནང་དུ་འོངས་པ་ལས་མི་དེ་བཙོན་དུ་བཟུང་བ་མཐོང་ནས། (MB H 347, *mdo sde*, sa 237v7)
> "At that time, a minister, upon coming in from outside, saw that man taken prisoner."

If the verb is reduplicated, ལས་ marks a continuing action. The converb can be literally translated as "upon V-ing" (with v2) or "while V-ing" (with v1).

> སྲས་གསུམ་པོ་ཚལ་གྱི་ནང་དུ་ཏོང་ཏོང་བ་ལས། སྟག་མོ་ཞིག་མཐོང་ནས། (MB D 139r4)
> "Three sons, upon going further and further into the forest, saw a tigress."

ཏོང་ཏོང་ is a reduplication that serves the intensification (see Lesson 17). In this clause it literally means "were going and going".

> འདུག་འདུག་པ་ལས། རྒྱང་མ་ནས་དེ་བཞིན་གཤེགས་པ་ཤིང་དྲུང་ན་དབང་པོ་ཀུན་ཞི་ཞིང་བདེ་བར་བཞུགས་པ་མཐོང་ངོ། (MB D 270v5)
> "While [he] was sitting [there], from afar [he] saw Tathāgata sitting under a tree with all [his] senses calm and peaceful."

Locative

When locative ན་ follows a nominalised verb, it serves to form temporal clauses.

> ཉི་མའི་འོད་ཟེར་ཤར་བ་ན།། འབྱུང་པོའི་བྱ་རྣམས་ལོང་བར་འགྱུར།། (SSP 3c–d)
> "When rays of the sun have risen, the birds of demons (i.e. owls and other nocturnal birds) become blind."

> བཅོམ་ལྡན་འདས་ཀྱིས་ལེགས་པར་འོངས་སོ་ཞེས་བཀའ་སྩལ་པ་ན། སྐྲ་དང་ཁ་སྤུ་རང་བྱི་སྟེ། གོས་ཀྱང་ངུར་སྨྲིག་ཏུ་གྱུར་ཏོ། (MB D 138v4–5)
> "When the Victorious One replied: 'Welcome!',[13] [their] head hair and beard fell off by itself [and their] clothes even turned yellowish-red."

Dative

The dative particle attached to a nominalised v1-stem expresses the simultaneity of the action of that verb with the action of the main verb:

> ཟས་དེ་ཡོན་ཏན་ཅན་ཞིག་འདུག་པ་ལ། ངས་ཀྱང་ཟ། (GLR 27r6)
> "As this food is excellent, I will eat [it] too."

If the nominalised verb is a v2-stem or temporal adverbs like "earlier" and "later" are used, ལ་ marks the anteriority of that action:

> སྐྲ་དང་པོ་གསེར་གཡུའི་རལ་པ་ཉིལ་ལེ་བ་ལ། ཕྱིས་སྐྱ་བོ་སེང་སེང་ཤིག་སྲོའི་རལ་པ་ཉིལ་ལེ་བ་བྱུང་བས། (ML D 11r)
> "The hair, once (དང་པོ་) dangling locks [plaited with] (lit. of) gold and turquoise, later (ཕྱིས་) pale and thin, became dangling locks [full] of lice and nits."

> མཆིམས་བཟའ་ཀླུ་རྒྱལ་དེ་དང་པོ་ཤིན་ཏུ་མཛེས་པ་ཞིག་ཡོད་པ་ལ། ཧྲིང་དུ་སྔོ་ལ་རིད་པར་བྱུང་བས། (GLR 27r3–4)
> "After Klu-rgyal, the lady from the Mčhims [family], was at first (དང་པོ་) very beautiful, later (ཧྲིང་དུ་) [she] seemed green and emaciated."

Reading

Beginning with Lesson 12 students will read a story from the canonical collection called མཛངས་བླུན་ཞེས་བྱ་བའི་མདོ། (short: མཛངས་བླུན།; usually translated as the *Sutra of the Wise and the Fool*). The story is titled སེམས་ཅན་ཆེན་པོས་སྟག་མོ་ལ་ལུས་བྱིན་པ། *How Sems-čan-čhen-po offered his body to a tigress*.[14] The collection was originally translated from Chinese into Old Literary Tibetan (OLT).[15] The OLT version was later revised and adapted to Classical Tibetan standards. It was included in the བཀའ་འགྱུར།, i.e. the part of the Tibetan Buddhist collection that contains words presumably spoken by the Buddha.

For the presented text the following editions were consulted: HL (Hahn 1996: 144, 158, 174, 191, 205), D (Sde-dge: D 341 *mdo sde*, a 138r5–140v7), N (Snar-thaṅ: N 326 *mdo sde*, sa 211r4–215r),[16] H (Lha-sa: H 347 *mdo sde*, sa 222v3–227r1), C (Čo-ne: C 980 *mdo maṅ*, a 154v1–157r4), and U (Urga: U 341 mdo sde, a 138r5–140v7). In order to reduce the editorial notes (which are not obligatory in a textbook), only those that could bring considerable changes to the interpretation of the text were included. Variations in punctuation marks were left out as unnoticed; this concerns diverging usage of ཤད་. In general the punctuation of the Sde-dge edition has been retained, with minor corrections from other redactions that should enhance the readability of the text flow for students. The folio numeration corresponds to that of the Sde-dge edition.

The reading exercises are provided with typographical support that should facilitate the analysis of the text. Elements of a clause are separated from each other by means of the degree symbol < ° > according to the following rules: modifiers are treated together with their head words (attributes with the head noun, adverbs with verbs and adjectives, genitive phrases and appositives with their head NP), modal verbs (see Lesson 13) together with their main verbs, postpositional phrases and analytical constructions (see Lesson 16) as one element. In addition, the story is supplied with markers for quotations (" ") that indicate direct speech (see Lesson 13).

From this lesson on, no word lists are provided at the end of the lessons. Instead, students should consult the Glossary at the end of the textbook or Tibetan dictionaries. There are three dictionaries that can be recommended for the reading exercises: Jäschke (J), Das (1902), and WTS. Several reprints of the first two dictionaries are now available, including pocketbook editions. The third dictionary is in progress; until now (December 2021) fifty-one fascicles have been published comprising letters *k–ph*. All three dictionaries have their advantages. Jäschke is the only dictionary which provides very valuable grammatical information that frequently helps to interpret difficult structures. Furthermore, it contains the majority of the vocabulary from three texts, excerpts from which have been chosen as reading exercises in this textbook: མཛངས་བླུན།, རྒྱལ་རབས་གསལ་བའི་མེ་ལོང་།, and མི་ལ་རས་པའི་རྣམ་ཐར།. Currently it is the dictionary that provides the most complete information on a lexeme based on solid methodological foundations. Das' dictionary includes more Buddhist terminology than Jäschke and might be more useful in this respect. WTS is certainly the most comprehensive dictionary in terms of the number of lexical entries and examples it provides.[17]

སེམས་ཅན་ཆེན་པོས་སྟག་མོ་ལ་ལུས་བྱིན་པ།

འདི་སྐད་ ◦ བདག་གིས་ ◦ ཐོས་པ་[18] ◦ དུས་གཅིག་ན། བཅོམ་ལྡན་འདས་ ◦ མཉན་དུ་ཡོད་པ་ན་ ◦ (138r6) རྒྱལ་བུ་རྒྱལ་བྱེད་ཀྱི་ཚལ་མགོན་མེད་ཟས་སྦྱིན་གྱི་ཀུན་དགའ་ར་བ་ན་ ◦ བཞུགས་སོ། །དེའི་ཚེ་ ◦ བཅོམ་ལྡན་འདས་ ◦ བསོད་སྙོམས་ཀྱི་དུས་ལ་ ◦ བབ་ནས། ཤམ་ཐབས་དང་ཆོས་གོས་ ◦ བགོས་ནས་ ◦ ལྷུང་བཟེད་ ◦ བསྣམས་ཏེ། ཀུན་དགའ་བོ་དང་ ◦ བསོད་སྙོམས་ལ་ ◦ གཤེགས་སོ། །དེའི་ཚེ་ན་ ◦ (138r7) གྲོང་ཁྱེར་དེ་ན་ ◦ རྒན་མོ་ཞིག་ལ་ ◦ བུ་རྟག་ཏུ་རྐུ་བ་གཉིས་ཤིག་ ◦ ཡོད་དེ། ནོར་བདག་གིས་ ◦ ཟིན་ནས་ ◦ ཞལ་ཆེ་པའི་མདུན་དུ་ ◦ ཁྲིད་དེ། ཁྲིམས་དང་ ◦ སྦྱར་ནས་ ◦ གསད་པ་ལ་ ◦ ཐུག་ནས། རིགས་ངན་ ◦ བསྐྲི་[19]སྟེ་ ◦ གསོད་པའི་གནས་སུ་ ◦ ཁྲིད་པ་ལས། བཅོམ་ལྡན་འདས་རྒྱང་མ་ནས་གཤེགས་པ་ ◦ རྒན་མོ་མ་ (138v1) སྐད་གསུམ་གྱིས་ ◦ མཐོང་ནས། སངས་རྒྱས་གཤེགས་པའི་ཕྱོགས་སུ་ ◦ ཕྱག་འཚལ་ནས།

Notes

1 Since the quotation comes from a metrical passage, the final particle is omitted after བརྟོན་.

2 Lit. "[He] becomes a one of stronger intellect."

3 དང་ is used in addition to the imperative particle in older texts and texts that were translated from other languages (usually Sanskrit). In later native texts the imperative particle is simply replaced by དང་ (Schneider 2017).

4 For the causative verb ཆུག་ (v1 འཇུག་), see Lesson 13.

5 For the complex verb construction བསྣན་པར་བྱ་, see Lesson 16.

6 Lit. "increase joy in them".

7 Cf. also Schneider (2017: 428–9).

8 Exceptions are encountered in metrical texts.

9 Lit. "so that there was nothing left".

10 ལྷག་ལུས་མེད་པར་, lit. "so that there are no remains".

11 According to Buddhism, an *anāgāmin* (lit. "one who does not come back again") is a person who will not return to this world anymore. She is reborn in a special heavenly plane not accessible to any other beings. From there she will attain *nirvāṇa*.

12 The particle ན་ does not convey any meaning here; for double case particles, see Lesson 15.

13 ལེགས་པར་འོངས་སོ་ཞེས་ is direct speech (see Lesson 13), lit. "[You] have arrived well". This is an official greeting formula used for admissions to the Buddhist order.

14 The story is more popularly known as "The Hungry Tigress", which, however, does not properly convey the message of this Buddhist legend that tells of a *bodhisattva* who sacrifices his life in order to save the life of a tigress and her two cubs.

15 Parts of the Old Tibetan collection were discovered at the beginning of the 20th century in the Mogao caves of Dunhuang. Unfortunately the present story has not been preserved.

16 The Snar-thaṅ edition of མཛངས་བླུན། available via BDRC is poorly preserved and was included only in cases that raised absolutely no doubt as to the reading.

17 There are some other Tibetan-English dictionaries on the market but their usefulness for reading Classical Tibetan texts is usually limited. Most of them do not distinguish between data from the classical language and modern literature or even spoken dialects. The same applies to the majority of Tibetan-Tibetan dictionaries, including the བོད་རྒྱ་ཚིག་མཛོད་ཆེན་མོ། (BTC). These dictionaries can be used by students with already sound experience in reading Classical Tibetan texts, who can recognise and avoid the methodological shortcomings and pitfalls of these works. However, they should not be used by beginners. For the same reasons it is also strongly advised *not* to use online Tibetan-English dictionaries.

18 D/C/U: པའི་. འདི་སྐད་བདག་གིས་ཐོས་པ་ is a phrase distinct from the following one. Otherwise one would have to translate: "At the time when I heard these words [. . .]" The phrase introduces the whole story as known from hearing. Strictly speaking, everything that follows ཐོས་པ་ is a direct quotation that should end with ཞེས་ཐོས་སོ་, that is, however, omitted.

19 D: སྒྲག་; C/U: སྐྲག་; H: བགྲི་; HL: སྒྲོག་.

Lesson 13

- Direct speech
- Indirect speech
- Interjections
- Compounds
- Modal verbs
- Causative verb འཇུག་

Direct speech

Direct speech is a written or spoken text that reports words exactly as they were spoken or thought by the speaker. In European languages direct speech is usually enclosed in quotation marks in texts. Classical Tibetan possesses a special particle, the so-called quotative particle (QUOT), to mark directly quoted words. This particle takes the following forms depending on the final letter of the preceding syllable:

ཅེས་	after	-ག, -ད, -བ, *-ད་དྲག་
ཞེས་	after	-ང, -ན, -མ, -འ, -ར, -ལ, -vowel
ཤེས་	after	-ས

In Classical Tibetan, the passage containing direct speech takes the position of an object of a verb of speaking, hearing, or thinking, like སྨྲ་ "to speak", རྗོད་ "id.", འདྲི་ "to ask", སེམས་ "to think", etc. The prototypical clause that embeds a quotation has the following structure:

Speaker$_{\text{ERG}}$ – Direct speech$_{\text{QUOT}}$ – Verb of speaking

DOI: 10.4324/9781003224198-16

དེས་དབྱིག་པ་ཅན་ལ་གླང་ག་རེ་ཞེས་བྱས་པ་དང་། (MB D 271v1–2)
"He said to Dbyig-pa-čan: 'Where is the ox?'"

ཕུ་བོ་གཉིས་ཀྱིས་ཁྱོད་ཟེར་བ་བདེན་ནོ་ཞེས་ཟེར་རོ། (MB D 139r5)
"The two elder brothers said: 'What you are saying is true.'"

བཅོམ་ལྡན་འདས་ཀྱིས་ལེགས་པར་འོངས་སོ་ཞེས་བཀའ་སྩལ་པ་ན། (MB D 138v4)
"When (པ་ན་) the Victorious One replied: 'Welcome,' [. . .]."[1]

དེ་, ཕུ་བོ་གཉིས་, and བཅོམ་ལྡན་འདས་, marked with ergative, are the subjects of the verbs བྱས་, ཟེར་, and བཀའ་སྩལ་, whereas གླང་ག་རེ་, ཁྱོད་ཟེར་བ་བདེན་ནོ་, and ལེགས་པར་འོངས་སོ་ (direct speech ending with the quotative ཞེས་) fill in the object slots of the verbs.

Direct speech is formulated as a complete clause. That is, it takes a clause-ending particle: either the final particle འོ་ (བདེན་ནོ་ and འོངས་སོ་ in the above clauses), the imperative particle /ཅིག་/, or the interrogative particle འམ་. If the quotation is a question with an interrogative word, then the interrogative particle is omitted (see the first example and Lesson 11).

These examples also demonstrate that although the end of a direct speech is usually marked with the quotative particle, its beginning may remain unmarked. In such cases only the proper analysis of the clause can give us clues as to where the quotation begins. Still, Classical Tibetan does possess means to mark the beginning of a quotation:

དེ་ནས་བྲག་སྲིན་མོ་ལངས་ཏེ། སྤྲེའུ་ལ་འདི་སྐད་ཅེས་ཟེར་རོ།། (GLR 22r6)
"Thereafter, having risen, the rock-ogress said the following words to the monkey."

The idiomatic phrase འདི་སྐད་ཅེས་ announces a direct speech that follows immediately after the respective clause. In the last example, the words that the rock-ogress spoke begin right in the next clause. དེ་སྐད་, the counterpart of འདི་སྐད་, refers back to words that have just been quoted:

སྟག་གིས་ཟོས་སོ་ཞེས་སྨྲས་སོ། །ལྷ་མོ་དེས་དེ་སྐད་སྨྲས་པ་ཐོས་ནས། (MB D 139v7–140r1)
"[The brothers] said: 'A tiger ate [him].' When (ནས་) the queen had heard these words uttered, [. . .]."

དེ་སྐད་ in the second clause refers to the direct speech སྟག་གིས་ཟོས་སོ་ of the preceding clause. We know that the direct speech ends with ཟོས་སོ་ because it is immediately followed by the quotative particle ཞེས་. However, the quotative particle can be left out if the context makes it clear that a quotation is embedded in the clause. This usually happens when a dialogue between two or more speakers continues:

> བྲག་སྲིན་མོ་ན་རེ། ཁྱེད་ངའི་ཁྱོ་མི་བྱེད་ན་ང་ཆེའི་དུས་བྱེད་དོ་ཟེར་ནས། (GLR 22r6)
> "The rock-ogress replied, 'If you don't become my husband, I will die.'"

ན་རེ་ (HON ཞལ་ན་རེ་) is another speech marker used to indicate that a conversation continues and the words that follow ན་རེ་ tie in with the preceding communication. In this particular example the quotative particle has been omitted after the quotation, but in general a quotation can be introduced by ན་རེ་ and end with a quotative particle. ན་རེ་ always stands after a subject in absolutive.[2]

ཅེས་བྱ་བ་ – *the "so-called"*

Another related function of the quotative particle is to introduce proper names or terms that are explained immediately after. In this function /ཅེས་/ occurs in idiomatic phrases like ཅེས་བྱ་བ་, ཅེས་ཟེར་བ་, or ཅེས་བགྱི་བ་:

> འཛམ་བུ་གླིང་འདི་ན་རྒྱལ་པོ་ཤིང་རྟ་ཆེན་པོ་ཞེས་བྱ་བ་ཞིག་ཡོད་དེ། (MB D 139r2)
> "In this continent, there was a king called Śiṅ-rta-čhen-po."

ཅེས་བྱ་བ་, etc., can usually be rendered as "the so-called" or "called". Nominalised verbs that follow the quotative particle in this construction are always derived from a v3-stem (cf. བྱ་ and བགྱི་ earlier). ཅེས་བྱ་བ་ can sometimes be reduced to the sole quotative particle:

> དེའི་མིང་ཡང་འཇང་གི་བུ་རུ་ལ་སྐྱེས་ཞེས་གྲགས་སོ།། (GLR 25v1)
> "As for his name, [he] was called Ru-la-skyes, the son of Ɣǰaṅ."

or to the nominalised verb:

> ནགས་མ་བྱ་ཚོགས་བྱ་བ། (GLR 23r4) "the forest called Bya-chogs (lit. Flock of birds)"
> ཞིང་སྐལ་བྲེ་པེ་སྟན་ཆུང་བྱ་བ་ (ML D 11v) "a field share called Pre-pe-stan-čhuṅ"

ཞལ་ནས་

ཞལ་ནས་, lit. "from the mouth", belongs to the honorific register (see Lesson 8). Strictly speaking, it is a postposition and replaces the ergative particle of an agent if the person speaking is of higher social standing. It is attached via a genitive particle to the person who speaks and is followed by a quotation:

> འཕགས་པའི་ཞལ་ནས། བྲག་སྲིན་མོའི་ཁྱོ་གྱིས་ཤིག་གསུངས། (GLR 22v5)
> "The Noble One ordained (གསུངས་): 'Become the husband of the rock-ogress!'"

Here the quoted words are presented as direct speech ending with the imperative particle ཤིག་.

Indirect speech

Classical Tibetan differentiates between direct and indirect speech, although the latter construction is far less common. Indirect speech reproduces the content of utterances without quoting them verbatim. There are no special markers for indirect speech similar to the quotative particle /ཅེས་/ of direct speech. Instead, the sentences that should be reproduced are nominalised by means of the པ་/བ་ particle, added the terminative -ར, and made a complement of a verb of speaking/hearing/thinking, etc.

> ཆོས་ཀྱི་འཁོར་ལོ་བསྐོར་བར་གསོལ་བ་དང་། (BS; *apud* Schwieger 2006: 200)
> "[They] asked that the wheel of Dharma is set in motion."

The clause ཆོས་ཀྱི་འཁོར་ལོ་བསྐོར་ is the content of indirect speech. It is nominalised (བ་) and the terminative -ར is added to it so that it can be made a complement of the verb གསོལ་.[3] In the following example, indirect speech is embedded between the reference to the source from which the quotation comes (བུ་སྟོན་རིན་པོ་ཆེའི་ཆོས་འབྱུང་ན།) and a verb of saying (གསུངས་):

> བུ་སྟོན་རིན་པོ་ཆེའི་ཆོས་འབྱུང་ན། ཀོ་ས་ལའི་རྒྱལ་པོ་གསལ་རྒྱལ་གྱི་བརྒྱུད་ལྔ་ཚིགས་སམ། རྒྱལ་པོ་གཟུགས་ཅན་སྙིང་པོའི་བརྒྱུད་ལྔ་ཚིགས་སམ། ཡང་ན་བད་ས་ལའི་རྒྱལ་པོ་འཆར་བྱེད་ཀྱི་བུ། སྐྱེས་བུ་ཆེན་པོའི་མཚན་དང་ལྡན་པ་ཞིག་ཡིན་པར་གསུངས་ལ། (GLR 24r6–v1)
> "In Bu-ston Rin-po-čhe's *Čhos ɣbyuṅ* it is said that (པར་)[4] [the first king of Tibet] was either the third out of five[5] [sons in] the lineage of Gsal-rgyal (Skt. Prasenajit), the king of Ko-sa-la (Skt. Kośala); or the third out of five [sons in] the lineage of king Gzugs-čan-sñiṅ-po (Skt. Bimbisāra); or again, the son of Ɣčhar-byed (Skt. Udayana), the king of Bad-sa-la (Skt. Vatsa), [the son who] was endowed with characteristic marks of a great person."

Interjections

Interjections (Intrj) stand at the beginning of a quotation and express a spontaneous thought or emotion. ཀྱེ་[6] serves to catch attention and may be followed by a form of address in absolutive, in which case the interjection emphasises the vocative function of the address (see Lesson 2: Absolutive). In the story *The descent of Tibetan people from a monkey and a rock-ogress* (see Reading II), the variant ཀྱེ་མ་ is also used:

ཀྱེ་མ་སྤྲེའུའི་རྒྱལ་པོ་ཆེན་པོ་ཁྱེད།། (GLR 22r6)

"Alas, you, the great king of monkeys!"

The interjection འོ་ན་ is used to express a new thought or idea:

འོ་ན་ཁོ་བོའི་ཕྲིན་ཞིག་ཀྱང་རྒྱལ་པོ་ལ་སྤྲོས་ཤིག (MB D 272r3)

"Well then (འོ་ན་), also deliver my message to the king!"

Compounds[7]

Compounds are complex lexical units that express one coherent concept, and their constituents represent at least two distinct lexemes. In Classical Tibetan compounding is a very popular and productive means of forming new lexical words from existing ones. Many compounds can be found explained in dictionaries. However, in order to be able to analyse and understand those compounds that have not been glossed anywhere, it is advisable to learn a few basic rules governing compounding.[8]

Rules of compounding

In Classical Tibetan compounds are formed according to the following rules:

1 If two lexemes, consisting of one syllable each, are combined into one compound, both syllables are retained:

མ་ "mother" + སྨད་ "children" > མ་སྨད་ "mother and her children"

ལུས་ "body" + སྲོག་ "life" > ལུས་སྲོག་ "body and life"

2 If the underlying lexemes have a second syllable that is a nominal particle, this syllable is deleted from the compound:

ནོར་ "wealth" + བདག་པོ་ "owner" > ནོར་བདག་ "wealthy man", lit. "owner of wealth"

བྱམས་པ་ "benevolence" + མགོན་པོ་ "protector" > བྱམས་མགོན་ "protector of benevolence"

3 If one of the lexemes consists of two syllables, neither of which is a nominal particle, the first syllable of the lexeme is usually retained in the compound:

དགའ་བ་ "(to be) happy" + བཤེས་གཉེན་ "spiritual advisor" > དགའ་བཤེས་ "spiritual friend"

ཉི་མ་ "the sun" + དཀྱིལ་འཁོར་ "disc" > ཉི་དཀྱིལ་ "solar disc"

Classification of compounds

The vast majority of Classical Tibetan compounds belong to one of the following classes:

Determinative compounds

In determinative compounds the second constituent is modified by the first one and the underlying structure can be reconstructed as a genitive (i.e. determinative) phrase. Usually both constituents of the compound are nouns.

ཁ་སྤུ་ "beard hair" < *ཁའི་སྤུ་, lit. "hair of the face"

བྱམས་མགོན་ "protector of benevolence" < *བྱམས་པའི་མགོན་པོ་ "id."

རྟ་རྫི་ "horse-keeper" < *རྟའི་རྫི་བོ་ "id."

Attributive compounds

In attributive compounds the second constituent, an adjective, modifies the first one, a noun:

ཁྱོ་བཟང་ "good husband" < *ཁྱོ་བཟང་པོ་ "id."

མི་ངན་ "bad man" < *མི་ངན་པ་ "id."

Coordinate compounds

Coordinate compounds coordinate two or more lexemes by means of the underlying conjunction དང་ "and" if the constituents are nouns, or ལ་ "and" if they are adjectives:

མ་སྨད་ "mother and her children" < *མ་དང་སྨད་ "id."

ཕ་མ་ "parents" < *ཕ་དང་མ་ "father and mother"

རྒྱལ་བློན་ "king and minister" < རྒྱལ་པོ་དང་བློན་པོ་ "id."

The lexemes that form a coordinate compound are co-hyponyms, i.e. their meanings are included in the meaning of another word, a hypernym. For instance, "father" and "mother" belong to a more general group of "parents".

Synonymic compounds

Synonymic compounds are a subclass of coordinate compounds. They are peculiar because the constituents of such a compound are synonyms or near-synonyms.

མང་དུ་ "many" < *མང་ལ་དུ་མ་, lit. "many and many"
ཚེ་སྲོག་ "life" < *ཚེ་དང་སྲོག་, lit. "lifetime and life"
བདེ་སྐྱིད་ "to be happy" < *བདེ་ལ་སྐྱིད་, lit. "to be cheerful and happy"

Modal verbs

Classical Tibetan possesses a small group of verbs that are used to indicate various modalities: necessity, obligation, ability, capacity, etc. This group of verbs is distinguished from action verbs by the lack of inflected forms: modal verbs have only one stem. Another peculiarity is that modal verbs are usually attached directly to the verb, of which the particular modality they should express. Alternatively, the main verb might acquire either པར་/བར་ (nominal particle /པ་/ + terminative -ར་) or directly acquire a terminative particle. Modal verbs always follow the main verb and function as its auxiliary:

བྱེད་ "to do" བྱེད་དགོས་ "should do"
ཟ་ "to eat" ཟ་རུ་འདོད་ "want to eat"

These constructions are negated with མ་ (in past contexts) or མི་ (in non-past contexts) inserted directly before the modal verb:

ཟ་མ་ནུས་ "not able to eat" (MB D 139v3)
སྨོན་མི་དགོས་ "do not need to desire" (ML D 10v)

Modal verbs cannot be modified by adverbs. However, they can be nominalised:

མི་ཉམས་པར་བྱེད་ནུས་པ་ཡོད་དམ། (MB D 139r7)
"Is there anybody able to do [this] without getting hurt [himself]?"

Here, the clause མི་ཉམས་པར་བྱེད་ནུས་ with the modal verb ནུས་ "to be able" is nominalised by means of the particle པ་ and subsequently used as the subject of the verb ཡོད་.

In the following the most frequently used modal verbs of Classical Tibetan are discussed.

དགོས་

དགོས་ expresses necessity and can be translated as "to be necessary, have to, need". It is attached directly to the stem of the main verb:

> ཁྱོད་ཀྱིས་ངའི་འཐབ་ཡ་བྱེད་དགོས་ཟེར་ནས། (GLR 24v6)
> "[The king] said: 'You have to act as my adversary.'"

> ཟས་དེ་ཡོན་ཏན་ཅན་ཞིག་འདུག་པ་ལ། ངས་ཀྱང་ཟ་དགོས་བསམས་ཏེ། (GLR 27r6)
> "[The king] thought: 'As this food is excellent, I too must eat [it].'"

ནུས་

ནུས་ is a modal verb of ability. It can be translated with "to be able, capable; can". Most commonly ནུས་ is attached directly to the verb, but it can also follow a nominalised verb in terminative.

> སྟག་མོ་ཁ་ཐམས་པས་ཟ་མ་ནུས་སོ། (MB D 139v2–3)
> "The tigress was not able to eat with a closed mouth."

> ཨ་ཞང་གིས་ནི་ཨ་ཁུ་ལ་བུ་མང་པོ་ཡོད་པས་རྒོལ་མ་ནུས། (ML D 12v)
> "Because the paternal uncle had many sons, the maternal uncle was not able to fight [against them]."

འདོད་

འདོད་ is a modal verb of wish, desire, and can be translated as "to wish, want". It follows either a plain verb stem, a verb stem in terminative, or a nominalised verb in terminative.

> སྟག་མོ་འདི་ནི་ [. . .] ཕྲུ་གུ་བྱུང་མ་ཐག་པ་ཡང་ཟ་རུ་འདོད་དོ། (MB D 139r5)
> "The Tigress wants to eat [her] newborn (lit. occurred) cubs."

ཆོག་

As a modal verb ཆོག་ has the meaning "to be allowed, permitted; may" and is usually attached directly to the verb.

> ཐར་ལམ་དུ་འགྲོ་ཆོག (KR 74; *apud* Schwieger 2006: 88)
> "[You] are allowed to tread the path of release."

ཐུབ་

ཐུབ་ is another verb of ability and can be translated as “to be able, capable; can”. ཐུབ་ is usually attached to a nominalised verb in terminative although it can also directly follow the main verb.

> ནང་པ་འདེད་ཐུབ་ནའང་། (TS 145; *apud* Schwieger 2006: 85)
> “Even if (ནའང་) [one] is able to drive away the Naṅ-pa [. . .].”

ཤེས་

ཤེས་ is yet another verb of ability and can be translated as “to be able, capable; can”. It is usually attached directly to the main verb although it can also follow a nominalised verb in terminative.

> སྨྲ་ཤེས་ནས་མིར་གྱུར་ཏོ། (GLR 23v4–5)
> “After [they] were able to speak, [they] became humans.”

> རྡུལ་དང་འདྲེས་པའི་ལྕགས་ཕྱེ་རྣམས།། ཁབ་ལེན་རྡོ་ཡིས་ལེན་པར་ཤེས།། (SSP 2c–d)
> “A lodestone is able to attract iron filings that are mixed with dust.”

Modal verbs as event verbs

In Classical Tibetan some of the modal verbs can be likewise used as normal event verbs. Compare hereto Eng. *I want to go home* (*want* = modal verb) and *I want a cookie* (*want* = event verb). The following examples illustrate the case in Classical Tibetan:

> ངེད་ལ་ནོར་དགོས་ཟེར། (ML D 12v)
> “[You] say ‘We need [our] possessions.’”

> གྱོས་པོའི་ཁྱིམ་འདོད། (MB D 272r6)
> Lit. “[I] wish the house of [my] father-in-law.”

> ངེད་རང་གིས་མི་ཐུབ་ཅེས་སྨྲས་སོ། (GLR 25r2–3)
> “‘I can’t match [him].’ Thus [he] said.”

> སྲས་རྣམས་ཀྱིས་རིམ་པ་བཞིན་ཆིབས་ཁ་ཐུབ་ཙ་ན། (GLR 24v4)
> “As soon as (ཙ་ན་) the sons, one after the other, had the command of bridle [. . .].”[9]

Causative verb འཇུག་

The causative verb འཇུག་ is attached to another verb to indicate that the subject causes someone or something to act or behave in a desired way. The causative verb follows the main verb in terminative.[10] The main verb has to be controllable because otherwise the subject could not cause the action to be carried out. In this function འཇུག་ may be translated as "to cause; to let". The causative འཇུག་ is derived from the action verb འཇུག་ "to put into" and retains its forms: v1 འཇུག་, v2 བཅུག་, v3 གཞུག་, v4 ཆུག་.

རྒྱལ་བུས་ཤིང་གི་ཚལ་བ་རྣོན་པོས་ལུས་ལ་ཁྲག་ཕྱུང་ནས། སྟག་མོ་ལ་བལྡག་ཏུ་བཅུག་པ་དང་། (MB D 139v3)
"The prince with a sharp wooden splinter made blood come out of (lit. on) [his] body. Then (ནས་) [he] let (བཅུག་) the tigress lick [the blood]."

རྒྱལ་བུས་ཀྱང་ངང་པའི་སྐད་ཤེས་པས། མགུལ་ནས་ཡི་གེ་བཀྲོལ་ཏེ་ཀློག་ཏུ་བཅུག་གོ། (MB H 347, *mdo sde*, sa 391v7–392r1; *apud* BCRD)
"Because the prince recognised the voice of the goose, having untied the letter from [its] neck, [he] let (བཅུག་) read [the letter]."

དེ་ལྟག་གི་ནོར་རྣམས་ཀུན་ཁ་འཆམ་པར་མྱང་ཚ་དཀར་རྒྱན་རང་ཚགས་བྱེད་དུ་ཆུག (ML D 11r)
"As agreed, let (ཆུག་) Myaṅ-cha Dkar-rgyan herself (རང་) save all the remaining wealth!"

Reading

"ལྷའི་ནང་ན་གཙོ་བོ་ ◦ ཐུགས་བརྩེ་བར་ ◦ དགོངས་ཏེ། བདག་གི་བུ་དགུམ་པ་ལ་ཐུག་པ་འདིའི་སྐབས་ ◦ མཛད་དུ་ ◦ གསོལ་ཞེས་" སྨྲས་པ། བཅོམ་ལྡན་འདས་ཀྱིས་ ◦ གསན་ནས། དེ་བཞིན་གཤེགས་པའི་[11] (138v2) ཐུགས་རྗེ་ཆེན་པོས་ ◦ དེ་དག་ལ་ ◦ ཐུགས་བརྩེ་བར་ ◦ དགོངས་ཏེ། དེ་དག་གི་སྡིག་བསྐྱབ་པའི་སླད་དུ་ ◦ བཅོམ་ལྡན་འདས་ཀྱིས་ ◦ ཀུན་དགའ་བོ་ལ་ ◦ བཀའ་ ◦ སྩལ་ཏེ། རྒྱལ་པོ་ལ་ ◦ གསོལ་བ་ ◦ འདེབས་སུ་ ◦ བཏང་བ་དང་། རྒྱལ་པོས་ཀྱང་ ◦ བཅོམ་ལྡན་འདས་ཀྱི་བཀའ་བཞིན་དུ་ ◦ དེ་དག་ ◦ བཏང་ངོ་། དེ་ (138v3) དག་ ◦ བཅོམ་ལྡན་འདས་ཀྱི་བཀའ་དྲིན་ ◦ དྲན་ཞིང་ ◦ རབ་ཏུ་དགའ་བ་ ◦ སྐྱེས་ནས། བཅོམ་ལྡན་འདས་གང་ན་བ་དེར་ ◦ སོང་སྟེ་ ◦ ཕྱིན་པ་དང་། ཞབས་ལ་ ◦ སྤྱི་བོས་ ◦ ཕྱག་འཚལ་ནས་ ◦ ཐལ་མོ་ ◦ སྦྱར་ཏེ་ ◦ བཅོམ་ལྡན་འདས་ལ་ ◦ འདི་སྐད་ཅེས་ ◦ གསོལ་ཏོ།།

Notes

1 The converbal particles པ་ན་ that follow the verb བཀའ་སྩལ་ inform us that the clause is not finished and the main clause will follow.

2 As against previous interpretations of ན་རེ་ (cf. Simon 1968: 555ff.), the phrase should be analysed as a complex particle that developed from the grammaticalised emphatic *ནར་རེ་; cf. ནར་མ་ "continuous, without interruption" (J: 304a) and the modern dialectal

NCA verb ནར་ "to become long, to lengthen; to get stretched" (CDTD.V: 709). ན་རེ་ always follows the speaker-subject in absolutive because the verb from which it derives, ནར་, is non-controllable.

3 For terminative as a converbal particle forming complement clauses, see Lesson 12.

4 པར་ after ཡིན་ marks indirect speech.

5 The construction 'uneven numeral + ཚོགས་' denotes the median of the group; e.g. ལྔ་ཚོགས་ means "the third out of five", because three is the median in a group of five elements.

6 ཀྱེ་ is a clipped form of the original ཀུ་ཡེ་. Both forms are attested in texts.

7 A detailed discussion and classification of Tibetan compounds can be found in Bialek (2018a). Although the latter work concentrates on Old Tibetan compounds, the rules of compounding and the classification of compounds likewise apply to Classical Tibetan.

8 In the following, only compounds consisting of two syllables will be discussed. Nevertheless, the reader should be aware of the existence of compounds of three or four syllables alike.

9 For ཙ་ན་, see Lesson 15: Other Converbal Particles.

10 In older literature the main verb may be represented by its v3-stem (see the first example), whereas in later texts v1-stems prevail.

11 D/N/H/U: པ་. དེ་བཞིན་གཤེགས་པ་ in absolutive would have to be interpreted as either the subject or the object of the verb དགོངས་. As it cannot be the object in the given context, only the subject role remains. However, the verb དགོངས་, meaning "to think", needs the subject in ergative. This analysis supports the reading དེ་བཞིན་གཤེགས་པའི་.

Lesson 14

- Passive
- Possessive attributes
- Complex attributes
- Ellipsis
- Omission of coreferential arguments
- Impersonal clause
- Other pronouns

Passive

When discussing the meanings of single verb stems in Lesson 4 it was stated that v3-stems, characteristic of transitive and controllable verbs (class I), have passive meaning. Passive verbs are used in constructions in which the action is reported from the perspective of the patient as affected by the action – compare the two English clauses:

active The king killed the treacherous servant.
passive The treacherous servant was killed (by the king).

Passive verbs by definition have only one argument which is their subject (*the treacherous servant* in the last example). Passive in Classical Tibetan does not require any special clause construction apart from a v3-stem. The subject of a passive verb stands in absolutive. A passive clause can also have other elements; for instance, one expressing an agent. In the aforementioned English example it is the bracketed phrase, *by the king*, which is optional.

མཁས་པ་ཤེས་རབ་ཀྱིས་བསྲུང་ན།། དགྲ་བོ་མང་ཡང་ག་ལ་ཚུགས།། (SSP 11a–b)
"If a wise one is guarded (v3 བསྲུང་) by [his] wisdom, enemies, even though plenty, to whom [can they] cause harm?"

DOI: 10.4324/9781003224198-17

ཁྱོད་ཀྱི་རིགས་རྒྱུད་རྣམས་ངས་བསྲུང་ངོ། (GLR 23v3)
"Your race will be guarded (v3 བསྲུང་) by me."

སྤྲེའུ་ལ་ཁྱོད་དང་ང་གཉིས་བཟའ་མི་བྱའོ་ཟེར་བས། (GLR 22r5)
"[The rock-ogress] said to the monkey: 'You and me, both, will be made (v3 བྱ་) husband and wife.'"

In later works passive is more commonly expressed with the analytical construction 'v3 + པར་/བར་ + བྱ་/བགྱི་/མཛད་' (see Lesson 16):

དེ་ནས་བོད་རྒྱལ་པོའི་གདུང་རབས་རིམ་པར་བྱོན་པ་རྣམས་བཤད་པར་བྱ་སྟེ། (GLR 24r3)
"Thereafter, generations of kings [of] Tibet, who appeared in succession, are explained (བཤད་པར་བྱ་)."

In addition, some verbs require a v3-stem as their complement:

དེའི་ཚེ་ཞིང་དག་ཀྱང་བརྔ་རན་ནས། (MB D 270v3)
"At that time, it was the season for fields to be reaped (བརྔ་)."

Possessive attributes

Possessive attribute is an attribute that expresses a certain feature as possessed by the referent of the noun phrase to which the attribute is applied. Possessive attribute, like any other attribute, always follows the noun phrase (HEAD) which it modifies. For instance, གཏིང་ཟབ་པོ་, lit. "a deep bottom", in itself is a noun phrase formed from the noun གཏིང་ "bottom" and the adjective ཟབ་པོ་ "deep". When used as a possessive attribute, it is attached to another noun, e.g. ཆུ་བོ་ "river", which constitutes the HEAD of the whole phrase:

ཆུ་བོ་གཏིང་ཟབ་པོ་ (MB D 271v6) "a deep river", lit. "a river with a deep bottom"

གཏིང་ཟབ་པོ་ is here a possessive attribute because the phrase ཆུ་བོ་གཏིང་ཟབ་པོ་ can be reworded as "a river that has a deep bottom".

The general structure of a simple noun phrase with a possessive attribute can be sketched as:

HEAD + [N+A]$_{\text{POSS.ATTR}}$

དངོས་པོ་ངོ་མཚར་ཆེ་བ་ (MB D 138v6) "wonderful things", lit. "things of great miracles"

སྤྲེའུ་ཕྲུག་རྣམས་སྤྱོད་ལམ་མི་འདྲ་བ་དྲུག་ (GLR 23r1–2) "monkey-children of six different modes of life"

A possessive attribute is in fact a noun phrase that can be used attributively. The following example contains a possessive attribute embedded in another possessive attribute:

ཁྲོན་པ་གཏིང་རྒྱ་ཤིན་ཏུ་ཆེ་བ་ (BGGB 544f; *apud* Schwieger 2006: 175) "a very broad well", lit. "a well with a bottom, the size of which is very great"

ཁྲོན་པ་ "well" is the main noun which is modified by གཏིང་རྒྱ་ཤིན་ཏུ་ཆེ་བ་. གཏིང་ "bottom" is likewise a noun modified by རྒྱ་ཤིན་ཏུ་ཆེ་བ་. The latter phrase again consists of a noun, རྒྱ་ "size", which is modified by ཤིན་ཏུ་ཆེ་བ་ "very big":

ཤིན་ཏུ་ཆེ་བ་ "very big"
རྒྱ་ཤིན་ཏུ་ཆེ་བ་ "very big size"
གཏིང་རྒྱ་ཤིན་ཏུ་ཆེ་བ་ "a bottom that has a very big size"
ཁྲོན་པ་གཏིང་རྒྱ་ཤིན་ཏུ་ཆེ་བ་ "a well with a bottom of very big size"

This example is taken from a story about an elephant that fell into a "very broad well". The attribute རྒྱ་ཤིན་ཏུ་ཆེ་བ་ describes the well as broad enough for an elephant to fall into.

Complex attributes

Since in Classical Tibetan a noun phrase can be modified in two ways, by genitive and attributive modifiers, very complex phrases can emerge. In literature translated from Sanskrit these can acquire immense length (see the example in Hahn 1996: 142f.), but indigenous Tibetan literature also abounds in such constructions. The following examples serve as an illustration.

བདག་གི་བུ་དགུམ་པ་ལ་ཐུག་པ་འདི་ (MB D 138v1) "these sons of mine who are about to be executed."

The head of this phrase is བུ་ "sons" which acquires the modifier བདག་གི་ "my" and the complex attribute དགུམ་པ་ལ་ཐུག་པ་, lit. "nearly killed ones". The latter is a nominalised clause དགུམ་པ་ལ་ཐུག "to come close to be killed". As an additional element the demonstrative pronoun འདི་ "this; these" ends the whole phrase.

> སྟག་མོ་བུ་བྱུང་ནས་ཞག་དུ་མ་ལོན་པ་བཀྲེས་ཤིང་སྐོམ་པས་ཉེན་ཏེ། ཕྱིར་ཡང་བུ་ཟ་ལ་ཐུག་པ་ཞིག (MB D 139r4)
> "a tigress, that, many days after getting cubs, being pained due to hunger and thirst, was also about to eat the cubs."

Everything that follows the first word, སྟག་མོ་, is its attribute. This complex attribute consists of two nominalised sentences: བུ་བྱུང་ནས་ཞག་དུ་མ་ལོན། "Many days passed after cubs had occurred," and བཀྲེས་ཤིང་སྐོམ་པས་ཉེན་ཏེ། ཕྱིར་ཡང་བུ་ཟ་ལ་ཐུག "Being pained due to hunger and thirst, [the tigress] was also about to eat the cubs." Lit. "Being pained, because [she] was hungry and thirsty, [she] was also about to eat [her] cubs."

> ཨ་མ་ལ་ཕ་མས་བྱིན་པའི་ཞིང་སྐལ་ཕྲེ་པེ་སྟན་ཆུང་བྱ་བ་མིང་མི་སྙན་རུང་སྟོན་ཐོག་གཞུན་པོ་ཡོང་བ་ཞིག་ཡོད་པ་དེ་ (ML D 11v)
> "the (དེ་) field share that was there (ཡོད་པ་) [and] that parents gave to [my] mother, though of unpleasant name, called Pre-pe-stan-čhuṅ, was yielding excellent harvest"

The head of the phrase is ཞིང་སྐལ་. It is modified by the relative clause ཨ་མ་ལ་ཕ་མས་བྱིན་པའི་ "that parents gave to [my] mother" and by the postposed attribute ཕྲེ་པེ་སྟན་ཆུང་བྱ་བ་མིང་མི་སྙན་རུང་སྟོན་ཐོག་གཞུན་པོ་ཡོང་བ་ཞིག. The latter consists of a nominalised sentence derived from the clause ཕྲེ་པེ་སྟན་ཆུང་བྱ་བ་མིང་མི་སྙན་རུང་སྟོན་ཐོག་གཞུན་པོ་ཡོང་། "A one called Pre-pe-stan-čhuṅ, although of unpleasant name, was a one yielding excellent harvest."

Ellipsis

Ellipsis is a construction in which certain words are omitted from a clause but are nevertheless understood from the context. In Classical Tibetan ellipsis is readily applied in dialogues or more generally within direct speech. All the examples quoted next stem from such contexts (the bracketed elements have been added in the translations):

> ང་ནི་མི་འགྲོན། འདི་དག་གིས་ང་ཁྲིད་དོ།། གང་དུ་ཁྲིད། རྒྱལ་པོའི་དྲུང་དུའོ།། (MB D 272r3)

– "For myself, [I] am not going [voluntarily]; they are leading me."
– "Whither are [they] leading [you]?"
– "[They are leading me] to the king."

The last clause of this dialogue does not even contain a verb, but it is understood as being the same as in the preceding clause, i.e. ཁྲིད་.

> ཁྱོད་ཀྱིས་གླང་བརྟས་སམ། བརྟས་སོ། (MB D 272r7)

– "Did you borrow the ox?"
– "[I] did borrow [the ox]."

Here the person answering the question only confirms the action of borrowing without stating the object that was borrowed or the person who borrowed it. This information is understood from the context.

> འདིའི་ཁྱོ་བྱས་ན་ནི་སྡོམ་པ་འཆོར་ལ། མ་བྱས་ན་ནི་སྡིག་ཚབས་ཆེ་བར་འདུག་སྙམ་ནས། (GLR 22v3)
> "[The *bodhisattva*-monkey] thought: 'If [I] become her husband, [my] vow will perish. If I do not [become her husband], the sin will be very great.'"

In the first clause of the second part འདིའི་ཁྱོ་ has been omitted so that only the negated verb མ་བྱས་ན་ is left.

> ཁྱོད་ཀྱིས་ངའི་གླང་བོར་གྱིས། གླང་སླར་བྱིན་ཅིག་ཅེས་སྨྲས་པ་དང་། དེས་སྨྲས་པ། ངས་མ་བོར་རོ།། (MB D 271v2)
> "'Because you lost my ox, give [me another] ox back!' Thus [he] replied. [Dbyig-pa-čan] answered: 'I did not lose [it].'"

In the last sentence the object (གླང་) of the verb བོར་ is omitted because its identity is obvious from the context.

Ellipsis is a process distinct from argument omission (see next section). Its only motivation is the fact that the omitted information has already been mentioned and can be easily retrieved from the context.

Omission of coreferential arguments

One of the major difficulties in understanding and translating Classical Tibetan texts is the correct identification of the main participants (i.e. subject and object) of an action. Namely, the information concerning the participants might be omitted from the text in linked clauses that share the elements which might then be left out. Contrary to ellipsis, omission of coreferential arguments is omnipresent and not restricted to dialogues or direct speech situations. Consider the following example:

> རྒྱལ་བུ་སེམས་ཅན་ཆེན་པོ་དེ་དེར་ཚེ་འཕོས་ནས། དགའ་ལྡན་ལྷའི་གནས་སུ་སྐྱེས་སོ།། (MB D 140r2–3)
> "After the prince Sems-čan-čhen-po had passed away there, [he] was reborn in Dgaɣ-ldan, a deities' place."

The sentence consists of two clauses, each ending with an intransitive verb: ཚེ་འཕོས་ and སྐྱེས་. The clauses are connected through the converbal particle ནས་. As the verbs are intransitive, they only require a subject. Whereas the subject of ཚེ་འཕོས་ is explicitly stated in the clause as རྒྱལ་བུ་སེམས་ཅན་ཆེན་པོ་དེ་, སྐྱེས་ lacks an overt subject. This happens because the subject of སྐྱེས་ is identical (i.e. coreferential) with the subject of the preceding clause and therefore could be omitted. We can sketch this process as S → $S_{\emptyset}$, meaning that the subject of the first clause is also the subject of the second clause but is represented by zero ($_{\emptyset}$) in the latter. An analogous situation occurs in the following sentence:

> བདག་གིས་ལུས་ཀྱིས་སྟག་མོ་ལྟོགས་པ་བསྐོད་པས་དགའ་ལྡན་ལྷའི་གནས་སུ་སྐྱེས་སོ།། (MB D 140r6)
> "Because I fed a hungry tigress with my body, [I] was born in Dgaɣ-ldan, a deities' place."

This sentence differs from the preceding one only in the fact that the first verb (བསྐོད་) is transitive and requires a subject (བདག་གིས་) and an object (སྟག་མོ་ལྟོགས་པ་). It is the subject of the first verb that is taken over by the second verb (སྐྱེས་) as its subject. Thus, we have again S → $S_{\emptyset}$. A reversed situation occurs in:

> བདག་ཡུན་རིང་པོ་ནས་འཁོར་བ་ན་འཁོར་ཞིང་། ལུས་སྲོག་གྲངས་མེད་པ་ཞིག་ཆུད་གསན་ཏེ། (MB D 139r7)
> "For a long time I've been roaming in the cycle of existence, having wasted innumerable bodies and lives."

The first verb (འཁོར་) is intransitive and the second one transitive (ཆུད་གསན་) but the subject remains the same: S → $S_{\emptyset}$.

The subject may remain unexpressed in more clauses that follow each other:

> བྲག་སྲིན་མོ་ཞིག་དེར་འོངས་ནས། ཆགས་པ་འདོད་པའི་བརྡ་མང་དུ་བསྟན་ནས་སོང་ངོ་། (GLR 22r5)
> "A rock-ogress made her way there. Having shown many signs of [her] desire for love [towards the monkey], [she] went back."

This sentence consists of three clauses with the following verbs: intransitive འོངས་, transitive བསྟན་, and intransitive སོང་. Only the first clause contains an overt subject: བྲག་སྲིན་མོ་ཞིག་. We may sketch the situation in the sentence as S → $S_{\emptyset}$ → $S_{\emptyset}$.

The situation can become even more complicated because sometimes other arguments of a clause, like the object, may be omitted as well. This happens again when these are coreferential with a subject of a linked clause.

> རྒྱལ་བུས་ཤིང་གི་ཚལ་བ་རྣོན་པོས་ལུས་ལ་ཁྲག་ཕྱུང་ནས། སྟག་མོ་ལ་བལྡག་ཏུ་བཅུག་པ་དང་། ཁ་ཡང་ཕྱེས་ནས་ལུས་ཀྱི་ཤ་མ་ལུས་པར་ཟོས་སོ། (MB D 139v3)

"The prince with a sharp wooden splinter made blood come out of (lit. on) [his] body. Then [he] let the tigress lick [the blood]. [She] even opened the mouth [and] completely ate the flesh of [his] body."

This sentence consists of four clauses that share some of their arguments but the relationship between the arguments within the consecutive clauses is complex. The subject of ཕྱུང་ and བཅུག་ is the same: S → $S_ø$. The second clause then introduces an indirect object (སྟག་མོ་ལ་) that becomes the subject of the subsequent clause: O_2 → $S_ø$. The last two clauses have the same subject, the tigress, and each end with a transitive verb (ཕྱེས་ and ཟོས་).

དེ་ནས་འཕགས་པ་སྤྱན་རས་གཟིགས་དེས། རྫུ་འཕྲུལ་སྟོན་པའི་སྤྲེའུ་ཞིག་ལ། དགེ་བསྙེན་གྱི་སྡོམ་པ་བྱིན་ནས། བོད་ཁ་བ་ཅན་གྱི་རྒྱལ་ཁམས་སུ་བསྒོམ་དུ་བཏང་ངོ། (GLR 22r3–4)

"At that time, after the Noble One, Spyan-ras-gzigs, had conferred the vow of a lay practitioner upon a monkey that was displaying magic tricks, [he] sent it (i.e. the monkey) to the realm of the snow-clad Tibet to meditate."

Here two arguments of the first clause are omitted from the following clause: the subject (འཕགས་པ་སྤྱན་རས་གཟིགས་དེས་) and the indirect object (སྤྲེའུ་ཞིག་ལ་). The subject of the transitive verbs བྱིན་ and བཏང་ remains the same (S → $S_ø$), but the function of the indirect object of the first clause changes in the second clause – it becomes the direct object: O_2 → $O_{1/ø}$. This change is only superficial because བཏང་ is a transitive verb (བྱིན་ is ditransitive) and per definition does not take an indirect object.

In yet another case, the basic word order SOV may be reversed to OSV if the clause is connected with another one and the object of the first clause is coreferential with the subject of the second clause (O → $S_ø$):

རྒྱལ་པོ་གྲི་གུམ་བཙན་པོ་དེ། ཐུགས་གདོན་གྱིས་བསླུས་ཏེ། བློན་པོ་ལོང་ངམ་རྟ་རྫི་ཟེར་བ་ཞིག་ལ། [. . .] ཟེར་ནས། (GLR 24v6)

"A demon bewitched king Gri-gum Bcan-po; [the king] said to a minister called Loṅ-ṅam-rta-rji: [. . .]."

The two clauses share one argument: རྒྱལ་པོ་གྲི་གུམ་བཙན་པོ་. However, it is the object of the first verb (བསླུས་) but the subject of the second one (ཟེར་). Its fronting in the first clause marks that it is omitted from the second clause: O → $S_ø$. An analogously formed sentence in English would be: "Gri-gum Bcan-po, bewitched by a demon, said to a minister called Loṅ-ṅam-rta-rji: [. . .]." Instead of fronting an argument as Classical Tibetan does, English uses passive to omit a coreferential argument. In Classical Tibetan the reversal is applied first of all if arguments might otherwise be misinterpreted. For instance, if the first clause had the word order SOV, then its subject (ཐུགས་གདོན་) would have to be interpreted as the subject of the next verb (ཟེར་) as well. Reversing the word order serves mainly to disambiguate the roles of the core arguments in the linked clauses.

A different situation arises when one of the arguments has a human referent of higher social position, i.e. requiring the honorific register. Here the argument may be freely omitted because its function is clear from the speech register of the verbs used:

> ཁྱི་མོ་དེས་རྒྱལ་པོ་ལ་དེ་བཞིན་དུ་ཞུས་པས། དེ་ལྟར་བྱེད་གསུངས་ཏེ། (GLR 25r3)
> "Because the bitch reported this accordingly to the king, [he] said: '[I] shall do like that.'"

Verbs ཞུས་ and གསུངས་ have one coreferential argument: རྒྱལ་པོ་; it is the indirect object of the first verb, but the subject of the second one: $O_2 \rightarrow S_{\emptyset}$. The identity of the speaker in the second clause is ascertained by the honorific register of the verb གསུངས་. In such cases, pragmatic factors like the speech register govern the identification of the omitted arguments.

For a proper analysis of linked clauses the most important consideration is: which arguments are coreferential and may be omitted, and which are not. The argument that can be omitted in the next clause precedes other arguments of its own clause. Whatever its function in the first clause, the argument becomes the subject of the following clause and can be omitted. The relationship between the main arguments of linked clauses may be very complicated and the previous examples do not represent all possible variations. The earlier discussion must be seen as a mere outline of the problematique.[1]

Impersonal clause

An impersonal clause contains an undetermined subject which is not expressed in the clause but assumed on the semantic level:

> དེའི་ཚེ་བཅོམ་ལྡན་འདས་བསོད་སྙོམས་ཀྱི་དུས་ལ་བབ་ནས། ཤམ་ཐབས་དང་ཆོས་གོས་བགོས་ནས། (MB D 138r6)
> "At that time, when the time for alms came, the Victorious One put on a lower garment and a monk-robe."

The verb phrase དུས་ལ་བབ་ can be literally translated as "[it] fell down on the time". The verb བབ་, frequently encountered in similar constructions, does not have a subject; the latter has to be assumed as "it".

སྲས་རྣམས་ཀྱིས་རིམ་པ་བཞིན་ཆིབས་ཁ་ཐུབ་ཙ་ན།
ཡབ་རྣམས་རིམ་པ་བཞིན་དུ་རྨུ་ཐག་ལ་འཇུས་ནས།
ནམ་མཁའ་ལ་འཇའ་ཡལ་བ་བཞིན་འགྲོ་ཡང་ཟེར། (GLR 24v4–5)

"[It] is said (ཟེར་) that as soon as the sons, one after the other, had the command of bridle
The fathers successively seized the *rmu*-rope [and]
[Then] were going like a rainbow disappearing in the sky."

The subject of the verb ཟེར་ remains unspecified; it could be the whole society, a single group, or an unknown person.

Another type of impersonal construction is used when something considered a general truth is expressed:

སྡིག་པ་བྱས་ན་སེམས་ཅན་དམྱལ་བར་ལྟུང་གི། དགེ་བ་བྱས་ན་མཐོ་རིས་སུ་སྐྱེ་སྟེ། (MB D 140r7)
"If [one] committed an offence, [one] goes (lit. falls) to hell. Whereas if [one] committed virtuous deeds, [one] is reborn in heaven."

From the point of view of the Buddhist teachings, any living being will be reborn in a place that corresponds to the moral value of its current deeds. This truth concerns everybody and therefore the subject of the verbs may be left as unspecified.

Alternatively, the subject is omitted if general events are discussed for which no concrete person(s) can be made responsible. This construction is readily used in historiographical works:

སོལ་བས་རྡོ་གསུམ་བཞུས་ནས། དངུལ་ཟངས་ལྕགས་གསུམ་བཏོན།
ཤིང་ལ་བུག་པ་ཕུག་ནས་གཤོལ་དང་གཉའ་ཤིང་བཅོས།།
མཐུར་གཉིས་གཉའ་རུ་བསྦེབས་པས་ཐང་རྣམས་ཞིང་དུ་རྨོས།།
རྒྱ་མཚོ་ཡུར་ལ་དྲངས་ནས་ཞིང་ལ་ས་བོན་བཏབ།། (GLR 26r5)

"[One] melted the three ores with the charcoal [and] thereby obtained silver, copper, [and] iron.
[One] bored holes into wood [and] thereby prepared ploughs and yokes.
As [one] had joined two halters to the yokes, [one] ploughed plains into fields.
[One] led ocean['s waters] in channels [and] then sowed seeds on the fields."

Other pronouns

Demonstrative (Lesson 1), personal (Lesson 2), possessive (Lesson 3), and interrogative (Lesson 11) pronouns have already been introduced. These are the most important types of pronouns but not all by far. In the following sections indefinite and relative pronouns will be discussed.[2]

Indefinite pronouns

Indefinite pronouns are pronouns that refer to non-specific (i.e. indefinite) objects or persons. In Classical Tibetan they are formed from interrogative pronouns གང་, ཅི་, and སུ་ by adding either the indefinite or the concessive particle:

གང་ཞིག་ "anyone, anything" གང་ཡང་ "whoever, whatever"
ཅི་ཞིག་ "anything, something" ཅི་ཡང་/ཅིའང་/ཅང་ "whatever"
སུ་ཞིག་ "somebody" སུ་ཡང་/སུའང་ "whoever"

ལེགས་པ་ཅི་ཞིག་ (MB D 138v6) "anything good"

ང་ལ་ཉེས་པའི་སྐྱོན་གང་ཡང་མེད། (MB D 270v7)
"I do not have any bad faults whatsoever."

Other indefinite pronouns can be formed from an interrogative word and the concessive particle:

གང་ནའང་ "wherever" གང་ལའང་ "whomever"
ཅིས་ཀྱང་ "by whatever means"

བུ་འདི་ཡོན་ཏན་ཞིག་སློབ་ཏུ་ཅིས་ཀྱང་གཏོང་ངོ་། (ML D 13r)
"By all means (ཅིས་ཀྱང་) [I] will send this child to learn a good skill."

Relative pronouns

Classical Tibetan does not have special relative pronouns because its relative clauses are usually formed from nominalised clauses in genitive (see Lesson 11). Other constructions however exist that share some characteristics with relative clauses as known from European languages. Consider, for instance, the following passage:

རྫ་ལ་དབྱུག་གུས་མ་བསྣུན་པ།། དེ་སྲིད་གཞན་དང་ཁྱད་ཅི་ཡོད།། (SSP 6c–d)
"[As long as one] has not beaten a drum with a stick, is there any difference to any other [drum]?"

The meaning of the couplet is that as long as one has not played a drum, no difference between the drum and any other drum can be established concerning their sounds. དེ་སྲིད་ "so long" is a correlate of ཇི་སྲིད་ "as long as" which is omitted from the text. The clause can be reformulated as: *ཇི་སྲིད་རྔ་ལ་དབྱུག་གུས་མ་བརྡུན་པ།། དེ་སྲིད་གཞན་དང་ཁྱད་ཅི་ཡོད།།, lit. "As long as one has not beaten a drum with a stick, so long is there a difference to another [drum]?"

Most commonly used interrogative pronouns are: ཅི་, གང་, སུ་, ཇི་ལྟར་, or ཇི་བཞིན་:

བཅོམ་ལྡན་འདས་ཀྱིས་ཅི་རིགས་པའི་ཆོས་བསྟན་ནས། (MB D 138v5)
"The Victorious One taught [them] doctrine that was suitable [for them]."

བུའི་མ་གང་ཡིན་པ་དེ་ (MB D 273r5)
"the one who was child's mother"

Sometimes constructions are encountered that contain elements of typical relative clauses with genitive (see Lesson 11) and a relative pronoun, cf.:

བུ་གཉིས་དང་བཙུན་མོ་དང་། ཕོ་བྲང་གི་སླས་སུ་བཅས་ཏེ་མྱུར་བར་རྒྱལ་བུ་གང་དུ་ཚེ་འཕོས་པའི་གནས་སུ་སོང་ངོ་། (MB D 140r1)
"The two sons and the queen, in company of the court, went quickly to the place where the prince had died."

The clause རྒྱལ་བུ་ཚེ་འཕོས་ is nominalised and connected to གནས་ with the genitive particle but in addition the relative pronoun གང་དུ་ is used. This usually happens when the element that is modified with a relative clause is neither the object nor the subject of the verb; in the last example it is གནས་ "place", a locative adjunct.

Reading

"བཅོམ་ལྡན་འདས་ཀྱི་བཀའ་དྲིན་ཆེན་པོས་ ◦ བདག་ (138v4) ཅག་གི་ཚེ་སྲོག་ལྷག་མ་ཙམ་ཞིག་ ◦ ལུས་པར་གྱུར་ན། ལྷའི་གཙོ་བོ་ ◦ ཐུགས་བརྩེ་བར་ ◦ དགོངས་ཏེ། བདག་ཅག་ ◦ ཆོས་ལ་ ◦ རབ་ཏུ་འབྱུང་བར་ ◦ ཅི་ ◦ གནང་ཞེས་" གསོལ་པ་དང་། བཅོམ་ལྡན་འདས་ཀྱིས་ "ལེགས་པར་འོངས་སོ་ཞེས་" བཀའ་ ◦ སྩལ་པ་ན། སྐྲ་དང་ཁ་སྤུ་ ◦ རང་ ◦ བྱི་སྟེ། གོས་ཀྱང་ ◦ ངུར་སྨྲིག་ཏུ་ ◦ (138v5) གྱུར་ཏོ། །དེ་དག་ ◦ ཤིན་ཏུ་དད་པའི་སེམས་བརྟན་པར་ ◦ གྱུར་ནས། བཅོམ་ལྡན་འདས་ཀྱིས་ ◦ ཅི་རིགས་པའི་ཆོས་ ◦ བསྟན་ནས་ ◦ རྡུལ་དང་དྲི་མ་ ◦ ཟད་དེ། དགྲ་བཅོམ་པར་ ◦ གྱུར་ཏོ། །དེའི་མ་རྒན་མོ་དེ་ཡང་ ◦ ཆོས་ ◦ ཐོས་པས་ ◦ ལན་ཅིག་ཕྱིར་མི་ལྡོག་པར་ ◦ གྱུར་ཏོ། །དེའི་ཚེ་ ◦ ཀུན་དགའ་བོས་ ◦ དེ་ལྟ་ (138v6) བུའི་དངོས་པོ་ངོ་མཚར་ཆེ་བ་དག་ ◦ མཐོང་ནས། "དེ་བཞིན་གཤེགས་པ་ནི་ ◦ ཡོན་ཏན་དེ་

སྙེད་ཅིག་ ◦ མངའོ་ཞེས་" བསྔགས་ཏེ། ཡང་འདི་ ◦ སྙམ་དུ་ "རྒན་མོ་མ་སྨད་གསུམ་པོ་ འདིས་ ◦ སྔོན་ ◦ ལེགས་པ་ཅི་ཞིག་ ◦ བགྱིས་ན། ད་ལྟར་ ◦ བཅོམ་ལྡན་འདས་དང་ ◦ ཕྲད་དེ། ཉེས་པ་ ཆེན་པོ་ལས་ཀྱང་ ◦ ཐར་ལ། (138v7) མྱ་ངན་ལས་འདས་པའི་བདེ་བ་ ◦ ཐོབ་ནས་ ◦ ལུས་གཅིག་གིས་ ཕན་པ་དང་། བདེ་བའི་དོན་ཐོབ་པ་ ◦ ལེགས་སོ་" སྙམ་དུ་ ◦ བསམས་པ་དང་། བཅོམ་ལྡན་འདས་ ཀྱིས་ ◦ མཁྱེན་ནས་ ◦ ཀུན་དགའ་བོ་ལ་ ◦ འདི་སྐད་ཅེས་ ◦ བཀའ་ ◦ སྩལ་ཏོ།།

Notes

1. Some recent studies suggest that in Classical Tibetan certain converbal particles could participate in establishing whether an argument is coreferential and can be omitted (see Beer 2019; Haller 2009). However, their conclusions have been invalidated by examining a more encompassing text corpus for the purposes of the textbook.
2. Classical Tibetan does not have special forms that would correspond to English reflexive (*myself*, *himself*, *themselves*, etc.) or reciprocal pronouns (*each other*).

Lesson 15

- Morphology of transitive and intransitive verbs
- Other converbal particles
- Light verbs
- Incorporation
- Idioms
- Measure words
- Comparative and superlative
- Double case particles
- Ergative in quotations

Morphology of transitive and intransitive verbs

In Classical Tibetan some verbs occur in pairs: one transitive, the other intransitive. Without going into historical details, one can roughly distinguish between two main groups:

I Transitive with a base letter representing a voiceless consonant (‘K’) vs intransitive with a base letter representing a voiced consonant (‘G’):[1]

Transitive ‘K’	Intransitive ‘G’
*ɣgums/ b**k**um/ dgum/ khums* “to kill”	*ɣgum/ **g**um* “to die”
*ɣbebs/**ph**ab/ dbab/phob* “to throw down”	*ɣbab/**b**ab* “to fall down”
*ɣbyed/**ph**ye/ dbye/ phyes* “to open”	*ɣbye/ **b**ye* “to open (itself)”
*ɣǰig/ b**ś**ig/ gźig/ śig* “to destroy”	*ɣǰig/ **ź**ig* “to collapse”

II Transitive with the superscript *s-* vs intransitive with the prescript *ɣ-* in v1-stems (the base letter being the same):[2]

Transitive *s-*	Intransitive *ɣ-*
***s**kor/ b**s**kor/ b**s**kor/ **s**kor* “to encircle”	***ɣ**khor/ **ɣ**khor* “to turn round”

DOI: 10.4324/9781003224198-18

skol/ bskol/ bskol/ skol "to boil"	*γkhol/ khol* "to boil (itself)"
sgyur/ bsgyur/ bsgyur/ sgyur "to change"	*γgyur/ gyur* "to change (itself)"
sgrub/ bsgrub/ bsgrub/ sgrubs "to complete"	*γgrub/ grub* "to accomplish (itself)"
sdud/ bsdus/ bsdu/ sdus "to gather"	*γdu/ γdus* "to come together"

This is a simplified view.[3] However, it is crucial that students are aware of the differences for they are frequently ignored, leading to severe errors in translations into European languages. The following clauses exemplify the difference:

སྐོར་ (TR) "to encircle, to surround"
བདག་ཚེ་འཕོས་པའི་རུས་བུ་ཚལ་ན་འདུག་པ་ལ་ཕ་མས་བསྐོར་ཏེ། (MB D 140r3)
"[My] parents surrounded (བསྐོར་) my bones[4] that lie in the wood."

འཁོར་ (INTR) "to turn round; to roam"
བདག་ཡུན་རིང་པོ་ནས་འཁོར་བ་ན་འཁོར་ཞིང་། (MB D 139r7)
"For a long time I've been roaming (འཁོར་) in the cycle of existence."

In the first clause the verb བསྐོར་ is transitive (it has the superscript *s*-) and therefore beside a subject in ergative (ཕ་མས་), it requires an object in dative (རུས་བུ་ཚལ་ན་འདུག་པ་ལ་).[5] འཁོར་, on the other hand, is intransitive (it has the prescript *γ*- in v1) and therefore requires only one argument: subject in absolutive (བདག་). The next example contains a transitive verb (བསྡུས་) and its intransitive (འདུ་) counterpart in one sentence:

སྐྱེ་བོ་ཀུན། །མ་བསྡུས་པར་ཡང་རང་ཉིད་འདུ།། (SSP 8a–b)
Lit. "All men gather (འདུ་) by themselves even though [nobody] has gathered them (བསྡུས་)."

Whether a verb is transitive or intransitive must not be judged solely from the value of its base letter (voiceless vs voiced) or whether it has the superscript *s*- or prescript *γ*-. One has to check whether the verb has an equivalent characterised by the opposite value. The dictionary of Jäschke always provides the equivalents; e.g. when looking after འགྱུར་ (J: 96, s.v. འགྱུར་བ་), one finds the information that the verb is cognate with སྒྱུར་བ་ and s.v. སྒྱུར་བ་ (J: 118) one is referred to འགྱུར་བ་.[6]

Other converbal particles

In addition to proper converbal particles (discussed in Lessons 8–10), Classical Tibetan possesses several more particles that serve to connect two clauses with each other. They usually express anteriority of the events reported in the clause to which they are attached. The following discussion concerns the most commonly used ones that also occur in the Readings.

- ཙ་ན་ "as soon as, when"[7]

  མི་གོ་ཆོད་རེ་མེད་ཙ་ན་ (ML D 11v)
  "When there is no capable man [. . .]."
  གཉིད་སད་ཙ་ན། (GLR 25r5)
  "When [she] awoke [. . .]." Lit. "When the dream ceased [. . .]."

- དུས་ "when, after"

  དབྱར་ཞིང་ལས་བྱེད་དུས་ཨ་ཁུའི་གཡོག །དགུན་བལ་ལས་བྱེད་དུས་ཨ་ནེའི་གཡོག (ML D 11r)
  Lit. "When doing field-works in the summer, [we were] servants of the paternal uncle; [and] when doing the spinning of wool in the winter, [we were] servants of the paternal aunt."

  ཞག་འགའ་སོང་དུས་བལྟས་པས། (GLR 25r6–v1)
  "As [she] examined [it], after a few days had passed [. . .]."

- མ་ཐག་(ཏུ་) "immediately thereafter"

  སྟག་མོ་འདི་ནི་ཤིན་ཏུ་སྡུག་བསྔལ་གྱིས་གཟིར་ཏེ། ཉམ་ཆུང་ལ་རིད་པས་ཤི་ལ་ཐུག་པ་འདི་ལྟ་བུ་བུ་བྱུང་མ་ཐག་པ་ཡང་ཟ་རུ་འདོད་དོ། (MB D 139r5)
  "This tigress is pained with great affliction[8] [and] about to die due to weakness and starvation, thus [she] even wants to eat [her] newborn (བྱུང་མ་ཐག་) cubs."

  དེའི་ཚེ་ན་བཙུན་མོ་ཡུམ་མནལ་བའི་རྨི་ལམ་ན། [. . .] སླམ་རྨིས་མ་ཐག་ཏུ་སད་ནས། (MB D 139v5–6)
  Lit. "At that time the queen mother woke up immediately after (མ་ཐག་ཏུ་) [she] had dreamt that [. . .]."

Light verbs

Light verbs are verbs that, having themselves little semantic content, form a predicate with a noun.[9] The most common light verbs in Classical Tibetan are བྱེད་, འདེབས་, འབོར་, རྒྱབ་, and གཏོང་. Light verbs allow denoting an action for which no simple verb usually exists in a language. In some cases a light verb construction is used because Classical Tibetan lacks an analogous honorific verb (cf. སྐྱབས་མཛད་ "(HON) to save" for སྐྱོབ་ "to guard; to save"). In the following, exemplary phrases with light verbs are provided:

- བྱེད་/མཛད་ "to do"

  དབང་བྱེད་ "to rule"
  གཙོ་བྱེད་/མཛད་ "to lead"
  བརྩོན་འགྲུས་མཛད་ "to strain oneself"
  གཏམ་བྱེད་ "to talk; to give a speech"
  ཕྲིན་བྱེད་ "to deliver a message"
  རྗེ་མཛད་ "to be a ruler"

- འདེབས་ "to cast"

  གསོལ་བ་འདེབས་ "to submit a request"
  སོ་སྒྲ་འདེབས་ "to whistle"
  ཚ་ངེས་འདེབས་ "to lament, cry"
  ས་བོན་འདེབས་ "to sow seeds"

- གཏོང་ "to send; to give"

  བག་མར་གཏོང་ "to give in marriage"
  སེམས་གསོ་གཏོང་ "to console"

- འབོར་ "to throw"

  དམོད་འབོར་ "to pronounce a prayer"

- རྒྱབ་ "to throw"

  སྒོ་རྒྱབ་ "to close the door"

Nouns in constructions with light verbs cannot be modified with postposed attributes, but in contrast to incorporations (see next section) they fill one argument slot of the light verb:

> འཛམ་བུ་གླིང་འདི་ན་རྒྱལ་པོ་ཤིང་རྟ་ཆེན་པོ་ཞེས་བྱ་བ་ཞིག་ཡོད་དེ། རྒྱལ་ཕྲན་ལྔ་སྟོང་སྐྱིད་ལ་དབང་བྱེད་དོ། (MB D 139r2)
> "There was a king called Śiṅ-rta-čhen-po in this continent; [he] was ruling over about five thousand vassals."

བྱེད་ is a transitive verb and therefore requires a direct object. The only element in absolutive is དབང་ and so it is the direct object of བྱེད་.

The most commonly used phrases with light verbs can be found in dictionaries under the respective noun. In general, interpreting new phrases is not difficult. To this end it is helpful to consult already well-known phrases.

Incorporation

In Classical Tibetan incorporation is a type of verb construction in which a simple verb 'incorporates' one of the clause elements to form a complex verb. Usually such an element initially used to be a subject or a direct object of the verb. Incorporation concerns then a phrase (a verb plus another element) that frequently co-occurs in close neighbourhood in a clause. The meaning of such a complex verb is more specific than that of a simple verb, i.e. incorporation results in narrowing down of the meaning. Despite the incorporation, the incorporating verb retains its original argument structure. That is, if before incorporation a verb required two arguments, after the incorporation it still requires two arguments.

ཚེ་འཕོ་ "to die" < *"for [one's] life to change"

> རྒྱལ་བུ་སེམས་ཅན་ཆེན་པོ་དེ་དེར་ཚེ་འཕོས་ནས། (MB D 140r2–3)
> "After the prince Sems-čan-čhen-po had passed away there [. . .]."

འཕོ་ is an intransitive verb and therefore accepts only one argument which is then its subject. Strictly speaking, the previous clause has two elements in absolutive: རྒྱལ་བུ་སེམས་ཅན་ཆེན་པོ་དེ་ and ཚེ་. However ཚེ་ (originally the subject of འཕོ་) is incorporated in the verb. The slot of the subject argument of ཚེ་འཕོ་ is free and so the complex verb can take རྒྱལ་བུ་སེམས་ཅན་ཆེན་པོ་དེ་ as its subject.

ལུས་ངལ་ "to be/become tired" < *"for the body to be tired"

> དེ་ལུས་ངལ་ནས། (MB D 272r1)
> "As they got tired [. . .]."

Yet another type of incorporation concerns verbs with a direct object that is etymologically related to the verb:

> དེ་ན་ཁྱིམ་བདག་ནི་ཟན་ཟ་སྟེ། (MB D 271v1)
> "As for the householder, [he] was eating there."

Lit. "As for the householder, [he] was eating a meal there." The noun ཟན་ "food, meal" is derived from the verb ཟ་ "to eat".

> དེའི་རྡུང་ན་ཐ་ག་པ་ཞིག་ཐགས་འཐག་ཅིང་འདུག་པ་དེའི་སྟེང་དུ་ལྷུང་ནས། (MB D 271v5)
> "[Dbyig-pa-čan] fell down [on the other side] onto a weaver who sat close by it (i.e. close to the wall) weaving (lit. weaving a texture)."

The noun ཐགས་ "texture" is etymologically related to the verb འཐག་ "to weave". In both examples the subject stands in absolutive although the verbs (ཟ་ and འཐག་) are basically transitive. The complex verbs ཟན་ཟ་ and ཐགས་འཐག་ can be understood as incorporations, resulting, however, in intransitive verbs that take only one argument – the subject in absolutive. These constructions can be conceived as intermediate between light verb constructions and incorporations: the complex verb incorporated its original object into its semantics but has lost its transitive argument structure, becoming intransitive.[10]

Idioms

As with any other language, Classical Tibetan abounds in idiomatic phrases. They differ from other collocations and phrases of the language in the fact that their exact meaning cannot be easily retrieved from the single elements of the phrase. Many of the idioms are glossed in dictionaries. However, some have found their way into written language from spoken vernaculars and are not included in the more general lexicographical works. In these cases one has to either consult native lists of rare vocabulary or try to unravel the meaning of the idiom from the textual context in which it is used. The following list contains only a small collection of verbal idioms from the Readings of the textbook.[11] The right column presents the literal translation of the idiom, if known.

བཀའ་སྩོལ་ "(HON) to speak"	lit. "to give a word"
མགོ་འདོན་ "to sustain"	lit. "to put out the head"
ངོ་ཤེས་ "to recognise"	lit. "to know the face"
ཆུད་གསན་ "to waste"	
གདན་འདྲེན་ "to invite"	lit. "to pull a mat"
ཕྱག་འཚལ་ "to pay homage; to bow"	
བྱིན་གྱིས་རློབ་ "to bless"	
དབུ་རྙེད་ "(HON) to introduce"	lit. "to find the head"

Measure words

Measure words are nouns that in combination with a numeral (NUM) or a quantifier indicate amount of something. A typical construction with a measure word in Classical Tibetan has the following structure:

NP + measure word + NUM

ནས་ "barley" + ཕུལ་ "a handful" + གང་ "full" (ML D 12v)
"a (full) handful of barley"

རས་ཡུག་གཅིག་ (MB D 273r6) "one piece of cotton cloth"
རིན་པོ་ཆེ་སྣ་བདུན་ (MB D 140v2) "seven kinds of jewel"
འགྲོ་བ་རིགས་དྲུག་ (GLR 23r1) "six states (lit. kinds) of existence"

It is characteristic that measure words are attached directly to the noun phrase without any case particle. This is different in English, where a measure word always requires the preposition *of*, e.g. *three glasses **of** wine.*

Comparative and superlative

Classical Tibetan does not have degree of comparison as a grammatical category of adjectives comparable to English:

positive	*good*	*big*
comparative	*better*	*bigger*
superlative	*best*	*biggest*

Comparative

In Classical Tibetan comparison is expressed by means of a construction involving either the delative particle (see Lesson 6) or the comparative particle པས་/བས་. The particle follows the term which is compared, and the quality for which it is compared follows the particle:

N པས་/ལས་ A
"[more] A than N"

If the adjective (A) has a nominal particle, it is replaced by པ་/བ་:

མགྲོགས་པོ་ > མགྲོགས་པ་
ཆེན་པོ་ > ཆེ་བ་

Delative particle of comparison

གཞན་ལས་ཆེ་བ་ (SBM; *apud* Schwieger 2006: 315) "bigger (ཆེ་བ་) than the other one"

ཅི་ཕན་བྱེད་པ་ལས་འོས་མེད། (ML D 13r)
"There is nothing [more] suitable (འོས་) than (ལས་) to do what is useful."

སྲོག་ཆགས་གྲོག་མ་མིག་མེད་ཀྱང་།། མིག་ལྡན་གཞན་ལས་ལྷག་པར་མགྲོགས།། (SSP 14c–d)
"Even though animals [such as] ants have no eyes, [they] are much quicker than (ལས་) other [animals] that have eyes."

Comparative particle

གླང་པོ་ཆེ་བས་སྟོབས་ཆེ་བ་ (ML D 17r) "stronger than (བས་) an elephant", lit. "of greater strength than an elephant"[12]

མཁས་པ་རང་གི་ཡུལ་བས་ཀྱང་།། ཡུལ་ཁམས་གཞན་ན་མཆོད་པ་ཐོབ།། (SSP 23a–b)
"Rather than (བས་) in his own country, a wise one obtains honours in a foreign country."

འོ་ན་ཁྱེད་ཀྱི་ཆ་ལུགས་སྤྲང་པོ་བས་ངན་པ་འདི་འདྲའི་ཆོས་པ་སྔར་མ་མཐོང་། (ML D 67v)
"Now, as for your appearance worse than (བས་) that of a beggar, I have never seen such a follower of Dharma."

In the latter clause the phrase སྤྲང་པོ་བས་ངན་པ་, lit. "worse from a beggar", is an attribute of ཆ་ལུགས་ "appearance".

There is no apparent difference in the use of delative or comparative particle to express comparison apart from the fact that the latter particle is more common in this function.

Superlative

In order to form a construction similar to the English superlative, an adjective is added the superlative particle ཤོས་ and the nominal particle of the adjective is elided. In the following example ཆུང་ཤོས་ is formed from the base form ཆུང་ངུ་.

དམག་བརྒྱ་པ་ལ་བུ་གསུམ་བྱུང་བའི་ཆུང་ཤོས་ (GLR 24r5) "the youngest of three sons born to Dmag-brgya-pa"

Yet another superlative construction involves a genitive phrase or a postpositional phrase with the meaning "among", cf.:

ལྷ་ཡི་མཆོག་ (SSP Ia) "the most excellent ones among deities"
ལྷའི་ནང་ན་གཙོ་བོ་ (MB D 138v1) "the most eminent one among deities"
བདག་གི་བུ་ནང་གི་སྡུག་པ་ (MB D 139v6) "the dearest of my sons"
ནང་གི་ཆུང་ངུ་ (MB D 139v5) "the youngest of them"

Double case particles

In rare instances two different case particles may follow each other:

མདོར་ན་མི་ནོར་གཞན་ལ་སྨོན་མི་དགོས་པ་ཡོད་པས། (ML D 10v)
"In short, because I do not need to desire another man's wealth [. . .]."

In this clause, the terminative -ར in མདོར་ is followed by the locative ན་ without any recognisable change of the meaning; མདོར་ already means "in brief" (lit. "in a short form").

Similarly in the common phrase དེས་ན་ "for that reason", the ergative -ས in དེས་ expresses the cause (see Lesson 5) making ན་ redundant. Whereas the meaning of ན་ in མདོར་ན་ can be deemed adequate to the meaning of the phrase, the locative ན་ in དེས་ན་ has no relevance for the meaning of the phrase because ན་ has never denoted causality. The same concerns པས་ན་ in:

> ཁྱིམ་བདག་ཀྱང་གླང་འོངས་པར་མཐོང་བ་ལས་མ་བཏགས་པས་ན། མིག་ཕྱུང་ཞིག་ཅེས་བཅད་དོ།། (MB D 272v1)
> "Because (པས་ན་) the householder, upon seeing that the ox comes in, did not bind [it], gouge out [his] eyes!"

As the examples with པས་ན་ and དེས་ན་ demonstrate, the use of the second particle cannot always be rationally explained. The same can be said about ན་ in the numeral adverbs such as གཅིག་ཏུ་ན་ or གཉིས་སུ་ན་ which are synonymous with གཅིག་ཏུ་ and གཉིས་སུ་, respectively.[13]

Ergative in quotations

The ergative particle may sometimes be encountered at the end of direct speech, between the last verb of the utterance and the quotative particle. In these cases ergative is a sentence final and not a converbal particle.[14] The ergative then follows the v3-stem of a transitive but the v1-stem of an intransitive verb.

There is no agreement among scholars regarding the exact meaning and function of ergative in this position. Examples in works translated from Sanskrit demonstrate that the construction 'V + ERG' rendered Sanskrit future forms.[15] Another meaning is suggested in:

> བདག་གི་བུ་ནང་གི་སྡུག་པ་ལ་བཀྲ་མི་ཤིས་ངེས་ཀྱིས་ཞེས་ (MB D 139v6)
> "[I] am certain (ངེས་ཀྱིས་) that [some] mischief has happened to the dearest of my sons."

What seems to connect all the heretofore collected examples of this construction[16] is that they express certainty about a predicted event. The event is most commonly projected into the future and has not yet been witnessed by the speaker. Therefore, it may sometimes be possible to conceive of the construction as expressing promise or prediction:

> འོ་ན་ངས་མར་པ་དང་སྤྲད་ཀྱིས། (ML D 27r)
> "Well then, I shall introduce [you] to Mar-pa."

སྡུག་རེས་བྱུང་ན་ལབ་རེས་ཀྱིས་ (ML D 11v)
"When misery occurred once, gossip [follows] in turn."

Reading

"མ་སྨད་གསུམ་པོ་འདི་ནི་ ◦ ངས་ ◦ ད་ལྟར་འདི་འབའ་ཞིག་གི་དུས་སུ་ ◦ གསོས་ (139r1) པར་ ◦ མ་ཟད་ཀྱི། སྔོན་འདས་པའི་དུས་ན་ཡང་ ◦ ངའི་བཀའ་དྲིན་གྱིས་ ◦ གསོས་སོ།" །ཀུན་དགའ་བོས་ ◦ གསོལ་པ། "བཅོམ་ལྡན་འདས་ ◦ སྔོན་འདས་པའི་དུས་ན་ཡང་ ◦ མ་སྨད་གསུམ་པོ་འདི་དག་ ◦ ཅི་ལྟར་ ◦ གསོས་པ་ ◦ བཅོམ་ལྡན་འདས་ཀྱིས་ ◦ བསྟན་དུ་ ◦ གསོལ།" (139r2) བཅོམ་ལྡན་འདས་ཀྱིས་ ◦ ཀུན་དགའ་བོ་ལ་ ◦ བཀའ་ ◦ སྩལ་པ། "སྔོན་འདས་པའི་དུས་བསྐལ་པ་གྲངས་མེད་པའི་ཕ་རོལ་ན། འཛམ་བུ་གླིང་འདི་ན་ ◦ རྒྱལ་པོ་ཤིང་རྟ་ཆེན་པོ་ཞེས་བྱ་བ་ཞིག་ ◦ ཡོད་དེ། རྒྱལ་ཕྲན་ལྔ་སྟོང་སྐྱིད་ལ་ ◦ དབང་བྱེད་དོ། །རྒྱལ་པོ་དེ་ལ་ ◦ སྲས་གསུམ་ ◦ (139r3) མངའ་སྟེ། རབ་ནི་ ◦ སྒྲ་ཆེན་པོ་ཞེས་ ◦ བྱའོ། །འབྲིང་པོ་ནི་ ◦ ལྷ་ཆེན་པོ་ཞེས་ ◦ བྱའོ། ཐ་ཆུངས་ནི་ ◦ སེམས་ཅན་ཆེན་པོ་ཞེས་ ◦ བྱ་སྟེ། སྲས་ཐ་ཆུངས་དེ་ ◦ ཆུང་ངུ་ནས་ ◦ བྱམས་པ་དང་སྙིང་རྗེར་ ◦ ལྡན་ཏེ། ཐམས་ཅད་ལ་ ◦ བུ་གཅིག་པ་དང་ ◦ འདྲའོ། །དེའི་ཚེ་ ◦ རྒྱལ་པོ་དེ་ ◦ བློན་པོ་དང་ ◦ བཅས། བཙུན་ (139r4) མོ་དང་སྲས་སུ་ ◦ བཅས་ཏེ། ཕྱི་རོལ་ཏུ་ ◦ འཆག་ཅིང་ ◦ དོང་བ་ལས། ཅུང་ཟད་ཅིག་ ◦ ངལ་བསོ་བའི་བར་དུ་ ◦ སྲས་གསུམ་པོ་ ◦ ཚལ་གྱི་ནང་དུ་ ◦ དོང་དོང་བ་ལས། སྟག་མོ་བུ་བྱུང་ནས་ཞག་དུ་མ་ལོན་པ་བཀྲེས་ཤིང་སྐོམ་པས་ཉེན་ཏེ། ཕྱིར་ཡང་བུ་ཟ་ལ་ཐུག་པ་ཞིག་ ◦ མཐོང་ནས། རྒྱལ་ (139r5) བུ་ཐ་ཆུངས་ཀྱིས་ ◦ ཕུ་བོ་གཉིས་ལ་ ◦ སྨྲས་པ།

Notes

1 The distinction between the base consonants concerns the consonants of v2-stems. The respective base letters are marked bold in the following list.

2 The superscript *s*- is retained in all stems, whereas the prescript *ɣ*- may be lost in v2-stems. If the base letter is voiceless, then the superscript *s*- is followed by an unaspirated consonant (*k*, *t*, *p*), and the prescript *ɣ*- by its aspirated equivalent (*kh*, *th*, *ph*). If the base letter is voiced (*g*, *d*, *b*) no alternation occurs.

3 The features are treated in more detail in Bielmeier (1988) and Bialek (2020a).

4 Lit. "bones of the dead me".

5 Subject in ergative and object in dative is not a prototypical argument structure of transitive verbs, but is by no means an unusual one.

6 Traditionally, Tibetan verbs are listed in dictionaries in their nominalised forms, for example, འགྱུར་བ instead of འགྱུར. This custom is not followed in the Glossary of the textbook and has also been abandoned in some modern dictionaries, like the Tibetan-German dictionary WTS.

7 ཙ་ན་ is a simplified form of ཙམ་ན་. ཙམ་ is a determiner (see Lesson 17) that grammaticalised most probably from the verb རྩོམ་ (√rtsam) "to set about, to be about".

8 Lit. "because this tigress is very afflicted, [she] is pained".

9 Compare Eng. "to *take* advantage", "to *do* a review", etc.

10 These constructions are known as *figura etymologica* in rhetoric or *cognate object constructions* in modern linguistics.

11 All idioms that occur in the textbook are listed in the Glossary.

12 སྟོབས་ཆེ་བ་ is a possessive attribute (see Lesson 14) with the literal meaning "having great strength".

13 Other combinations of two case particles are likewise possible, although seldom encountered in indigenous non-metrical works; for some examples, see Hahn (1996: 201f).

14 In some cases the ergative lacks the final -ས and so becomes identical with the genitive.

15 Hoffmann (1955).

16 See Hoffmann (1955), Beyer (1993: 353f.), and Schwieger (2006: 120).

Lesson 16

- Auxiliary particle ཀྱིན་
- Analytical verb constructions
- Concessive auxiliary རུང་
- Purposive particle རྒྱུ་

Auxiliary particle ཀྱིན་

The form of the auxiliary particle ཀྱིན་ depends on the last letter of the preceding syllable:

ཀྱིན་	after	-ད, -བ, -ས, *-ད་དྲག་
གིན་	after	-ག, -ང, -འ, -vowel
གྱིན་	after	-ན, -མ, -ར, -ལ

The sole function of this particle is to connect the main verb with the following auxiliary verb. However, only a few analytical verb constructions 'main verb + auxiliary' use the particle. Those are basically the constructions with ཡིན་, ཡོད་, or འདུག་ as auxiliaries. Their common trait is that they express the progressive aspect.

Analytical verb constructions

An analytical verb construction is a complex syntactic construction in which an auxiliary verb (AUX) is added to the main verb. For example, Eng. *I am working* contains an analytical verb construction formed with the auxiliary *am* and the main verb *work* (+ *-ing* suffix). In Classical Tibetan analytical verb constructions can take one of the following forms:

- Main verb + auxiliary verb
- Main verb + auxiliary particle /ཀྱིན་/ + auxiliary verb

DOI: 10.4324/9781003224198-19

- Main verb + coordinative particle /ཅིང་/ + auxiliary verb
- Nominalised main verb + auxiliary verb
- Nominalised main verb + terminative -ར + auxiliary verb

An important characteristic of the constructions is that no other words or syllables are allowed between the main verb and the auxiliary, apart from those mentioned earlier and the negations མི་ and མ་. The latter usually stand directly before the auxiliary. Auxiliary verbs cannot be modified by an adverb. In metrical texts particles that usually stand between the main verb and the auxiliary may be omitted. In addition, both main verb and auxiliary may use various available stems to express differing meanings.

In Classical Tibetan analytical verb constructions came into being mainly to express grammatical meanings which the bare verb stems could not express.[1] However, they were not all created at one time; they developed successively starting as early as in the 9th century. The consequence is that Classical Tibetan texts composed in different times will use analytical constructions to varying degrees; in general, the younger the text, the more analytical constructions it uses. Similarly, the meaning of a particular construction might have likewise undergone changes. Another factor complicating the reading is the genre of the text: different types of analytical constructions are preferred in different genres. All these variations are reflected even in this textbook's sample selection of readings – the text of Mi-la Ras-pa's biography uses constructions not encountered in རྒྱལ་རབས་གསལ་བའི་མེ་ལོང་། and vice versa. Accordingly, the following discussion can only give a most general overview of analytical verb constructions encountered in the readings of the textbook.[2] Below, the analytical verb constructions will be discussed according to the auxiliary they take. The grammatical meaning of the particular construction is provided next to the construction.[3]

འགྱུར་

འགྱུར་ as an auxiliary requires the main verb to be nominalised and have the terminative -ར added, irrespective of whether འགྱུར་ itself occurs as a v1- or v2-stem.[4]

I. v1 + པར་/བར་ *+* འགྱུར་ *– Future tense*

When added to a v1-stem of the main verb, the v1-stem འགྱུར་ is used to express future. This can be compared with Ger. *werden* "to become" that likewise developed to an auxiliary to denote future events, cf. *Ich werde morgen meine Mutter anrufen.*

སེམས་ཅན་སྲིན་པོས་ཟ་བར་འགྱུར།། (GLR 22v2)

"The ogress will eat [all] sentient beings."

ཁྱོད་ཀྱི་བུ་དེ་ཀུན་ལས་རྒྱལ་བར་འགྱུར་རོ།། (GLR 25v3)
"Your son will be victorious over all."

II. v2 + པར་/བར་ *+* གྱུར་ *– Perfective aspect*

This construction expresses the accomplishment of an event:

སྲིན་པོའི་ཕྲུ་གུ་དཔག་མེད་སྐྱེས་གྱུར་ནས།།	"After [I] have given birth to innumerable children by (lit. of) the ogre,
ཁ་བ་ཅན་གྱི་རྒྱལ་ཁམས་འདི་ཉིད་དུ།།	[And] after this very realm of the snow-clad [Tibet] as such
སྲིན་པོའི་གྲོང་ཁྱེར་དག་ཏུ་གྱུར་ནས་ནི།།	Has turned to an ogres' domain (lit. towns),
གང་ཡོད་སེམས་ཅན་སྲིན་པོས་ཟ་བར་འགྱུར།།	Wherever [they] may be, the ogress will eat [all] sentient beings." (GLR 22v2)

སྐྱེས་གྱུར་ (metrically for *སྐྱེས་པར་གྱུར་) in the first line means that the children were born before the town turned to an ogres' town and their birth was the condition for the change of the character of the town.

བདུད་རིགས་སྲིན་མོ་ཆགས་པའི་འདུ་ཤེས་ཅན།།	"An ogress [from] a demon-race, obsessed with passion,
གདུང་བའི་སྨྲེ་སྔགས་སྣ་ཚོགས་བརྗོད་གྱུར་ནས།།	Uttered various kinds of doleful lamentations." (GLR 22v4)

III. v1 + པར་/བར་ *+* གྱུར་ *– Past progressive*

This construction denotes an event that was ongoing in the past.

ཟས་སུ་མ་རྨོས་པའི་ལོ་ཐོག་ཟ་ཞིང་། གོས་སུ་ཤིང་ལོ་གོན་པར་གྱུར། (GLR 23v5)
"[They] were eating the crops that [one] had not sown and ploughed as [their] food, and wearing tree-leaves as [their] clothes."

The coordinative particle ཞིང་ coordinates ཟ་ and གོན་ so that the auxiliary refers to both verbs: *ཟ་པར་གྱུར་ and གོན་པར་གྱུར་.

ཡིན་

ཡིན་ may be replaced by ལགས་ if the context requires an honorific or a humble verb. When negated, ཡིན་ is replaced by མིན་ or the negation is put before the main verb.

I. v2 + པ་/བ་ *+* ཡིན་ *– Perfective aspect*

This construction indicates a completed action.

ཁོ་རང་འཆི་ཁར་ནོར་བདག་པོ་ལ་སྤྲད་པ་ཡིན། (ML D 12v)
"After he died, [the things] returned to the wealth's owner."

རྒྱལ་པོ་དེས་དམ་པ་ཆོས་ཀྱི་དབུ་བརྙེས་པ་ཡིན་ནོ། (GLR 27r1–2)
"This king has introduced the Noble Dharma [in Tibet]."

II. V + པ་/བ་ *+* ཡིན་ *– Egophoric*

This construction is used to indicate that the speaker has a personal (egophoric) knowledge of the events described. As opposed to the egophoric construction with the auxiliary བྱུང་ (see later), 'V + པ་/བ་ + ཡིན་' can be used only when the subject is the 1st person.

སྔར་ཡབ་མི་ལ་ཤེས་རབ་རྒྱལ་མཚན་བཞུགས་པའི་ཚེ། མི་དྲག་ཞན་ཀུན་ངེད་ཀྱི་ཞལ་འཛུམ་དཀར་ནག་བལྟ་བ་ཡིན་ཏེ། ཕྱིས་ནོར་ཡོད་རྒྱལ་པོའི་ཚུལ་དུ་སོང་ནས། ཨ་ཁུ་དང་ཨ་ནེའི་ཞལ་འཛུམ་དཀར་ནག་བལྟ་བ་བྱུང་། (ML D 11v)
"Previously, when [my] father Mi-la Śes-rab Rgyal-mchan was alive, all the people, high and low, were looking for whether our smile was friendly or unfriendly. Later, after [they] became wealthy like kings, the smile of [my] paternal uncle and aunt, whether friendly or unfriendly, was looked for [by us]."

The passage contrasts བལྟ་བ་ཡིན་ with བལྟ་བ་བྱུང་. In the first case the speaker (Mi-la Ras-pa) relates people's behaviour towards himself and his family, and therefore the egophoric auxiliary ཡིན་ is appropriate. The literal translation would read: "Our smile, whether friendly or unfriendly, was looked for by all the people, high and low." The use of the egophoric auxiliary ཡིན་ confirms that ངེད་ཀྱི་ཞལ་འཛུམ་ is the subject of the clause that, due to the v3 བལྟ་, has to be interpreted as a passive clause (see Lesson 14). The action in the second part of the passage concerns Mi-la Ras-pa's uncle and aunt and so བྱུང་ is used (for its explanation see the section on འབྱུང་).

ང་ཡང་གཏམ་ཚིག་གསུམ་པ་ཞིག་གཏོང་བ་ལགས་པས། (ML D 12r)
"I also have a few words to say." Lit. "I also give a few words."

III. ཡོད་པ་ཡིན་ – Emphasis

པ་ཡིན་ adds emphasis to the main verb ཡོད་ without changing the grammatical meaning of the verb.

> ཁྱེད་ཀྱི་ནོར་རྫས་དེ་གང་ན་ཡོད་པ་ཡིན། (ML D 12v)
> "What is your possession or where is it?"

ཡོད་

The verbs ཡོད་, མཆིས་ (HML), and མངའ་ (HON) are used in the same analytical constructions; the only difference being the speech register of the respective formations.

I. v2 + ཡོད་ – Perfect

The construction indicates that an action has been completed and its outcome is relevant for the actual situation:[5]

> དེ་ལྟར་ན་བོད་ཁ་བ་ཅན་པ་མི་འདི་རྣམས་པ་སྤྲེའུ་དང་། མ་བྲག་སྲིན་མོ་གཉིས་ལས་ཆད་པ་ཡིན་པས། རིགས་གཉིས་སུ་བྱེ་ཡོད་དོ། (GLR 23v5)
> "In that way, because these people, the inhabitants of the snow-clad Tibet, had descended from both a father-monkey and a mother rock-ogress, [they] have divided into two kinds."

བྱེ་ is a v2-stem of the intransitive འབྱེ་ "to divide". བྱེ་ཡོད་ means that the inhabitants of Tibet have divided into two kinds and this is a fact still recognised at the time of the story telling.

II. v1 (seldom v3) + པ(ར)་/བ(ར)་ + ཡོད་ – Assertive

This construction indicates that the speaker is certain about the contents of her statement. The statement may relate to the present or future events. It may also express a general truth.

> མདོར་ན་མི་ནོར་གཞན་ལ་སྨོན་མི་དགོས་པ་ཡོད་པས། (ML D 10v)
> "In short, because I do not need to desire another man's wealth [. . .]."

This is a statement made by Mi-la Ras-pa's father on his deathbed. As it concerns his own assets, he may be certain about the truth of his words.

III. v1 + auxiliary particle + ཡོད་ *– Progressive aspect*

Progressive denotes an ongoing action:

> ཆོས་ཟབ་མོ་སྟོང་པ་ཉིད་ལ་མོས་པར་བྱེད་གིན་ཡོད་དུས། (GLR 22r4)
> "While [the monkey] was devoting itself to the profound Buddhist teaching, the voidness, [. . .]."

> ཕག་ཏུ་སོག་གིན་ཡོད་པ་ཡང་མང་རབ་ཏུ་སོང་བ་ལ་ཤ་མང་པོ་ཉོས། (ML D 11v)
> "For what [he] had been collecting (སོག་གིན་ཡོད་པ་) secretly [he] bought great quantities (lit. much) of meat for the surplus."

བྱེད་

The verbs བྱེད་, བགྱིད་ (HML), and མཛད་ (HON) are used in the same analytical constructions; the only difference being the speech register of the respective formations.

I. V + པར་/བར་ *+* བྱེད་ *– Causative*

This construction is used to form causative meanings from verbs that cannot form causatives with འཇུག་ (see Lesson 13) because they are non-controllable. For instance, བདེ་ means "to be happy". It expresses an emotional state which, by definition, cannot be controlled. When used in the analytical construction བདེ་བར་བྱེད་, it can be translated as "to make sb. happy".[6]

> ངས་སྔོན་ཡང་ཡུན་རིང་པོ་ནས་བགེགས་ལས་ཐར་བར་བྱས་ཏེ་སྲོག་བསྐྱབས་ནས་བདེ་བར་བྱས་སོ།། ད་མངོན་པར་སངས་རྒྱས་ནས་ཀྱང་བགེགས་ལས་ཐར་བར་མཛད་ནས། (MB D 140v5–6)
> "Earlier, having saved [them] from difficulties a long time ago, I rescued [their] lives [and] made them happy. Now, after [I] had achieved manifesting enlightenment, I saved [them] from difficulties [again]."

The main verbs བདེ་ and ཐར་ are non-controllable. The passage quotes Buddha's words. In the first sentence ཐར་བར་བྱས་ is used, that is contrasted with ཐར་བར་མཛད་ in the second sentence. In both instances the Buddha relates his own actions, but the second action follows his enlightenment and therefore the honorific auxiliary མཛད་ was chosen.

> ཆོས་ཟབ་མོ་སྟོང་པ་ཉིད་ལ་མོས་པར་བྱེད་གིན་ཡོད་དུས། (GLR 22r4)
> "While [the monkey] was devoting itself to the profound Buddhist teaching, the voidness, [. . .]."

Here the analytical construction མོས་པར་བྱེད་, lit. "to make sb. admire", is embedded in another construction 'V + auxiliary particle + ཡོད་' which adds the progressive meaning to it (see section on ཡོད་). Sometimes the auxiliary follows immediately after the main verb:

> ཁྱོད་ཀྱི་ཁྱོ་བྱས་ན་ངའི་སྡོམ་པ་འཆོར་བྱས་པས། (GLR 22r6)
> "If [I] became your husband, my vow would be lost." Lit. "[. . .] [I] would make my vow escape."

The same construction can be used to form imperatives from non-controllable verbs which, by definition, do not have v4-stems:

> རྒྱལ་པོ་ཆེན་པོ་འདི་ལྟར་མཁྱེན་པར་མཛོད་ཅིག (MB D 140r6)
> "Great king, understand [it] this way!"

མཁྱེན་ is a non-controllable verb and cannot be used in imperative constructions. Here the auxiliary verb མཛོད་ allows to express an action that can be controlled by the subject. One cannot cause anybody to understand anything, but one can figuratively say "make [it] so that [you] understand", as the clause does.

When used with controllable verbs the analytical construction does not influence the meaning of the verb; it is then just a periphrastic form of the main verb:

> མི་ངན་ལ་དབང་བསྐུར་ན་ཆུ་ལ་བྲེས་འཇལ་བྱེད། (ML D 12v)
> "If [one] granted power to wicked men, [they] will measure out water by the manger."

> སྟན་ལ་ཧར་ལངས་བྱས། (ML D 12v)
> "[He] suddenly rose from (lit. on) the seat."

II. v2/v3 + པར་ /བར་ + བྱ་ – Passive

The construction was probably created in order to disambiguate the stem of the main verb. Namely, many examples from earlier literature concern such event verbs whose v2-stems were identical with v3-stems, e.g. བཤད་ (in the following example), བསྟན་, and བསྐྱེད་ (see Schwieger 2006: 134). The resulting analytical construction was unanimous with the meaning of v3-stems and expressed passive voice (see Lesson 14).

> དེ་ནས་བོད་རྒྱལ་པོའི་གདུང་རབས་རིམ་པར་བྱོན་པ་རྣམས་བཤད་པར་བྱ་སྟེ། (GLR 24r3)
> "Thereafter, generations of kings of Tibet, who appeared in succession, are explained (བཤད་པར་བྱ་)."

འདུག་

I. V + (པར་/བར་) + འདུག་ – *Sensory evidence*

འདུག་ indicates that the action or its result are available to the agent (3rd person) through her personal experience.

> སྤྲེའུ་བྱང་ཆུབ་སེམས་དཔའ་བལྟར་ཕྱིན་པས། ལས་ཀྱི་དབང་གིས་སྤྲེལ་ཕྲུག་ལྔ་བརྒྱར་འཕེལ་འདུག་གོ། (GLR 23r4–5)
> "Because the *bodhisattva*-monkey went to inspect [them], [he] realised (འདུག་) that perforce of [their previous] actions the [number of] monkey-children had increased to five hundred."

In this passage the *bodhisattva* visits a place where he left his monkey-children and sees that in the meantime their number has increased. The use of the auxiliary འདུག་ in འཕེལ་འདུག་ indicates that the increase (འཕེལ་) is witnessed by the *bodhisattva*. A similar explanation can be provided for the next passage:

> ཞག་འགའ་སོང་དུས་བལྟས་པས། ཁྱེའུ་ཞིག་བྱུང་འདུག (GLR 25r6–v1)
> "As [the mother] examined [it], after a few days had passed a boy appeared [to her]."

The mother wrapped a clot of blood, which was born to her, with clothes and put it aside. After a while she looked for it and saw that a boy emerged out of the clot. བྱུང་འདུག་ indicates that she personally saw the boy.

II. V + (པ (ར)་/བ (ར)་) + འདུག་ – *Assertive*

This construction indicates that the speaker is certain about the contents of her statement. The statement may relate to the present or future events. It may also express a general truth. In this function the auxiliary may be replaced by གདའ་ (see the last example).

> ང་ད་ལན་གྱི་ནད་འདིས་མི་གཏོང་བ་འདུག་ཅེང་། (ML D 10v)
> "The present illness does not leave me."

> མ་བྱས་ན་ནི་སྡིག་པ་ཚབས་ཆེ་བར་འདུག་སྙམ་ནས། (GLR 22v3)
> "'If [I] do not [become her husband], the sin will be very great.' [Thus he] thought."

> ང་ཤི་དུར་ཁུང་ནས་བལྟའོ་གསུང་བ་དེ་ད་གཟིགས་པའི་དུས་ལ་བབ་གདའོ། (ML D 12v)
> "The time has indeed come to regard now what [you once] said: '[You] will be watched from the grave [when] I die.'"

III. V + coordinative particle + འདུག་ – Progressive aspect

Progressive denotes an ongoing action. In this function the verbs མཆིས་ and བཞུགས་ can sometimes replace འདུག་.

ངུ་ཞིང་འགྱེལ་ནས་ཁྲི་ལོག་ལོག་བྱེད་ཅིང་འདུག (ML D 12v)
"Weeping [she] fell down [and] was rolling back and forth [on the ground]."

འབྱུང་ – *Past/egophoric*

The construction 'v1/v2 + བྱུང་' expresses an action completed in the past, of which the speaker has personal knowledge. The speaker can be identical with the subject, direct object, or indirect object of the verb. With the v1-stem the construction can be interpreted as past imperfective; the v2-stem indicates that the action was completed in the past.

ལས་དལ་མེད་བྱེད་དགོས་བྱུང་བས་ཡན་ལག་རྣམས་སེར་གར་སོང་། (ML D 11r)
"Because [we] had to work without rest, [our] limbs became cracked."

Here Mi-la Ras-pa relates the hardship he and his family experienced while working for his paternal uncle and aunt. The verb བྱུང་ indicates that Mi-la Ras-pa also had to labour.

ཁྱད་པར་མཛེས་སེའི་ཕ་མས་རྒྱགས་ཀྱུ་སྔོར་མེ་ཤིང་ཡན་བསྐུར་ནས། ང་ཀློག་སློབ་སར་མཛེས་སེ་མོ་རང་སེམས་གསོ་ལ་ཡང་ཡང་བཏང་བྱུང་། (ML D 13v)
"In particular, Mjes-se's parents gave [us] provisions, meat,[7] and firewood, and then in order to console [me], [they] sent Mjes-se herself again and again to the place where I was learning to read."

In this passage Mi-la Ras-pa recounts how Mjes-se's parents sent Mjes-se to his place; the speaker (i.e. Mi-la Ras-pa) was the beneficiary of the action. In Mi-la Ras-pa's biography we also find constructions with identical meanings but with a nominalised main verb, 'V + པ་/བ་ + བྱུང་':

སྔར་ཡབ་མི་ལ་ཤེས་རབ་རྒྱལ་མཚན་བཞུགས་པའི་ཚེ། མི་དྲག་ཞན་ཀུན་ངེད་ཀྱི་ཞལ་འཛུམ་དཀར་ནག་བལྟ་བ་ཡིན་ཏེ། ཕྱིས་ནོར་ཡོད་རྒྱལ་པོའི་ཚུལ་དུ་སོང་ནས། ཨ་ཁུ་དང་ཨ་ནེའི་ཞལ་འཛུམ་དཀར་ནག་བལྟ་བ་བྱུང་། (ML D 11v)
"Previously, when [my] father Mi-la Śes-rab Rgyal-mchan was alive, all the people, high and low, were looking for whether our smile was friendly or unfriendly. Later, after [they] became wealthy like kings, the smile of [my] paternal uncle and aunt, whether friendly or unfriendly, was looked for [by us]."

The passage contrasts བལྟ་བ་ཡིན་ with བལྟ་བ་བྱུང་. The use of the egophoric auxiliary ཡིན་ confirms that ངེད་ཀྱི་ཞལ་འཛུམ་ is the subject of the clause that, due to the v3 བལྟ་, has to be interpreted as a passive clause (see Lesson 14). The action in the second part of the passage concerns Mi-la Ras-pa's uncle and aunt. As the clause is passive (v3 བལྟ་), ཨ་ཁུ་དང་ཨ་ནེའི་ཞལ་འཛུམ་ is its only argument – the subject. The egophoric བྱུང་ indicates that it was the speaker, i.e. Mi-la Ras-pa (and maybe also his mother and sister), who was watching whether the smile of his uncle and aunt was friendly. The phrase "by us" has to be added to the translation due to the auxiliary བྱུང་.

> རང་ལས་ཞན་པ་ཀུན་གྱིས་རྒྱབ་ནས་འཛུ་བ་བྱུང་། (ML D 11v)
> "All [our] own (རང་) ordinary workers were laughing behind [our] backs."
>
> མྱང་ཚ་དཀར་རྒྱན་མ་སྨད་ནོར་སློངས་བྱེད་པ་ཡིན་པ་འདུག་ཟེར་བ་བྱུང་། (ML D 11v)
> "'[This] is the source of wealth [for] Myaṅ-cha Dkar-rgyan, mother and [her] children.' [He] said."
>
> ངེད་མིང་སྲིང་གཉིས་ཀྱིས་ནི་ར་མདའ་ངུ་བ་མིན་པ་མ་བྱུང་། (ML D 12v)
> "We two, the brother and the sister, could do nothing but cry for help."

In these passages the speaker (Mi-la Ras-pa) is present in the action; in the first example as an object of laughing, in the second one as receiver of a message, and in the third one as an agent. The v1-stems འཛུ་ and ངུ་ indicate that the action was ongoing.

འོང་ – *Future tense*

འོང་ (also ཡོང་) is used to express future. It occurs in various constructions, like the following:

- V + འོང་/ཡོང་
- V + པ་/བ་ + འོང་/ཡོང་
- V + པར་/བར་ + འོང་/ཡོང་

The main verb (V) may be represented by a v1-, v2-, or (seldomly) v3-stem. The distinctive features of the single constructions have not been determined yet.

> ཅི་ཙམ་སྲིད་པ་དང་བཅས་པའི་ཆོས་ནི་མཐར་འཇིག་པར་འོང་ངོ་། (MB D 140r6)
> "Things that are possessed of existence so much will eventually perish."
>
> ཨ་ཁུ་དང་ཨ་ནེ་གཉིས་ཀྱིས་ཀྱང་ཅི་དྲག་རེ་སྟེར་ཡོང་། (ML D 13r)
> "Even the paternal uncle and aunt will give [you] what is expedient."

སོང་ – *Perfective/sensory evidence*

The construction 'v2 + སོང་' expresses a completed action that was witnessed by the speaker who was not personally involved in the event. It is another evidential construction.

> ཉུང་ན་མཐུ་ཐོང་ཟེར་ཞིང་ཐོན་སོང་། དེའི་ཕྱི་བཞིན་ཁོང་ལ་དགར་མི་རྣམས་ཀྱང་ཐོན་སོང་། (ML D 13r)
> "'If [you] are few, cast spells!' Saying this, [paternal uncle and aunt] went out (ཐོན་སོང་). People who were loyal towards them followed them out."

In the quotation, Mi-la Ras-pa describes a meeting of family and friends, from which his paternal uncle and aunt withdrew. Mi-la Ras-pa also participated in the meeting and saw when they left the meeting. The use of the auxiliary སོང་ informs the reader that Mi-la Ras-pa relates something that he himself witnessed: he has first-hand knowledge of the event.

ཟིན་ – *Perfective aspect*

The construction 'v2 + (པར་/བར་) + ཟིན་' emphasises the accomplishment of an action:

> དེའི་ཚེ་སྟག་མོས་རྒྱལ་བུའི་ཤ་ནི་ཟད་པར་ཟོས་ཟིན་གྱིས། (MB D 140r1–2)
> "Because at that time the tigress has completely eaten the flesh of the prince['s body], [. . .]."

The same function may be fulfilled by the verb ཚར་, v2-stem of འཚར་ "to be finished, completed".

Concessive auxiliary རུང་

The main verb རུང་ has the meaning "to be suitable, right", yet when attached directly to another verb it functions as an auxiliary with concessive meaning. The complex constructions with རུང་ are not proper analytical verb constructions because they do not express any additional grammatical meaning but only add concessive meaning to a clause.

> ཨ་ཁུ་དང་ཨ་ནེ་གཉིས་ཅི་ལ་མི་འཆམ་རུང་ལྟོ་ལ་འཆམ་པ་དང་། (ML D 12r)
> "Although the paternal uncle and aunt never agreed on anything, [they] did agree on food."

> ཨ་ཁུ་དང་ཨ་ནེས་ངེད་རང་གི་ནོར་ཆ་གཅིག་སླད་རུང་སྟེར་དགོས་མེད། (ML D 13r)
> "Even though the paternal uncle and aunt [would] return [us] a single possession, [they] do not need to give [it] back."

Purposive particle རྒྱུ་

རྒྱུ་ is another auxiliary particle that stands between the main verb and the auxiliary. Depending on the auxiliary, the meaning of རྒྱུ་ may vary but its constant element is that it expresses an action that shall be done. In this respect, the constructions often resemble gerundive or future passive participle of Sanskrit.

> ངེད་མ་བུ་གསུམ་ལ་ནོར་དབང་རྒྱུ་མ་བྱུང་བ་ (ML D 11r)
> "no goods for us three (mother and children) to be controlled"

> གཞན་ཟ་རྒྱུ་མེད་ནས། (GLR 23r5)
> "There was nothing else to eat."

> ནོར་ཁྱེད་རང་ལ་འདུག་པ། ཡུལ་མི་ཁྱིམ་མཚེས་ལ་ཤ་ཆང་ཕངས་མེད་གཞིག་ནས་སྟོན་མོ་བཤམ་རྒྱུ་འདུག་པ། ཁྱེད་ཀྱི་ནོར་རམ་དེ་ངེད་ལ་མེད། (ML D 12v–13r)
> "The possessions that you have, the means [you] have for preparing a feast for [your] countrymen [and] neighbours after having wasted abundant meat and beer, is it your possession? We do not have it."

སྟོན་མོ་བཤམ་རྒྱུ་འདུག་པ་ can be literally translated as "what is there for a feast to be prepared". The clause is nominalised and therefore the literal meaning is lost in the translation.

Sometimes the auxiliary after རྒྱུ་ is left out:

> དེས་ན་ངའི་བུ་འདི་ཡང་ད་ལྟར་ཆུང་འདུག་པས། ཨ་ཁུ་དང་ཨ་ནེས་གཙོ་བྱས་པའི་གཉེན་བཤེས་ཀུན་ལ་བཅོལ་གཏམས་བྱ་རྒྱུ་ལ། (ML D 10v)
> "For that reason (དེས་ན་), because this son of mine is still young, [he] shall be entrusted to all the friends and relatives led by the paternal uncle and aunt."

Reading

"སྟག་མོ་འདི་ནི་ ◦ ཤིན་ཏུ་སྡུག་བསྔལ་གྱིས་གཟིར་ཏེ། ཉམ་ཆུང་ལ་རིད་པས་ཤི་ལ་ཐུག་པ་འདི་ལྟ་བུ་ ◦ བུ་བྱུང་མ་ཐག་པ་ཡང་ ◦ ཟ་རུ་འདོད་དོ་ཞེས་" སྨྲས་པ་དང་། ཕུ་བོ་གཉིས་ཀྱིས་ "ཁྱོད་ཟེར་བ་ ◦ བདེན་ནོ་ཞེས་" ཟེར་རོ། །ནུ་བོས་ཡང་ ◦ ཕུ་བོ་ (139r6) གཉིས་ལ་ ◦ སྨྲས་པ། "སྟག་མོ་འདིས་ ◦ ཟས་སུ་ ◦ ཅི་ ◦ ཟ་ཞེས་" དྲིས་ན། ཕུ་བོ་གཉིས་ཀྱིས་ "བསད་མ་ཐག་པའི་ཤ་རློན་པ་དང་། ཁྲག་དྲོན་མོས་ ◦ དེའི་ཡིད་ ◦ ཚིམ་པར་ ◦ འགྱུར་རོ་ཞེས་" སྨྲས་སོ། །ཡང་ ◦ སྨྲས་པ། "གང་ ◦ སུ་ཡང་ ◦ རུང་

སྟེ་ ◦ དེ་ལྟ་བུའི་དངོས་པོས་ ◦ འདིའི་སྲོག་ ◦ བསྐྱབས་ཏེ། (139r7) མི་ཉམས་པར་ ◦ བྱེད་ནུས་པ་ ◦ ཡོད་དམ།" ཕུ་བོ་གཉིས་ཀྱིས་ ◦ སྨྲས་པ། "དེ་ནི་ ◦ ཤིན་ཏུ་ཡང་དཀའ་བས་ ◦ མེད་དོ།" །དེ་ནས་ ◦ རྒྱལ་བུ་ཐ་ཆུངས་དེས་ ◦ ཡིད་ལ་ ◦ འདི་ ◦ སྙམ་དུ་ ◦ བསམས་སོ། "།བདག་ ◦ ཡུན་རིང་པོ་ནས་ ◦ འཁོར་བ་ན་ ◦ འཁོར་ཞིང་། ལུས་སྲོག་གྲངས་མེད་པ་ཞིག་ ◦ ཆུད་གསན་ཏེ། (139v1) བར་འགའ་ནི་ ◦ འདོད་ཆགས་ཀྱི་ཕྱིར། བར་འགའ་ནི་ ◦ ཞེ་སྡང་གི་ཕྱིར། བར་འགའ་ནི་གཏི་མུག་གི་ཕྱིར། ལུས་ ◦ བཏང་ཡང་ ◦ ཆོས་ཀྱི་ཕྱིར་ ◦ བསོད་ནམས་ཀྱི་ཞིང་དང་། ལན་འགའ་ཡང་ ◦ མ་ཕྲད་པའི་ལུས་འདི་ ◦ ཅི་ ◦ རུང་" སྙམ་བསམས་ནས། གསུམ་ཀར་ ◦ འགྲོགས་ཏེ་ ◦ སོང་བ་ལས། རིང་པོར་མ་(139v2) ཕྱིན་པར་ ◦ ཕུ་བོ་གཉིས་ལ་ ◦ འདི་སྐད་ཅེས་ ◦ སྨྲས་སོ། "།མཆེད་གཉིས་ ◦ སྔར་གཤེགས་ཤིག་དང་། བདག་ ◦ དོན་ཞིག་ ◦ གཉེར་ཏེ། སླད་བཞིན་པར་ ◦ མཆིའོ་ཞེས་" སྨྲས་སོ། །ལམ་དེ་ཉིད་དུ་ ◦ ཞུགས་ཏེ་ ◦ སྟག་མོའི་ཚང་གང་ན་ཡོད་པར་ ◦ མྱུར་དུ་སོང་ནས། སྟག་མོའི་དྲུང་དུ་ ◦ ཉལ་བ་དང་། སྟག་ (139v3) མོ་ ◦ ཁ་ཐམས་པས་ ◦ ཟ་མ་ནུས་སོ།།

Notes

1 Recall that a Classical Tibetan verb could have only up to four different stems and many verbs had only one or two stems.

2 Analytical constructions of Classical Tibetan still await a thorough linguistic examination. For the most comprehensive overview to date, see Schwieger (2006: 97ff.).

3 An overview of all discussed analytical verb constructions can be found in Appendix F.

4 Apart from the meanings discussed later, འགྱུར་ frequently renders passive voice in the literature translated from Sanskrit (Hahn 1996: 166).

5 Sometimes the elative particle stands between the main verb and ཡོད་. This might have been the original construction (see Lesson 12 for resultative meaning of ནས་) from which 'v2 + ཡོད་' evolved.

6 The construction !བདེར་འཇུག་ is not allowed because བདེ་ is a non-controllable verb; one cannot (effectively) order anybody to be happy.

7 ཆུ་སྟོར་, lit. "that what gives substance (སྟོར་) to water".

Lesson 17

- Clause chaining
- Determiners
- Reduplication
- Numerals

Clause chaining

In Classical Tibetan clause chaining is a type of construction in which two or more clauses (usually with some shared arguments) are located next to each other without any converbal particle; cf.:

> བཙུན་མོས་ནི་མགོ་ནས་བཟུང་། རྒྱལ་པོས་ནི་ལག་པ་ནས་བཟུང་སྟེ། ཆོ་ངེས་བཏབ་ནས་ངུས་པ་དང་། (MB D 140r2)
> "The queen seized [his] head [and] the king seized [his] hand; [they] lamented and cried."

The passage describes a situation in which parents see the corpse of their son and react by seizing the different parts of the body. The two actions form part of one event. The gerundial particle སྟེ་ has both verbs བཟུང་ in its scope. The literal translation of the passage would be "The queen, having seized [his] head, [and] the king, having seized [his] hand, lamented and cried."

> འབྲོང་རུ་དྲོན་མོ་ཞིག་ཏུ་བཙུག གོས་ཐུང་གི་ངར་པས་དྲིལ་བཞག་པས། (GLR 25r6)
> "[She] put [the clot] into a warm horn of a wild yak, wrapped up in (lit. with) a leg of trousers, [and] laid down."

This complex clause consists of the following simple clauses:

> འབྲོང་རུ་དྲོན་མོ་ཞིག་ཏུ་བཙུག "[She] put [the clot] into a warm horn of a wild yak,"

DOI: 10.4324/9781003224198-20

གོས་སྣུང་གི་དར་པས་དྲིལ་ "wrapped up in a leg of trousers,"

བཞག་པས་ "laid down."

The verbs བསྒྲུག་ and དྲིལ་ are followed neither by a converbal particle nor by any particle that is allowed to end a clause, but they remain in the scope of the converbal particle པས་ that follows the last verb. All three verbs have the same subject and direct object and describe a single event. The latter feature is typical of chained clauses.

Determiners

When discussing the structure of a noun phrase in Classical Tibetan (see Lesson 1), it was stated that the word order within a noun phrase is fixed and so-called determiners are the last elements of a noun phrase. Determiners express the reference of a noun which they modify. They may indicate whether the noun is to be understood as definite or indefinite, whether it is closer or more distant to the speaker, or what its quantity is. Until now two determiners have been discussed:

- Demonstrative དེ་ (Lesson 1)
- Indefinite /ཅིག་/ (Lesson 1)[1]

There are however other determiners that may also occur after adjectives and numerals in a noun phrase:

- ཙམ་ "about (with reference to quantity)"
  སྲོག་ཆགས་སྟོང་ཙམ་ (GLR 22v2) "about one thousand living beings"
  ལོ་བདུན་ཙམ་ (ML D 10r) "about seven years"
- རེ་ "each, every"
  སེམས་ཅན་ཁྲི་རེ་ (GLR 22v2) "each ten thousand sentient beings"
  ནུབ་རེ་ (GLR 22v2) "every night"
- ཉིད་ "the very same"[2]
  རྒྱལ་ཁམས་འདི་ཉིད་ (GLR 22v2) "this very realm"
  ལམ་དེ་ཉིད་ (MB D 139v2) "the very same road"
- རང་ "only, mere"
  ངེད་མ་སྨད་ལ་སྡུག་པོ་རང་བཏང་བས། (ML D 11r)
  "Because [they] caused only misery to us, mother and children, [. . .]"

- སྙེད་ "about (with reference to quantity)"

  རྒྱལ་ཕྲན་ལྔ་སྟོང་སྙེད་ (MB D 139r2) "about five thousand vassals"
- (རྣམ་པ་) སྣ་ཚོགས་ "various (kinds)"

  ཚིག་སྙན་པ་རྣམ་པ་སྣ་ཚོགས་ (MB D 140r5) lit. "various kinds of nice words"
- ཐམས་ཅད་ "all"

  འཁོར་མང་པོ་ཐམས་ཅད་ (MB D 140v6) "all the numerous attendants"
  རྩོད་པ་དེ་དག་ཐམས་ཅད་ (MB D 272r7) "all the conflicts"
- འབའ་ཞིག་ "mere, sole; only"

  འདི་འབའ་ཞིག་ (MB D 138v7) "only now"
  རུས་པ་དང་ཁྲག་འབའ་ཞིག་ (MB D 140r2) "mere bones and blood"

Reduplication

Classical Tibetan knows two types of reduplication: lexical and grammatical reduplication.

Lexical reduplication

Lexical reduplication consists of doubling one word or a syllable in order to coin a new word.[3] The new word usually expresses intensification of a quality possessed by the base word; cf.:

རྩོག་རྩོག་པ་ (MB D 139v4) "completely dirty"	< རྩོག་པ་ (also བཙོག་པ་) "unclean, dirty"
ཡང་ཡང་ (ML D 11v) "again and again"	< ཡང་ "again"
ནར་ནར་ (ML D 12v) "continuously"	< ནར་མ་ "continuous"

Apart from the most basic pattern of reduplication in which one or more syllables are repeated in the same form, one also encounters various changes in vowels or insertion of additional syllables between the reduplicated syllables:

ཁྲག་ཁྲུག་ "complicate, confused"	< འཁྲུག་ "to be disturbed"
ཐ(ར)་རེ་ཐོ(ར)་རེ་ "scatteredly"	< འཐོར་ "to be scattered"
ལྷབ་ལྷུབ་ "wide, flowing"	< ལྷུབ་ "width"

Grammatical reduplication

Grammatical reduplication does not produce new words but has either intensifying/distributive (with nouns) or iterative/progressive meaning (with verbs).

> དུམ་བུ་དུམ་བུར་འཆད་ (MB D 140v1) "to be cut to bits and pieces"

དུམ་བུ་དུམ་བུ་ is a reduplicated form of དུམ་བུ་ "piece" and connotes multitude of pieces.

> ངུ་ཞིང་འགྱེལ་ནས་ཁྲེ་ལོག་ལོག་བྱེད་ཅིང་འདུག (ML D 12v)
> "Weeping [she] fell down [and] was rolling back and forth [on the ground]."

As in the last example, reduplication of verbs usually indicates that the action continued for a while. This type of reduplication commonly occurs with the converbal particle ལས་:

> སྲས་གསུམ་པོ་ཚལ་གྱི་ནང་དུ་དོང་དོང་བ་ལས། (MB D 139r4)
> "The three sons continued on into a forest." Lit. "While the three sons were going and going into a forest [. . .]."

> ཞིང་ཐོག་ཏུ་སོང་སོང་བ་ལས། (MB D 270v3)
> "[The Brahmin] was going back and forth on the field."

Numerals

This section presents simple numerals as well as the basic rules for forming complex numerals. Their knowledge is relevant not only for proper understanding of texts but also for identifying pages of the traditional Tibetan དཔེ་ཆ་ print format.

Numerals always follow the word to which they apply (see Lesson 1). If there is an adjective in the noun phrase, numerals stand after the adjective.

> མ་སྨད་གསུམ་པོ་ (MB D 138v7) "mother and [her] children, the three"
> གདུང་རབས་ཉི་ཤུ་རྩ་བདུན་ (GLR 24r4) "twenty-seven generations"

Beside their attributive function, numerals may also be used as nouns:

> གསུམ་ཀར་འགྲོགས་ཏེ་སོང་བ་ལས་ (MB D 139v1) "The three went on together." Lit. "Accompanied as the three, [they] went."

Cardinal numerals

Classical Tibetan has a decimal numeral system; the basic numerals are presented in Table 17.1.

Table 17.1 Basic numerals

Number	*CT number*	*Numeral*	*Variant*	*Abbreviation*
1	༡	གཅིག་	ཅིག་	
2	༢	གཉིས་	ཉི་	ཉེར་
3	༣	གསུམ་	སུམ་	སོ་
4	༤	བཞི་		ཞེ་
5	༥	ལྔ་		ང་
6	༦	དྲུག་		རེ་
7	༧	བདུན་		དོན་
8	༨	བརྒྱད་		གྱ་
9	༩	དགུ་		གོ་
10	༡༠	བཅུ་	ཅུ་/བཅོ་/ཤུ་	

Variant forms are used in some numerals of higher order and will be discussed together with these. They may also be used in a few idioms like ཅིག་ཤད་ "single *śad*", ཅིག་རྐྱང་ "separate, single", or ཉིས་ཤད་ "double *śad*" (see chapter Tibetan Script). Abbreviations are applied to form higher numerals (see later).

Tibetan also has a special name for the numeral zero: ཀླད་ཀོར་. The numerals གསུམ་ and དགུ་ are sometimes used with the meaning "some" or "all":

> གཏམ་ཚིག་གསུམ་པ་ཞིག་ (ML D 12r) "a few words"

The numerals 11–19 are formed by postposing numerals 1–9 to བཅུ་ "ten":

Table 17.2 Numerals 11–19

11	༡༡	བཅུ་གཅིག་	16	༡༦	བཅུ་དྲུག་
12	༡༢	བཅུ་གཉིས་	17	༡༧	བཅུ་བདུན་
13	༡༣	བཅུ་གསུམ་	18	༡༨	བཅོ་བརྒྱད་
14	༡༤	བཅུ་བཞི་	19	༡༩	བཅུ་དགུ་
15	༡༥	བཅོ་ལྔ་			

Numerals "fifteen" བཅོ་ལྔ་ and "eighteen" བཅོ་བརྒྱད་ use the variant བཅོ་ of the numeral བཅུ་. This results from the assimilation of *u* in བཅུ་ to the vowel *a* of the following syllable.

The multiples of 10 are formed by postposing བཅུ་ "ten" to numerals 1–9:

Table 17.3 Multiples of 10

20	༢༠	ཉི་ཤུ་	60	༦༠	དྲུག་ཅུ་
30	༣༠	སུམ་ཅུ་	70	༧༠	བདུན་ཅུ་
40	༤༠	བཞི་བཅུ་	80	༨༠	བརྒྱད་ཅུ་
50	༥༠	ལྔ་བཅུ་	90	༩༠	དགུ་བཅུ་

Here the variants of the numerals 2, 3, and 10 (see Table 17.1) are used according to the following rules:

- After a final vowel of the first syllable the form བཅུ་ is used
- After a final consonant of the first syllable the variant ཅུ་ is used
- After ཉི་, the variant ཤུ་ is used[4]

The multiples of 10, including the numeral 100, frequently have the determiner ཐམ་པ་ "complete, full" added: སུམ་ཅུ་ཐམ་པ་ can be translated as "exactly (ཐམ་པ་) thirty".

The numerals 21–99 (apart from the multiples of 10) are formed according to one of the following patterns:

1. Multiple of 10 + numerical particle རྩ་ + numeral 1–9
2. Multiple of 10 + abbreviation + numeral 1–9
3. Abbreviation + numeral 1–9

The numerical particle རྩ་ is used exclusively to form higher numerals. Table 17.4 contains several examples of numerals 21–99:

Table 17.4 Numerals 21–99

		1	*2*	*3*
21	༢༡	ཉི་ཤུ་རྩ་གཅིག་		ཉེར་གཅིག་
23	༢༣	ཉི་ཤུ་རྩ་གསུམ་		ཉེར་གསུམ་
35	༣༥	སུམ་ཅུ་རྩ་ལྔ་	སུམ་ཅུ་སོ་ལྔ་	སོ་ལྔ་
47	༤༧	བཞི་བཅུ་རྩ་བདུན་	བཞི་བཅུ་ཞེ་བདུན་	ཞེ་བདུན་
61	༦༡	དྲུག་ཅུ་རྩ་གཅིག་	དྲུག་ཅུ་རེ་གཅིག་	རེ་གཅིག་
89	༨༩	བརྒྱད་ཅུ་རྩ་དགུ་	བརྒྱད་ཅུ་གྱ་དགུ་	གྱ་དགུ་

Pattern 1 is most commonly applied in Classical Tibetan texts. Pattern 2 is primarily used in spoken language but may also be encountered in texts. This pattern can be used for the numerals 31–99; the numerals 21–29 are always formed with the numerical particle རྩ་. Pattern 3 is preponderantly used in pagination of traditional Tibetan དཔེ་ཆ་ prints.

Classical Tibetan has special terms for powers of ten:

Table 17.5 Powers of 10

100	བརྒྱ་	100,000	འབུམ་
1,000	སྟོང་	1,000,000	ས་ཡ་
10,000	ཁྲི་	10,000,000	བྱེ་བ་

Higher numerals can be found in various lexicographical sources, like the earliest Tibetan-Sanskrit dictionary *Mahāvyutpatti* (Mvy: chapter CCXLIX, entries 7947–8006).

Multiples of powers of ten are formed from numerals 1–9 with a postposed power of ten:

200	ཉི་བརྒྱ་
3,000	སུམ་སྟོང་
80,000	བརྒྱད་ཁྲི་

In these numerals the variant forms of གཅིག་, གཉིས་ and གསུམ་, i.e. ཅིག་, ཉི་ and སུམ་, are used. In exceptional cases the order of numerals might be reversed, cf.:

འཇིག་རྟེན་སྟོང་གསུམ་ (*apud* Hahn 1996: 196) "the three thousand worlds"

As an example, a few higher numerals are provided in Table 17.6:[5]

Table 17.6 Higher numerals

120	༡༢༠	བརྒྱ་ཉི་ཤུ་	བརྒྱ་དང་ཉི་ཤུ་
187	༡༨༧		བརྒྱ་དང་བརྒྱད་ཅུ་རྩ་བདུན་
654	༦༥༤		དྲུག་བརྒྱ་དང་ལྔ་བཅུ་རྩ་བཞི་
84000	༨༤༠༠༠	བརྒྱད་ཁྲི་བཞི་སྟོང་	

Numerals over 100 sometimes make use of the comitative particle དང་ (cf. numerals in the rightmost column of Table 17.6).

Ordinal numerals

Ordinal numerals are regularly formed by adding the nominal particle པ་ to the corresponding cardinal numeral (see Lesson 7). The only exception is the numeral "first" which has an irregular form དང་པོ་:[6]

Table 17.7 Ordinal numerals

གཅིག་ "one"	དང་པོ་ "first"
དྲུག་ "six"	དྲུག་པ་ "sixth"
བཅུ་གཉིས་ "twelve"	བཅུ་གཉིས་པ་ "twelfth"

Collective numerals

Collective numerals are formed by means of the nominal particles ཀ་/ཁ་/ག་ or པོ་. The particles, added to a cardinal numeral, denote a particular group of objects or persons as a collective:

མ་སྨད་གསུམ་པོ་ (MB D 138v7) "mother and [her] children, the three"
བདུད་བཞི་པོ་ (SBM; *apud* Schwieger 2006: 58) "the four demons"

The nominal particle ཀ་/ཁ་/ག་ may have an additional deictic meaning:

ལུས་ངག་ཡིད་གསུམ་ཀ་ (SBM; *apud* Schwieger 2006: 58) "body, speech, and mind, these three"
རྒྱུད་སྡེ་བཞི་ཀ་ (SBM; *apud* Schwieger 2006: 58) "these/the four classes of Tantra"

Distributive numerals

Distributive numerals are words that answer the questions "how many times each?" or "how many at a time?" In Classical Tibetan they are formed by reduplicating the corresponding cardinal numeral:

གཉིས་གཉིས་ (SBM; *apud* Schwieger 2006: 62) "doubly"
ལྔ་བཅུ་ལྔ་བཅུ་ (SBRG 4v; *apud* Schwieger 2006: 62) "fifty each"

When forming a distributive numeral from a complex numeral only tens and units are reduplicated:

ཉིས་བརྒྱ་ལྔ་བཅུ་ལྔ་བཅུ་ (SBRG 7v; *apud* Schwieger 2006: 62) "two hundred fifty each"

Multiplicative numerals

Multiplicative numerals are formed with the noun ལན་ "time, times" and a postposed cardinal numeral:

ལན་གཉིས་ (SBM; *apud* Schwieger 2006: 63) "twice, two times"
ལན་བདུན་ (SBM; *apud* Schwieger 2006: 62) "seven times"

Numeral adverbs

As numerals can be used as adjectives (attributively) or as nouns, it is possible in Classical Tibetan to derive various adverbs from them. This happens by adding the adverb-forming case particle terminative to a base numeral.

Cardinal numeral + terminative

གཅིག་ཏུ་ "firstly; on the one hand" གཉིས་སུ་ "secondly; on the other hand"

Here an additional case particle, the locative, is sometimes added; གཅིག་ཏུ་ན་ or གཉིས་སུ་ན་ are synonyms of གཅིག་ཏུ་ and གཉིས་སུ་.

Ordinal numeral + terminative

དང་པོར་ "in the first place; firstly" གཉིས་པར་ "secondly"

Collective particle ཕྲག་

The collective particle ཕྲག་ has two main functions: collective and multiplicative. In the first function it is used to form collective numerals:

རིག་གནས་བཅུ་ཕྲག་ (SBM; *apud* Schwieger 2006: 59) "the ten sciences"
བརྒྱ་ཕྲག་ "a hundred", i.e. a set that consists of one hundred (བརྒྱ་) elements
བདུན་ཕྲག་ "a group of seven [days]", i.e. a week

If the particle stands between two numerals, then it has the multiplicative function (NUM_1 is a multiplier, NUM_2 is a multiplicand):

NUM_1 ཕྲག་ NUM_2

སྟོང་ཕྲག་ཉི་ཤུ་ (SBRG; *apud* Schwieger 2006: 59) "1,000 × 20"
འབུམ་ཕྲག་བཅུ་གཉིས་ (SBRG; *apud* Schwieger 2006: 59) "100,000 × 12"

What happens here is that the first numeral is turned into a collective numeral, to which an attribute is then added. The first example could be reanalysed literally as "twenty thousands"; སྟོང་ཕྲག་ = head of the noun phrase, ཉི་ཤུ་ = attribute.

ཕྱེད་ *"half"*

ཕྱེད་ "half" is an adjective used to express half of a unit. It is used in a special construction with a postposed comitative particle and a numeral:

> ཕྱེད་དང་གསུམ་ "two and a half", lit. "with a half [of the unit it yields] three"

The corresponding noun ཕྱེད་ཀ་ "a half" forms numerals according to the following pattern:

> དྲུག་དང་ཕྱེད་ཀ་ (*apud* Schwieger 2006: 57) "six and (དང་) a half"

Fractions

Unit fractions are formed with the word ཆ་ "part":

> བརྒྱ་ཆ་ or བརྒྱའི་ཆ་ "one hundredth"

Multiples of unit fractions are formed by adding a numeral after ཆ་:

> ལྔ་ཆ་བཞི་ "four fifths"
> བརྒྱ་ཆ་གསུམ་ "three hundredths"

Dates

Classical Tibetan uses cardinal numerals for calendar days:

> ས་རྟ་ལུག་ཟླའི་ཚེས་བརྒྱད་ལ་ (VOHD 13 1599; *apud* Schwieger 2006: 61) "on the eighth day of the sheep-month [of the] Earth-Horse [year]"
> ས་གའི་ཟླ་བའི་ཚེས་བཅོ་ལྔའི་ནུབ་མོ་ (TST 42; *apud* Schwieger 2006: 61) "the evening of the fifteenth day of the Sa-ga-month"

Traditionally a few different calendars were in use in Tibet. Depending on the calendar used the format of the date may vary. For instance, in the first example the name of the month is ལུག་ཟླ་ "sheep month" but in the second it is ས་གའི་ཟླ་བ་,

lit. "the month of the Sa-ga [constellation]" (ཟླ་བ་ "month"). These two names belong to different calendar systems. In addition, months can also be counted, like ཟླ་བ་དང་པོ་ "the first month".

Likewise two calendars for counting years existed: a duodenary and a sexagenary. The duodenary calendar is based on a twelve-year cycle in which each year is referred to by the name of an animal:

Table 17.8 Twelve-year cycle

1	བྱི་	Rat	5	འབྲུག་	Dragon	9	སྤྲེ་	Monkey
2	གླང་	Ox	6	སྦྲུལ་	Snake	10	བྱ་	Hen
3	སྟག་	Tiger	7	རྟ་	Horse	11	ཁྱི་	Dog
4	ཡོས་	Hare	8	ལུག་	Sheep	12	ཕག་	Swine

In the sexagenary calendar a cycle consists of sixty years, i.e. to each animal year one of the five elements (ཤིང་ "wood", མེ་ "fire", ས་ "earth", ལྕགས་ "iron", ཆུ་ "water") is added.[7] In the first example the year is called ས་རྟ་ (for *ས་རྟ་ལོ་; ལོ་ "year") which identifies a year within the sexagenary cycle as "Earth-Horse [year]". Sometimes gender markers མོ་ "female" and ཕོ་ "male" are added in between: ཤིང་མོ་ཕག་ལོ་ "female (མོ་) Wood-Swine year". However, they do not change the identification of the year; a particular combination of an animal year and an element is ascribed one concrete gender marker so that the Wood-Swine year is always female.

Reading

དེའི་ཚེ་ ◦ རྒྱལ་བུས་ཤིང་གི་ཚལ་བ་རྣོན་པོས་ ◦ ལུས་ལ་ ◦ ཁྲག་ ◦ ཕྱུང་ནས། སྟག་མོ་ལ་ ◦ བལྡག་ཏུ་ བཅུག་པ་དང་། ཁ་ཡང་ ◦ ཕྱེ་ནས་ ◦ ལུས་ཀྱི་ཤ་ ◦ མ་ལུས་པར་ཟོས་སོ། །ཕྲུ་བོ་གཉིས་ཀྱིས་ ◦ བསྡད་ ནས། རིང་ཞིག་ཏུ་ ◦ མ་འོངས་པས། ཕྱིར་ ◦ རྗེས་བཞིན་དུ་ ◦ (139v4) ཚལ་དུ་[8] ◦ འོང་བ་ ལས། སྤུར་སྨྲས་པའི་ཚུལ་ ◦ བརྟགས་ན་ "གདོན་མི་ཟ་བར་ ◦ སྟག་མོ་ལྟོགས་པ་ ◦ སྔོན་དུ་སོང་ངོ་" སྙམ་བསམས་ནས་ ◦ དེར་ ◦ ཕྱིན་ཏེ་ ◦ བལྟས་ན། ནུ་བོ་ཐ་ཆུངས་ ◦ སྟག་གིས་ ◦ ཟོས་ཏེ། ཤ་དང་ ཁྲག་གིས་ ◦ ཀུན་ཏུ་ ◦ བསྒོས་ནས། རྩོག་རྩོག་པ་ལྟར་ ◦ འདུག་པར་ ◦ མཐོང་ངོ་། །ལུས་ ◦ ས་ ལ་ ◦ བརྡབས་ཏེ་ ◦ (139v5) བརྒྱལ་ལོ། །རིང་ཞིག་ ◦ ལོན་པ་དང་། དབུགས་ ◦ ཕྱིར་ ◦ ཕྱུང་ ནས། ཚོ་ངེས་ ◦ འདེབས་ཏེ་ ◦ ས་ལ་ ◦ འགྲེ་ཞིང་ ◦ ཁམས་པར་གྱུར་ཏོ། །དེའི་ཚེ་ན་ ◦ བཙུན་མོ་ཡུམ་ མནལ་བའི་རྨི་ལམ་ན། ཕུག་རོན་གསུམ་ཞིག་ ◦ ཀུན་ཏུ་ ◦ འཕུར་ཞིང་ ◦ རྩེ་བ་ལས། ནང་གི་ཆུང་དུ་

གཅིག་ ◦ ཁྲས་ ◦ ཁྲིར་བ་ ◦ སྙམ་རྨིས་མ་ (139v6) ཐག་ཏུ་ ◦ སད་ནས། སྐྲག་དངངས་ཏེ་ ◦ རྒྱལ་པོ་ལ་ ◦ བསྙད་དོ།། “བདག་གིས་ ◦ གཏམ་དུ་ ◦ ཐོས་ན། ཕུག་རོན་ནི་ ◦ བུ་ཕོའི་བླ་སྟེ། ཕུག་རོན་ནང་གི་ཆུང་ངུ་ ◦ ཁྲས་ ◦ ཁྲིར་བ་ན། བདག་གི་བུ་ནང་གི་སྡུག་པ་ལ་ ◦ བཀྲ་མི་ཤིས་ ◦ ངེས་ཀྱིས་ཞེས་” དེ་མ་ཐག་ཏུ་ ◦ ཀུན་ཏུ་ ◦ རྩོལ་བ་བཏང་བ་ལས། རིང་པོར་ ◦ མ་ལོན་ (139v7) པར་ ◦ རྒྱལ་བུ་གཉིས་ནི་ ◦ འོངས་ཀྱིས། “བུ་ནང་གི་སྡུག་པ་ ◦ ཅང་ ◦ མ་ཉེས་སམ་ ◦ ག་རེ་ཞེས་” དྲིས་ན། ཕུ་བོ་གཉིས་ ◦ སྐད་ཀྱིས་ ◦ བརྟངས་ཏེ། རིང་ཞིག་ཏུ་ ◦ དབུགས་ཀྱང་ ◦ མ་ཕྱིན་ ◦ སྨྲ་ཡང་མ་ནུས་ནས། དེའི་འོག་ཏུ་ ◦ དབུགས་ ◦ ཕྱིན་པ་དང་། “སྟག་གིས་ ◦ ཟོས་སོ་ཞེས་” སྨྲས་སོ། །ལྷ་མོ་དེས་ ◦ དེ་སྐད་ (140r1) སྨྲས་པ་ ◦ ཐོས་ནས་ ◦ ཁམས་ཏེ། ས་ལ་ ◦ འགྱེལ་ནས་ ◦ རིང་ཞིག་ ◦ ལོན་པ་དང་། དབུགས་ ◦ ཕྱིན་ཏེ། བུ་གཉིས་དང་བཙུན་མོ་དང་། ཕོ་བྲང་གི་སླས་སུ་ ◦ བཅས་ཏེ་ ◦ མྱུར་བར་ ◦ རྒྱལ་བུ་གང་དུ་ཚེ་འཕོས་པའི་གནས་སུ་ ◦ སོང་ངོ་། དེའི་ཚེ་ ◦ སྟག་མོས་ ◦ རྒྱལ་བུའི་ཤ་ནི་ ◦ ཟད་པར་ཟོས་ཟིན་ (140r2) གྱིས། རུས་པ་དང་ཁྲག་འབའ་ཞིག་གིས་ས་ལ་རྩོག་རྩོག་པ་ལྟར་འདུག་པ་ ◦ མཐོང་ངོ་། །བཙུན་མོས་ནི་ ◦ མགོ་ནས་ ◦ བཟུང་། །རྒྱལ་པོས་ནི་ ◦ ལག་པ་ནས་ ◦ བཟུང་སྟེ། ཚོ་ངེས་ ◦ བཏབ་ནས་ ◦ ངུས་པ་དང་། དེར་ཡང་ ◦ ཁམས་ནས་ ◦ རིང་ཞིག་ ◦ ལོན་ཏེ། ཕྱིར་ ◦ སངས་སོ། །རྒྱལ་བུ་ (140r3) སེམས་ཅན་ཆེན་པོ་དེ་ ◦ དེར་ ◦ ཚེ་འཕོས་ནས། དགའ་ལྡན་ལྷའི་གནས་སུ་ ◦ སྐྱེས་སོ། །དེ་ “ཅིའི་ཕྱིར་ ◦ བདག་ ◦ ཅི་ ◦ སྤྱད་པས་ ◦ འདིར་ ◦ སྐྱེས་” སྙམ་བསམས་ཏེ། ལྷའི་མིག་གིས་ ◦ རྒྱུད་ལྔ་ ◦ ཀུན་ཏུ་བལྟས་ན། བདག་ཚེ་འཕོས་པའི་རུས་བུ་ཚལ་ན་འདུག་པ་ལ་ ◦ ཕ་མས་ ◦ བསྐོར་ཏེ། ཤིན་ཏུ་ ◦ ཡིད་ལ་ ◦ (140r4) གཅགས་པས། མྱ་ངན་གྱི་ཟུག་རྔུས་ ◦ སྡུག་བསྔལ་ཞིང་ ◦ ཚོ་ངེས་ ◦ འདེབས་པ་ ◦ མཐོང་ནས། ལྷས་ ◦ བསམས་པ། “བདག་གི་ཕ་མ་ ◦ འདི་ལྟར་ ◦ མི་དགའ་བའི་རྐྱེན་གྱིས་ ◦ གལ་ཏེ་ན་ ◦ ལུས་དང་སྲོག་གི་བར་ཆད་དུ་ ◦ འགྱུར་གྱིས། དེ་ལ་ ◦ སྤྲོ་བ་ ◦ བསྐྱེད་ཅིང་ ◦ གཏམ་བྱར་ ◦ འགྲོའོ་” སྙམ་བསམས་ (140r5) ནས། ནམ་མཁའ་ལས་ ◦ བབས་ཏེ་ ◦ སྟེང་གི་ནམ་མཁའ་ལས་ ◦ ཚིག་སྙན་པ་རྣམ་པ་སྣ་ཚོགས་ཀྱིས་ ◦ ཕ་མ་གཉིས་ལ་ ◦ སྤྲོ་བ་ ◦ བསྐྱེད་དོ།།

Notes

1 In the later section Numerals, yet another determiner, ཐམ་པ་ “complete, full”, is discussed.

2 This ཉིད་ should be distinguished from ཉིད་ added to a word to form an abstract noun, e.g. སྟོང་པ་ཉིད་ (GLR 22r4) “voidness”.

3 A detailed discussion of lexical reduplication can be found in Uray (1954).

4 ཤུ་ is an assimilated form of ཙུ་ that originally followed the final -ས of *ཉིས་. Compare hereto the assimilation rules of the indefinite, quotative, or coordinative particles that change their first consonants to ཤ when attached to a syllable with the final -ས.

5 More examples can be found in Schwieger (2006: 55f.).
6 གཅིག་པ་ is a distinct word with the meaning “the same”.
7 One cycle of sixty years is called རབ་བྱུང་.
8 As constructions ‘to go to V’ require v1 or v3 (see Lesson 12), one would expect here v3 བཙལ་ or v1 འཚོལ་ instead of v4 ཚོལ་, but all editions agree on the latter form.

Lesson 18

- Impact of Sanskrit on Classical Tibetan
- Metrics

Impact of Sanskrit on Classical Tibetan

Early on in their history Tibetans started translating works from foreign languages. When their interests turned to Buddhism in the 8th century, intense translation work began with the aim of rendering Buddhist literature into Tibetan. Soon after, at the beginning of the 9th century, strict rules for translating were fixed and it was agreed that all works should be translated directly from Sanskrit. As the time passed the language of translations became more and more standardised. The translations have left a lasting trace in the Classical Tibetan language, to the extent that even works written by Tibetan Buddhist authors make use of vocabulary that was originally coined with the aim of rendering Buddhist technical terms from Sanskrit. Thus Classical Tibetan abounds in words that initially emerged in the translations. In addition, plenty of loanwords were borrowed into Tibetan. The following list serves only as an illustration, based on the texts from the readings of the textbook.

Loan translations

Loan translations (also called calques) are words borrowed from another language (from Sanskrit in the case of Classical Tibetan) by a literal translation that is supposed to mirror the etymology of the original. In Classical Tibetan loan translations from Sanskrit primarily concern nouns (including proper nouns) and verbs.

Nouns

ཀུན་དགའ་བོ་ "Ānanda" = Skt. Ānanda, the name of the favourite disciple of the Buddha

DOI: 10.4324/9781003224198-21

དགྲ་བཅོམ་པ་ "Arhat"; the translation was based on a traditional etymology of Skt. *arhant* which explained it as **ari-han*, lit. "enemy-killer"

བཅོམ་ལྡན་འདས་ "the Victorious One", translates Skt. *bhagavant*, an epithet of the Buddha

དེ་བཞིན་གཤེགས་པ་ "Tathāgata"; the Tibetan term is a literal translation of Skt. *tathāgata*, lit. "the one who came/went this way"

ཕྱིར་མི་ལྡོག་པ་ "one who does not come back again" = Skt. *anāgāmin*; the oldest Tibetan-Sanskrit Dictionary, the *Mahāvyutpatti*, glosses *anāgāmin* with ལན་ཅིག་ཕྱིར་མི་འོང་བ་ལ་འཇུག་པ་ (Mvy: 5130), which means that both variants, ལན་ཅིག་ཕྱིར་མི་འོང་བ་ and ལན་ཅིག་ཕྱིར་མི་འཇུག་པ་, are attested and acknowledged. Notice the difference between these standard translations and the earlier version ལན་ཅིག་ཕྱིར་མི་ལྡོག་པ་ attested in the story *How Sems-čan-čhen-po offered his body to a tigress* (see Reading in Lesson 14).

སངས་རྒྱས་ "Buddha"; translates Skt. *buddha*, lit. "awoken"

སེམས་ཅན་དམྱལ་བ་ "hell" = Skt. *naraka*; the compound སེམས་ཅན་ "sentient being" was added to the native Tibetan term དམྱལ་བ་ "hell" by analogy with Skt. *nara-* in *naraka* that was apparently associated with the unrelated *nara* "man"

Verbs

Many verbs coined after a Sanskrit model have an adverb attached to them. The most commonly applied adverbs are ཀུན་ཏུ་, ཀུན་ནས་, མངོན་པར་, མཆོག་ཏུ་, རྗེས་སུ་, ཉེ་བར་, རྣམ་པར་, ཡང་དག་པར་, ཡོངས་སུ་, རབ་ཏུ་, ལེགས་པར་, ཤིན་ཏུ་, and ལྷག་པར་. By means of the adverbs Tibetans attempted to render Sanskrit verbal prefixes.

རབ་ཏུ་འབྱུང་ "to become a monk" < Skt. *pra-*√vraj "to go forth, to proceed; to become a monk"

མངོན་པར་སངས་རྒྱས་ "to attain manifesting enlightenment" < Skt. *abhi-saṃ-*√budh "to attain complete enlightenment"

In these examples རབ་ཏུ་ and མངོན་པར་ render Sanskrit prefixes *pra-* and *abhi-saṃ-*, respectively.

Loanwords

Loanwords are borrowed from another language and adopted to the phonetics of the target language. As the following examples demonstrate, the orthography of loanwords does not always correspond to the standard orthography of Classical Tibetan. Compare hereto the selected variants in the following examples:

པདྨ་ ~ པད་མ་ "lotus"	< Skt. *padma* "id."
པཎྜིཏ་ ~ པཎྜི་ཏ་ "scholar"	< Skt. *paṇḍita* "scholar, learned man"
མཎྜལ་ ~ མཎ་ཌལ་ "circle"	< Skt. *maṇḍala* "disc, circle"
ཙནྡན་ ~ ཙན་དན་ "sandal-tree"	< Skt. *candana* "id."
ཤཱཀྱ་ "Śākya"	< Skt. (PN) Śākya
ཨུཏྤལ་ ~ ཨུཏ་པལ་ "blue lotos"	< Skt. *utpala* "id."[1]

As the examples of loan translations and loanwords demonstrate, Tibetans followed various strategies in adding new vocabulary to the stock of their language. There are even words that combine the two approaches:

འཛམ་བུ་གླིང་ (MB D 139r2) = Skt. Jambudvīpa, name of a continent in Indian cosmology

The syllables འཛམ་བུ་ were borrowed from Skt. *jambu*, whereas གླིང་ "island" translates Skt. *dvīpa* "id". In the following example ཤཱཀྱ་ is a loanword from Skt. Śākya, whereas ཐུབ་པ་ translates Skt. *muni*:

ཤཱཀྱ་ཐུབ་པ་ = Skt. Śākyamuni, lit. "the sage of the Śākyas".

For beginners this part of Classical Tibetan vocabulary should not pose any problems since the most popular terms are usually glossed in all dictionaries. However, as soon as one starts reading translational literature, additional reference works (such as Tibetan-Sanskrit dictionaries) have to be consulted. Unless the student knows Sanskrit, the words should be learnt by heart because most of them are not analysable in Classical Tibetan.

Metrics

Metrical passages are encountered not only in texts translated from Sanskrit but also in indigenous Tibetan literature. Therefore, it is necessary that students have at least some general knowledge of Tibetan metrics before they start reading texts.[2] This section provides the most basic rules for the understanding of poetic meters. The following explanations are an almost literal translation of Lesson 20 from Hahn's *Lehrbuch* (1996: 221ff.; adapted with a permission from the publisher) extended, whenever possible, by examples taken from the chapter Readings of the present textbook. If no bibliographical data is provided for an example, the example has been taken from Hahn.

Structure of stanzas

Four-line stanzas dominate in literature translated into Classical Tibetan from Sanskrit or Chinese.[3] Usually all four lines of a stanza have the same number of syllables. Each verse of such stanzas consists most commonly of seven syllables. A stanza composed of four seven-syllable lines forms the Tibetan blank verse (or Tibetan *śloka*) and can be encountered, for instance, in Buddhist teachings, legends, scientific works, proverbial literature, and epics. In this form the Sa-skya Paṇḍita's work ལེགས་པར་བཤད་པ་རིན་པོ་ཆེའི་གཏེར། was written; its first chapter has been supplied as Reading IV in the textbook. In translational literature, deviations from the standard of four-line stanzas by either adding or subtracting one verse are sporadic. Stanzas consisting of six verses might have come into being when the original was more extensive than usual.

This rigid structure of stanzas, encountered in literature translated from foreign languages, can be juxtaposed with much less standardised composition of stanzas in Tibetan native works. Apart from precise four-lines stanzas, Tibetan authors also make use of stanzas of irregular numbers of verses, within which the number of syllables may likewise fluctuate. One such example are metric passages in Reading II. There seems to have been no obligatory rules for the verse composition.

Composition of verses

Composition of verses is most transparent in works translated from foreign languages. Apart from rare exceptions, there tends to be an odd number of syllables in a line, fluctuating between seven and twenty-one syllables. Such verses are composed of three to ten metrical feet, each of which consists of two syllables, and an additional syllable at the end of the line. Within the metrical foot the first syllable is always strong and the second one weak (strong syllables are underlined in the following examples). Hence, one can also call these 'trochee'. They form the basic modules of the Tibetan verse. Tibetan authors also use verses with an even number of syllables. Most popular are those consisting of eight syllables; a number that can be achieved in two ways: (1) through an addition of a metrically weak syllable at the beginning of a line with uneven number of syllables:

བདག་བློ་ཡི་པད་མོ་ཁ་ཕྱེ་སྟེ། *bdag bló yi pád mo khá phye sté* |
"The lotus of my understanding opened." Lit. "[. . .] opened [its] mouth."

or (2) through the use of a three-syllable metrical foot like a dactyl (-́ - -):

> འཁོར་བ་ལ་ཕྱི་ཕྱག་འཚལ་བ་ཡིན།   *<u>ykhór</u> ba la <u>phyí</u> phyag <u>ychál</u> ba <u>yín</u>* |
> "He said goodbye to the cycle of existence."

The fragment of Sa-skya Paṇḍita's work ལེགས་པར་བཤད་པ་རིན་པོ་ཆེའི་གཏེར། (provided as Reading IV in the textbook) delivers examples of stanzas with differing numbers of syllables in a line: in the first stanza of the introduction the lines have eleven syllables, in the second stanza nine, and the main part of the work is built upon seven-syllable lines.

Composition of trochee

The popularity of trochee (-́ -) as a basic module of Tibetan metrics is understandable when one considers that a great part of Tibetan vocabulary consists of lexical words of the structure 'a root syllable + a particle'. Tibetan authors simply made the sequence of a meaningful root syllable followed by a 'meaningless' syllable (i.e. a particle) to the standard of their poetic meters. However, in two cases this basic sequence may be 'disturbed': (1) compounded words consisting of two or more root (i.e. meaningful) syllables; and (2) two or more particles may follow each other (e.g. a number particle plus a case particle). For this reason the sequences 'root syllable + root syllable' or 'particle + particle' are likewise allowed. Here the first syllables are considered strong by virtue of their position. In consequence, due to the dominance of trochee in Tibetan metrics the first of two root syllables and the first of two particles (metrically) overbalance the second one.

Trochees structure the contents of a verse in such a way that their two syllables form one lexical or grammatical unit. Stretching over one trochee is possible only within phrases or words that consist of more than two syllables, cf.:

> རིན་པོ་ཆེ་ལྔ་   *<u>rín</u> po <u>čhé</u> lṅa* "five jewels"

This disarranging only seldomly occurs in consecutive segments of a verse. The following passage contains allowed sequences, but is disruptive and misleading:

> རིན་པོ་ཆེ་ལྔ་རྣམས་ཀྱིས་   *<u>rín</u> po <u>čhé</u> lṅa <u>rnáms</u> kyis*

It suggests a division into two dactyls: *<u>rín</u> po čhe <u>lṅá</u> rnams kyis*.

The sequence 'particle + root syllable' is only exceptionally permitted in cases, in which a very close grammatical relationship to the preceding metrical foot can be detected; cf.:

ཤིང་རྟ་ལ་གནས་ *śiṅ rta lá gnas* "to stay in a chariot"

སྲིད་གསུམ་ལ་ཕན་ *srid gsum lá phan* "to be beneficial for the triple world"

In these examples *lá gnas* and *lá phan* form the sequence 'particle + root syllable'. The four-syllable framing apparently mitigates the harshness of such sequences.

In addition to particles, other words are likewise considered metrically weak. These have one feature in common: they are attached to the right end of a base word.

- Words of comparison: ལྟར་, འདྲ་, མཚུངས་, བཞིན་
- Possessive adjectives or verbs བཅས་, ལྡན་, འཁོར་, འབྲེལ་, and their negative equivalents: འབྲལ་ and མེད་
- Pronouns such as གང་, ཅི་, དེ་, འདི་, སུ་
- Postpositions such as ཕྱིར་; སླད་
- Determiners such as ཉིད་, ཙམ་
- Auxiliary and modal verbs such as དགོས་, འགྱུར་, འབྱུང་

The metrical weakness of these words is confirmed by the fact that when they stand on the thesis (i.e. the first syllable) they are only infrequently followed by a root syllable, just like particles in this position. On the other hand, they may follow each other or a particle. The metrical valence of the latter sequences is comparable to that of the sequence 'particle + particle'.

The variants of the concessive particle, the interrogative particle, and the final particle that follow a vowel (i.e. འང་, འམ་, and འོ་) are generally not considered independent syllables. They are usually attached directly to the preceding syllable without the ཚེག་:[4]

ཐོབ་པའང་གང་ན་ *thób payaṅ gáṅ na*

When necessary, the clause-final particles (i.e. the final and the interrogative particle) may be used as independent syllables as well. In these cases they are mostly divided from the preceding syllable by a ཚེག་:

རྟགས་ཀྱིས་བརྗོད་པ་འོ། *rtágs kyis brǰód pa yó |*

Means of composition

As the word order of Tibetan clauses is not completely arbitrary (the verb is always the last element of a clause), one needs additional means that would facilitate formation of trochees. To this end four major procedures are applied:

omission, contraction, lengthening, and insertion of expletives. All four means of composition are frequently used. Moreover, they may occur in various combinations.

Omission

The following particles can be omitted (in the transliteration the omitted words have been added in square brackets):

a Nominal particles (together with case particles if present)

ཡིན་ཕྱིར་ཆུ་བོ་ཐམས་ཅད་འབབ། (SSP 1d)
yín [paɣi] phyir čhú bo thám̃s čad ɣbáb |

b Case particles

འགྲོ་བའི་གཙོ་བོ་ཀུན་མཁྱེན་དེ་ལ་བདག་ཕྱག་འཚལ། (SSP Id)
ɣgró baɣi gcó bo kún mkhyen dé la bdág [gis] phyag ɣchál [lo] |

c Converbal particles

གཅིག་པུ་ཡིན་ཡང་ཀུན་ལས་རྒྱལ། (SSP 16b)
gčíg pu yín [na] yaṅ kún las rgyál |

d Final particle

བདག་ནི་ལས་ཀྱི་དབང་གིས་སྲིན་མོའི་རིགས་སུ་སྐྱེས།། (GLR 22v1)
bdág ni lás kyi dbáṅ gis srín moɣi rígs su skyés [so] ||

Moreover, sometimes even copula verbs may be omitted:

བཤད་པ་འདི་ནི་ལེགས་བཤད་རིན་ཆེན་གཏེར། (SSP IId)
bśád pa ɣdí ni légs bśad rín čhen gtér [yin] ||

Contraction

Contraction used in poetic meters is just another facet of compounding (see Lesson 13). Classical Tibetan makes extensive use of compounds and this fact facilitates the employment of compounded forms in versified passages. For example:

སྟོབས་ལྡན་ (SSP 5b) or སྟོབས་ལྡན་པ་ (SSP 25c) "strong" for སྟོབས་དང་ལྡན་པ་, lit. "possessed with strength"

Other well-known examples are:

ཐེག་ཆེན་ for ཐེག་པ་ཆེན་པོ་ Skt. *mahāyāna*
བྱང་སེམས་ for བྱང་ཆུབ་སེམས་དཔའ་ Skt. *bodhisattva*
མྱང་འདས་ for མྱ་ངན་ལས་འདས་པ་ Skt. *nirvāṇa*

Lengthening

All particles that have alternating forms after vowels may use the longer form in order to create an additional syllable:

a Genitive particle

ཆུ་ཡི་ (SSP 1c) instead of *ཆུའི་

b Ergative particle

རི་ཡིས་ (GLR 23v1) instead of *རིས་

c Terminative particle

དོན་འཁོར་མདའ་རུ་ (GLR 27v3) instead of *དོན་འཁོར་མདར་

d Diminutive particle

ཆར་འདོད་བྱི་འུ་ (SSP 13c) instead of *ཆར་འདོད་བྱིའུ་
སེ་འུ་ (SSP 22c) instead of *སེའུ་

Insertion of expletives[5]

The following particles can be inserted as expletives:

a Focus particle ནི་

འཕགས་རྒྱལ་གྱི་ནི་བྲམ་ཟེ་ (SSP 11c) instead of *འཕགས་རྒྱལ་གྱི་བྲམ་ཟེ་
ཡུང་བ་དང་ནི་ཚ་ལེ་ (SSP 15c) instead of *ཡུང་བ་དང་ཚ་ལེ་

b Number particle དག་

ཁྱོད་ཀྱི་སྐུ་དག་ instead of *ཁྱོད་ཀྱི་སྐུ་

c The locative particle ན་ (after ergative or terminative)

བྱས་པས་ན་ instead of བྱས་པས་
ཇི་ལྟར་ན་ instead of ཇི་ལྟར་

d The terminative particle སུ་ (after elative)

བྱས་ནས་སུ་ instead of བྱས་ནས་

e Concessive particle

རང་གི་ཡུལ་བས་ཀྱང་ (SSP 23a) instead of *རང་གི་ཡུལ་བས་

Caesura

The end of a line in a stanza may, but does not have to, coincide with a thematic or syntactic break. Apart from stanzas in which every line serves as a marking for the division of contents, one also finds stanzas where one multi-syllable word stretches across the end of a verse. In these cases, the fixed number of syllables in a verse overrides the division of a stanza according to the contents of its lines.

Reading

ཕ་མ་གཉིས་ཀྱིས་ ◦ ནམ་མཁའ་ལ་ ◦ བལྟས་ནས། “ལྷ་ ◦ ཁྱོད་སུ་ཞིག་ལགས་པ་ ◦ བདག་ལ་ ◦ སྨྲོས་ཤིག་ཅེས་” སྨྲས་པ་དང་། ལྷས་ ◦ སྨྲས་པ། (140r6) “བདག་ནི་ ◦ རྒྱལ་བུ་སེམས་ཅན་ཆེན་པོ་ཞེས་བྱ་བ་ ◦ ཡིན་ཏེ། བདག་གིས་ ◦ ལུས་ཀྱིས་ ◦ སྟག་མོ་ལྟོགས་པ་ ◦ བསྐྱོད་པས་ ◦ དགའ་ལྡན་[6]ལྷའི་གནས་སུ་ ◦ སྐྱེས་སོ། །རྒྱལ་པོ་ཆེན་པོ་ ◦ འདི་ལྟར་ ◦ མཁྱེན་པར་མཛོད་ཅིག །ཅི་ཙམ་སྲིད་པ་དང་བཅས་པའི་ཆོས་ནི་ ◦ མཐར་ ◦ འཇིག་པར་འོང་ངོ་། །སྐྱེ་བ་ (140r7) ◦ ཡོད་ན་ ◦ ངེས་པར་ ◦ འཇིག་གོ། །སྡིག་པ་ ◦ བྱས་ན་ ◦ སེམས་ཅན་དམྱལ་བར་ ◦ ལྟུང་གི། །དགེ་བ་ ◦ བྱས་ན་ ◦ མཐོ་རིས་སུ་ ◦ སྐྱེ་སྟེ། སྐྱེ་བ་དང་འཇིག་པ་ ◦ ཀུན་ལ་ ◦ སྲིད་ན། ཅིའི་སླད་དུ་ ◦ བདག་འབའ་ཞིག་གི་ཕྱིར་ ◦ མྱ་ངན་གྱི་རྒྱ་མཚོར་ལྟུང་བ་ ◦ མི་ཚོར་རམ། དགེ་བའི་ཕྱོགས་ལ་ ◦ བརྩོན་འགྲུས་མཛོད་ཅིག་ (140v1) ཅེས་” པ་དང་། དེའི་ཕ་མས་ ◦ སྨྲས་པ། “ཁྱོད་ནི་ ◦ སྙིང་རྗེ་ཆེན་པོས་ ◦ སྟག་མོ་བསྐྱོད་དེ་ ◦ ཐམས་ཅད་ལ་ ◦ སྙིང་བརྩེ་བ་ ◦ ཡིན་ན། བདག་ཅག་ ◦ བཏང་སྟེ། ཚེའི་དུས་ ◦ བྱས་པས། ངེད་ནི་ ◦ ཁྱོད་དྲན་པའི་ཕྱིར་ ◦ ཤ་ཡང་ ◦ དུམ་བུ་དུམ་བུར་ ◦ ཆད་པ་ཙམ་དུ་ ◦ སྡུག་བསྔལ་གྱིས་ ◦ གདུངས་ན། སྙིང་རྗེ་ཆེན་པོ་ (140v2) སྐྱོད་པ་ཁྱོད་ ◦ འདི་ལྟར་ ◦ བྱ་བའི་ ◦ རིགས་སམ།” དེ་ནས་ཡང་ ◦ ལྷ་དེས་ ◦ ཚིག་སྙན་པ་རྣམ་པ་སྣ་ཚོགས་ཀྱི་སྒོ་ནས་ ◦ བཞམས་ཏེ། སྤྲོ་བ་ ◦ བསྐྱེད་པས་ ◦ དེའི་ཕ་མ་ཡང་ ◦ སྤྲོ་བ་ཅུང་ཟད་ ◦ སྐྱེས་ནས། རིན་པོ་ཆེ་སྣ་བདུན་གྱི་སྒྲོམ་ ◦ བྱས་ཏེ། རུས་བུ་ ◦ དེའི་ནང་དུ་ ◦ བཅུག་སྟེ་ ◦ སྦས་པའི་སྟེང་དུ་ ◦ མཆོད་རྟེན་ ◦ བྱས་སོ། །(140v3) ལྷ་ཡང་ ◦ ཕྱིར་ ◦ གནས་སུ་ ◦ སོང་ངོ་། །རྒྱལ་པོ་དང་འཁོར་མང་པོ་རྣམས་ཀྱང་ ◦ ཕྱིར་ ◦ ཕོ་བྲང་དུ་ ◦ སོང་ངོ་།”[7] །བཅོམ་ལྡན་འདས་ཀྱིས་ ◦ ཀུན་དགའ་བོ་ལ་ ◦ བཀའ་ ◦ སྩལ་པ། “ཁྱོད་ཀྱི་ཡིད་ལ་ ◦ ཅི་ ◦ སྙམ་དུ་ ◦ སེམས། དེའི་ཚེ་དེའི་དུས་ན་ ◦ རྒྱལ་པོ་

ཤིང་རྟ་ཆེན་པོ་དེ་ ◦ སུ་ ◦ ཡིན་ ◦ སྙམ་དུ་ ◦ སེམས། དེ་ནི་ ◦ ད་ལྟར་ ◦ (140v4) ངའི་ཡབ་རྒྱལ་པོ་ཟས་གཙང་མ་ ◦ ཡིན་ནོ། །དེའི་ཚེ་དེའི་དུས་ན་ ◦ རྒྱལ་པོ་དེའི་བཙུན་མོ་དེ་ནི་ ◦ ད་ལྟར་ ◦ ངའི་ཡུམ་སྒྱུ་མ་ལྷ་མཛེས་ ◦ ཡིན་ནོ། །དེའི་དུས་ན་ ◦ སྲས་རབ་སྒྲ་ཆེན་པོ་དེ་ནི་ ◦ བྱམས་པ་ ◦ ཡིན་ནོ། །སྲས་འབྲིང་པོ་ལྷ་ཆེན་པོ་ནི་ ◦ བ་སུ་མི་ཏྲ་ ◦ ཡིན་ནོ། །དེའི་ཚེ་དེའི་དུས་ན་ ◦ རྒྱལ་བུ་ཐ་ཆུངས་ (140v5) སེམས་ཅན་ཆེན་པོ་ནི་ ◦ གཞན་དུ་ ◦ མ་སེམས་ཤིག །ད་ལྟར་ ◦ ང་ ◦ ཡིན་ནོ། །དེའི་ཚེ་དེའི་དུས་ན་ ◦ སྟག་ཕྲུག་ནི་ ◦ མི་འདི་གཉིས་ ◦ ཡིན་ཏེ། ངས་ ◦ སྔོན་ཡང་ ◦ ཡུན་རིང་པོ་ནས་ ◦ བགེགས་ལས་ ◦ ཐར་བར་བྱས་ཏེ་ ◦ སྲོག་ ◦ བསྐྱབས་ནས་ ◦ བདེ་བར་བྱས་སོ། །ད་ ◦ མངོན་པར་སངས་རྒྱས་ནས་ཀྱང་ ◦ བགེགས་ (140v6) ལས་ ◦ ཐར་བར་མཛད་ནས། འཁོར་བའི་སྡུག་བསྔལ་ཆེན་པོ་ལས་ ◦ ཡོངས་སུ་གྲོལ་ལོ།" །དེའི་ཚེ་ན་ ◦ ཀུན་དགའ་བོ་དང་། འཁོར་མང་པོ་ཐམས་ཅད་ ◦ བཅོམ་ལྡན་འདས་ཀྱིས་གསུངས་པ་ལ་ ◦ ཡི་རངས་ཏེ་ ◦ མངོན་པར་བསྟོད་དོ།།

སེམས་ཅན་ཆེན་པོས་ ◦ སྟག་མོ་ལ་ ◦ ལུས་ ◦ བྱིན་པའི་ལེའུ་སྟེ་ ◦ (140v7) གཉིས་པའོ།།

Notes

1 The most comprehensive list of loanwords in Classical Tibetan remains Laufer's pioneering study (1916); see also Schneider (2019: 50ff.).

2 In the selection of readings provided in the textbook, two texts make use of metrics: Saskya Paṇḍita's ལེགས་པར་བཤད་པ་རིན་པོ་ཆེའི་གཏེར། (SSP) and Bsod-nams Rgyal-mchan's རྒྱལ་རབས་གསལ་བའི་མེ་ལོང་། (GLR).

3 A line of a stanza is sometimes also called a 'verse'. The two terms will be used alternately here.

4 However, sometimes even spellings like པའང་ have to be read as two syllables, despite the 'lacking' ཚེག་.

5 Expletive is a word or phrase added to the clause although not necessary for the expression of the proper construction or meaning of the clause.

6 All editions read དགའ་ལྡན་གྱི་ལྷའི་གནས་སུ་, lit. "in the place of deities of Dgaɣ-ldan", but on another occasion (in D 140r3) we read དགའ་ལྡན་ལྷའི་གནས་སུ་, lit. "in Dgaɣ-ldan, the place of deities". The latter phrase, which is an apposition, is deemed internally more coherent.

7 Here ends the story the Victorious One was telling Kun-dgaɣ-bo (see D 139r2 in Lesson 15).

Readings

Reading I

Householder Dbyig-pa-čan

The story of the householder Dbyig-pa-čan comes from the canonical collection མཛངས་བླུན།. Other variants of this Indian story are likewise preserved in Buddhist literature. Contrary to the story *How Sems-čan-čhen-po offered his body to a tigress* (see Reading exercise in Lesson 12), an Old Tibetan version of the Dbyig-pa-čan story has been preserved in a manuscript now kept in Bibliothèque Nationale de France with the shelf mark PT 943. There are interesting differences in grammar between this version and the later canonical ones which attest to language change and the standardisation of the written language. The version of the text presented next is based on the following editions: HL (Hahn 1996: 227–32), D (Sde-dge: D 341 *mdo sde*, a 270v1–4r2), H (Lha-sa: H 347 *mdo sde*, sa 433v5–439r6), C (Čo-ne: C 980 *mdo maṅ*, a 305r3–308v7), and DH (Dunhuang: PT 943: 19r2–24v6).[1] In general, the punctuation of the Sde-dge edition has been retained with minor corrections from other redactions that should enhance the readability of the text flow for students. The folio numeration corresponds to that of the Sde-dge edition.

འདི་སྐད་བདག་གིས་ཐོས་པ་དུས་གཅིག་ན། བཅོམ་ལྡན་འདས་མཉན་ཡོད་ན། རྒྱལ་བུ་རྒྱལ་བྱེད་ཀྱི་ཚལ་མགོན་མེད་ཟས་སྦྱིན་གྱི་ཀུན་དགའ་ར་བ་ན་བཞུགས་སོ། །དེའི་ཚེ་ཡུལ་དེ་ན་བྲམ་ཟེ་ཕྱིན་ཏེ་ལོ་ཤུ་ཤ་ཞེས་བྱ་བ་ཞིག་ཡོད་དེ། (270v2) བྲམ་ཟེ་དེའི་ཆུང་མ་དེ་རབ་ཏུ་མི་སྡུག་ཅིང་མིག་གཉིས་ཀྱང་མི་མཐོང་སྟེ། མི་མཐོང་བ་དེ་ལ་བུ་ཕོ་ནི་མེད་ཀྱི། བུ་མོ་བདུན་ཡོད་དེ། རབ་ཏུ་དབུལ་ཕོངས་སོ། བྲམ་ཟེའི་བུ་མོ་དེ་དག་ཀྱང་སོ་སོར་བག་མར་བཏང་སྟེ། ཕྱིས་དམག་པ་དག་འདུས་ནས། བྲམ་ཟེའི་ཆུང་མ་ (270v3) ཡང་ཁྲོ་ཞིང་གཏུམ་མོ་ཞིག་སྟེ། བུ་མོ་དང་། དམག་པ་དག་འོང་བ་ལ་ཁྲོས་ནས། བུ་མོ་དག་ཀྱང་ཕྱིར་མ་ལ་གཤེའོ། །དེའི་ཚེ་ཞིང་དག་ཀྱང་བརྔ་རན་ནས། ཁྱིམ་མཆེས་ལས་[2]བ་ལང་ཞིག་བརྙས་ཏེ། ཞིང་ཐོག་ཏུ་སོང་སོང་བ་ལས། ལེགས་པར་མ་བསྲུངས་པས་སྟོར་ཏོ། (270v4) །དེའི་ཚེ་ན་ཕྱིན་ཏེ་ལོ་ཤུ་ཤས་འདི་སྙམ་དུ་བསམས་སོ། །བདག་གིས་སྟོན་ཉེས་པ་ཅི་ཞིག་བྱས་ན། ཁྱིམ་དུ་འོང་ན་ནི། ཆུང་མས་རྟག

DOI: 10.4324/9781003224198-23

ཏུ་སྨྲེ་ཞིང་བུ་མོ་བདུན་དང་། དམག་པ་རྣམས་ཀྱིས་འདུག་ཏུ་མི་སྟེར། ད་ཁྱིམ་མཚེས་ཀྱི་བ་ལང་བརྙས་ན་ནི། སྟོར་བར་གྱུར་ཏེ། བདག་གིས་བཙལ་ཀྱང་ (270v5) མ་རྙེད་ན། ཇི་ལྟར་བྱ་སྙམ་མྱ་ངན་གྱིས་ཡི་མུག་སྟེ་འདུག་འདུག་པ་ལས། རྒྱང་མ་ནས་དེ་བཞིན་གཤེགས་པ་ཤིང་དྲུང་ན་དབང་པོ་ཀུན་ཞི་ཞིང་བདེ་བར་བཞུགས་པ་མཐོང་ངོ་། བྲམ་ཟེ་དེས་འཁར་བ་ལ་སྙོམ་ཚུགས་བཅས་ཏེ། རྒྱང་ཚད་ཀྱི་བར་དུ་བརྟགས་ནས་ཀྱང་འདི་སྙམ་དུ་བསམས་སོ། (270v6) དགེ་སློང་གཽ་ཏ་མ་ནི་རབ་ཏུ་བདེ་སྐྱིད་དོ། །དེ་ལ་ཆུང་མས་སྤྱོ་བ་ཡང་མེད། བུ་མོ་ངན་པ་དང་། དམག་པས་གཙེ་བ་ཡང་མེད། ཞིང་བརྔ་རན་ཏེ་གླང་བརླག་ཡང་མི་དགོས་ཏེ་མྱ་ངན་མེད་དོ་སྙམ་བསམས་ནས། བཅོམ་ལྡན་འདས་ཀྱིས་ (270v7) དེའི་བསམ་པ་ཐུགས་ཀྱིས་མཁྱེན་ནས། འདི་སྐད་ཅེས་བཀའ་སྩལ་ཏོ། །ཁྱོད་ཀྱིས་བསམས་པ་བཞིན་ཏེ། ང་ལ་ཡང་དག་པར་ཉེས་པའི་སྐྱོན་གང་ཡང་མེད། ཆུང་མ་ངན་པ་ཡང་མེད་ན། གཞི་ཞིང་སྤྱོ་བ་ལྟ་ཅི་སྨོས། བུ་མོ་བདུན་གྱིས་འཚེ་བ་ཡང་མེད། དམག་པ་ (271r1) ཁྱིམ་དུ་འདུ་བ་ཡང་མེད། ཞིང་བརྔ་རན་པ་དང་། གླང་སྟོར་བའི་མྱ་ངན་བྱེད་པ་ཡང་མེད་དོ། །ཁྱོད་རབ་ཏུ་འབྱུང་བར་དགའ་འམ་ཞེས་བཀའ་སྩལ་པ་དང་། བྲམ་ཟེས་བཅོམ་ལྡན་འདས་ལ་འདི་སྐད་ཅེས་གསོལ་ཏོ། །བདག་ད་ལྟར་ཁྱིམ་ལ་དུར་ཙམ་དུ་འཛིན་ཏེ། ཆུང་མ་དང་། (271r2) བུ་མོ་ལ་དགྲ་ཙམ་དུ་སེམས་སོ། །བཅོམ་ལྡན་འདས་ཀྱིས་རབ་ཏུ་འབྱུང་བར་གནང་ན་བདག་རབ་ཏུ་འབྱུང་ངོ་ཞེས་གསོལ་པ་དང་། བཅོམ་ལྡན་འདས་ཀྱིས་ལེགས་པར་འོངས་སོ་ཞེས་བཀའ་སྩལ་པས། སྐྲ་དང་ཁ་སྤུ་རང་བྱི་སྟེ་དགེ་སློང་དུ་གྱུར་ཏོ། །དེ་ནས་བཅོམ་ལྡན་འདས་ (271r3) ཀྱིས་ཅི་རིགས་པར་ཆོས་བསྟན་ནས། དེ་ཉིད་དུ་དྲི་མ་ཀུན་ཟད་དེ་དགྲ་བཅོམ་པར་གྱུར་ཏོ། །དེ་ནས་ཀུན་དགའ་བོས་བཅོམ་ལྡན་འདས་ལ་གསོལ་པ། ལེགས་སོ། །བཅོམ་ལྡན་འདས་སེམས་ཅན་གྱི་དོན་མཛད་པ་བསམ་གྱིས་མི་ཁྱབ་བོ། །བྲམ་ཟེ་འདིས་སྔོན་ལེགས་པ་ཅི་ཞིག་ (271r4) བགྱིས་ན། ཉེས་པའི་སྐྱོན་ཀུན་དང་བྲལ་ཏེ། རས་དཀར་པོ་གཙང་མ་ལ་ཚོན་ཞེན་པ་སླ་བ་ལྟར་དགེ་བ་ལ་ཕན་པའི་དོན་ཐོབ་པར་གྱུར།[3] །བཅོམ་ལྡན་འདས་ཀྱིས་ཀུན་དགའ་བོ་ལ་བཀའ་སྩལ་པ། བྲམ་ཟེ་འདི་ལ་ད་ལྟར་འབའ་ཞིག་ངས་ཕན་བཏགས་ཏེ། བདེ་བར་བྱས་པར་མ་ཟད་ཀྱི། སྔོན་ (271r5) འདས་པའི་དུས་ན་ཡང་ཉེས་པ་ཀུན་ལས་ཐར་ཞིང་བདེ་བར་བྱས་སོ། །ཀུན་དགའ་བོས་གསོལ་པ། འདས་པའི་དུས་ན་བྲམ་ཟེ་འདི་ལ་ཇི་ལྟར་བདེ་བར་མཛད་པ་རྒྱས་པར་བསྟན་དུ་གསོལ།[4] བཅོམ་ལྡན་འདས་ཀྱིས་བཀའ་སྩལ་པ། ཁྱོད་ཤིན་ཏུ་ལེགས་ (271r6) པར་ཉོན་ལ་ཡིད་ལ་ཟུངས་ཤིག་དང་། ཁྱོད་ལ་བསྟན་པར་བྱའོ། །ཀུན་དགའ་བོས་གསོལ་པ། དེ་བཞིན་དུ་ཐོས་པར་འཚལ་ལོ་ཞེས་གསོལ་པ་དང་། བཅོམ་ལྡན་འདས་ཀྱིས་ཀུན་དགའ་བོ་ལ་འདི་སྐད་ཅེས་བཀའ་སྩལ་ཏོ། །

སྔོན་འདས་པའི་བསྐལ་པ་གྲངས་མེད་ཚད་མེད་པའི་ (271r7) ཕ་རོལ་ན་རྒྱལ་པོ་མཛེས་པ་ཞེས་བྱ་བ་ཞིག་བྱུང་སྟེ། ཆོས་བཞིན་དུ་སྲིད་འཚོའོ། །དེའི་ཚེ་ཡུལ་དེ་ན་བྲམ་ཟེ་དབྱིག་པ་ཅན་ཞེས་བྱ་བ་ཞིག་འདུག་སྟེ། རབ་ཏུ་དབུལ་ཕོངས་པ། བཟའ་བ་དང་བགོ་བ་མེད་པ་ཞིག་གོ། དེས་ཁྱིམ་བདག་ཅིག་ལས་གླང་ཞིག་བརྙས་ཏེ། ཉིན་པར་སྤྱད་ནས་གླང་དེ་ཁྲིད་དེ་ (271v1) ཁྱིམ་བདག་དེའི་ཁྱིམ་དུ་སོང་བ་དང་། དེ་ན

ཁྱིམ་བདག་ཉི་ཟན་ཟ་སྟེ། དབྱིག་པ་ཅན་གྱིས་གླང་དེ་ཁྱིམ་གྱི་ནང་དུ་བཏང་བ་དང་། གླང་སྒོ་གཞན་དུ་སོང་ནས་སྟོར་ཏོ། །ཁྱིམ་བདག་དེ་ཟན་ཟོས་ནས་ལངས་པ་དང་། དེ་ན་གླང་མ་མཐོང་ནས། དེས་དབྱིག་པ་ཅན་ལ་གླང་ (271v2) ག་རེ་ཞེས་བྲུས་པ་དང་། དེས་སྨྲས་པ། ཁྱོད་ཀྱི་ཁྱིམ་དུ་བཏང་ངོ་། །ཁྱོད་ཀྱིས་ངའི་གླང་བོར་གྱིས། གླང་སླར་བྱིན་ཅིག་ཅེས་སྨྲས་པ་དང་། དེས་སྨྲས་པ། ངས་མ་བོར་རོ། །དེ་ནས་དེ་གཉིས་འགྲོགས་ཏེ་རྒྱལ་པོའི་ཐད་དུ་འདོང་དང་། ཨུ་བུ་ཅག་གི་རིགས་པ་དང་མི་ (271v3) རིགས་པ་རྟོག་པར་འགྱུར་རོ་ཞེས་སྨྲས་ནས་དེ་གཉིས་དོང་བ་དང་། མི་གཞན་ཞིག་གི་རྟ་རྒོད་མ་ཞིག་བྲོས་ནས། དེས་དབྱིག་པ་ཅན་ལ་སྨྲས་པ། རྒོད་མ་མ་བཏང་ཞེས་སྨྲས་ནས། དེས་རྡོ་ཞིག་བླངས་ཏེ་འཕངས་པ་དང་། རྟའི་རྐང་པ་ལ་ཕོག་ནས་རྐང་པ་ཆག་གོ །དེས་སྨྲས་པ། (271v4) ཁྱོད་ཀྱིས་ངའི་རྟ་བསད་ཀྱིས། ངའི་རྟ་བྱིན་ཅིག །ཅིའི་ཕྱིར་རྟ་སྦྱིན། དེས་སྨྲས་པ། ཚུར་ཤོག་རྒྱལ་པོའི་དྲུང་དུ་འདོང་དང་། དེས་ཨུ་བུ་ཅག་གི་ཞལ་ཆེ་གཅོད་དོ་ཞེས་སྨྲས་ནས། དེ་དག་དེར་སོང་བ་དང་། དབྱིག་པ་ཅན་དེ་འབྲོས་པར་བརྩམས་ཏེ། དེས་རྩིག་པ་ (271v5) ཞིག་གི་སྟེང་དུ་མཆོངས་པ་དང་། དེའི་དྲུང་ན་ཐག་པ་ཞིག་ཐགས་འཐག་ཅིང་འདུག་པ་དེའི་སྟེང་དུ་ལྷུང་ནས་ཐག་པ་དེ་ཆེ་འཕོས་པ་དང་། ཐག་པའི་ཆུང་མས་དབྱིག་པ་ཅན་དེ་བཟུང་ནས། ཁྱོད་ཀྱིས་ངའི་ཁྱོ་བསད་ཀྱིས། ངའི་ཁྱོ་བྱིན་ཅིག་ཅེས་སྨྲས་པ་དང་། ངས་ཁྱོད་ཀྱི་ཁྱོ་ཅི་ལྟར་སྦྱིན་ཞེས་སྨྲས་ (271v6) ནས། ཚུར་ཤོག་རྒྱལ་པོའི་དྲུང་དུ་འདོང་དང་། དེས་ཨུ་བུ་ཅག་གི་ཞལ་ཆེ་གཅོད་དོ་ཞེས་དེ་དག་དོང་བ་ལས། ལམ་གྱི་བར་དེ་ན་ཆུ་བོ་གཏིང་ཟབ་པ་ཞིག་ཡོད་དེ། ཆུ་དེའི་ནང་ནས་ཚུར་ཤིང་མཁན་ཞིག་སྟེའུ་ཁ་ནས་ཁྱེར་ཏེ་འོང་ངོ་། དེ་ལ་དབྱིག་པ་ཅན་གྱིས་ཆུའི་གཏིང་ཅི་ཙམ་ཞེས་དྲིས་པ་ (271v7) དང་། ཆུ་གཏིང་ཟབ་པོ་ཞེས་སྨྲས་པས། སྟེའུ་ཆུར་ལྷུང་སྟེ། སྟེའུ་མ་རྙེད་པ་དང་། དེས་དབྱིག་པ་ཅན་བཟུང་ནས། ཁྱོད་ཀྱིས་ངའི་སྟེའུ་ཆུར་བསྐྱུར་རོ། །དེས་སྨྲས་པ། ངས་མ་བསྐྱུར་རོ། །ཚུར་ཤོག་རྒྱལ་པོའི་དྲུང་དུ་འདོང་དང་། དེས་ཨུ་བུ་ཅག་གི་ཞལ་ཆེ་གཅོད་དོ་ཞེས་ (272r1) སྨྲས་ནས་དོང་ངོ་། དེ་ལུས་ངལ་ནས་ཆང་ཚོང་གི་ཁྱིམ་དུ་སོང་སྟེ་ཆང་བསླངས་ནས། ཆང་ཚོང་མ་དེ་ལ་བུ་ཕོ་ཞིག་བཙས་ཏེ། བུ་གོས་ཀྱིས་གཡོགས་ཏེ་བསྙལ་པ་ལས། དབྱིག་པ་ཅན་དེའི་སྟེང་དུ་འདུག་པ་དང་། ཁྱེའུ་དེ་སྲོག་དང་བྲལ་བར་གྱུར་ཏོ། (272r2) །དེས་ཀྱང་དབྱིག་པ་ཅན་དེ་བཟུང་སྟེ། ཁྱོད་ཀྱིས་ངའི་བུ་བསད་ཀྱིས། ངའི་བུ་བྱིན་ཅིག །དེས་སྨྲས་པ། ངས་མ་བསད་ན། ཁྱོད་ཀྱི་བུ་ངས་ཇི་ལྟར་སྦྱིན། དེས་ཚུར་ཤོག་རྒྱལ་པོའི་དྲུང་དུ་འདོང་དང་། དེས་ཨུ་བུ་ཅག་གི་ཞལ་ཆེ་གཅོད་དོ་ཞེས་སྨྲས་ནས། དེ་དག་དོང་བ་ལས། གནས་གཞན་ཞིག་ (272r3) ན་ཤིང་ཤ་གོ་ཏ་ཀ་ལ་བྱ་རོག་གཅིག་[5]འདུག་པ་དེས་དབྱིག་པ་ཅན་དེ་མཐོང་ནས་གར་འགྲོ་ཞེས་སྨྲས་པ་དང་། ང་ནི་མི་འགྲོ་ན། འདི་དག་གིས་ང་ཁྲིད་དོ། །གང་དུ་ཁྲིད། རྒྱལ་པོའི་དྲུང་དུའོ། །འོ་ན་ཁོ་བོའི་ཕྲིན་ཞིག་ཀྱང་རྒྱལ་པོ་ལ་སྨྲོས་ཤིག །གནས་འདི་ཞེས་བགྱི་བ་ན། (272r4) ཤིང་ཤ་གོ་ཏ་ཀ་དེ་ལ་བྱ་རོག་གཅིག་འདུག་པ། བདག་ཤིང་གཞན་གྱི་ཁ་ན་འདུག་པའི་ཚེ་སྐད་མི་སྙན་ལ། ཤིང་འདིའི་ཁར་འོངས་ན་སྐད་ངོ་མཚར་དུ་སྙན་ན། དེ་ཅིའི་ཕྱིར་ཞེས་དེ་སྐད་མཆིའོ་ཞེས་སྨྲོས་ཤིག །དེ་ནས་ཡང་གནས་གཞན་ཞིག་ཏུ་སྦྲུལ་ཞིག་མཐོང་ནས། སྦྲུ་མ་(272r5)

བཞིན་དུ་བདག་གི་ཕྱིན་འདི་ཞུས་ཤིག །བདག་ནམ་ཁྱུང་ནས་ཕྱིར་འབྱུང་བའི་ཚེ་ནི་བདེ། སླར་འཇུག་པའི་ཚེ་སྡུག་བསྔལ་ན། ཅིའི་ཕྱིར་དེ་ལྟར་གྱུར་ཅེས་ཞུས་ཤིག །དེ་དག་དོང་བ་ལས། གནས་གཞན་ཞིག་ན་ན་ཆུང་གཞོན་ནུ་ཞིག་གིས་མཐོང་ནས། སྔོ་མ་བཞིན་དུ་ལོ་མའི་ཕྱིན་ཡང་ (272r6) ཞུས་ཤིག །ནམ་ལོ་མོ་ཕ་མའི་ཁྱིམ་ན་འདུག་པའི་ཚེ་གྲོས་པོའི་ཁྱིམ་འདོད། གྲོས་པོའི་ཁྱིམ་ན་འདུག་པའི་ཚེ་ཕ་མའི་ཁྱིམ་འདོད་ན། དེ་ཅིའི་ཕྱིར་ཞུས་ཤིག་ཅེས་སྨྲས་ནས། དེ་དག་དོང་བ་ལས། རྒྱལ་པོའི་དྲུང་དུ་ཕྱིན་པ་དང་། དེ་དག་རྒྱལ་པོའི་རྐང་པ་ལ་མགོ་བོས་ཕྱག་འཚལ་ཏེ་ (272r7) ཕྱོགས་གཅིག་ཏུ་འདུག་གོ། །དེ་ནས་རྒྱལ་པོས་དེ་དག་ལ་ཁྱོད་ཅི་ལ་འོངས་ཤེས་དྲིས་པ་དང་། དེ་དག་གིས་དབྱིག་པ་ཅན་དང་ཁྱིམ་བདག་རྗོད་པ་དེ་དག་ཐམས་ཅད་སྨྲས་སོ། །རྒྱལ་པོས་དབྱིག་པ་ཅན་ལ་སྨྲས་པ། ཁྱོད་ཀྱིས་གླང་བརྣས་སམ། བརྣས་སོ། (272v1) འོ་ན་ཕྱིར་བྱིན་ནམ། ཁྱིམ་བདག་གིས་མཐོང་བར་བྱིན་ཏེ། ཁས་ནི་མ་གཏད་དོ། །རྒྱལ་པོས་སྨྲས་པ། དབྱིག་པ་ཅན་འདིས་གླང་ཕྱིར་བྱིན་ཏེ་མ་སྨྲས་པས། ལྕེ་ཆོད་ཅིག །ཁྱིམ་བདག་ཀྱང་གླང་འོངས་པར་མཐོང་བ་ལས་མ་བཏགས་པས་ན། མིག་ཕྱུང་ཞིག་ཅེས་བཅད་དོ། (272v2) །ཁྱིམ་བདག་གིས་སྨྲས་པ། དབྱིག་པ་ཅན་གྱིས་གཅིག་ཏུ་ན་བདག་གི་གླང་ཕྲོགས། གཉིས་སུ་ན་བདག་གི་མིག་ཕྱུང་བ་བས། དབྱིག་པ་ཅན་རྒྱལ་བར་གྱུར་ཀྱང་བླའོ། །མི་གཅིག་གིས། ལྷ་དབྱིག་པ་ཅན་གྱིས་བདག་གི་རྟ་རྒོད་མ་བཀུམ་མོ་ཞེས་སྨྲས་པ་དང་། རྒྱལ་ (272v3) པོས་དབྱིག་པ་ཅན་ལ་ཁྱོད་ཀྱིས་རྟ་ཇི་ལྟར་བསད་ཅེས་དྲིས་ན། བདག་ལམ་དུ་ཞུགས་ཏེ། །མཆི་མཆི་བ་ལས། མི་འདིས་རྟ་མ་བཏང་ཞིག་ཅེས་མཆི་ནས། བདག་གིས་རྡོ་བ་ཞིག་བླངས་ཏེ་འཕངས་པས་རྟ་གུམ་མོ། །རྒྱལ་པོས་སྨྲས་པ། རྟ་བདག་གིས་རྟ་མ་ (272v4) བཏང་ཞིག་ཅེས་སྨྲས་པས། རྟ་བདག་ནི་ལྕེ་ཆོད་ཅིག་དབྱིག་པ་ཅན་རྡོ་བ་འཕངས་པས་ལག་པ་ཆོད་ཅིག །མི་དེས་སྨྲས་པ། གཅིག་ཏུ་ན་བདག་གི་རྟ་བསད། གཉིས་སུ་ན་བདག་གི་ལྕེ་བཅད་པ་བས་དབྱིག་པ་ཅན་རྒྱལ་བར་གྱུར་ཀྱང་བླའོ། །ཤིང་མཁན་ (272v5) གྱིས་སྨྲས་པ། དབྱིག་པ་ཅན་གྱིས་བདག་ལ་ཆུའི་གཏིང་ཅི་ཙམ་དུ་ཟབ་ཅེས་དྲིས་པས། །ཁ་ནས་སྟེའུ་ཐོགས་པ་ཆུར་ལྷུང་ངོ་ཞེས་གསོལ་པ་དང་། རྒྱལ་པོས་སྨྲས་པ། རྫས་ཅི་འཁྱེར་ཡང་ཕྲག་པ་ལ་བཀུར་བའི་རིགས་ཀྱི་ཁ་ནས་ཁྱེར་བས། ཤིང་མཁན་གྱི་མདུན་སོ་གཉིས་ (272v6) ཆོག་ཅིག །དབྱིག་པ་ཅན་ནི་ཆུའི་གཏིང་ཟབ་བམ་ཞེས་དྲིས་པས་ལྕེ་ཆོད་ཅིག །ཤིང་མཁན་གྱིས་སྨྲས་པ། གཅིག་ཏུ་ན་བདག་གི་སྟེའུ་སྟོར། གཉིས་སུ་ན་བདག་གི་སོ་བཅག་པ་བས་དབྱིག་པ་ཅན་རྒྱལ་བར་གྱུར་ཀྱང་བླའོ། །ཆང་ཚོང་མས་སྨྲས་པ། དབྱིག་ (272v7) པ་ཅན་གྱིས་བདག་གི་བུ་བསད་དོ། །དབྱིག་པ་ཅན་གྱིས་སྨྲས་པ། བདག་ངལ་བས་ཆང་སློང་[6]དུ་མཆིས་པས་སྟན་ལ་མ་བལྟས་པར་སྟན་ལ་འདུག་པས། འོག་ན་བུ་མཆིས་པ་མ་ཚོར་ཏེ་བུ་གུམ་མོ། །རྒྱལ་པོས་སྨྲས་པ། ཆང་ཚོང་མ་ཁྱོད་བུ་གོར་བསླལ་ལ་གོས་ (273r1) ཀྱིས་མི་མངོན་པར་གཡོགས་པས་ཉེས་སོ། །དབྱིག་པ་ཅན་ཁྱོད་སྟན་ལ་མི་རྟོག་པར་འདུག་པ་ཡང་ཉེས་ཀྱིས། དབྱིག་པ་ཅན་ཁྱོད་ཁྱོ་བྱོས་ལ་བུ་ཡོད་པར་གྱིས་ཤིག་ཅེས་སྨྲས་སོ། །ཆང་ཚོང་མས་སྨྲས་པ། གཅིག་ཏུ་ན་བདག་གི་བུ་བསད། གཉིས་སུ་ན་བདག་གི་ཁྱོ་ (273r2) བྱས་པ་བས་དབྱིག་པ་ཅན་རྒྱལ་བར་གྱུར་ཀྱང་བླའོ། །ཐ་ག་པའི་ཆུང་མས་སྨྲས་

པ། དབྱིག་པ་ཅན་གྱིས་བདག་གི་ཁྱོ་བཀུམ་མོ། །དབྱིག་པ་ཅན་གྱིས་སྨྲས་པ། བདག་ལ་དགྲ་མངས་པས་འཇིགས་ཏེ་རྩིག་པ་ལས་བརྒལ་ནས་བྲོས་པ་ལས། ཕག་ན་ (273r3) མི་ཡོད་པ་མ་མཐོང་སྟེ་གུམ་མོ། རྒྱལ་པོས་སྨྲས་པ། སོང་ལ་འདི་ཉིད་ཁྱོད་ཀྱི་ཁྱོ་གྱིས་ཤིག །དེས་སྨྲས་པ། གཅིག་ཏུ་ན་བདག་གི་ཁྱོ་བསད། གཉིས་སུ་ན་འདི་བདག་གི་ཁྱོ་བྱས་པ་བས་དབྱིག་པ་ཅན་རྒྱལ་བར་གྱུར་ཀྱང་བླའོ། །དེ་དག་སོ་སོ་ནས་ཞལ་ཆེ་བཅད་དེ། (273r4) དབྱིག་པ་ཅན་ཡུས་བྱིན་ནས་ཉེས་པ་ཀུན་ལས་ཐར་ཏོ། །རྒྱལ་པོ་དེ་ལ་ཡང་བུད་མེད་གཉིས་ཤིག་བུ་གཅིག་ལ་རྩོད་དེ། རྒྱལ་པོ་བློ་མཁས་པས་བརྟགས་ནས། བུད་མེད་གཉིས་ལ་འདི་སྐད་ཅེས་བསྒོའོ། །ཁྱོད་གཉིས་བུའི་ལག་པ་རེ་རེ་ནས་བཟུང་སྟེ། དྲོངས་ལ་ (273r5) གང་གིས་ཐོབ་པའི་བུར་འགྱུར་ཅིག་ཅེས་བསྒོ་བ་དང་། བུའི་མ་མ་ཡིན་པ་དེས་ནི་བུ་ལ་སྙིང་རྗེ་མེད་པས་སྡུད་ཀྱིས་མི་དོགས་ཏེ་མཐུ་ཅི་ཡོད་པས་དྲངས་སོ། །བུའི་མ་གང་ཡིན་པ་དེ་ནི་བུ་ལ་བྱམས་པས་སྡུད་ཀྱིས་དོགས་ཏེ་སྟོབས་ཀྱིས་ཐུབ་ཀྱང་དྲག་ཏུ་མི་འདྲེན་ནོ། །རྒྱལ་ (273r6) པོས་ཀྱང་རྟོགས་ནས་དྲག་ཏུ་དྲངས་པ་དེ་ལ་འདི་ནི་ཁྱོད་ཀྱི་བུ་མ་ཡིན་ཏེ། བུད་མེད་གཅིག་ཤོས་ཀྱི་བུ་ཡིན་པས་ན། དྲང་པོར་སྨྲོས་ཤིག་ཅེས་སྨྲས་པ་དང་། དལ་གྱིས་འདྲེན་པའི་བུ་ཡིན་པར་གྱུར་ཏེ་བུ་ཁྱེར་རོ། །དེ་ནས་ཡང་མི་གཉིས་ཤིག་རས་ཡུག་གཅིག་ལ་རྩོད་དོ། (273r7) །རྒྱལ་པོའི་དྲུང་དུ་ལྷགས་པ་ལས། རྒྱལ་པོས་བརྟགས་ནས་ཞལ་ཆེ་གོང་མ་བཞིན་དུ་བཅད་དོ། །དེ་ནས་དབྱིག་པ་ཅན་གྱིས་རྒྱལ་པོ་ལ་འདི་སྐད་ཅེས་གསོལ་ཏོ། །འདི་དག་གིས་བདག་བཟུང་སྟེ་ཁྲིད་ཅིང་མཆི་བ་ན། སྦྲུལ་ཞིག་ཕྲིན་དུ་འདི་སྐད་ཅེས་མཆིའོ། །བདག་ (273v1) ཁུང་བུ་ནས་ཕྱིར་འབྱུང་བའི་ཚེ་ནི་བདེ། སླར་འཛུག་པའི་ཚེ་ནི་སྡུག་བསྔལ་ན། ཅིའི་ཕྱིར་དེ་ལྟར་གྱུར་པ་ཞུས་ཤིག་ཅེས་མཆིའོ། །རྒྱལ་པོས་སྨྲས་པ། སྦྲུལ་དེ་ལ་ཁྱོད་ཀྱིས་འདི་སྐད་ཅེས་གྱིས་ཤིག །ཁྱོད་མི་ཁྲོ་ཞིང་བཀྲེས་པས་ཁུང་ནས་འབྱུང་བའི་ཚེ་ནི་བདེའོ། (273v2) །ཕྱིར་བྱུང་ནས་ཁ་ཟས་མང་དུ་ཟོས་ལ་བྱ་རྣམས་ཀྱིས་གཙེས་པས། ཁྱོད་ཁྲོས་ནས་སྦོམ་པོར་གྱུར་པས་སླར་འཛུག་པའི་ཚེ་ཁུང་བུ་ལ་ཐོགས་ནས་སྡུག་བསྔལ་ལོ་ཞེས་གྱིས་ཤིག །ཁྱོད་ཀྱིས་ད་སྟེ་ཁ་ཟས་ཀྱི་ཚོད་ཤེས་ལ་མི་ཁྲོ་ན། ཇི་ལྟར་ཕྱིར་འབྱུང་བ་དང་འདྲ་བར་བདེ་བར་འཛུག་ (273v3) གོ་ཞེས་སྨྲོས་ཤིག །དེ་ནས་ན་ཆུང་གཞོན་ནུའི་ཕྲིན་སྨྲས་པ་དང་། རྒྱལ་པོས་སྨྲས་པ། ན་ཆུང་གཞོན་ནུ་དེ་ལ་ཁྱོད་ཀྱི་ཕ་མའི་ཁྱིམ་ན་མཛའ་བོ་ཞིག་འདུག་སྟེ། ནམ་གྱོས་པོའི་ཁྱིམ་ན་འདུག་པའི་ཚེ་མཛའ་བོ་ལ་ཆགས་པས་ཕ་མའི་ཁྱིམ་དུ་འགྲོ་འདོད་དོ། ནམ་ཕ་མའི་ཁྱིམ་ན་ (273v4) འདུག་པའི་ཚེ་མཛའ་བོ་ལ་སྐྱོ་སྟེ་ཁྱོ་ལ་ཆགས་པས་གྱོས་པོའི་ཁྱིམ་དུ་འགྲོ་འདོད་པ་ཡིན་གྱིས། གནས་གཅིག་སྡོངས་ལ་གཅིག་ལེགས་པར་ཟུངས་ཤིག་དང་། དེ་ལྟ་བུའི་གནོད་པ་མེད་པར་འགྱུར་རོ་ཞེས་སྨྲོས་ཤིག །གནས་གཞན་ཞིག་ན་ཤིང་ཤ་གོ་ཏ་ཀ་ལ་བྱ་རོག་གཅིག་འདུག་པའི་ (273v5) ཕྲིན་སྨྲས་པ་དང་། རྒྱལ་པོས་སྨྲས་པ། ཤིང་དེའི་འོག་ན་གསེར་ཡོད་པས་ཁྱོད་ཀྱི་སྐད་སྙན་པ་ཡིན་ནོ། །ཤིང་གཞན་གྱི་དྲུང་ན་གསེར་མེད་པས་སྐད་མི་སྙན་ནོ་ཞེས་གྱིས་ཤིག །རྒྱལ་པོས་དབྱིག་པ་ཅན་ལ་སྨྲས་པ། ཁྱོད་ལ་ཉེས་པ་མང་དུ་བྱུང་ཡང་ངས་བཏང་ (273v6) ངོ་། །ཁྱོད་ནི་དབུལ་ཕོངས་ཀྱིས། ཤིང་གི་འོག་ན་གསེར་གྱི་གཏེར་ཡོད་པ་རྐོས་ལ་ཁྱེར་ཅིག །དབྱིག་པ་ཅན་གྱིས་རྒྱལ་པོས་བསྒོ་བ་བཞིན་དུ་སོ་སོའི་ཕྲིན་ཡང་བསྒོ་ནས། ཤིང་དྲུང་

ནས་གསེར་ཡང་ཕྱུང་སྟེ་ཁྲེར་རོ། །དེ་ཕྱིན་ཆད་སོ་ཚོས་ཚུགས་ནས་ཅིས་ཀྱང་མི་བྲེལ་ཏེ་ (273v7) ཚེ་གཅིག་ཏུ་ཕྱུག་ཅིང་བདེ་སྐྱིད་པར་གྱུར་ཏོ། །ཀུན་དགའ་བོ། དེའི་ཚེ་དེའི་དུས་ན་རྒྱལ་པོ་མཛེས་པ་དེ་ལ་གཞན་དུ་མ་སེམས་ཤིག །དེ་ནི་ད་ལྟར་ང་ཡིན་ནོ། །དེའི་ཚེ་དེའི་དུས་ན་བྲམ་ཟེ་དབྱིག་པ་ཅན་དེ་ནི་བྲམ་ཟེ་ཕྱིན་ཏེ་ལོ་ཤུ་ཤ་ཡིན་ནོ། །ངས་སྔོན་ཡང་སྡུག་བསྔལ་ལས་ (274r1) ཐར་བར་བྱས་ཏེ། རིན་པོ་ཆེ་བྱིན་ནས་བདེ་སྐྱིད་པར་བྱས་སོ། །ད་མངོན་པར་སངས་རྒྱས་ནས་ཀྱང་སྡུག་བསྔལ་ལས་ཐར་བར་བྱས་ཏེ་ཟད་མི་ཤེས་པའི་ཆོས་རིན་པོ་ཆེའི་གཏེར་བྱིན་ནོ། །བཅོམ་ལྡན་འདས་ཀྱིས་དེ་སྐད་ཅེས་བཀའ་སྩལ་ནས། ཚེ་(274r2) དང་ལྡན་པ་ཀུན་དགའ་བོ་དང་འཁོར་མང་པོ་རྣམས་བཅོམ་ལྡན་འདས་ཀྱིས་གསུངས་པ་ལ་རྗེས་སུ་ཡི་རངས་ནས་མངོན་པར་དགའོ། །

ཁྲིམ་བདག་དབྱིག་པ་ཅན་ཞེས་བྱ་བའི་ལེའུ་སྟེ་སུམ་ཅུ་དགུ་པའོ། །

Notes

1 The Snar-thaṅ (N 326 *mdo sde*, sa 422r6–427r1) and Urga (U 341 *mdo sde*, a 270r7–274r2) editions available via BDRC are hardly legible and therefore have been omitted from the collation.

2 All editions read ལ་ but in another passage, DH, D, and C read ལས་ (cf. D 271r7).

3 Notice the lack of the final particle at the end of direct speech.

4 Notice the lack of the final particle at the end of direct speech.

5 DH has གཅིག་ but the remaining editions attest to ཅིག་. The indefinite particle ཅིག་ is a misspelling because the noun phrase ends with the determiner དེ་ (གནས་གཞན་ཞིག་ན་ཤིང་ཤ་ཀོ་ཏ་ཀ་ལ་བྱ་རོག་གཅིག་འདུག་པ་དེས་, lit. "the one crow that was sitting in another place on a *śa ko ta ka*-tree").

6 Although final clauses with verbs of going require a v3-stem of a transitive verb: 'go to do sth.', v1-stems (like སྐྱོང་ here) are also encountered (see Lesson 12).

Reading II

The descent of Tibetan people from a monkey and a rock-ogress

རྒྱལ་རབས་གསལ་བའི་མེ་ལོང་། "The Mirror Illuminating the Royal Genealogies" (GLR), from which the following reading comes, is one of the most important and influential Buddhist historiographical works in the history of Tibetan literature.[1] It was compiled by Bla-ma Dam-pa Bsod-nams Rgyal-mchan (1312–1375) at Bsam-yas in 1368. The work belongs to the genre of ཆོས་འབྱུང་།, i.e. the history of Buddhist teachings in Tibet. Regarding its contents, the work draws on themes and histories found already in earlier works of other authors. Its compositional character reveals the considerable extent to which Bla-ma Dam-pa made use of available sources. As Per Sørensen put it, "Bla-ma dam-pa's work is in fact a well-balanced compilation of sources used by the author, passages and themes being carefully chosen, quoted and again patched together by him so as to form a new consecutive unity" (1994: 35).

Two pre-modern editions of རྒྱལ་རབས་གསལ་བའི་མེ་ལོང་། have been preserved: (1) the Lha-sa edition printed in 1478, extant in only one rather poorly preserved copy (Bsod-nams Rgyal-mchan 1966: XIX–XX); and (2) the Sde-dge edition printed in ca. 1750–60, of which some more copies are known. Preparing the edition of chapter 7 for Reading II, I have mainly relied on the Sde-dge edition (GLR) that has kindly been put at my disposal by Per Sørensen as a microfilm.

The orthography of the Sde-dge edition is nearly faultless, but one peculiarity seen in both editions calls for reflection. This is the almost invariable usage of the form ཅིག་ of the indefinite particle, especially after a final vowel of the preceding syllable. According to the Classical Tibetan orthography, after a vowel the form ཞིག་ should be applied. In chapter 7 of the work, ཅིག་ is practically the only form of the indefinite particle, therefore a misspelling for གཅིག་ can be excluded. Another orthographic anomaly concerns the concessive particle, the form of which often violates the assimilation rules too. Most commonly the form ཀྱང་ is used instead of the expected ཡང་. As this is a textbook for beginners I have amended forms of the particles so that they conform to the standard of Classical Tibetan.

DOI: 10.4324/9781003224198-24

The story of the descent of Tibetans from a monkey seems to have been inspired by Indian sources, especially by the figure of Hanūmān, the ape-king occurring in *Rāmāyana*. The latter text was already translated into Tibetan during the Old Tibetan phase of the language and thus has a very long tradition of reception in Tibet (Sørensen 1994: 127, fn. 329). The story of the descent of Tibetans from a monkey has always been a very popular literary motif and has found its way into various works of Tibetan authors, historiographical and religious.

དེ་ནས་འཕགས་པ་སྤྱན་རས་གཟིགས་དེས། (22r4) རྫུ་འཕྲུལ་སྟོན་པའི་སྤྲེའུ་ཞིག་ལ། དགེ་བསྙེན་གྱི་སྡོམ་པ་བྱིན་ནས། བོད་ཁ་བ་ཅན་གྱི་རྒྱལ་ཁམས་སུ་བསྒོམ་དུ་བཏང་ངོ་། །དེར་སྤྲེའུ་དེས། བྲག་རོག་པོ་ཞིག་ (D: གཅིག་)[2]ལ་བསྒོམས་ཏེ། དེའང་བྱམས་སྙིང་རྗེ་བྱང་ཆུབ་ཀྱི་སེམས་བསྒོམས་པ་དང་། ཆོས་ཟབ་མོ་སྟོང་པ་ཉིད་ལ་མོས་པར[3] བྱེད་གིན་ཡོད་དུས། (22r5) ལས་ཀྱིས་མནར་བའི་བྲག་སྲིན་མོ་ཞིག་དེར་འོངས་ནས། ཆགས་པ་འདོད་པའི་བརྡ་མང་དུ་བསྟན་ནས་སོང་ངོ་། །རྗེས་ལ་བྲག་སྲིན་མོ་དེ་བུད་མེད་ཀྱི་ཆས་སུ་བྱས་ཏེ། སྤྲེའུ་ལ་ཁྱོད་དང་ང་གཉིས་བཟའ་མི་བྱའོ་ཟེར་བས། སྤྲེའུ་ན་རེ། ང་འཕགས་པ་སྤྱན་རས་གཟིགས་ཀྱི་དགེ་བསྙེན་ཡིན་ (22r6) པས། ཁྱོད་ཀྱི་ཁྱོ་བྱས་ན་ངའི་སྡོམ་པ་འཆོར་བྱས་པས། བྲག་སྲིན་མོ་ན་རེ། ཁྱོད་ངའི་ཁྱོ་མི་བྱེད་ན་ང་ཆེའི་དུས་བྱེད་དོ་ཟེར་ནས། སྤྲེའུའི་རྩར་ཉལ་ལོ། །དེ་ནས་བྲག་སྲིན་མོ་ལངས་ཏེ། སྤྲེའུ་ལ་འདི་སྐད་ཅེས་ཟེར་རོ། །

ཀྱེ་མ་སྤྲེའུའི་རྒྱལ་པོ་ཆེན་པོ་ཁྱེད། །[4]
ཚུར་ཟད་བདག་ལ་དགོངས་ཤིང་ (22v1) གསན་དུ་གསོལ། །
བདག་ནི་ལས་ཀྱི་དབང་གིས་སྲིན་མོའི་རིགས་སུ་སྐྱེས། །[5]
འདོད་ཆགས་རྒྱས་པས་ཁྱེད་ལ་ཞེན་ཞིང་ཆགས། །
ཆགས་པའི་དབང་གིས་ཁྱེད་ལ་བསྐོར་ཅིང་གསོལ། །
བདག་ནི་ཁྱེད་དང་ཁྱིམ་ཐབ་མི་བྱེད་ན། །
ཐ་མ་སྲིན་པོ་ཞིག་དང་འགྲོགས་ནས་ཀྱང་། །
ཉིན་རེ་ (22v2) ལ་འང་སེམས་ཅན་ཁྲི་རེ་གསོད། །
ནུབ་རེ་ལ་འང་སྲོག་ཆགས་སྟོང་ཚམ་ཟ། །
སྲིན་པོའི་ཕྲུ་གུ་དཔག་མེད་སྐྱེས་གྱུར་ནས། །
ཁ་བ་ཅན་གྱི་རྒྱལ་ཁམས་འདི་ཉིད་དུ། །
སྲིན་པོའི་གྲོང་ཁྱེར་དག་ཏུ་གྱུར་ནས་ནི། །
གང་ཡོད་སེམས་ཅན་སྲིན་པོས་ཟ་བར་འགྱུར། །
དེ་བས་བདག་ལ་དགོངས་ (22v3) ནས་ཐུགས་རྗེས་ཟུངས། །

ཞེས་གདུང་བའི་སྐད་ཀྱིས་མཆི་མ་ཕྱུང་བས། དེར་བྱང་ཆུབ་སེམས་དཔའ་སྤྲིའུ་སྙམ་ན། འདིའི་ཕྲུ་བྱས་ན་ནི་སྡོམ་པ་འཆོར་ལ། མ་བྱས་ན་ནི་སྡིག་པ་ཆབས་ཆེ་བར་འདུག་སྙམ་ནས། སྐད་ཅིག་ལ་རི་བོ་པོ་ཏ་ལར་འཕགས་པའི་དྲུང་དུ་ཕྱིན་ནས་འདི་སྐད་ཅེས (22v4) གསོལ་ཏོ། །

ཀྱེ་མ་འགྲོ་བའི་མགོན་པོ་ཐུགས་རྗེ་ཅན། །
བདག་ནི་དགེ་བསྙེན་སྡོམ་པ་སྲོག་བཞིན་བསྲུངས། །
བདུད་རིགས་སྲིན་མོ་ཆགས་པའི་འདུ་ཤེས་ཅན། །
གདུང་བའི་སྨྲེ་སྔགས་སྣ་ཚོགས་བཏོན་གྱུར་ནས། །
བདག་ལ་བསྐོར་ཅིང་སྡོམ་པ་འཕྲོག་ཏུ་བྱུང་། །
དེ་ལ་ཅི་ལྟར (22v5) བྱས་ན་སྡོམ་པ་བསྲུང་། །
བྱམས་མགོན་ཐུགས་རྗེ་ཅན་ཁྱོད[6]དགོངས་སུ་གསོལ། །

ཞེས་གསོལ་བ་བཏབ་པས། འཕགས་པའི་ཞལ་ནས། བྲག་སྲིན་མོའི་ཁྱོ་གྱིས་ཤིག་གསུངས། རྗེ་མོ་ཁྲོ་གཉེར་ཅན་དང་། རྗེ་མོ་སྒྲོལ་མ་གཉིས་ཀྱིས་ཀྱང་། ནམ་མཁའ་ནས་དེ་ནི་ཤིན་ཏུ (22v6) ལེགས་སོ་གསུང་ངོ་། །དེ་ནས་འཕགས་པས་སྤྲིའུ་དང་། བྲག་སྲིན་མོ་གཉིས་བཟའ་མིར་བྱིན་གྱིས་བརླབས་ནས། ཁ་བ་ཅན་འདིར་ཡོན་ཏན་གསུམ་དང་ལྡན་ཏེ། མ་འོངས་པའི་དུས་སུ་སངས་རྒྱས་ཀྱི་བསྟན་པ་དར་ཞིང་རྒྱས་ལ་ཡུན་རིང་དུ་གནས་པ་དང་། དགེ་བའི་བཤེས་གཉེན (23r1) རྒྱུན་ཆད་མེད་པར་འབྱུང་བ། རིན་པོ་ཆེའི་གཏེར་ཁ་བྱེ་བ། ཕན་བདེ་དང་དགེ་ལེགས་ཕྱོགས་བཅུར་རྒྱས་པ་སོགས་བྱིན་གྱིས་བརླབས་སོ། །དེ་ནས་སྤྲིའུ་དང་། བྲག་སྲིན་མོ་གཉིས་བཟའ་མི་བྱས་པས། འགྲོ་བ་རིགས་དྲུག་ནས་ཚེ་འཕོས་པའི་སྤྲིའུ་ཕྲུག་རྣམས་སྤྱོད་ལམ་མི (23r2) འདྲ་བ་དྲུག་སྐྱེས་སོ། །དེ་ཡང་། སེམས་ཅན་དམྱལ་བ་ནས་ཚེ་འཕོས་པའི་སྤྲིའུ་ཕྲུག་དེ། ངོ་ནག་ལ་སྡུག་སྲན་ཆེ་བ་ཞིག་འདུག །ཡི་དགས་ཀྱི་གནས་ནས་ཚེ་འཕོས་པའི་སྤྲིའུ་ཕྲུག་དེ། བཞིན་མི་སྡུག་ལ་ཟས་ལ་གདུང་བ་ཞིག་འདུག །དུད་འགྲོའི་གནས་ནས་ཚེ་འཕོས་པའི་སྤྲིའུ་ཕྲུག་དེ། (23r3) གླེན་ལ་རྡོད་ངན་པ་ཞིག་འདུག །མིའི་གནས་ནས་ཚེ་འཕོས་པའི་སྤྲིའུ་ཕྲུག་དེ། ཤེས་རིག་རྒྱས་ལ་སེམས་ཆུང་བ་ཞིག་འདུག །ལྷ་མ་ཡིན་གྱི་གནས་ནས་ཚེ་འཕོས་པའི་སྤྲིའུ་ཕྲུག་དེ། ཐུ་ལ་ཕྲག་དོག་ཆེ་བ་ཞིག་འདུག །ལྷའི་གནས་ནས་ཚེ་འཕོས་པའི་སྤྲིའུ་ཕྲུག་དེ། ངང་རྒྱུད་རིང་ལ་སེམས (23r4) དགེ་བ་ཞིག་འདུག་གོ། །དེར་སྤྲིའུ་ཕྲུག་དྲུག་པོ་དེ་ནི་ཕ་བྱང་ཆུབ་སེམས་དཔའ་སྤྲིའུས། ནགས་མ་བྱ་ཚོགས་བྱ་བ། ཤིང་ཐོག་མེད་པ་ཞིག་ཏུ་བསྐྱལ་ནས་ལོ་གསུམ་བཞག་གོ། །ལོ་གསུམ་ལོན་པ་དང་། སྤྲིའུ་བྱང་ཆུབ་སེམས་དཔའ་བལྟར་ཕྱིན་པས། ལས་ཀྱི་དབང་གིས་སྤྲིལ (read: སྤྲིའུ) ཕྲུག (23r5) ལྔ་བརྒྱར་འཕེལ་འདུག་གོ། །དེ་ནས་ཤིང་ཐོག་རྣམས་ཟད། གཞན་ཟ་རྒྱུ་མེད་ནས་ཕ་མས་ཅི་ཡང་མ་ཟོས་ཀྱང་། ཕ་ཅི་ཟ་མ་ཅི་ཟ་ཟེར་ཞིང་། ལག་གདེངས་ལ་ཉམས་ཐག་སྟེ། དབུལ་

ཕོངས་སོ། །དེར་བྱང་ཆུབ་སེམས་དཔའ་སྤྲེའུ་སྙམ་ན། ང་ཉོན་མོངས་པའི་དབང་དུ་སོང་བ་ནི་མིན། (23r6) འཕགས་པའི་བཀའ་བསྒྲུབས་པས་སྤྲེའུ་ཕྲུག་འདི་ཙམ་དུ་སོང་འདུག་སྙམ་ནས། སྐད་ཅིག་ལ་རི་བོ་པོ་ཏ་ལར་ཕྱིན་ནས། འཕགས་པ་ལ་འདི་སྐད་ཅེས་གསོལ་ཏོ། །ཀྱེ་མ།

ཁྱིམ་ཐབ་འཁོར་བའི་བཙོན་རར་མ་ཞེས་ཞིང་། །
བུད་མེད་བདུད་ཀྱིས་བསླུས་པ་མ་ཞེས་པས། །
བུ་ཚས་འཁོར་བའི་འདམ་ (23v1) དུ་བདག་ཚུད་དོ། །
འདོད་པ་དུག་གི་ཡོ་མར་མ་རྟོགས་པས། །
སྙིང་རྗེས་ཆགས་པར་གྱུར་བས་བདག་བསླུས་སོ། །
འདོད་པས་བསྡམས་ཤིང་སྡུག་བསྔལ་རི་ཡིས་ནོན། །
ཉོན་མོངས་དུག་ཟོས་ལས་ངན་རིམས་ཀྱིས་བཏབ། །
སྡུག་བསྔལ་ཕུང་པོས་བདག་ཉིད་མནར་གྱུར་ན། །
ཀྱེ་མ་ (23v2) ཀྱི་ཧུད་བྱམས་མགོན་ཐུགས་རྗེ་ཅན། །
ད་ནི་ཇི་ལྟར་བྱས་ན་བུ་ཚ་གསོ། །
འཕགས་པས་གནང་བས་བདག་ནི་འདི་ལྟར་འགྱུར། །
ད་ལྟ་ཡི་དགས་གྲོང་ཁྱེར་ལྟ་བུར་འདུག །
ཕྱི་མ་དམྱལ་བར་སྐྱེ་བར་ཐེ་ཚོམ་མེད། །
དེ་ཕྱིར་བདག་ལ་ཐུགས་རྗེས་བསྐྱབ་ཏུ་གསོལ། །

ཞེས་གསོལ་བ་བཏབ་ (23v3) པས། འཕགས་པའི་ཞལ་ནས་ཁྱོད་ཀྱི་རིགས་རྒྱུད་རྣམས་ངས་བསྐྱང་ངོ་གསུངས་ནས། འཕགས་པ་ཡར་བཞེངས་ཏེ། ནས། གྲོ། སྲན་མ། བྲ་བོ། སོ་བ་རྣམས་རི་རབ་ཀྱི་ཁོང་སེང་ནས་བླངས་ཏེ། ས་ལ་གཏོར་བས་ཡུལ་དེར་མ་རྨོས་པའི་ལོ་ཐོག་གིས་གང་བར་གྱུར་ཏོ། དེ་ནས་སྤྲེའུ་ (23v4) བྱང་ཆུབ་སེམས་དཔའ་དེས་སྤྲེའུ་ཕྲུག་རྣམས་དེར་ཁྲིད་དེ། མ་རྨོས་པའི་ལོ་ཐོག་ལ་གཏད་ནས། ད་ཟོ་དང་བྱས་པས། ཟོ་དང་གོང་པོ་རི་ཡིན་ཟེར་རོ། །དེ་ནས་སྤྲེའུ་ཕྲུག་རྣམས་ཀྱིས་ལོ་ཐོག་ཟོས་པས་ཚིམ་པར་གྱུར་ནས། སྤུ་ཡང་ཐུང་དུ་སོང་། མཇུག་མ་ཡང་ཐུང་དུ་སོང་སྟེ། སྨྲ་ཤེས་ (23v5) ནས་མིར་གྱུར་ཏོ། །ཟས་སུ་མ་རྨོས་པའི་ལོ་ཐོག་ཟ་ཞིང་། གོས་སུ་ཤིང་ལོ་གོན་པར་གྱུར། དེ་ལྟར་ན་བོད་ཁ་བ་ཅན་པ་མི་འདི་རྣམས་ཕ་སྤྲེའུ་དང་། མ་བྲག་སྲིན་མོ་གཉིས་ལས་ཆད་པ་ཡིན་པས། རིགས་གཉིས་སུ་བྱེ་ཡོད་དོ། །དེ་ལ་ཕ་སྤྲེའུ་བྱང་ཆུབ་སེམས་དཔའི་རིགས་སུ་གྱུར་ (23v6) པ་ནི། ངང་རྒྱུད་རིང་པ། དད་པ་ཆེ་བ། སྙིང་རྗེ་ཆེ་ལ་བརྩོན་འགྲུས་ཆེ་བ། དགེ་བ་ལ་དགའ་བ། ཚིག་འཇམ་པ། སྨྲ་མཁས་པ་དེ་ནི་ཕའི་རིགས་སོ། །མ་བྲག་སྲིན་མོའི་རིགས་སུ་གྱུར་པ་ནི། འདོད་ཆགས་དང་ཞེ་སྡང་ཆེ་བ། ཚོང་དང་ཁེ་སྤོག་ལ་སེམས་པ། བློ་འདོད་དང་འགྲན་སེམས་ (24r1) ཆེ་བ། གད་མོ་ཆེར་དགོད་པ། ལུས་སྟོབས་

དང་སྙིང་སྟོབས་ཆེ་བ། སྤྱོད་པས་སྐད་ཅིག་ཀྱང་མི་ཚུགས་པ། བློ་སྣ་མང་བ། བྱེད་སྒྲིན་པ། དུག་ལྷ་ཀྱུས་པ། གཞན་གྱི་སྐྱོན་ཐོས་ན་དགའ་བ། ཁྲོ་གཏུམ་པ་དེ་ནི་མའི་རིགས་སོ། །དེའི་དུས་དེར་རི་རྣམས་ནི་ (24r2) ཤིང་ནགས་སུ་སོང་། ཀླུང་ཐམས་ཅད་ནི་ཆུས་ཁེངས་ཡོད་པ། སྐོང་ཆུ་ལག་ཁ་ཕྱེ་ནས། ཆུ་ཐམས་ཅད་དེར་སོང་སྟེ། སྐོང་ཆུ་ལག་ཏུ་ཐིམ་མོ། །དེ་ནས་ཐང་ཐམས་ཅད་ལ་ཞིང་བྱས། གྲོང་ཁྱེར་མང་པོ་བརྩིགས། དེ་ནས་རིང་པོར་མ་ལོན་པར། རྗེ་གཉའ་ཁྲི་བཙན་པོ་བོད་ཀྱི་རྒྱལ་ (24r3) པོ་ལ་བྱོན་ནས། རྗེ་དང་འབངས་སུ་བཅོས་སྐད་དོ། །

བོད་ཀྱི་མི་བརྒྱུད་སྤྲེའུ་དང་བྲག་སྲིན་མོ་ནས་ཆད་པའི་ལེའུ་སྟེ་བདུན་པའོ། །

Notes

1 The following brief introduction to རྒྱལ་རབས་གསལ་བའི་མེ་ལོང་། is based on Sørensen's description of the work (1994: 1–39). Students are encouraged to consult the excellent study of Per Sørensen that provides invaluable information on miscellaneous topics covered by the work of Bla-ma Dam-pa, from history, to textual history, to philology.

2 གཅིག་ might be an isolated case of hypercorrection of an editor who noticed the inconsistency of the spelling with the acknowledged rules of the Classical Tibetan orthography.

3 Both editions attest to སོས་པ་ but Sørensen amended it with the more plausible སོས་པར་ (1994: 127; see also Lesson 16).

4 The Sde-dge edition clearly reads སྤྲེའུའི་ and thus the verse has eight syllables only. The original might have had སྤྲེའུ་ཡི་ instead.

5 This verse consists of eleven syllables; it is possible that the first two syllables, བདག་ནི་, were added later.

6 The transmitted ཁྱོད་ is the only case of the non-honorific register used in words that are addressed to Spyan-ras-gzigs in the story.

Reading III

The death of Mi-la Ras-pa's father

The biography of Mi-la Ras-pa, མི་ལ་རས་པའི་རྣམ་ཐར།, is one of the most renowned pieces of Tibetan literature. It was composed by Gcaṅ-smyon He-ru-ka (1452–1507), a tantric master from Central Tibet. The work has been translated many times into Western languages and has enjoyed great popularity among students of Tibetan language and culture.

Mi-la Ras-pa was a historical person, although certainly not all details of his biography are based on facts. There is even disagreement concerning the dates of his birth and death which are variously given as 1028–1111, 1040–1123, or 1052–1135. He was born in Skya-rṅa-rca, a small village in southern Tibet. After an eventful and turbulent young-adulthood Mi-la Ras-pa became a fervent student of the Buddhist teacher Mar-pa (1012?–97). He spent great part of his adulthood living as a hermit in caves of southern Tibet.

The text presented herewith is based on the critical edition by Jan Willen de Jong (ML: 31–5) with some minor amendments. The second chapter of the first part of the work relates the death of Mi-la Ras-pa's father and the difficulties Mi-la Ras-pa and his mother experienced from their own family afterwards.

གཉིས་པ་ནི། ཡང་རས་ཆུང་པས་ཞུས་པ། བླ་མ་ལགས། དང་པོ་ཡབ་དང་བྲལ་བས་འོ་བརྒྱལ་མང་པོ་ཐུགས་ཉམས་སུ་བཞེས་གསུང་བ་ཅི་འདྲ་བཞེས་ལགས་ཞུས་པས། དེ་ནས་ངས་ལོ་བདུན་ཙམ་འགྲོ་བའི་ཚེ།[1] ཡབ་མི་ལ་ཤེས་རབ་རྒྱལ་མཚན་དེ་སྙུན་གཞི་དྲག་པོ་རང་ཞིག་གིས་ཟིན་ནས། སྨན་པ་ (D 10v) དང་མོ་མ་རྣམས་ཀྱིས་ཀྱང་མི་འཚོ་བར་ལུང་བསྟན་ཞིང་བོར། གཉེན་ཉེ་འབྲེལ་རྣམས་ཀྱིས་ཀྱང་མི་འཚོ་བར་ཤེས། ཁོང་རང་ཀྱང་མི་འཚོ་བར་ཁོ་ཐག་ཆོད་ནས། ཨ་ཁུ་དང་ཨ་ནེ་ལ་སོགས་གཉེན་ཉེ་རིང་གྲོགས་དགའ་བཤེས་ཡུལ་མི་ཁྱིམ་མཚེས་དྲག་པ་ཀུན་བསགས་ཏེ། བུ་སྨད་ནོར་དང་བཅས་པ་བཅོལ་གཏམས་བྱས་ནས། མཐར་ཕ་ཤུལ་བུས་འཛིན་དུ་འཇུག་པའི་ཁ་ཆེམས་ཀྱི་ཡི་གེ་རྒྱས་པར་བྱས་ཏེ་ཀུན་གྱིས་ཐོས་པར་བསྒྲགས། དོན་བསྡུ་ལ་ངག་ཏུ་ང་ད་ལན་གྱི་ནད་འདིས་མི་གཏོང་བ་འདུག་ཅིང་། དེས་ན་ངའི་བུ་འདི་ཡང་

DOI: 10.4324/9781003224198-25

ད་ལྟར་ཆུང་འདུག་པས། ཨ་ཁུ་དང་ཨ་ནེས་གཙོ་བྱས་པའི་གཉེན་བཤེས་ཀུན་ལ་བཙོལ་གཏམས་བྱ་རྒྱུ་ལ། ངའི་ཕུ་ན་ནོར་གནག་རྟ་ལུག་གསུམ། མདའ་ན་འོར་མ་གྲུ་གསུམ་གྱིས་གཙོ་བྱས་པའི་ཞིང་སྐྱོང་[2] མིག་ཏུ་མི་ཚུད་པ་འགའ། ཁང་པའི་འོག་ན་ཕྱུགས་བ་[3]ར་བོང་གསུམ། སྟེང་ཁང་ན་རྫིག་གསེར་དངུལ་ཟངས་ལྕགས། གཡུ་དང་གོས་དར་འབྲུའི་བང་མཛོད་ལ་སོགས་ཏེ། མདོར་ན་མི་ནོར་གཞན་ལ་སློན་མི་དགོས་པ་ཡོད་པས། འདི་རྣམས་ཀྱི་སྟེང་ནས་ཆ་ཤས་ཅིག་ང་རང་གི་རྗེས་སུ་ཐོང་། དེ་ལྷག་རྣམས་ཁྱེད་འདིར་ཚོགས་ཀུན་ལ་ང་རང་གི་བུ་འདིས་ཁྱིམ་སོ་མ་ཟིན་གྱི་བར་ལ་བཙོལ་ལོ། །ཁྱད་པར་དུ་ཨ་ཁུ་དང་ཨ་ནེ་གཉིས་ལ་བཙོལ་ལོ། །བུ་འདིས་ཁྱིམ་སོ་ཕེར་བ་དང་། མཛེས་སེ་དང་ཆུང་གཉེན་བསྒྲིགས་ཡོད་པས་མོ་རང་མནའ་མར་བསྙུ། ནོར་རྣམས་ལྷག་ལུས་མེད་པར་ཕོག་ལ་ཕ་ཤུལ་བུས་འཛིན་དུ་ཆུག་ཅིག་དེ་བར་ལ་ངའི་བུ་སྨད་གསུམ་གྱི་སྐྱིད་སྡུག་ཁྱེད་ཨ་ཁུ་དང་ཨ་ནེས་གཙོ་བྱས་པའི་གཉེན་ཚན་ཀུན་ཤེས་སོ། །སྡུག་ཏུ་མ་འཇུག་ཅིག །ང་ཤི་དུར་ཁུང་ནས་བལྟའོ་ཞེས་གསུངས་ནས་གྲོངས་སོ། །དེ་ནས་ཡབ་ (D 11r) ཀྱི་གཤེགས་རྫོངས་རྣམས་བྱས། དེ་ལྷག་གི་ནོར་རྣམས་ཀུན་ཁ་འཆམ་པར་སྨྱུང་ཚ་དཀར་རྒྱན་རང་ཚགས་བྱེད་དུ་ཆུག །ཁ་འཛིན་དགོས་པ་ཀུན་གྱིས་ཟུར་ནས་ཅི་ལེགས་ཀྱིས་ཟེར་བ་ལ། ཨ་ཁུ་དང་ཨ་ནེ་གཉིས་ན་རེ། མི་ཉེ་བྱས་རུང་དུང་པོ་ཉེ། ཁོང་མ་སྨད་ངེད་ཀྱིས་སྡུག་ཏུ་མི་འཇུག །ནོར་རྣམས་ཁ་ཆེམས་བཞིན་ངེད་ཀྱིས་ཚགས་བྱེད་ཟེར་ནས། ངའི་ཞང་པོ་དང་མཛེས་སེའི་ཕ་མིང་གིས་ལོ་རྒྱུས་བྱས་རུང་མ་ཉན་པར་ཕོ་ནོར་རྣམས་ཨ་ཁུས་བྱས། མོ་ནོར་རྣམས་ཨ་ནེས་བྱས། གཞན་རྣམས་ཕྱེད་མར་བགོས་ཏེ། ཁྱེད་མ་སྨད་རྣམས་གསོ་རིས་བྱེད་ཟེར་ནས། ངེད་མ་བུ་གསུམ་ལ་ནོར་དབང་རྒྱུ་མ་བྱུང་བའི་ཁར། དབྱར་ཞིང་ལས་བྱེད་དུས་ཨ་ཁུའི་གཡོག །དགུན་བལ་ལས་བྱེད་དུས་ཨ་ནེའི་གཡོག །ལྟོ་ཁྱིའི་ལྟོ། ལས་བོང་བུའི་[4] ལས། གོས་རྡུལ་ཕྲུག་ཐག་ཆད་པ་ལ་དྲིས་མའི་སྣ་རགས་བཅིངས་པ་གྱོན་ནས། ལས་དལ་མེད་བྱེད་དགོས་བྱུང་བས་ཡན་ལག་རྣམས་སེར་གར་སོང་། ལྟོ་གོས་ངན་པའི་སྟོབས་ཀྱིས་ཁ་མདོག་སྐྱ་ལ་ཤ་རིད་པ། སྐྲ་དང་པོ་གསེར་གཡུའི་རལ་པ་ཉིལ་ལི་བ་ལ། ཕྱིས་སྐྲ་བོ་སེང་སེང་ཤིག་སྤྲེའི་རལ་པ་ཉིལ་ལི་བ་བྱུང་བས། མཐོང་བ་དང་ཐོས་པའི་མི་སེམས་ཆུང་ཀུན་མཆི་མ་འཁོར་བ་དང་། ཨ་ཁུ་དང་ཨ་ནེ་ལ་ལྐོག་ལབ་དིར་རེ་བ་བྱུང་རུང་འཛེམ་མེད་བྱས། ངེད་མ་སྨད་ལ་སྡུག་པོ་རང་བཏང་བས། ཨ་མས་ཨ་ནེ་ལ་ཁྲུང་ཚ་དཔལ་འདྲེན་དུ་མི་འདུག་བདུད་མོ་སྡུག་འདྲེན་དུ་འདུག་བྱས་པས། ཨ་ནེ་ལ་བདུད་མོ་སྡུག་འདྲེན་དུ་མིང་ཆགས། དེ་དུས་འཇིག་རྟེན་པའི་གཏམ་དཔེ་ལ། མི་བདག་བདག་ཏུ་རེ་བདག་པོ་སྐྱོ་ཁྲིར་འདོན་ (D 11v) ཟེར་བ་དེ་ངེད་མ་སྨད་ལ་བྱུང་། སྔར་ཡབ་མི་ལ་ཤེས་རབ་རྒྱལ་མཚན་བཞུགས་པའི་ཚེ། མི་དྲག་ཞང་ཀུན་ངེད་ཀྱི་ཞལ་འཛུམ་དཀར་ནག་བལྟ་བ་ཡིན་ཏེ། ཕྱིས་ནོར་ཡོད་རྒྱལ་པོའི་ཚུལ་དུ་སོང་ནས། ཨ་ཁུ་དང་ཨ་ནེའི་ཞལ་འཛུམ་དཀར་ནག་བལྟ་བ་བྱུང་། ཨ་མ་ལ་ཡང་མི་རྣམས་ཀྱིས་ལྐོག་ལབ་ཏུ། ཁྲོ་ཕྱུག་ཆུང་མ་གྲུང་། བལ་འཇམ་སྣུམ་བུ་ལེགས་ཟེར་བ་དེ་བདེན་པར་འདུག་སྟེ། མི་གོ་ཆོད་རེ་མེད་ཙ་ན་དཔེ་འདི་དང་འདྲ། དང་པོ་སྨྱུང་ཚ་དཀར་རྒྱན་ཁྲོ་བཟང་གིས་མགོ་འདོན་དུས་མོ་བློ་ཁོག་ཆེ་ལ་གྲུང་། ལག་བཙུད་ཆེ་ཟེར་བ་ཡོད་དེ། ད་གྲུང་ཞན་གྱི་ཤན་ཕྱེད་ནས་གདའོ་ཟེར། སྡུག་རེས་བྱུང་ན་ལབ་རེས་ཀྱིས་[5]དཔེ་

དེར། རང་ལས་ཞན་པ་ཀུན་གྱིས་རྒྱབ་ནས་འཕྱ་བ་བྱུང་། ང་ལ་མཛེས་སེའི་ཕ་མས་གོས་ལྷམ་སོ་མ་རེ་བྱིན་ནས། མི་ནོར་དུ་མ་སོང་ན་ནོར་མི་རྟག་རྒྱ་ཁའི་ཟེལ་པ་བྱ་བ་ཡིན་པས་ནོར་མེད་སྙམ་པ་མི་དགོས། དང་པོ་ཡབ་མེས་རྣམས་ལའང་ནོར་རྟེང་སོར་བྱུང་བ་ཡིན། ཁྱེད་རང་ཚོ་ལའང་ནོར་ཡོད་པའི་དུས་ཡོང་ཟེར་ནས་སེམས་གསོ་ཡང་ཡང་བཏང་། དེ་ནས་ངས་ལོ་བཅོ་ལྔ་ཙམ་ལོན་པའི་ཚེ། ཨ་མ་ལ་ཕ་མས་བྱིན་པའི་ཞིང་སྐལ་པྲི་པེ་སྟན་ཆུང་བྱ་བ་མིང་མི་སྙན་རུང་སྟོན་ཐོག་གཞུན་པོ་ཡོང་བ་ཞིག་ཡོད་པ་དེ། ཞང་པོས་སོ་ནམ་བྱས་པའི་ནས་སྐྱེ་འཕེལ་དུ་ཅི་འགྲོ་བྱས་ནས་ཕག་ཏུ་སོག་གིན་ཡོད་པ་ཡང་མང་རབ་ཏུ་སོང་བ་ལ་ཤ་མང་པོ་ཉོས། ནས་དཀར་མོ་མང་པོ་ལ་ཕྱེ་བྱས། ནག་མོ་མང་པོ་ཆང་དུ་བཙོས་པས། སྐྱུང་ཚ་དཀར་རྒྱུན་མ་སྨད་ནོར་སློངས་བྱེད་པ་ཡིན་པ་འདུག་ཟེར་བ་བྱུང་། དེ་ནས་ངེད་རང་གི་ཁང་པ་ཀ་བཞི་གདུང་བརྒྱད་མ་དེར་གདན་མང་པོ་གཡར་ནས་བཏིང་སྟེ། ཨ་ཁུ་དང་ (D 12r) ཨ་ནེས་གཙོ་བྱས་པའི་གཉེན་ཉེ་འཁོར་གྲོགས་དགའ་བཞེས་ཡུལ་མི་ཁྱིམ་མཚེས་རྣམས་དང་། ཁྱད་པར་ཡབ་མི་ལ་ཤེས་རབ་རྒྱལ་མཚན་སྐུ་གཤེགས་ཁར་ཞལ་ཆེམས་ཀྱི་ཡི་གེ་རྒྱུས་ཡོད་པ་རྣམས་བོས་ཏེ། ཨ་ཁུ་དང་ཨ་ནེ་ལ་ཞ་ཁོག་འཛུགས། གཞན་གཟུག་ཐོབ་པ་ལ་གཟུག །ལྷུ་ཐོབ་པ་ལ་ལྷུ། ཆང་དཀར་ཡོལ་གྱི་གཡང་ཚེ་དང་བཅས་པའི་སྟོན་མོ་བཟང་པོ་དྲངས་ནས། ཨ་མས་གྲལ་གྱི་དབུས་སུ་ལངས་ཏེ། འོ་ལགས་སོ། བུ་སྐྱེས་པ་ལ་མིང་། ཆང་དྲངས་པ་ལ་གཏམ་བྱ་བར་གདའ་བས། ང་ཡང་གཏམ་ཚིག་གསུམ་པ་ཞིག་གཏོང་བ་ལགས་པས། ཡབ་མི་ལ་ཤེས་རབ་རྒྱལ་མཚན་སྐུ་ཐེམ་ཁར་ཞལ་ཆེམས་གསུངས་པ་རྒྱུས་ཡོད་ཀྱི་མི་བགྲེས་པ་ཨ་ཁུ་དང་ཨ་ནེས་གཙོ་མཛད། འདིར་བཞུགས་ཀྱི་གྲལ་པ་རྣམས་སྙན་གསན་པར་ཞུ་ཞེས་བརྗོད་ནས། ཞང་པོས་ཡབ་ཀྱི་ཞལ་ཆེམས་ཀྱི་ཡི་གེ་བཀླགས་པའི་མཐར། ཨ་མས་ཡི་གེ་འདིའི་དོན་གསུང་དག་དང་བཅས་པ་འདིར་བཞུགས་ཀྱི་བགྲེས་པ་ཀུན་གྱི་ཐུགས་ལ་གསལ་བས་རྒྱས་པར་ཞུ་མི་དགོས་པར་གདའ། དོན་དྲིལ་བ་ལ་སྔར་ཕན་ཨ་ཁུ་དང་ཨ་ནེ་གཉིས་ཀྱིས་ངེད་མ་སྨད་གསུམ་ལ་མགོ་འདྲོན་ཡང་དག་མཛད་པ་ཐུགས་ལ་བཏགས། ད་ང་རང་གི་བུ་དང་མཛེས་སེ་གཉིས་ཀས་ཁྱིམ་སོ་ཟིན་པ་འདུག་པས་ངེད་རང་གི་ནོར་བཅོལ་རྣམས་སྤྲོད་པ་དང་། མཛེས་སེ་ཡང་མནའ་མར་བསུ་ནས་ཡབ་ཀྱི་ཞལ་ཆེམས་བཞིན་ཕ་ཤུལ་བུས་འཛིན་དུ་འཇུག་པར་ཞུ་བྱས་པས། ཨ་ཁུ་དང་ཨ་ནེ་གཉིས་ཅི་ལ་མི་འཆམ་རུང་ལྟོ་ལ་འཆམ་པ་དང་། ང་བུ་གཅིག་པོར་སོང་བ་དང་། ཨ་ཁུ་ལ་ (D 12v) བུ་མང་པོ་ཡོད་པའི་སྟབས་ཀྱིས། ཨ་ནེ་དང་ཨ་ཁུ་གཉིས་གཅིག་ཏུ་དྲིལ་ནས་ཁྱེད་ཀྱི་ནོར་རམ་དེ་གང་ན་ཡོད་པ་ཡིན། དང་པོ་མི་ལ་ཤེས་རབ་རྒྱལ་མཚན་ཁོ་རང་ཁམས་བཟང་རིང་ལ། ཁང་ཞིང་གསེར་གཡུ་མཛོ་རྟ་གནག་ལུག་རྣམས་ངེད་ཀྱིས་གཡར་བཏང་བ་ཁོ་རང་འཆི་ཁར་ནོར་བདག་པོ་ལ་སྤྲད་པ་ཡིན། ཁྱེད་རང་དབང་བའི་ནོར་གསེར་སེ་གཅིག་གམ། ནས་ཕུལ་གང་ངམ། མར་ཉག་གཅིག་གམ། གོས་དར་རྐྱང་སྣ་གཅིག །དུད་འགྲོ་ཚེ་འཛུགས་གཅིག་ཀྱང་མིག་གིས་མ་མཐོང་བ་ལ་ད་འདི་འདྲ་ཟེར་བ། ཁྱོད་ཀྱི་ཁ་ཆེམས་ཀྱི་ཡི་གེ་སུས་བྲིས། སྡུག་མད་ཚོ་ལྟོགས་གྲིར་མ་བསད་པར་གསོས་པ་ངེད་རབ་ཡིན། ལར་མི་ངན་ལ་དབང་བསྐྱུར་ན་ཆུ་ལ་བྲིས་འཇལ་བྱེད་བྱ་བ་དེ་འདི་འདྲ་ལ་ཟེར་བ་ཡིན་ཟེར། སྣ་ཕུས་[6]སྟན་ལ་ཏར་ལངས་བྱས། སེ་གོལ་གཏོགས། ཐུ་བ་སྤྲུགས། རྐང་པ་བརྡབས་ནས། ནན་ཏར་མ་སོང་ན་ཁང་པ་ཡང་ངེད་དབང་བས། དོ་

སྨད་ཚོ་ཕྱིར་སོང་ཟེར་ཞིང་ཨ་མ་ཐལ་ལྡུག་གིས་བརྡུངས། ངེད་མིང་སྲིང་གཉིས་ཕུ་དུང་[7]གི་ལྡུག་གིས་བརྡུངས། དེའི་ཚེ་ཨ་མ་ནི། ཡབ་མི་ལ་ཤེས་རབ་རྒྱལ་མཚན་ངེད་མ་སྨད་ཀྱི་ལས་བསྐོས་[8]ལ་གཟིགས་དང་། ང་ཤི་དུར་ཁྲུང་ནས་བལྟའོ་གསུང་བ་དེ་ད་གཟིགས་པའི་དུས་ལ་བབ་གདའོ་ཟེར། ངུ་ཞིང་འགྲིལ་ནས་བྲེ་ལོག་ལོག་བྱེད་ཅིང་འདུག །ངེད་མིང་སྲིང་གཉིས་ཀྱིས་ནི་ར་མདའ་ངུ་བ་མིན་པ་མ་བྱུང་། ཨ་ཞང་གིས་ནི་ཨ་ཁུ་ལ་བུ་མང་པོ་ཡོད་པས་རྒོལ་མ་ནུས། གཞན་ཡུལ་མི་ངེད་རང་ལ་དགར་བ་རྣམས་ནི་མ་སྨད་ཚོའི་སྙིང་རྗེ་བ་ལ་ཟེར་མི་ངུ་བ་མི་འདུག །གཞན་རྣམས་ཀྱང་ཤུགས་རིང་ནར་ནར་འདུག །ཨ་ཁུ་དང་ཨ་ནེ་ནི་ངེད་ལ་ནོར་དགོས་ཟེར། ནོར་ཁྱེད་རང་ལ་འདུག་པ། (D 13r) ཡུལ་མི་ཁྲིམ་མཆོས་ལ་ཤ་ཆང་ཕངས་མེད་བཞིག་ནས་སྟོན་མོ་བཤམ་རྒྱུ་འདུག་པ། ཁྱེད་ཀྱི་ནོར་རམ་དེ་ངེད་ལ་མེད། ཡོད་ནའང་མི་གཏོང་བས་དོ་སྨད་ཚོ་མང་ན་དམག་དྲོངས། ཉུང་ན་མཐུ་ཐོང་ཟེར་ཞིང་ཐོན་སོང་། དེའི་ཕྱི་བཞིན་ཁོང་ལ་དགར་མི་རྣམས་ཀྱང་ཐོན་སོང་། ཨ་མ་ནི་དེ་ནས་ཀྱང་ངུ་ཐག་མ་ཆོད་པར་འདུག་པ་ལ། ཞང་པོ་དང་མཛེས་སེའི་ཕ་མིང་སོགས་ངེད་རང་ལ་དགར་མི་ཀུན་ཨ་མའི་སེམས་གསོ་ཕྱིར་བསྡད་ནས། ཆང་ལྡུག་རྣམས་འཐུང་ཞིང་ཨ་མ་ལ་ད་མ་ངུ་ངུས་པས་མི་ཕན། དེ་རིང་འདིར་སྟོན་གྲལ་དུ་ཚོགས་པ་ཀུན་ལ་ནོར་སློངས་རེ་གྱིས། ངེད་འདི་ན་ཡོད་པ་ཀུན་གྱིས་ཀྱང་ཅི་དྲག་རེ་སྐྱེར། ཨ་ཁུ་དང་ཨ་ནེ་གཉིས་ཀྱིས་ཀྱང་ཅི་དྲག་རེ་སྐྱེར་ཡོང་ཟེར་བ་ལ། ཨ་ཞང་ན་རེ་དེ་ཀ་གྱིས་ལ་བུ་འདི་ཡོན་ཏན་ཅིག་སློབ་ཏུ་ཐོང་། ཁྱེད་རང་མ་སྨད་ངའི་སར་སྡོད་ལ་ཞིང་གི་སོ་ནམ་གྱིས། ཅི་ཕན་བྱེད་པ་ལས་འོས་མེད། གང་ནའང་ཨ་ཁུ་དང་ཨ་ནེ་ལ་ངོ་མི་ཚ་ཞིག་བྱེད་དགོས་ཟེར་བ་ལ། ཨ་མ་ན་རེ་རང་གི་ནོར་ལ་དབང་རྒྱུ་མ་བྱུང་བའི་སྐྱོང་བྱས་པའི་ནོར་གྱིས་བུ་ཚ་མི་སོས། ཨ་ཁུ་དང་ཨ་ནེས་ངེད་རང་གི་ནོར་གྱི་ཆ་གཅིག་སྤྲད་རུང་སྐྱེར་དགོས་མེད། བུ་འདི་ཡོན་ཏན་ཞིག་སློབ་ཏུ་ཅིས་ཀྱང་གཏོང་། ངེད་མ་སྨད་ལ་ཨ་ཁུ་དང་ཨ་ནེས་གཤའ་མ་རང་མ་བཙོལ་བའི་རྗེད་ལ། ཛ་གདང་རྒྱུག་དང་དུད་པ་ལང་རྒྱུག་བྱས་ནས། ཁོང་གཉིས་ཀྱི་མངོན་བློ་འཆར་བ་ཡིན། ཞིང་གི་སོ་ནམ་ཡང་འདི་ག་ནས་བྱེད་ཟེར་ནས། རྟའི་མི་ཐོད་གད་ཁ་བྱ་བ་ན་སྔགས་རྙིང་མ་པའི་སློབ་དཔོན་ཀླུ་བརྒྱུད་མཁན་གྲོང་ཆོག་ལ་ཤིན་དུ་བྲིན་པ་ཞིག་ཡོད་པ་དེར་ང་ཀློག་སློབ་ཏུ་བཏང་། དེ་དུས་གཉེན་ (D 13v) རྣམས་ཀྱིས་ཀྱང་ནོར་སློངས་སྣ་རེ་སྣ་གཉིས་བྱིན་འདུག །ཁྱེད་པར་མཛེས་སེའི་ཕ་མས་རྒྱུགས་ཀུ་སྡོར་མི་ཤེང་ཡན་བསྐུར་ནས། །ང་ཀློག་སློབ་སར་མཛེས་སེ་མོ་རང་སེམས་གསོ་ལ་ཡང་ཡང་བཏང་བྱུང་། ཨ་ཞང་གིས་ཨ་མ་དང་སྲིང་མོ་མི་ལས་དང་སྤྲང་དུ་མི་འགྲོ་བའི་དུས་ཀྱི་ལྟོ་བྱིན། ཨ་མ་སྤྲང་དུ་ཨ་ཞང་གིས་མ་བཅུག་པར་མིའི་ལས་ཉིན་འཁལ་ཉིན་འཐག་བྱེད་ཅིང་། ངེད་མིང་སྲིང་ལ་ཅི་ཕན་དང་ནོར་ཅི་སོགས་བྱས། སྲིང་མོས་ཅི་ལྟོགས་ཀྱི་མི་གཡོག་དང་། ཛ་གདང་རྒྱུག་དུད་པ་ལང་རྒྱུག་བྱས་ནས་ལྟོ་གོས་ཅི་རྙེད་བྱས་རུང་། ལྟོ་སྐྱ་ལ་གོས་རྡུལ་བ་ཡིད་འཕམ་པ་ལས་སྐྱིད་པོ་རང་མ་སྐྱོང་གསུངས་པས། དེའི་ཚེ་ཚོས་ཉན་དུ་གྱུར་ཚད་ཐུགས་སྐྱོ་ཤས་དང་ངེས་འབྱུང་གི་སྒོ་ནས་མཆི་མ་འདོན་ཞིང་དར་ཅིག་ཀུན་ཁ་རོག་པར་འདུག་གོ །

སྡུག་བསྔལ་གྱི་བདེན་པ་ཕུལ་ཕྱིན་ཐུགས་ཉམས་སུ་བཞེས་པའི་མཛད་པ་སྐྱེ་གཉིས་པའོ། །

Notes

1 Here and below in a similar passage all editions have ངས་: ངས་ལོ་བདུན་ཙམ་འགྲོ་ (D 10r) and ངས་ལོ་བཅོ་ལྔ་ཙམ་ལོན་ (D 11v).

2 All editions consulted by de Jong read སྦྱང་ (ML: 31) instead of the correct སྦྲང་.

3 All editions read པ་ (ML: 31). However, the context of the phrase and the otherwise lexicographically attested བ་ར་བོང་གསུམ་ "the three: cow, goat, [and] donkey" (cf. BTC: 1803b), support the amendment with བ་.

4 The B edition has བོང་བུའི་ (ML: 32), whereas the remaining editions attest to བོང་. The reading བོང་བུའི་ establishes a parallel between this phrase and the preceding ཁྱིའི་.

5 For ergative in quotations, see Lesson 15. Actually, all editions read ཀྱི་ which is a common scribal error for ཀྱིས་.

6 All editions read བུས་ (ML: 34) instead of the correct ཕུས་.

7 The context makes it clear that ཕུ་དུང་ is meant instead of the attested ཕུ་རུང་ (ML: 34).

8 Although according to de Jong all editions read ལས་སྐྱོས་ (ML: 34), Jäschke quotes the phrase as ངེད་མ་སྨད་ཀྱི་ལས་བསྐྱོས་ (J: 24a, s.v. སྐྱོ་བ་). I amend the text in accordance with Jäschke.

Reading IV

Investigation of wise ones

Sa-skya Paṇḍita was an honorary title of Kun-dgaɣ Rgyal-mchan (1181–1252), a hierarch and scholar of the Sa-skya school. His most renowned work, ལེགས་པར་བཤད་པ་རིན་པོ་ཆེའི་གཏེར།, is a collection of aphorisms of worldly wisdom. It consists of 457 stanzas divided into nine thematically ordered chapters. Sometimes famous motifs from Indian literature are also alluded to in the work. Reading IV presents the first chapter of Sa-skya Paṇḍita's work preceded by introductory stanzas. This chapter is devoted to the sagacity of wise ones. The version presented herewith to students basically follows the critical edition prepared by Eimer (see SSP). Only sporadically has a differing reading been proposed.

རྒྱ་གར་སྐད་དུ། སུ་བྷཱ་ཥི་ཏ་ར་ཏྣ་ནི་དྷི་ནཱ་མ་ཤཱ་སྟྲ།
བོད་སྐད་དུ། ལེགས་པར་བཤད་པ་རིན་པོ་ཆེའི་གཏེར་ཞེས་བྱ་བའི་བསྟན་བཅོས།

འཕགས་པ་འཇམ་དཔལ་གཞོན་ནུར་གྱུར་པ་ལ་གུས་པས་ཕྱག་འཚལ་ལོ། །

ལྷ་ཡི་མཆོག་དང་ཀླུ་དབང་གྲུབ་པ་རིག་འཛིན་གཙོ། །
དྲང་སྲོང་རྒྱས་པ་གྲོག་མཁར་བ་དང་རྐང་མིག་སོགས། །
ཀུན་ནས་དགའ་བའི་གཙུག་གི་ནོར་བུས་ཞབས་མཆོད་པ། །
འགྲོ་བའི་གཙོ་བོ་ཀུན་མཁྱེན་དེ་ལ་བདག་ཕྱག་འཚལ། ༡ །

རིགས་པས་དཔྱད་ན་ཆོས་ལུགས་མི་འགལ་ཞིང་། །
འཇིག་རྟེན་བྱ་བ་ཀུན་ནས་ལེགས་བསྒྲུབ་པ། །
དམ་པ་རྣམས་ཀྱི་སྤྱོད་ཚུལ་ཅི་འདྲ་ཞིག །
བཤད་པ་འདི་ནི་ལེགས་བཤད་རིན་ཆེན་གཏེར། ༢ །

DOI: 10.4324/9781003224198-26

མཁས་པ་ཡོན་ཏན་མཛོད་འཛིན་པ། །དེ་དག་ལེགས་བཤད་རིན་ཆེན་སྡུད། །
རྒྱ་མཚོ་ཆེན་པོ་ཆུ་ཡི་གཏེར། །ཡིན་ཕྱིར་ཆུ་བོ་ཐམས་ཅད་འབབ། ༡ །

སྐྱེ་བོ་ཡོན་ཏན་ཡོད་མེད་པའི། །བླང་དོར་བློ་གྲོས་ལྡན་པ་མཁས། །
རྟུལ་དང་འདྲེས་པའི་ལྕགས་ཕྱེ་རྣམས། །ཁབ་ལེན་རྡོ་ཡིས་ལེན་པར་ཤེས། ༢ །

ལེགས་བཤད་མཁས་པའི་བློ་གྲོས་ཀྱིས། །གོ་ཡི་བླུན་པོས་དེ་ལྟ་མིན། །
ཉི་མའི་འོད་ཟེར་ཤར་བ་ན། །འབྱུང་པོའི་བྱ་རྣམས་ལོང་བར་འགྱུར། ༣ །

ཤེས་རབ་ལྡན་པས་ཉེས་པ་དག །སེལ་བར་ནུས་ཀྱི་བླུན་པོས་མིན། །
ནམ་མཁའ་ལྡིང་གིས་དུག་ཅན་སྦྲུལ། །གསོད་པར་ནུས་ཀྱི་ཁྭ་ཏས་མིན། ༤ །

བློ་གྲོས་ཆེན་པོ་རྒུད་ན་ཡང་། །ལྷག་པར་བློ་གྲོས་སྤོབས་ལྡན་འགྱུར། །
རི་དྭགས་རྒྱལ་པོ་བཀྲེས་པ་ན། །གླང་ཆེན་སྤྱི་བོ་སྨུར་དུ་འགེམས། ༥ །

མཁས་པ་བརྟད་ཅིང་མ་དྲིས་པ། །དེ་ཡི་བར་དུ་གཏིང་མི་དཔོགས། །
རྔ་ལ་དབྱུག་གུས་མ་བསྣུན་པ། །དེ་སྲིད་གཞན་དང་ཁྱད་ཅི་ཡོད། ༦ །

རིག་པ་ནང་པར་འཆི་ཡང་བསླབ། །ཚེ་འདིར་མཁས་པར་མ་གྱུར་ཀྱང་། །
སྐྱེ་བ་ཕྱི་མར་བཅོལ་བ་ཡི། །ནོར་ལ་རང་ཉིད་ལེན་པར་འདྲ། ༧ །

ཡོན་ཏན་ལྡན་ན་སྐྱེ་བོ་ཀུན། །མ་བསྡུས་པར་ཡང་རང་ཉིད་འདུ། །
དྲི་ལྡན་མེ་ཏོག་རྒྱང་རིང་ཡང་། །བུང་བ་སྤྲིན་གྱི་ཚོགས་བཞིན་འཁོར། ༨ །

མཁས་པ་ཡོན་ཏན་ཀུན་བསླབས་པ། །མཐར་ཕྱིན་གཅིག་གིས་འཛིག་རྟེན་གསལ། །
གླེན་ངན་ཤེས་པ་མང་ན་ཡང་། །རྒྱུ་སྐར་བཞིན་དུ་གསལ་མི་ནུས། ༩ །

མཁས་པ་ཡོན་ཏན་དཔག་མེད་ཀྱང་། །གཞན་གྱི་ཡོན་ཏན་ཆུང་ངུའང་ལེན། །
དེ་ལྟར་རྒྱུན་དུ་སྦྱུད་པ་ཡིས། །མྱུར་དུ་ཐམས་ཅད་མཁྱེན་པར་འགྱུར། ༡༠ །

མཁས་པ་ཤེས་རབ་ཀྱིས་བསྲུང་ན། །དགྲ་བོ་མང་ཡང་ག་ལ་ཚུགས། །
འཕགས་རྒྱལ་གྱི་ནི་བྲམ་ཟེའི་བུ། །གཅིག་པུས་དགྲ་བོའི་ཚོགས་ཀུན་བཅོམ། ༡༡ །

བློ་ཆུང་གྲོས་ཉེས་འཁྲུགས་པའི་ཚེ། །བློ་ལྡན་ཐབས་ཀྱིས་བདེ་བར་གསོ། །
ཆུ་ཀླུང་རྙོག་པས་ཆུད་གསན་པ། །ཆུ་དྭངས་ནོར་བུས་དང་བར་བྱེད། ༡༢ །

མཁས་པ་ཇི་ལྟར་ཐབས་རྡུགས་ཀྱང་། །བླུན་པོ་འཇུག་པའི་ལམ་མི་འགྲོ། །
ཆར་འདོད་བྱིའུ་སྐོམ་ན་ཡང་། །ས་ལ་འབབ་པའི་ཆུ་མི་འཐུང་། ༡༣ །

ཤེས་རབ་ལྡན་པ་མགོ་བསྐོར་ཀྱང་། །བྱ་བའི་ཆ་ལ་རྨོངས་མི་འགྱུར། །
སྲོག་ཆགས་གྲོག་མ་མིག་མེད་ཀྱང་། །མིག་ལྡན་གཞན་ལས་ལྷག་པར་མགྱོགས། ༡༤ །

བློ་གྲོས་ལྡན་པ་གཉིས་བགྲོས་ན། །བློ་གྲོས་ལེགས་པ་གཞན་འབྱུང་སྲིད། །
ཡུང་བ་དང་ནི་ཚ་ལེ་ལས། །ཁ་དོག་གཞན་ཞིག་སྐྱེ་བར་འགྱུར། ༡༥ །

ཁོང་མཛངས་བསོད་ནམས་བསགས་པའི་མི། །གཅིག་པུ་ཡིན་ཡང་ཀུན་ལས་རྒྱལ། །
རི་དྭགས་རྒྱལ་པོ་སེང་གེ་དང་། །འཁོར་ཡོས་སྐྱུར་ལ་གྲོགས་མི་དགོས། ༡༦ །

ཐབས་ལ་མཁས་ན་ཆེན་པོ་ཡང་། །བྲན་དུ་བཀོལ་བ་ག་ལ་དཀའ། །
མཁའ་ལྡིང་མཐུ་རྩལ་ཆེ་ན་ཡང་། །གོས་སེར་ཅན་གྱི་བཞོན་པར་གྱུར། ༡༧ །

འཇིག་རྟེན་འདི་དང་ཕ་རོལ་གྱི། །བདེ་བ་སྒྲུབ་པ་ཤེས་རབ་ཡིན། །
རྒྱལ་བུ་ཟླ་བའི་ཤེས་རབ་ཀྱིས། །བྲན་བཟངས་འདི་དང་ཕྱི་མར་བསྒྲུབས། ༡༨ །

དཔའ་ཞིང་མཐུ་རྩལ་ཆེ་ན་ཡང་། །མཁས་པ་མིན་པས་དཔལ་མི་ཐོབ། །
འབྱོར་པ་ཐོབ་པར་གྱུར་ན་ཡང་། །བསོད་ནམས་མེད་ན་ག་ལ་རྟག ༡༩ །

ཡོན་ཏན་སྐྱོན་གཉིས་སུས་ཀྱང་གསལ། །འདྲིས་པ་འབྱེད་ཤེས་མཁས་པ་ཡིན། །
བ་ལས་འོ་མ་ཀུན་གྱིས་ལོངས། །ཆུ་ལས་འོ་མ་ངང་པས་ཕྱེད། ༢༠ །

སྨྲས་ཤིང་བསྐུལ་བར་གྱུར་པ་ན། །དུད་འགྲོ་ལ་ཡང་གོ་བ་སྐྱེ། །
མ་བསྐུལ་གཞན་གྱིས་མ་སྨྲས་པར། །བསམ་པ་ཤེས་ན་མཁས་པ་ཡིན། ༢༡ །

བློ་དང་ལྡན་ན་མ་སྨྲས་ཀྱང་། །རྣམ་འགྱུར་ཉིད་ལས་བསམ་པ་གོ། །
བལ་པོས་སེའུ་མ་ཟོས་ཀྱང་། །ཁ་དོག་ཉིད་ལས་བྲོ་བ་ཤེས། ༢༢ །

མཁས་པ་རང་གི་ཡུལ་བས་ཀྱང་། །ཡུལ་ཁམས་གཞན་ན་མཆོད་པ་ཐོབ། །
ནོར་བུ་གཞན་དུ་བྲིན་པ་ཙམ། །རྒྱ་མཚོའི་གླིང་དུ་ག་ལ་བྲིན། ༢༣ །

མཁས་པ་སློབ་པའི་དུས་ན་སྡུག །བདེ་བར་སྡོད་ལ་མཁས་མི་སྲིད། །
བདེ་བ་ཆུང་ལ་ཆགས་པ་དེས། །ཆེན་པོའི་བདེ་བ་ཐོབ་མི་སྲིད། ༢༤ །

བློ་དང་ལྡན་ན་ཉམ་ཆུང་ཡང་། །སྟོབས་ལྡན་དགྲ་བོས་ཅི་བྱར་ཡོད། །
རི་དྭགས་རྒྱལ་པོ་སྟོབས་ལྡན་པ། །རི་བོང་བློ་དང་ལྡན་པས་བསད། ༢༥ །

སེམས་ཅན་གཞན་དང་རྗེས་མཐུན་པའི། །སྤྱོད་པ་ཤེས་ན་མཁས་པ་ཡིན། །
དུད་འགྲོ་ཡིན་ཡང་རིགས་མཐུན་རྣམས། །ཁྱུ་གཅིག་ཏུ་ནི་མི་གནས་སམ། ༢༦ །

ངེས་པར་འབྱུང་བའི་བྱ་བ་འགའ། །མ་གྲུབ་པ་ན་དཔྱོད་པའི་ཚེ། །
མཁས་རྨོངས་གཉིས་ཀྱི་ཁྱད་པར་ཤེས། །གྲུབ་ནས་དཔྱོད་པ་བླུན་པོའི་ཚུལ། ༢༧ །

མཁས་པ་རྣམས་ཀྱིས་དཔྱད་པ་ཡི། །ཤེས་བྱ་ཤེས་ན་མཁས་པར་བགྲང་། །
བ་ལང་རྒན་གཞོན་དཔྱོད་པ་ལ། །བླུན་པོ་མཁས་ཀྱང་ཡོན་ཏན་མེད། ༢༨ །

རྒྱ་མཚོ་ཆུ་ཡིས་མི་ངོམས་ཤིང་། །རྒྱལ་པོའི་བང་མཛོད་ནོར་གྱིས་མིན། །
འདོད་ཡོན་སྤྱད་པས་མི་ངོམས་ཏེ། །མཁས་པ་ལེགས་བཤད་ཀྱིས་མི་ངོམས། ༢༩ །

ལེགས་བཤད་བྱིས་པ་དག་ལས་ཀྱང་། །མཁས་པ་རྣམས་ནི་ཡོངས་སུ་ལེན། །
དྲི་ཞིམ་བྱུང་ན་རི་དྭགས་ཀྱི། །ལྟེ་བ་ལས་ཀྱང་གླ་རྩི་ལེན། ༣༠ ། །།

ལེགས་པར་བཤད་པ་རིན་པོ་ཆེའི་གཏེར་ལས། མཁས་པ་བརྟག་པ་སྟེ་རབ་ཏུ་བྱེད་པ་དང་པོའོ།། །།

Translations of exercises and readings

Exercises

Lesson 1

1. *čhos zab mo* "profound (A) Buddhist teaching (N)"; 2. *chig ɣǰam pa* "mild (A) words (N)"; 3. *lo gsum* "three (NUM) years (N)"; 4. *rgyal po de* "the/that (DEM) king (N)"; 5. *sras tha čhuṅs de* "the (DEM) youngest (A) son (N)"; 6. *źag du ma* "many (NUM) days (N)"; 7. *śa rlon pa* "fresh (A) flesh (N)"; 8. *khrag dron mo* "warm (A) blood (N)"; 9. *rgyal bu tha čhuṅs de* "the (DEM) youngest (A) prince (N)"; 10. *yun riṅ po* "long (A) time (N)"; 11. *chal ba rnon po* "sharp (A) splinter (N)"; 12. *chig sñan pa* "kind (A) words (N)"; 13. *ñes pa čhen po* "great (A) moral faults (N)"; 14. *phug ron gsum źig* "(a) (INDF) three (NUM) doves (N)"; 15. *bu mo ṅan pa* "bad (A) daughters (N)".

Lesson 2

1. *rgyal bu sems čan čhen po de* "the prince Sems-čan-čhen-po"; 2. *stag mo ltogs pa* "hungry tigress"; 3. *sems čan khri* "ten thousand sentient beings"; 4. *srog čhags stoṅ* "one thousand living beings"; 5. *brda maṅ du* "many signs"; 6. *mgon po thugs rǰe čan* "compassionate protector"; 7. *spreɣu phrug lṅa brgya* "five hundred monkey-children"; 8. *khyim mches drag pa kun* "all noble neighbours"; 9. *lto gos ṅan pa* "bad food and clothing"; 10. *ston mo bzaṅ po* "excellent feast"; 11. *rgyal po čhen po* "great king"; 12. *ɣkhor maṅ po rnams* "many attendants"; 13. *bu mo de dag* "the daughters"; 14. *bdag rgyal bu sems čan čhen po yin/* "I am the prince Sems-čan-čhen-po." 15. *ṅa dge bsñen yin/* "I am a lay practitioner."

Lesson 3

1. *spreɣuɣi rgyal po čhen po* "great king of monkeys"; 2. *kha ba čan gyi rgyal khams ɣdi* "this realm of the snow-clad (i.e. Tibet)"; 3. *srin poɣi phru gu dpag*

DOI: 10.4324/9781003224198-27

med "innumerable children of the ogre"; 4. *srin poɣi groṅ khyer dag* "towns of ogres"; 5. *ɣgro baɣi mgon po* "protector of beings"; 6. *bud med kyi čhas* "woman's garments"; 7. *ṅaɣi sdom pa* "my vow"; 8. *ri rab kyi khoṅ seṅ* "inner caverns of Ri-rab"; 9. *bdag čag gi che srog* "our lives"; 10. *ɣbyuṅ poɣi bya rnams* "birds of demons"; 11. *bram ze deɣi čhuṅ ma de* "the wife of the Brahmin"; 12. *groṅ khyer de na rgan mo źig la bu gñis śig yod/* "In the town an old woman had two sons." 13. *ṅa spyan ras gzigs kyi dge bsñen yin/* "I am a lay practitioner of Spyan-ras-gzigs." 14. *qa khu la bu maṅ po yod/* "[My] paternal uncle had many sons." 15. *rgya mcho čhen po čhu yi gter yin/* "A vast ocean is a treasury of water." 16. *deɣi che yul de na bram ze phyin te lo śu śa yod do/* "At that time in the country there was a Brahmin called Phyin-te-lo-śu-śa." 17. *khyod kyi skad sñan pa yin no/* "Your voice is pleasant."

Lesson 4

1. Bones lie in the wood. 2. Thereafter the rock-ogress rose. 3. Innumerable children of the ogre were born. 4. Monkey-children were born. 5. Then, the fruits were consumed. 6. The Noble One rose. 7. I was born into the race of ogresses. 8. Wealth occurred to [your] ancestors. 9. This man has no sons. 10. Later, the sons-in-law gathered. 11. Clothes turned yellowish-red. 12. Two princes came. 13. The prince Sems-čan-čhen-po passed away there. 14. The deity went back to [its] place. 15. The two went. 16. They went there.

Lesson 5

1. [Their] head hair and beard fell off by itself. 2. Then, the youngest prince thought to himself (lit. thought this in [his] mind). 3. Then, with a sharp wooden splinter the prince let blood come out of (lit. on) [his] body. 4. The parents looked at the sky. 5. Birth and decay are intrinsic to (lit. exist in) everything. 6. Due to [my] offspring I've got into the swamp of the circle of rebirth. 7. I went as the only son. 8. The aunt and the paternal uncle united (lit. gathered as one). 9. The consort and her children went out. 10. The maternal uncle and Mjes-se's father and brothers stayed. 11. The ox went out through another door. 12. The leg broke. 13. You killed my husband. 14. The Victorious One taught a doctrine. 15. At that point Phyin-te-lo-śu-śa thought this in [his] mind. 16. [My] wife is always scolding. 17. The Victorious One discerned his thoughts with [his] mind. 18. You killed my horse. 19. The wife of the weaver seized Dbyig-pa-čan.

Lesson 6

1. Dust and impurities disappeared. 2. For a long time I've been roaming in the cycle of existence. 3. Give [me] an ox back! 4. Now, eat! 5. The limbs became cracked. 6. The mother stood up in the middle of the row. 7. The maternal uncle read the text of [my] father's testament. 8. Mɟes-se's parents sent firewood. 9. Birds of demons become blind. 10. The Victorious One is not comprehended (lit. comprised) by [human] thought. 11. He borrowed an ox from a householder. 12. In the middle of the road, there was a river. 13. The axe fell into the river. 14. Then, Kun-dgaɣ-bo saw things of this kind. 15. The wife of the Brahmin was ugly.

Lesson 7

I. འགྲོ་བ་ – present participle པ་ ~ བ་; བཙུན་མོ་ – feminine མོ་; ལྔ་པ་ – ordinal numeral པ་; སྲིན་མོ་ – feminine མོ་; ཇོ་མོ་ – feminine མོ་; གསོལ་བ་ – noun པ་ ~ བ་; སྨན་པ་ – affiliation པ་; བུ་མོ་ – feminine མོ་; དྲུག་པོ་ – collective པོ་; སྐྱེས་པ་ – perfective participle པ་ ~ བ་.

II.1. Perforce of [my previous] actions, I was born into the race of [rock]-ogresses. 2. At that time in the town an old woman had two constantly robbing sons. 3. The three, the old woman, the mother and [her] sons, saw the Victorious One coming from afar. 4. Rays of the sun have risen. 5. You lost my ox. 6. You let my axe fall (lit. sent) into the river. 7. They are leading me. 8. Knock out carpenter's two incisor (lit. front) teeth! 9. The meaning of this text is clear to the mind of all elders. 10. Thereafter, the *bodhisattva*-monkey led the monkey-children there. 11. Her mind is satisfied with fresh flesh and warm blood. 12. The queen heard these words uttered. 13. The blind one didn't have a son.

Lesson 8

1. Don't think any differently! 2. The teachings of the Buddha, while spreading, will increase. 3. The sole son of a Brahmin conquered all troops of enemies. 4. *Garuḍa*-[bird] became the riding-beast of Gos-ser-čan. 5. Then Kun-dgaɣ-bo together with the numerous attendants were happy. 6. The Brahmin rested [his] chin on a staff. 7. He will pass a judgement on (lit. of) us. 8. Deliver (lit. say) my message to the king! 9. Dbyig-pa-čan killed my mare. 10. One day (lit. time) the Victorious One was abiding in Mñan-du-yod-pa. 11. A rock-ogress made her way (lit. came) there. 12. Three doves were flying and playing

around. 13. The king together with [his] many attendants returned to [his] castle. 14. All relatives know the happiness and misery of my children and [their] mother, the three. 15. Now I take [my] house merely as grave.

Lesson 9

1. domesticated cattle: cows, goats, [and] donkeys, the three; 2. Regarding two princes, [they] came. 3. As for myself, [I] am the prince Sems-čan-čhen-po. 4. Regarding him, now it is my father, the king Zas-gcaṅ-ma. 5. Regarding the queen of that king in those days of yore, today it is my mother Sgyu-ma Lha-mɟes. 6. Then, as for these six children of the monkey, [their] father, the *bodhisattva*-monkey, brought [them] to the forest called Bya-chogs (lit. Flock of birds) [and] abounding in fruits. 7. I fed a hungry tigress with [my] body. 8. Now I take [my] house [merely] as grave [and] think of [my] wife and daughters as enemies only. 9. He took a stone and threw [it]. 10. In another place, a crow was sitting on a *śa ko ta ka*-tree. 11. As for yourself, due to [your] great compassion, having fed the tigress, [you] were kind to everybody [else]. 12. A dove is a sign for a son; the youngest among the doves was carried away by a falcon. 13. Monk Gau-ta-ma is utterly happy. 14. A mare of another man fled.

Lesson 10

1. The youngest son, being filled (lit. possessed) with love and compassion from childhood, seemed to all like [their] only child. 2. Indeed, the king did set them free according to the words of the Victorious One. 3. That eldest son Sgra-čhen-po of (lit. in) those days is Byams-pa. 4. [Their] hair grew shorter. [Their] tails grew shorter, as well. 5. A little joy rose (lit. grew) in his parents. 6. The daughters inveighed against [their] mother in return (ཕྱིར་, lit. back). 7. Earlier I did bad deeds. 8. Tathāgata was sitting under a tree. 9. Dbyig-pa-čan let the ox into the house. 10. Until then, you, all the relatives, [will] know the happiness and misery of my children and [their] mother, the three. 11. My maternal uncle and Mɟes-se's father and brothers recalled the account. 12. Thereafter, the *bodhisattva*-monkey, having led the monkey-children there, pointed towards the crops. 13. These people, the inhabitants (པ་) of the snow-clad Tibet, are those who descended from both a father-monkey and a mother rock-ogress. 14. All the water, having flowed therein, disappeared by being absorbed in the arms [of] Skoṅ-čhu. 15. The lord Gñaɣ-khri Bcan-po appeared to [become] the king of Tibet.[1] 16. Even if a Nepalese did not eat the pomegranate, [he] knows [its] taste from [its] very colour.

Lesson 11

1. During a short rest the three sons went into a forest. 2. What does this tigress eat as food? 3. [My] parents surrounded my bones (lit. bones of the dead me) that lie in the wood. 4. Why then, just because of me, don't [you] recognise [your] fall into the ocean of misery? 5. What do [you] think in your mind? 6. Who is [now] that king Śiṅ-rta-čhen-po of (lit. in) those days of yore? 7. Then Kun-dgaɣ-bo together with all the numerous attendants, having rejoiced hearing what the Victorious One said, praised [him]. 8. Monkey-children, reborn from six states of existence, were born. 9. Being a chapter on how Sems-čan-čhen-po offered [his] body to a tigress, this is the second [chapter]. 10. The Brahmin spoke to the Victorious One. 11. At that time, the Noble One, Spyan-ras-gzigs, conferred the vow of a lay practitioner upon a monkey that was displaying miracles. 12. The extremely poor was a one with neither food nor clothes. 13. He jumped onto a wall. 14. He has not even a scolding wife. 15. [My] father Mi-la Śes-rab Rgyal-mchan got infected with an illness.

Lesson 12 How Sems-čan-čhen-po offered his body to a tigress

[These are] the words I heard. One day (lit. time) the Victorious One was abiding in Mñan-du-yod-pa in the 'Grove of the Prince Rgyal-byed', a copse [founded by] (lit. of) Mgon-med-zas-sbyin. At that time, when the time for alms came, the Victorious One put on a lower garment and a monk-robe. Then, having taken up [his] alms-bowl, [he] went for alms with Kun-dgaɣ-bo. At that time in the town there was an old woman whose sons were always stealing;[2] [they] were seized by a wealthy man [and] led to a judge. After [their case] was assessed under (lit. compared with) the [existing] laws, [they] were [just] about to be executed. A hangman was assigned [with the execution and he] led [them] to the place of execution. Upon (ལས་) that the three, the old woman, the mother and [her] sons,[3] saw the Victorious One coming from afar. [They] paid homage to the coming Buddha.

Lesson 13

The Victorious One heard [the mother] saying: "Oh, the most eminent one among the deities, I beg [you], thinking [about us] kindly, to save these sons of mine, who are about to be killed."[4] [He] took pity on them[5] with the great compassion of a Tathāgata. In order to save their lives, the Victorious One, having spoken to Kun-dgaɣ-bo, sent [him] to submit a request to the king. As for the king, he did set them free according to the words of the Victorious One. As the kindness of the

Victorious One came to mind, great happiness arose [in them].[6] [They] went to the place where the Victorious One was staying; [when they] arrived [there], [they] bowed the top of [their] heads to [his] feet. Then, having joined the palms of [their] hands [in a gesture of devotion], [the sons] spoke with these words to the Victorious One:

Lesson 14

"Once this remnant of our life has been saved through the great kindness of the Victorious One, [oh] the most eminent among the deities, having thought kindly [of us], would [you] allow us to join the religion of the Buddha?" When the Victorious One replied: "Welcome!",[7] [their] head hair and beard fell off by itself [and their] clothes even turned yellowish-red. [They] became steadfast in their belief,[8] and the Victorious One taught [them] doctrine suitable [for them].[9] Hence, [their spiritual] dust and impurities disappeared [and they] became Arhats. Because their old mother also heard the teaching, [she] became a non-returning one. Then, after Kun-dgaɣ-bo had seen these miraculous things,[10] [he] said in praise (lit. praised): "Regarding Tathāgata, [he] possesses such excellent qualities." And again [he] thought: "What good deeds did the three, the old woman, the mother and her sons, accomplish earlier, so that now, having encountered the Victorious One, [they] have become free from great moral faults and achieved the happiness of *nirvāṇa*? The goal of benefit and happiness [they] achieved within a lifetime (lit. with one body) is good." The Victorious One discerned [his thoughts] and said these words to Kun-dgaɣ-bo:

Lesson 15

"Regarding the three, the mother and [her] sons, it is not only now, at that time, that I have taken care [of them],[11] but also earlier, in the past, [I] took care [of them] with my kindness." Kun-dgaɣ-bo replied: "Victorious One, [I] beg that the Victorious One teaches [me] how [he] took care of these three, the mother and [her] sons, also earlier, in the past." The Victorious One said to Kun-dgaɣ-bo:[12]

"Earlier, in days gone by, innumerable aeons ago, there was a king called Śiṅ-rta-čhen-po in this continent; [he] was ruling over about five thousand vassals. The king had three sons: the oldest was called Sgra-čhen-po; the middle one was called Lha-čhen-po,[13] [and] the youngest one was called Sems-čan-čhen-po. The youngest son, being filled (lit. possessed) with love and compassion from childhood, seemed to all like [their] only child. At that time, the king accompanied by [his] ministers, the queen, and [his] sons, went outside for a walk. They stopped to rest a bit,[14] [but] the three sons continued on into a forest. Thereupon [they] saw a tigress, that, many days after getting cubs, being pained due to hunger and thirst, was about to eat [her] cubs. Then, the youngest prince said to [his] two elder brothers:

Lesson 16

'Regarding this tigress, a one like this, pained with great affliction[15] [and] about to die due to weakness and starvation, even wants to eat [her] newborn cubs.' The two elder brothers responded (lit. said): 'What you are saying is true.' When the youngest brother also asked the elder brothers: 'What does this tigress [usually] eat as food?', the elder brothers answered: 'Her mind is satisfied with the fresh flesh and warm blood of what's just been killed.' And again [he] asked: 'Is there anybody who, being suitable [and] having saved [her] life by such means,[16] can do [this] without getting hurt [himself]?' The elder brothers replied: 'Regarding this, because this is very difficult, there is nobody [who could do this].' Then, the youngest prince thought to himself:[17] 'For a long time I've been roaming in the cycle of existence, having wasted innumerable bodies and lives, – although I have abandoned bodies, once due to passion, once due to hatred, and once due to ignorance, what is this body worth that for the sake of Buddhist teaching has not even once met with the field of virtue?' The three went on together.[18] Thereupon (ལས་), not having gone far, [the youngest prince] said these words to [his] two elder brothers: 'Oh, brothers, go on ahead! Having taken care of something, I will come after.' Having taken (lit. entered) the same road, [he] returned quickly to the place where the tigress' den was. He lay down near the tigress [but] the tigress was not able to eat with a [due to her weakness] closed mouth.

Lesson 17

Then, with a sharp wooden splinter the prince let blood come out of (lit. on) [his] body. Afterwards (ནས་) [he] let the tigress lick [the blood]. [She] even opened the mouth [and] completely[19] ate the flesh of [his] body. The two elder brothers waited [and] because [the youngest brother] did not come for a long time, retracing [their own] steps [they] went back to look [for him]. When they considered what [he] said earlier,[20] [they] thought: 'Surely, [he] went to feed the hungry tigress.' When, having arrived there, [they] looked, [they] saw that [their] youngest brother, being eaten by the tigress, completely smeared (lit. smudged) with flesh and blood, was lying [there] quite gruesomely.[21] Having fallen,[22] [they] fainted away. A long time passed before [they] recovered [their] consciousness (lit. breath). Then, crying [they] rolled on the ground and swooned. At that time the queen mother dreamed[23] that three doves had been flying and playing around, and the youngest of them[24] was carried away by a falcon. [She] woke up immediately in terror (སྐྲག་དངངས་) and told the king: 'I've heard it said[25] that a dove is a sign for a son; if the youngest among the doves was carried away by a falcon, [I] am certain that some mischief has happened to the dearest of my sons.' Immediately after this [they] organised (lit. let) thorough searches.[26] After a short while,[27] because the two princes came back, [the mother] asked: 'Is the dearest of [my] sons unhurt? Where is [he]?' The two sons were unable to utter a word;[28] they could neither breathe[29] nor speak for a long time. Thereafter, [their] breath returned (lit. come back) and [they] said: 'A tiger ate [him].' When the queen had heard these words uttered, [she] fainted away. [She] collapsed on the ground. After a long time[30] [her] breath recovered [and] the two sons and the queen, in company of the court, went quickly to the place where the prince had died. Because by that time the tigress had completely eaten the flesh of the prince['s body], they saw [it][31] lying on the ground, a mess of mere bones and blood.[32] The queen seized [his] head, the king seized [his] hand; [and they] lamented and cried. There [they] fainted away and after a long time woke up again. After the prince Sems-čan-čhen-po had passed away there (དེར་), [he] was reborn in Dgaɣ-ldan, a deities' place. He (དེ་) thought: 'Why? What did I do that I've been born here?' When [he] surveyed (lit. looked through) the five realms of existence with his divine eye, [he] realised (lit. saw): '[My] parents, having surrounded my bones[33] that lie in the wood, because [they] loved [me] much [in their] mind, are pained due to grief of misery and [so they] lament.'[34] The deity thought: 'Because a threat might occur to [their] bodies or lives on account of their unhappiness,[35] I will go to please them[36] and to talk to them.' Then (ནས་), having come down from the sky, [he] pleased [his] parents with various comforting words [said] from above.[37]

Lesson 18

After the parents looked at the sky, [they] said: 'Oh, deity, tell me[38] who are you?' The deity spoke: 'As for myself, [I] am the prince called Sems-čan-čhen-po – because I fed a hungry tigress with my body, [I] was born in Dgaɣ-ldan, a deities' place. Oh, great king, understand [it] this way: things that are possessed of existence so much will eventually perish. [Things[39] that] possess birth will certainly perish. If [one] committed an offence, [one] goes (lit. falls) to hell. Whereas (གི་) if [one] committed virtuous deeds, [one] is reborn in heaven. If birth and decay are intrinsic to (lit. exist in) everything, why then, just because of me, don't [you] recognise [your] fall into the ocean of misery? Strain [yourself] towards virtue!' His parents responded: 'As for yourself, due to [your] great compassion [you] fed the tigress; [but in] being kind to everybody [else], [you] abandoned [us]. Because [you] died, when we were recalling you[40] we were pained with misery as if [our] flesh would be cut to bits and pieces; oh, you who practice great compassion, was it suitable to act this way?' Then, the deity again [tried to] calm down [his parents] by means of various kind words; and because [he] pleased [them], a little joy rose in his parents. Having made a chest from seven kinds of jewel, [they] placed [his] bones inside of it [and] above the hidden [chest they] made a shrine. The deity went back to [its] place. The king together with [his] many attendants also returned to [his] palace."

The Victorious One said to Kun-dgaɣ-bo: "What do you think? What do [you] think: who is [now] that king Śiṅ-rta-čhen-po of (lit. in) those days of yore? Regarding him, now it is my father, the king Zas-gcaṅ-ma. Regarding the queen of that king in those days of yore, today it is my mother Sgyu-ma Lha-mȷes. That eldest son Sgra-čhen-po of (lit. in) those days is Byams-pa. The middle son Lha-čhen-po is Ba-su-mi-tra. Regarding the youngest prince Sems-čan-čhen-po of those days of yore, don't think any differently! Now it is me. The tiger cubs of those days of yore are these two men. Earlier, having also saved [them] from difficulties a long time ago, I rescued [their] lives [and] made them happy. Now, even (ཀྱང་) after [I] had achieved manifesting enlightenment, I saved [them] from difficulties [again]. [They] became absolutely free from the great misery of the cycle of existence." Then Kun-dgaɣ-bo together with all the numerous attendants, having rejoiced [hearing] what the Victorious One said, praised [him].

Second chapter: How Sems-čan-čhen-po offered [his] body to a tigress.[41]

Readings

Reading I. Householder Dbyig-pa-čan

[These are] the words I heard.[42] One day the Victorious One was abiding in Mñan-yod in the 'Grove of the Prince Rgyal-byed', a copse founded by (lit. of) Mgon-med-zas-sbyin. At that time in the country there was a Brahmin called Phyin-te-lo-śu-śa. The wife of the Brahmin was very ugly and also (ཀྱང་) blind in both eyes. The blind one, having seven daughters but no son, was very poor. [The couple] gave the daughters of the Brahmin in marriage[43] one after another (སོ་སོར་). Later, the sons-in-law gathered [in their house]. The wife of the Brahmin, being also a wrathful and hot-tempered woman (མོ་), raged at the visiting (lit. coming) daughters and sons-in-law. Thereupon (ནས་), the daughters inveighed against their mother in return (ཕྱིར་, lit. back). At that time, it was the season for fields to be reaped.[44] Having borrowed an ox from a neighbour, [the Brahmin] was going back and forth on the field [and], because [he] had not watched (lit. guarded) [the ox] properly, [it] got lost. At that point Phyin-te-lo-śu-śa thought this in [his] mind:

"What bad deeds did I do earlier so that when I return home [my] wife is always scolding and the seven daughters and the sons-in-law do not [even] allow me to stay? [And] now, when I borrowed [my] neighbour's ox, [it] got lost. Although I looked [for it], I have not found [the ox]. What should [I] do?"[45] While [he] was sitting [there], tormented with [these] worries, from afar [he] saw Tathāgata sitting under a tree with all [his] senses calm and peaceful. The Brahmin, rested [his] chin on a staff[46] and pondered for a while.[47] Then, [he] thought again: "Monk Gau-ta-ma is utterly happy. He has neither a scolding wife nor bad daughters and sons-in-law who harm [him].[48] Not having to borrow an ox when the time comes for fields to be reaped, [he] has no troubles." The Victorious One discerned his thoughts with [his] mind and spoke the following words: "[It] is [just] like you have thought; if I do not have any really bad faults,[49] nor do I have a bad wife, how much less [do I have] inveighing and scolding. [I] have neither seven harming daughters nor sons-in-law who gather in [my] house. [I] do not have any troubles because of a lost ox when the time comes for fields to be reaped.[50] Would you like to become a monk?" The Brahmin said to the Victorious One: "Now I take [my] house [merely] as grave [and] think of [my] wife and daughters as enemies only. If the Victorious One allows [me] to become a monk, then I will become a monk." Because the Victorious One said "Welcome!", the [Brahmin's] head hair and beard fell off by itself [and he] became a monk. Thereafter, the Victorious One taught [him] Buddhist teachings in an appropriate manner[51] [and] then at that very moment all [his mental] impurities disappeared and [he] became an Arhat. Then Kun-dgaɣ-bo said to the Victorious One: "[It] is excellent. The Victorious One, who works for the welfare of sentient beings,[52] is not comprehended (lit. comprised) by [human] thought. What good deeds did this Brahmin previously do that, free from all faults of bad deeds, [he] obtained that which is beneficial for [his] virtue[53] as easily as paint is applied to a clean white cotton cloth?"[54] The Victorious One replied to Kun-dgaɣ-bo: "It is not only now that, having supported this Brahmin, I made [him] happy, but also (ཡང་) earlier, in the past, [I] freed [him] from all bad deeds and made [him] happy." Kun-dgaɣ-bo pleaded: "I beg [you] to instruct [me] in detail how [you] made this Brahmin happy in the past." The Victorious One responded: "Listen very carefully (lit. well) and take [it] into [your] mind! [It] will be taught to you." Kun-dgaɣ-bo pleaded: "[I] wish to listen to exactly like that." The Victorious One said the following words to Kun-dgaɣ-bo:

"Earlier, before innumerable immeasurable aeons in (lit. of) the past, there was a king called Mɟes-pa;[55] [he] was ruling the dominion according to Buddhist teachings. At that time in the country there was a Brahmin called Dbyig-pa-čan – the extremely poor one had neither food nor clothes.[56] Having borrowed an ox from a householder, he used [it] during the daytime. Thereafter, [he] led the ox and [he] went to the house of the householder. As for the householder, [he] was eating[57] there. Dbyig-pa-čan let the ox into the house. The ox went out through another door and got lost. The householder, having eaten, stood up, and, not seeing the ox anywhere, said to Dbyig-pa-čan: 'Where is the ox?' The latter (lit. he) answered: '[I] let [it] into your house.' 'Because you lost my ox, give [me another] ox back!' Thus [he] replied. [Dbyig-pa-čan] answered: 'I did not lose [it].' Then the two said together[58] 'Let [us] go to the king! [He] will examine who of us is right and who is wrong.'[59] Having said thus, the two proceeded. When a mare of another man fled, he called out to Dbyig-pa-čan, 'Don't let the mare escape!' He (i.e. Dbyig-pa-čan) took a stone and threw [it towards the mare]. [He] hit the leg of the horse and the leg broke. [The horse-owner] said, 'Because you killed my horse, give [me] my horse [back]!' 'Why should [I] give [you another] horse?' He (i.e. the horse-owner) replied, 'Come here! Let [us] go to the king and he will pass a judgement on (lit. of) us.' Then, they went there (i.e. to the king). Dbyig-pa-čan planned to escape: he jumped onto a wall and fell down [on the other side] onto a weaver who sat close by it (i.e. close to the wall) weaving.[60] Thereupon the weaver died. The wife of the weaver seized Dbyig-pa-čan and said [to him]: 'Because you killed my husband, give [me] my husband back!' [Dbyig-pa-čan] asked (lit. said): 'How can I give [you] your husband back?' [She] replied (lit. said), 'Come here! Let [us] go to the king and he will pass a judgement on (lit. of) us.' Off they went. On the way,[61] there was a deep river. Holding an axe in [his] mouth a carpenter emerged out of (lit. from) the river. Dbyig-pa-čan asked him, 'How deep is the river?'[62] Because [the carpenter] spoke, 'The river is deep,'[63] the axe fell into the river. [The carpenter] could not find the axe and [therefore] seized Dbyig-pa-čan [saying] 'You let my axe fall[64] into the river.' He (i.e. Dbyig-pa-čan) replied, 'I did not throw [the axe into the river].' [The carpenter said]: 'Come here! Let [us] go to the king and he will pass a judgement on (lit. of) us.' So they went. As they got tired, [they] stopped at (lit. went to) a tavern and ordered beer. A beer-seller had just given birth to a son. Having covered the baby with a cloth, [she] laid [it] down [to sleep]. Thereupon (པ་ལས་), Dbyig-pa-čan sat down on it (i.e. on the baby) and the boy died.[65] Having seized Dbyig-pa-čan, she [said], 'Because you killed my son, give [me] my son back!' He replied, 'If I did not kill [your son], how could I give [you] your son back?' She (དེས་) said, 'Come here! Let [us] go to the king and he will pass a judgement on (lit. of) us.' They went. In another place a crow was sitting on a *śa ko ta ka*-tree – it saw Dbyig-pa-čan [and] said, 'Where [are] you going?' [He answered]: 'For myself, [I] am not going [voluntarily]; they are leading me.' 'Whither are [they] leading [you]?' 'To the king.' 'Well then, also deliver (lit. tell) my message to the king! "In the place called so-and-so, a crow sitting on the *śa ko ta ka*-tree is saying

(མཆིའོ་): 'When I was sitting on another tree [my] voice was not pleasant but when [I] came to this tree my voice is wonderfully pleasant. Why is this so?'" Ask it (lit. say) thus!' Then, at yet (ཡང་) another place [they] saw a snake. As before, [it said] 'Convey (lit. tell) this message of mine [to the king]! "Whenever I come out from [my] hole, [I] am happy. [But] when I go back in, [I] suffer. Why is this so?"[66] Ask [it] thus!' As they went [further], a young girl saw [them] at another place. As before, [she] said (སྨྲས་): 'Convey my message [to the king]! "When I stay in [my] parents' house I miss (lit. wish) the house of [my] father-in-law. When I stay in the house of [my] father-in-law I miss (lit. wish) the house of [my] parents. Why is this so?"' They went [further] and came to the king. Having bowed with [their] heads to king's feet, they sat down on one side. Then, the king asked them, 'Why did you come?'[67] They related all the conflicts between Dbyig-pa-čan and the householder.[68] The king asked (lit. said) Dbyig-pa-čan: 'Did you borrow the ox?' '[Yes, I] did.' 'Well, did [you] bring [it] back?' 'Having given [it] back so that the householder [could] see [it], I did not communicate [it].'[69] The king decided 'Because this Dbyig-pa-čan, having given back the ox, did not say [it aloud], cut off [his] tongue! Because the householder, upon seeing that the ox came in, did not bind [it], gouge out [his] eyes!' The householder said, 'First Dbyig-pa-čan took away my ox. Now it is better that Dbyig-pa-čan wins than if [one] gouged out my eyes in addition.'[70] The other (lit. one) man said, 'Lord, Dbyig-pa-čan killed my mare.' When the king asked Dbyig-pa-čan 'How did you kill the horse?' [Dbyig-pa-čan said,] 'Having entered the road, I was walking. After this man shouted (lit. said) "Don't let the horse free!", having seized a stone, I threw [it at the horse]. Therefore (བས་) the horse died.' The king said, 'Because the horse-owner shouted "Don't let the horse free!", regarding the horse-owner, cut off [his] tongue! Because Dbyig-pa-čan threw the stone, cut off [his] hand!' The man said: 'First Dbyig-pa-čan killed my horse. Now it is better that Dbyig-pa-čan wins than if [one] cut off my tongue in addition.' The carpenter said, 'Because Dbyig-pa-čan asked "How deep is the river?" the axe carried in [my] mouth[71] fell into the river.' The king said, 'Although it is appropriate to carry any portable object[72] on a shoulder [you] carried [the axe] in the mouth. Therefore (བས་), knock out [his] two incisor (lit. front) teeth! Because Dbyig-pa-čan asked "Is the river deep?" cut off [his] tongue!' The carpenter said, 'First my axe got lost. Now it is better that Dbyig-pa-čan wins than if [one] knocked out my teeth in addition.' The beer-seller said, 'Dbyig-pa-čan killed my child.' Dbyig-pa-čan replied (lit. said), 'Because I was tired, I went to order a beer. Without having looked at the mat, I sat on it. Not having recognised a child lying underneath, the child died.' The king said, 'You beer-seller, because [you] laid [your] child down

(གོར་, lit. on a spot) and (ལ་) covered [it] with a cloth so that [it] was invisible, [you] made a mistake. And because you, Dbyig-pa-čan (who sat down on the mat without examining [it]),[73] made a mistake, you, Dbyig-pa-čan, become [her] husband and cause [her] to have a baby!'[74] The beer-seller said, 'First [he] killed my child. Now it is better that Dbyig-pa-čan wins than if [he] became my husband in addition.' The weaver's wife said, 'Dbyig-pa-čan killed my husband.' Dbyig-pa-čan replied (lit. said), 'Because I had a lot of enemies, fearing [them], I crossed a wall and fled. Not having seen a man concealed behind [the wall],[75] the man died.' The king said, 'Go, and this one shall become your husband!'[76] She (i.e. the wife) said, 'First [he] killed my husband. Now it is better that Dbyig-pa-čan wins than if [he] became my husband in addition.' [The king] passed them the judgements individually, and after [they] had blamed Dbyig-pa-čan,[77] [he] became free from all offences. In that king's presence two women were arguing about a child. The perceptive king[78] examined [the case] and said these words to the women: 'You two, having each seized an arm of the child, pull [it] and take [it] as [your] own whoever obtains the child!'[79] Because the one (པ་) who was not the child's mother had no compassion for the child, and not fearing to hurt[80] [it], [she] pulled with all the strength [she] had. But the one who was child's mother, because [she] loved the child, and fearing to hurt [it], did not pull vehemently even though [she] could match [the other one] with [her] strength. After perceiving [this], the king said to the one who pulled vehemently, '[This] is not your child. Because [it] is the child of the other woman, speak honestly!' [It] was the child of the one who was pulling gently [and so she] took the child. Later, two men were also arguing about one piece of cotton cloth. Upon coming together to the king, the king considered [their case] and passed a judgement similar to the previous one. Then, Dbyig-pa-čan said the following to the king: 'When they, having seized me, were leading [me], a snake said the following words as a message: "When I come out from [my] hole, I am happy [but] when I creep (lit. enter) back in, I am pained. Ask why is [it] like that!"' The king said, 'Say to the snake: "Because, while not wrathful, you are hungry when coming out of the hole, you are happy. After [you] had come out and you had eaten a lot of food the birds tormented [you]. Therefore (པས་), [you] became angry [and] because [you] got plump, when coming back in, [you now] get stuck in the hole and are pained." Say it [to him]!: "If from now on you recognise the right amount of food, not being angry, [you] will come back as happy as when you went out." Say it thus!' Then [Dbyig-pa-čan] delivered (lit. told) the message of the young girl and the king replied: 'Say to the young girl: "In the house of your parents lives a lover; so when [you] are staying in the house of [your] father-in-law, because [you] are attached to the lover, [you] wish to return to the house of [your] parents. But when [you] are staying in the house of [your] parents, being vexed with the lover, [you] yearn for [your] husband, therefore [you] wish to go to the house of [your] father-in-law. For this reason (ཕྱིས་) abandon one place and stick properly (lit. well) to the [other] one and [you] will have no such pain."' [Dbyig-pa-čan] delivered the message of the crow sitting on the *śa ko ta ka*-tree in [yet] another place and the king replied, '"Because under the tree there is gold, your voice is pleasant. Because near the other tree there is no gold, [your] voice is not pleasant." Say it thus!' The king said to Dbyig-pa-čan, 'Even though many calamities happened to you, I set [you] free. Because you are poor, dig out the gold treasure which is under the tree and keep [it]!' According to king's order, Dbyig-pa-čan delivered the messages to (lit. of) everybody and then dug (lit. took) out the gold from below the tree and took [it for himself]. From then on [Dbyig-pa-čan's] household was established.[81] Thereafter, not lacking anything[82] within one life [he] became rich and happy.[83]

Kun-dgaɣ-bo, don't think about the king Mɟes-pa at that time any differently! Regarding him, now it's me. Regarding the Brahmin Dbyig-pa-čan of that time, [now he] is Brahmin Phyin-te-lo-śu-śa. Having already freed [him] from suffering earlier, I offered [him] the jewel [of Dharma] and made [him] happy. Now, after [I] had achieved manifesting enlightenment, I also freed [him] from suffering and gave [him] the treasure of jewels: i.e. the everlasting Dharma."[84] After the Victorious One had said these words, the venerable Kun-dgaɣ-bo together with numerous attendants were very pleased about the words of the Victorious One[85] and were delighted.

Thirty-ninth chapter: Householder Dbyig-pa-čan.

Reading II. The descent of Tibetan people from a monkey and a rock-ogress

At that time, after the Noble One, Spyan-ras-gzigs, had conferred the vow of a lay practitioner upon a monkey that was displaying miracles, [he] sent it (i.e. the monkey) to the realm of the snow-clad Tibet to meditate. There the monkey meditated on a black rock; namely (དེའང་), [it] contemplated benevolence, compassion, [and] the thought of enlightenment. While (དུས་) [the monkey] was devoting itself to the profound Buddhist teaching, the voidness, a rock-ogress who suffered from [her previous] actions, made her way there. Having shown many signs of [her] desire for love[86] [towards the monkey], [she] went [back]. Later, having appeared (lit. acted, བྱས་) in the form (lit. garment) of a woman, the rock-ogress said to the monkey, "You and me, both, will be made husband and wife." Therefore (བས་)[87] the monkey answered, "Because I am a lay practitioner of the Noble One,

Spyan-ras-gzigs, if [I] became your husband, [I] would lose my vow." Because (པས་) [he] said [so], the rock-ogress replied, "If you don't become my husband, I will die", and lay down before the monkey. Thereafter, having risen, the rock-ogress said the following words to the monkey:

"Alas, the great king of the monkeys,
Think a little about me: [I] beg you to listen [to my words].[88]
As for me, perforce of [my previous] actions, [I] was born into the race of [rock]-ogresses.
Due to [my] growing desire, longing for you [I] am attached [to you].
Perforce of [this] passion, while having besieged [you] I beg [you]:
As for me, if I don't establish a family[89] with you,
Eventually I shall come together with an ogre,
Kill ten thousand sentient beings every day,
[And] eat about one thousand living beings every night.
After [I] have given birth to innumerable children by (lit. of) the ogre,
[And] after (ནས་) this very realm of the snow-clad [Tibet] as such
Has turned to an ogres' domain (lit. towns),
Wherever [they] may be, the ogres will eat [all] sentient beings.
Therefore, having reflected on me, embrace (lit. seize) [me] with [your] compassion!"

Because (པས་) the doleful words caused tears to flow down (lit. come out) [his face], the *bodhisattva*-monkey thought: "If [I] become her husband, [my] vow will perish. If I do not [become her husband], the sin will be very great." Immediately (སྐད་ཅིག་ལ་), [he] went to the Po-ta-la mountain, to the Noble One, and spoke thus:

"Alas, compassionate Protector of Beings,
As for me, [I] protected the vow of a lay practitioner like [my own] life.
[However], an ogress [from] a demon-race, obsessed with passion,[90]
Uttered various kinds of doleful lamentation.
Thereafter (ནས་), having besieged me, [she] came (lit. occurred) to deprive [me] of [my] vow,
How should [I] act towards her in order for the vow to be protected?[91]
I beg you compassionate Protector of Benevolence to reflect [upon that]."

Because [he] filed [this] request, the Noble One ordained: "Become the husband of the rock-ogress!" From the sky, both goddesses Khro-gñer-čan and Sgrol-ma were also saying, "That (དེ་ནི་) would be excellent!" Then, the Noble One blessed both the monkey and the rock-ogress as husband and wife. [He] granted [his] blessings such as that in this snow-clad [Tibet] endowed with three excellent qualities in a future time the teachings of the Buddha will spread and increase, and last for a long time, and spiritual friends who are virtuous will occur without interruption; that mines [full] of precious stones will have opened;[92] [and] that happiness and prosperity will spread in ten directions.[93] Then, because both the monkey and the rock-ogress became husband and wife, monkey-children – reborn from six states of existence, who [therefore] had six different modes of life[94] – were born. Namely (དེ་ཡང་), the monkey-child reborn from hell was one with a black face and (ལ་) great hardiness. The monkey-child reborn from the place of hungry ghosts was one with an ugly face and (ལ་) [constantly] longing for food. The monkey-child reborn from the place of animals was one who was stupid and (ལ་) had a wicked constitution (རྩོད་). The monkey-child reborn from the place of men was one of great knowledge and (ལ་) faint-hearted.[95] The monkey-child reborn from the place of semi-gods was one who was malicious and (ལ་) of great envy. The monkey-child reborn from the place of deities was one with great (lit. long) forbearance and (ལ་) a virtuous mind. Then, as for these six children of the monkey, [their] father, the *bodhisattva*-monkey, brought [them] to the forest called Bya-chogs (lit. Flock of birds) [and] abounding in fruits and left [them there] for three years. The three years passed. When (lit. because) the *bodhisattva*-monkey went to inspect [them], [he] realised (འདུག་) that perforce of [their previous] actions the [number of] monkey-children had increased to five hundred. The fruits were consumed [and] there was nothing else to eat. Even though (ཀྱང་) [their] parents didn't eat anything, [the children], asking: "Father, what [shall we] eat? Mother, what [shall we] eat?" with arms raised in despair and exhausted, were suffering from poverty (lit. were poor). Then, the *bodhisattva*-monkey thought: "It is not me who has got into trouble. Because I accomplished the order of the Noble One, so many monkey-children have occurred," and in an instant [he] went to the Po-ta-la mountain and spoke thus to the Noble One: "Alas,

> Because (པས་) [I] recognised neither house and hearth as a prison of the circle of rebirth
> Nor that a demon conjured up the woman,
> Due to [my] offspring I've got into the swamp of the circle of rebirth.
> Because [I] did not apprehend passion as a poisoned leaf,
> Having become passionate out of compassion, [I] deluded myself.
> While fettered by passion, [I] feel overcome by a mountain of suffering.
> [I] have eaten the poison [of] misery [and] am underlaid by the plague of bad [previous] actions.[96]
> Having myself been pained with a heap of suffering,

Alas! Oh, compassionate Protector of Benevolence,
What shall [I] do now to train [my] offspring?[97]
Because of [the actions] sanctioned (lit. permitted) by the Noble One I have ended up like this.
Now, [Tibet] is like a town of hungry ghosts.
There is no doubt that later [they] will be reborn in hell.
Therefore, I beg [you] to stand guard over me out of compassion."

Because [he] made [this] request, the Noble One said, "Your race will be guarded by me." Then (ནས་), the Noble One, having risen, took barley, wheat, beans, buckwheat, [and] unhusked barley from the inner caverns of Ri-rab [and] scattered [them] on the ground. Hence (བས་), the country became filled with crops that [one] had not sown and ploughed there (དེར་). Thereafter, the *bodhisattva*-monkey, having led the monkey-children there, pointed towards the crops that [one] had not sown and ploughed [and] said: "Now, eat!" Because [he] said [that] (སྨྲས་པས་), [one] says "[This place] is Zo-daṅ-goṅ-po-ri."[98] Because the monkey-children had eaten the crops, [they] became satisfied. [Their] hair and tails grew shorter. After [they] were able to speak, [they] became humans. [They] were eating the crops that [one] had not sown and ploughed as [their] food, and wearing tree-leaves as [their] clothes. In that way, because these people, the inhabitants (པ་) of the snow-clad Tibet,[99] had descended from[100] both a father-monkey and a mother rock-ogress, [they] have divided into two kinds.

Concerning that, those who became the lineage of the father, the *bodhisattva*-monkey: those of great forbearance, great faithfulness, great compassion and (ལ་) great diligence, rejoicing in virtuous deeds, of mild words, [and] eloquent;[101] those are the father's line.

Those who became the lineage of the mother, the rock-ogress: of great lust and hatred, thinking of trade and profit, of great greed and quarrelsome temper, laughing aloud, with great physical strength and courage, unsettled in [their] behaviour, having [too] many thoughts, precipitate in acting, full of five poisons, rejoicing to hear of others' harm, furious with rage; those are the mother's line.

Then at that time, mountains that had turned into forests, [and] all the river valleys that had filled with water, opened up the mouths [of] the arms [of] Skoṅ-čhu[102] [and] all the water, having flowed therein, disappeared by being absorbed in the arms [of] Skoṅ-čhu.[103] Thereafter (དེ་ནས་), on all the plains [one] made [arable] fields [and] built many towns. After a short time,[104] the lord Gñaɣ-khri Bcan-po appeared to [become] the king of Tibet.[105] Then (ནས་), [he] made [Tibetans] lords and subjects. [So] it is said.[106]

Seventh chapter: The descent of Tibetan people from a monkey and a rock-ogress.[107]

Reading III. The death of Mi-la Ras-pa's father

This is the second [deed].[108] Further, because Ras-čhuṅ-pa asked: "Dear Lama, [would you] please (ལགས་) tell [me] what it was like[109] at the beginning [when], due to the loss of [your] father, [you] experienced (ཐུགས་ཉམས་སུ་བཞེས་) many difficulties?" [Mi-la Ras-pa said:][110]

"It was then (དེ་ནས་), when I was about seven years old, [my] father Mi-la Śes-rab Rgyal-mchan became infected with a serious illness.[111] Then, physicians and diviners predicted that [he] would not recover and abandoned [him]. [His] relatives also (ཀྱང་ . . . ཀྱང་) realised that [he] would not recover. He himself (རང་) was also (ཀྱང་) certain that [he] would not recover. Hence (ནས་), having gathered all noble near and distant relatives (including [my] paternal uncle and aunt), friends, spiritual advisors, countrymen, [and] neighbours, [he] entrusted [his] children and [their] mother together with [all] the wealth [to them]. Finally, having prepared in detail the text of a testament ordering the son to take over the patrimony, [he] promulgated [it] so that everyone [could] hear: 'Briefly and (ལ་) verbally, the present illness does not leave me. For that reason (དེས་ན་), because this son of mine is still young, [he] shall be entrusted to all the relatives and friends led by the paternal uncle and aunt. In my uplands, cattle: yaks, horses, [and] sheep, the three; in the downlands, some fields that have not attracted the eye of beggars,[112] of which the triangular Ɣor-ma is the most prominent; on the ground floor of the house, domesticated cattle: cows, goats, [and] donkeys, the three; on the upper story, valuables:[113] gold, silver, copper, iron, turquoise and silk clothes, [and] corn magazine, among others. In short, because I do not need to desire another man's wealth, spend (lit. give away) a portion from these [riches] after my [death]. The rest is entrusted to all of you gathered here until the household has not been taken over by my son. In particular, [it] is entrusted to both paternal uncle and aunt. This son will be able to bear the household and because [I] have arranged a child-marriage with Mȷes-se [he] will join her as [his] wife. Then give back the wealth completely and let my son take over the patrimony! Until then, you, all the relatives led by the paternal uncle and aunt, [will] know the happiness and misery of my children and [their] mother, the three. Do not lead [them] into misery! [You] will be watched from the grave [when I] die.' [He] spoke so and died thereafter. Then, [one] prepared a farewell ceremony for the father. [One] said: 'As agreed, let Myaṅ-cha Dkar-rgyan herself save all the remaining wealth. All needed assistants should do whatever is good for [their] part.' Thereupon (ལ་) the paternal uncle and aunt replied: 'Although (རུང་) [some] people are family, [we] are close relatives. We will not lead them, the mother and her children, into misery. We will save the goods according to the testament.' Though (རུང་) my maternal uncle and Mȷes-se's father and brothers recalled the account, without listening [to it] the paternal uncle prepared the men's goods, [and] the paternal aunt prepared the women's goods. Having divided other things in half, [they] said: 'You, mother and children, will support [us] each in turn.' In addition to [the fact that] (བར་) there were no goods for us three (mother and children) to be controlled, in the summer during field-works, [we were] servants of the paternal uncle; [and] in the winter during the time of spinning of wool, [we were] servants of the paternal aunt. [Our] food was dogs' food, [our] work was donkeys' work. [We] wore tattered robes with a girdle of *dres ma*-grass bound over [our] severed shoulder. Because [we] had to work without rest, [our] limbs became cracked. Due to (སྐྱོབས་ཀྱིས་) bad food and clothing [our] complexion [became] pale and bodies emaciated; the hair, once dangling locks [plaited with] (lit. of) gold and turquoise, later pale and thin, became dangling locks [full] of lice and nits. Hence (བས་), all timid people who saw and heard [us] were shedding tears. Though (རུང་) buzzing slanders[114] circulated (lit. occurred) about [my] paternal uncle and aunt, [they] acted without shame.[115] Because [they] caused only misery to us, mother and children, [my] mother said (ཞུས་) to the paternal aunt: '[You] are not Khyuṅ-cha Dpal-ɣdren ("Glorious Leader of the Khyuṅ's offspring") [but] Bdud-mo Stag-ɣdren ("Demoness Leading Tigers").' Therefore (ཕས་), the name Bdud-mo Stag-ɣdren attached to [my] aunt. In those days, a folk-proverb that said '[If] a false master (lit. non-master) wishes to be a master, [he] puts the [true] master as a door-guarding dog' appeared [true] for us, mother and children. Previously, when [my] father Mi-la Śes-rab Rgyal-mchan was alive, all the people, high and low, were looking for whether our smile was friendly or unfriendly.[116] Later, after [they] became wealthy like kings, the smile of [my] paternal uncle and aunt, whether friendly or unfriendly, was looked for [by us]. People talked slanderously about [my] mother: 'The saying "Rich husband, wise wife. Soft wool, good woollens" is true. [Now] when there is no capable man, it is [just] like [in] that proverb. At first, when a good husband was sustaining Myaṅ-cha Dkar-rgyan, she was confident[117] and wise. [One] was saying [she] was an excellent housewife.[118] Now that [she] does not differ from a weak-minded person, [she] is [just] there (གདའ་).' For instance (དཔེ་དེར་), all [our] own (རང་) ordinary workers were laughing behind [our] backs: 'When misery occurred once, gossip [follows] in turn.' Mjes-se's parents gave me new shoes and clothes and said: 'Because wealth, called "dew on (lit. of) the grass", is not durable, when many riches (lit. man's wealth) are gone [you] do not need to think [of yourself as] impoverished. Previously, wealth occurred [first] later (ཧྲིང་སོར་) to your ancestors. For you, too, a time of prosperity[119] will come.' [Saying this they] consoled us over and over again. Then I turned fifteen. There was a field share, that the parents gave to [my] mother, and though of an unpleasant name, called Pre-pe-stan-čhuṅ, [it] was yielding an excellent harvest.[120] [My] maternal uncle did whatever was suitable so that barley from (lit. of) the field cultivation grew and cropped; for what [he] had been collecting secretly, [he] bought great quantities of (lit. much) meat for the surplus.[121] Because (པས་) [he] made flour from[122] a great quantity of white barley [and] brewed a great quantity of black barley into beer, [he] said: '[This] is the source of wealth[123] [for] Myaṅ-cha Dkar-rgyan, mother and [her] children.' Then [he] borrowed many carpets [and] spread [them] in our house Ka-bźi-gduṅ-brgyad-ma (lit. "the one having four pillars [and] eight beams"). Having summoned [our] relatives led by the paternal uncle and aunt, kindreds, friends, spiritual advisors, countrymen, neighbours – and in particular those who had knowledge of the text of the testament [read] upon (བར་) the death of [my] father Mi-la Śes-rab Rgyal-mchan – [we] placed a body of a slaughtered animal in front of [my] paternal uncle and aunt. To others who deserved (lit. achieved) quarter shares [we offered] quarters, to those who deserved minor shares, [we offered] minor shares. After [we] had offered (lit. drawn) an excellent feast of beer in porcelain cups for life and fortune,[124] having stood up in the middle of the row, [my] mother said: 'All right, "A name for a born child, a speech for an offered (lit. drawn) beer." [This] being said, I also have a few words to say (གཏོང་, lit. give). [I] ask [you] elders acquainted with the testament proclaimed after the passing of the father Mi-la Śes-rab Rgyal-mchan, who are led by the paternal uncle and aunt, persons in a row sitting here, to please listen [to me].' Then (ནས་), after [my] maternal uncle had finished (lit. at the end of) reading the text of [my] father's testament, [my] mother said (ཟླས་): 'Since (བས་) the meaning of this text together with its wording is clear to the mind of all elders who are sitting here, it is not necessary to recount [it] extensively. Briefly,[125] until recently both paternal uncle and aunt interested [themselves] in us three, the mother and the children, taking utmost care [of us].[126] Now, because the household can be taken over by both my son and Mjes-se, [I] ask [you] to return (lit. give) our wealth entrusted [to you] and let the son possess (lit. seize) [his] patrimony according to [his] father's testament after [he] has joined Mjes-se as [his] wife.' Although the paternal uncle and aunt never agreed on anything, [they] did agree on food.[127] I went as the only son and because (སྐབས་ཀྱིས་) [my] paternal uncle had many sons, the aunt and the paternal uncle united. 'What is your possession or where is it? A house, fields, gold, turquoise, *mjo*s, horses, yaks, [and] sheep we previously (དང་པོ་) loaned [him] when (རིང་ལ་) Mi-la Śes-rab Rgyal-mchan was himself in good health, have returned to the wealth's owner after he (i.e. Mi-la Śes-rab Rgyal-mchan) died. The wealth you own, is it one gold nugget? Or a handful of barley? Or a lump of butter? Or one kind of a single silk cloth? Or one animal, a single she-goat? None did [we] see with [our] eyes. Now [you] speak like this. Who wrote the text of your testament? We, who nourished [you], true miserable ones, so that [you] did not starve to death, were the best. But as the saying goes "If [one] granted power to wicked men, [they] will measure out water by the manger."' [Thus the paternal uncle] said. [He] blew [his] nose [and] suddenly rose from (lit. on) [his] seat. [He] snapped [his fingers],[128] shook off [his] coat-flap, and stomped [his] feet. Then (ནས་) [he] said: 'If that's not enough, because we own even [this] house, you and your children go out!' While saying [this he] slapped [my] mother with [his] hand [and] gave us, brother and sister, a blow with [his] sleeve.[129] Then [my] mother cried out (lit. said): 'Oh father Mi-la Śes-rab Rgyal-mchan, look at the fate of us, mother and children! The time has indeed (གདའ་) come to regard now what [you once] said: "[You] will be watched from the grave [when] I die."' Weeping [she] fell down [and] was rolling back and forth[130] [on the ground]. We two, the brother and the sister, could do nothing but cry for help. Because the paternal uncle had many sons, the maternal uncle was not able to fight [against them]. Others, [our] countrymen who were loyal towards us, out of compassion for the mother and children said, 'Do not be so tearful.'[131] Others again sighed deeply (lit. continuously). [Then] the paternal uncle and aunt said: '[You] say "We need [our] possessions". The possessions that you have, the means [you] have for preparing a feast for [your] countrymen [and] neighbours after having wasted abundant meat and beer, is it your possession? We do not have it. [But] even if [we] had [it], [we] would not give [it to you]. Therefore (བས་), if you and [your] children are many, lead an army! If you are few, cast spells!' Saying this, [they] went out. People who were loyal towards them followed them out. When mother could not stop weeping even thereafter,[132] all the people who were loyal towards us, like the maternal uncle and Mjes-se's father and brothers, stayed in order to console her.[133] When drinking the rest of the beer [they] said to [my] mother: 'Now, do not cry! Crying is not helpful.[134] Ask something (lit. possessions) from all who are gathered here today in the feast-rows! We all who are here give [you] what is expedient (ཅི་དྲག་རེ་). Even the paternal uncle and aunt will give [you] what is expedient.' The maternal uncle continued: 'Do exactly that and send [your] son to learn a good skill! You, mother and daughter, stay at my place and cultivate fields! There is nothing more suitable than to do what is useful. In any case, [you] must not be ashamed[135] before the paternal uncle and aunt.' Then [my] mother replied: '[My] children will not be raised[136] with possessions that did not come from [my] control over our own possessions, but that come from begging.[137] Even though the paternal uncle and aunt [would] return [to us] one part of our possessions, [they] do not need to give [it] back. By all means (ཅིས་ཀྱང་) [I] will send this child to learn a good skill. Since (lit. after; ཧྲེང་ལ་) the paternal uncle and aunt did not return (lit. entrust) to us, mother and children, what was rightfully ours, [we] will run to [places where] drums resound (lit. open)[138] and smoke rises. Then real understanding will arise within them.[139] And as for the cultivation of fields, from now on [we] will do [it].' Thereafter [mother] sent me to study reading with (lit. to) Klu-brgyad-mkhan, a teacher of the Rñiṅ-ma-pa mantra tradition, who was staying in Mi-thod-gad-kha of Rca [and] was very much in demand for village rituals. At that time, [our] relatives gave [us] a few sources of wealth each. In particular, Mjes-se's parents gave [us] provisions, meat,[140] and firewood, and then in order to console [me], [they] sent Mjes-se herself again and again to the place where I was learning to read. [My] maternal uncle gave [my] mother and sister food when [they] were not going for labour or begging. In order for [my] maternal uncle not to have to send [my] mother begging, [she] did the work of men, so that what was spun during the day was that day woven. [She] provided whatever was useful and valuable to us, brother and sister. Meanwhile (གྱི་) [my] sister did whatever was possible: [she] served [other] people[141] and ran to [places where] drums resound and smoke rises. Although [she] obtained some food and clothes, [we] ourselves were not experiencing any happiness besides flavourless food, tattered clothes, [and] a despondent mind." Because (པས་) [Mi-la Ras-pa] had related (གསུངས་) thus, at that point all (ཚད་) those who have heard the teaching, being grieved and resigned, were shedding tears.[142] Then, in a moment, [they] were all silent.[143]

Second deed: Practising of the victorious truth of suffering.[144]

Reading IV. Investigation of wise ones

[Title][145]

A treatise titled *Subhāṣitaratnanidhināmaśāstra* in Sanskrit [and] *A Treasury of Aphoristic Jewels* in Tibetan.

[Invocation]

With reverence [I] pay homage to the Noble One, Ɣǰam-dpal Gźon-nur-gyur-pa.[146]

[Introduction]

[I] I pay homage to the Omniscient One, to the Chief of beings,[147]
[Whose] feet the most excellent ones among deities, the lords of serpents, the accomplished ones, the best among knowledge holders,[148]
The sages Rgyas-pa (Skt. Vyāsa), Grog-mkhar-ba (Skt. Vālmīki), and Rkaṅ-mig (Skt. Akṣapāda), among others,[149]
Worship with [their] surpassingly beautiful (lit. lovely) head-jewels.

[II] [The one that], if [one] has examined [it] methodically,[150] does not contradict the Buddhist religion and tradition,
[Through which] the affairs [of this] world were perfectly [and] correctly accomplished,
This one, that expounds any conduct of the Noble Ones, [is] the *Treasury of Aphoristic Jewels*.

[Chapter 1: Investigation of wise ones]

[1] The wise ones who hold the repository of virtues,
Collect [therein] jewels of aphorisms.
Because the vast ocean is the treasury of water,
All rivers flow (lit. fall) [into it].

[2] Those who have intelligence are skilled in
Attracting (བླང་) men possessed of virtues [and] repelling (དོར་) [those who] have none.[151]
A lodestone is able to attract iron filings that are mixed with dust.

[3] Whereas by means of the intelligence of a wise man [he] understands the aphorisms,
The fools do not.[152]
When rays of the sun have risen,
The birds of demons[153] become blind.

[4] Whereas those possessed of understanding
Are able to clean away [their] moral faults, the fools are not.[154]
Whereas the *garuḍa*-bird is able to kill a poisonous snake,
A crow is not.[155]

[5] Even if a man of great intellect grows weak,
[His] intellect becomes even stronger.[156]
When the king of animals (i.e. the lion) is hungry,
[He] quickly rips the crown of the head of an elephant.

[6] [As long as one] has not asked a wise one while debating,
So long the depth [of his intellect] cannot be measured.[157]
[As long as one] has not beaten (lit. stuck in) a drum with a stick,
Is there any difference to any other [drum]?[158]

[7] Even though [one] dies the day after tomorrow, knowledge should be gained (lit. learnt).
Even though [one] has not become wise in this life,
[Gaining knowledge] is just like obtaining wealth
That is entrusted to [one's] later life.

[8] If [one] possesses virtues, then all men
Gather by themselves [around one] without being gathered.[159]
Around a flower possessed with fragrance,[160] even if [it is] far away,
Bees will circle like a crowd of clouds.

[9] Owing to a single wise one who learned and fulfilled[161] all the virtues,
The world shines.
Even though those intelligent [but] evil-minded are many,
Just like lunar mansions, [they] are not able to shine.

[10] Although [his own] virtues are countless,
A wise one accepts the virtues of others, even if [they] are small.
Because [he] constantly acts like that,
Quickly [he] becomes one who knows everything.[162]

[11] If a wise one is guarded by [his] wisdom,
Enemies, even though plenty, to whom [can they] cause harm?
The sole son of the Brahmin from Ɣphags-rgyal
Conquered all troops of enemies.

[12] When a narrow-minded person was disturbed through a bad counsel,
An intelligent person makes (lit. restores) [him] happy [again] with a stratagem.
A river which is impure (lit. wasted) due to whirlpools
[One] makes clean [again] with a pure-water-jewel.

[13] However much [all his] means are worn out, a wise one
Does not go the way which a fool takes.
Even if a *cātaka*-nestling is thirsty,
[It] does not drink water that falls on the ground.

[14] Even though [one] turned the sage's head [away],
He will not have become confused concerning [his] part to be done.
Even though animals [such as] ants have no eyes,
[They] are much quicker than other [animals] that have eyes.

[15] When two intelligent persons have conferred,
[Then] another good understanding comes forth.
From [mixing of] turmeric and alum
[Yet] another colour will appear (lit. will be born).

[16] A man who has gathered inner knowledge and merit,
Even though alone, is victorious over all.
Lion, the king of beasts, and a universal emperor
Do not need companions.

[17] If [one] is skilled in means,
Where is the difficulty of appointing even a great one as [one's] servant?
Even though *garuḍa*-[bird] has great strength [and] physical skills,
[It] became the riding-beast of Gos-ser-čan.

[18] In (lit. of) this and the other world
One who achieves happiness is a wise one.[163]
The wisdom of prince Zla-ba
Saved Bran-bzaṅs in this and the next [world].

[19] Even though, being courageous and [one's] strength [and] physical skills are great,
Not being learned, [one] will not attain glory.
Even though [one] obtained wealth,
If there is no merit, where is [there] permanence?

[20] Everyone [knows] virtue and misdeed [when they] are [clearly] separated (lit. clear).[164]
Who knows [how] to separate a mixture [of them] is a wise one.
Everyone uses[165] cows' milk (lit. milk from cows),
[But only] geese separated milk from water.

[21] When [one] has spoken to and exhorted [it],
Understanding will arise even in an animal.
If, without being exhorted, [one] understands thoughts that the other has not expressed (lit. spoken),
[One] is wise.

[22] If [one] has intelligence, even if [the other] did not say anything,
[He] understands [another's] thoughts just from [his] facial expression.
Even if a Nepalese did not eat the pomegranate,
[He] knows [its] taste from [its] very colour.

[23] Rather than in his own country,
A wise one obtains honours in a foreign country.
As much as a jewel is precious elsewhere,
For whom [should it] be precious on an ocean's island?[166]

[24] A wise one is tormented during [his] studies.
It is not possible to become wise for [somebody who] lives comfortably (lit. easily).
Somebody who is attached to petty contentment
Is not able to obtain the happiness of great [contentment].

[25] If [one] has intelligence, even if [he is] weak,
What [can] a powerful enemy do [to him]?
A wise hare killed
The mighty king of beasts.

[26] If [one] knows a conduct that
Agrees with [that of] other sentient beings, [one] is wise.
Even though [they are] animals,
Do not [those of] one breed live in one flock?

[27] When examining some acts (that certainly occur)
Before [they] are completed,
[One] recognises the difference between (lit. of) the wise and the ignorant.
Examining after [acts] are completed [is] a way of a fool.

[28] If [one] understands the subject matter of knowledge
That was investigated by wise ones, [one] is considered wise.
Even if a fool is skilled in examining the age of oxen,
[He] is not possessed of merits.[167]

[29] While an ocean is not sated by water,
A king's treasury is not sated by wealth.
[One] is not sated by enjoying desired goods.
A wise one is not sated by aphorisms.

[30] Even from children
Wise ones accept aphorisms.
When a nice scent has arisen,
[One] accepts musk even from the navel of animals.

First chapter: Investigation of wise ones from *A Treasury of Aphoristic Jewels*.[168]

Notes

1 Lit. "The lord Gñaɣ-khri Bcan-po came for the king of Tibet."
2 Lit. "At that time in the town an old woman had two constantly stealing sons."
3 The phrase རྒན་མོ་མ་སྐྱིད་ is atypical for CT and might be a calque from Chinese.
4 The main verb of the direct speech is གསོལ་ "[I] beg", to which the verbal phrase སྐྱབས་མཛད་ "to save" is subordinate. However, the action of སྐྱབས་མཛད་ is additionally modified by ཐུགས་བརྩེ་བར་དགོངས་ཏེ, lit. "thinking kindly".
5 Lit. "thought about them kindly".
6 Lit. "While they were remembering the favour of the Victorious One, happiness arose [in them]." The second clause can be literally translated as "The state of (པ་) being very glad arose." རབ་ཏུ་ is an adverb and as such it can only modify adjectives and verbs. For this reason the phrase རབ་ཏུ་དགའ་ has to be interpreted as a verbal phrase ("to be utmost happy") that has been nominalised (པ་) to function as the subject of སྐྱེས་.
7 Lit. "[You] have arrived well" is an official greeting formula of an admission to the Buddhist order.
8 Lit. "They turned to those who have steadfast mind that is very believing."
9 Lit. "doctrine that was suitable".

10 Lit. "such things of great miracles". ངོ་མཚར་ཆེ་བ་ is a possessive attribute (see Lesson 14).

11 Lit. "while it is not over that I have taken care [of them] only now, at that time".

12 What follows is, strictly speaking, the direct speech of the Victorious One. His words end with ཕོ་བྲང་དུ་སོང་ངོ་ in D 140v3.

13 The preceding two sentences end with the final particle འོ་ because the next clause ends with the gerundial སྟེ་ in introductive function and is followed by explanations that refer only to the youngest son and not to all the sons.

14 ཅུང་ཟད་ཅིག་ངལ་བསོ་ means "to rest a bit". Here the clause is nominalised and added the postpositional phrase བར་དུ་ "within, during".

15 Lit. "because [she] is very (ཤིན་ཏུ་) afflicted, [she] is pained".

16 Lit. "through such things".

17 Lit. "thought this in [his] mind". འདི་ has a cataphoric function here; it informs that the content of the thoughts will be revealed in the next clause.

18 Lit. "Accompanied as the three, [they] went."

19 Lit. "without there being anything left".

20 Lit. "the way of what [he] said earlier".

21 One would rather expect the sentence to describe the tigress as smeared with blood, etc. (Hahn 2003c: 19, fn. 19). However, the Tibetan syntax makes it clear that the phrase ནུ་བོ་ཐ་ཆུངས་ remains the pivot, due to its fronted position at the beginning of the clause.

22 Lit. "having thrown [their] bodies on the ground".

23 Lit. "dreamed (སྙམ་རྨིས་) in a dream (རྨི་ལམ་) of the sleeping queen mother".

24 For this construction, see Lesson 15: Superlative.

25 Lit. "as a rumour (གཏམ་)".

26 Lit. "let search all around".

27 Lit. "without long time having passed".

28 Lit. "the words choked the two sons".

29 Lit. "[their] breath did not come".

30 Lit. "A long time passed."

31 As in the preceding clause ཤ་ is marked with the focus particle ནི་, I understand ཤ་ as also being the object of མཐོང་. This is confirmed by the following clauses in which the queen and the king seize the head and the hand of the prince's body, which is not explicitly mentioned.

32 Lit. "as if messed solely with bones and blood".

33 Lit. "bones of the dead me".

34 The passage is not a true direct speech because no words are quoted. It is the scene that the prince saw that is presented here from his point of view. For this reason the 1st person singular pronoun བདག་ is used.

35 Lit. "the fact that my parents are so unhappy".

36 Lit. "generate joy in them".

37 Lit. "from the sky of the top", i.e. atop of the parents.

38 བདག་ 1SG; from the following passage it occurs that the person speaking is the father.

39 This is a case of ellipsis (see Lesson 14) in which ཆོས་ has been omitted because it occurs in the preceding sentence.

40 Lit. "because of remembering [you]".

41 Lit. "Being a chapter on how Sems-čan-čhen-po offered [his] body to a tigress, this is the second [chapter]".

42 These introductory words are explained in fn. 20 for the reading exercise in Lesson 12.

43 བག་མར་བཏང་ lit. "gave as brides".

44 Lit. "it was right to reap".

45 Lit. "When, having looked [for], I have not found [the ox], how should [it] be acted?"

46 The difficulty in translating the clause consists in a correct interpretation of སྐྱོམ་རྩུགས་. For the first syllable the variants སྙོམ་ (DH) and རྐྱོམ་ (D) are also attested; compare hereto the multiple spellings attested in modern dialects: ཀུར་ཙོགས་ (CDTD: 24), སྐྱོག་སྐྱོ་ (CDTD: 280), and ཨོག་སྐྱོ་ (CDTD: 9402). The recurring syllable སྐྱོ་ and the second syllable ཙོགས་ suggest that the variant སྐྱོམ་རྩུགས་, even though probably not original, is the most appropriate from the available ones.

47 Hahn remarked that the phrase རྒྱང་ཚད་ཀྱི་བར་དུ་ corresponds to "for a long time" of a Chinese version of the story (1996: 228, fn. 3). The Old Tibetan manuscript reads རྒྱངས་ཅད་ (DH 19v3) instead of རྒྱང་ཚད་ but both have locative rather than temporal connotations.

48 Lit. "For him there is neither scolding by a wife, nor harming by bad daughters and sons-in-law."

49 Lit. "faults that are really bad".

50 Lit. "I don't have making troubles of a lost ox and of reaping of fields on time."

51 Lit. "so that [it] was suitable".

52 Lit. "makes welfare of sentient beings". སེམས་ཅན་གྱི་དོན་མཛད་པ་ is an attribute to བཅོམ་ལྡན་འདས་.

53 Lit. "obtained the goal that is beneficial for [his] virtue".

54 Lit. "as easily as paint penetrating a clean white cotton cloth."

55 The Indian version of the name was in Sanskrit Ādarśamukha "Mirror-face" (Hahn 1996: 229, fn. 1).

56 Lit. "was a one who had neither food nor clothes."

57 For the phrase ཟན་ཟ་, see Lesson 15: Incorporation.

58 དེ་ནས་དེ་གཉིས་འགྲོགས་ཏེ་, lit. "then, the two, having got together", cannot belong to the quotation because དེ་ in དེ་གཉིས་ is a 3rd person pronoun.

59 Lit. "[he] will examine the right one and the wrong one of us."

60 For the phrase ཐགས་འཐག་, see Lesson 15: Incorporation.

61 Lit. "in the middle of the road". བར་ is not a relator noun here because it is followed by the demonstrative དེ་.

62 Lit. "How far is the bottom of the river?"

63 Lit. "The river is of a deep bottom". གཏིང་ཟབ་པོ་ is a possessive attribute.

64 More literally བསྐྱུར་ means here "to let [sb.] convey [sth.]". It is the causative equivalent of the transitive འཁྱུར་ "to carry, to convey".

65 Lit. "the boy became deprived of life".

66 Lit. "Why does it happen this way?"

67 Lit. "What for did you come?"

68 Lit. "all that Dbyig-pa-čan and the householder were arguing about".
69 Lit. "did not deliver [it] up with the mouth."
70 Lit. "Even though Dbyig-pa-čan will have been victorious, this is better than [if one] secondly gouged my eyes out."
71 ཁ་ནས་ lit. "from the mouth". The elative marks here the mouth as agent that holds the axe. Compare in this respect the use of elative in the phrase ཞལ་ནས་ (see Lesson 13: Direct Speech).
72 རྫས་ཅི་འཁྱེར་ཡང་ lit. "whatever objects [one] carries".
73 Strictly speaking, སྟན་ལ་མི་རྟོག་པར་འདུག་པ་ཡང་, lit. "sitting on a mat without examining [it]," is an attribute to དབྱིག་པ་ཅན་ཁྱོད་.
74 Lit. "act so that [she] has a baby".
75 Lit. "a man who was in concealment".
76 Lit. "Go and make this one to your husband!"
77 Lit. "gave Dbyig-pa-čan the blame".
78 Lit. "the king having a skilled mind"; བློ་མཁས་པས་ is a possessive attribute.
79 གང་གིས་ཐོབ་པའི་བུ་ lit. "a child that whoever obtains".
80 The verb དོགས་ requires its object (verbal or nominal) in ergative.
81 སོ་ཚིས་ཚུགས་, lit. "housekeeping took roots".
82 ཅིས་ཀྱང་མི་བྲེལ་, lit. "not poor with anything".
83 Here ends the story that the Victorious One was relating to Kun-dgaɣ-bo.
84 ཟད་མི་ཤེས་པའི་ཆོས་རིན་པོ་ཆེའི་གཏེར་ is an appositional phrase of ཟད་མི་ཤེས་པའི་ཆོས་ and རིན་པོ་ཆེའི་གཏེར་; ཟད་མི་ཤེས་ lit. "not able to decline".
85 Lit. "about what the Victorious One had said".
86 Lit. "many signs that [she] desires love".
87 Lit. "Because (བས་) the rock-ogress said [. . .], the monkey answered [. . .]".
88 Lit. "[I] beg you to listen [to my words] while thinking a little about me."
89 Lit. "make house and hearth".
90 Lit. "having the thought of passion".
91 Lit. "If [I] have acted in what way towards her, will the vow be protected?"
92 བྱེ་ is a v2-stem of འབྱེ་, whereas the remaining verbs of the phrase either are (འབྱུང་) or shall be (གནས་, རྒྱས་) interpreted as v1. འབྱེ་ "to open" denotes a change in the status of the subject and the event is punctual. འབྱུང་, གནས་, and རྒྱས་ have durative meanings here. The durative meaning of འབྱུང་ is underscored by the adverbial phrase རྒྱུན་ཆད་མེད་པར་ "without interruption" that itself connotes duration.
93 The syntax of the sentence should be analysed an follows: [ཁ་བ་ཅན་འདིར་ ((ཡོན་ཏན་གསུམ་དང་ལྡན་ཏེ། མ་འོངས་པའི་དུས་སུ་སངས་རྒྱས་ཀྱི་བསྟན་པ་དར་ཞིང་རྒྱས་ལ་ཡུན་རིང་དུ་གནས་པ་) དང་། (དགེ་བའི་བཤེས་གཉེན་རྒྱུན་ཆད་མེད་པར་འབྱུང་བ།)) (རིན་པོ་ཆེའི་གཏེར་ཁ་བྱེ་བ།) (ཕན་བདེ་དང་དགེ་ལེགས་ཕྱོགས་བཅུར་རྒྱས་པ་སོགས་)] བྱིན་གྱིས་བརླབས་སོ།. The position of སོགས་ makes it clear that the elements listed before སོགས་ are counted as blessings (བྱིན་). Semantically the locative adjunct ཁ་བ་ཅན་འདིར་ "in this snow-clad [Tibet]" has to refer to all the events listed afterwards: "in this snow-clad [Tibet], the teachings of Buddha will last and spiritual friends will be occurring", "in this snow-clad [Tibet], mines will have

opened", and "in this snow-clad [Tibet], prosperity will spread". Thus, ཁ་བ་ཅན་འདིར་ belongs to the phrase that ends with སོགས་. To sum up, if the text of GLR as handed down to us is correct, the blessings were (1) "the teachings of the Buddha, while spreading, will increase and last for a long time and spiritual friends, who are virtuous, will be occurring without interruption"; (2) "mines [full] of precious stones will have opened"; and (3) "happiness and prosperity will spread in ten directions".

94 སྤྱོད་ལམ་མི་འདྲ་བ་དྲུག་, lit. "of six not-similar modes of life".

95 Lit. "of small heart".

96 Lit. "the plague of bad [previous] actions struck [me]".

97 Lit. "If [I] have acted how now will [I] train [my] offspring?".

98 The sentence ཟོ་དང་ "Eat!" is a wordplay on the place name Zo-daṅ-goṅ-po-ri. A place name Zo-thaṅ is attested in southern Tibet, in the Yar-kluṅ valley (Sørensen 1994: 132, fn. 349). The sound change ཐང་ "plain" > དང་ frequently occurs if the preceding syllable ends with a vowel as is the case with Zo-daṅ.

99 Although all text redactions attest to a genitive particle after བོད་ཁ་བ་ཅན་པ་, this has to be elided. The phrase བོད་ཁ་བ་ཅན་པ་ is derived from བོད་ཁ་བ་ཅན་ "snow-clad Tibet" and denotes an inhabitant of the latter, lit. "someone affiliated to the snow-clad Tibet" (for this function of པ་ see Lesson 7). The phrase has to be understood as forming apposition with མི་འདི་རྣམས་.

100 Lit. "were ones begotten from".

101 སྨྲ་མཁས་པ་, lit. "skilled in talking".

102 Skoṅ-čhu is a name of a river in the region usually spelled as Koṅ/Rkoṅ-po. This clause is analysed as follows: [དེའི་དུས་དེར་ (རི་རྣམས་ནི་ཤིང་ནགས་སུ་སོང་།) (ཀླུང་ཐམས་ཅད་ནི་ཆུས་ཁེངས་) ཡོད་པ།]$_S$ [སྐོང་ཆུ་ལག་ཁ་]$_O$ ཕྱེ་ནས།. The phrase ending with ཡོད་པ་ is the subject of the verb ཕྱེ་ (v2 < འབྱེད་) and སྐོང་ཆུ་ལག་ཁ་ is its object. The absolutive case (instead of ergative) of the subject can be explained by the fact that the acting forces are mountains and river valleys, i.e. natural resources that per definition do not have volition and cannot control any action that they cause.

103 This topos depicts how Tibet was formed when waters of the ocean, that once covered all the land, disappeared in the newly opened river mouths of the river Skoṅ-čhu.

104 Lit. "not having passed longly".

105 Lit. "arrived for the king of Tibet".

106 Lit. "[these] are the words."

107 Lit. "Being the chapter on the descent of human lineages of Tibet from a monkey and a rock-ogress, [it] is the seventh one".

108 The phrase གཉིས་པ་ནི།, together with the final sentence of the story, form the most general framework, within which the proper story as told by Mi-la Ras-pa is placed: གཉིས་པ་ནི། STORY སྡུག་བསྔལ་གྱི་བདེན་པ་ཕུལ་ཕྱིན་ཐུགས་ཉམས་སུ་བཞེས་པའི་མཛད་པ་སྟེ་གཉིས་པའོ།། lit. "Concerning the second one, being the deed of practising the victorious truth of suffering, the STORY is the second [deed of Mi-la Ras-pa]".

109 Lit. "how did [you] take it".

110 The quotation is not introduced in any way in the text, but it starts here and ends with the words གསུངས་པས་ (p. 243, l. 27; D 13v).

111 གཞི་དྲག་པོ་ is a possessive attribute to སྙུན་, lit. "an illness having a serious cause".

112 སྤྲང་མིག་ཏུ་མི་ཚུད་པ་, lit. "what (པ་) has not entered into the beggars' eye".

113 རྫིག་ is almost unknown in dictionaries. Its provided meanings are contextual and based on three passages from Mi-la Ras-pa's work. As རྫིག་ also encompasses clothes in the previous passage, I propose translating it as "valuables"; WTS glosses it as "Wertgegenstand, Besitztum" (38: 476a).

114 The B edition reads དི་རི་བ་ whereas the remaining editions attest to དི་ར་རི་བ་ (ML: 32). BTC explains དིར་རི་བ་ as "ལབ་གླེང་མང་བའི་ཚུལ་" (1.1256b), which could be rendered with "talkative". The word is apparently related to the verb ཧྲིར་ "to rush, to roar, of the wind; to roll" (J: 291a) and was coined as an adjective describing the noise caused by roaring wind. In the context here, དིར་རི་བ་ describes the noise made by crowds. The translation "buzzing" is only tentative.

115 Lit. "[they] acted as someone without shame".

116 Lit. "Our smile, whether friendly or unfriendly, was watched by all the people, high and low."

117 བློ་ཁོག་ཆེ་, lit. "of great intrinsic power of mind", is a possessive attribute functioning here as an attributive predicate coordinated (ལ་) with གྲུང་ "wise".

118 ལག་བཅུད་ཆེ་ is another possessive attribute, lit. "of great ལག་བཅུད་". BTC explains ལག་བཅུད་ཆེ་ as "ལྟོ་ཆས་གང་བཟོས་ན་ཡང་བྲོ་བ་ཆེན་པོ་ཡོད་པ་" (2749b), lit. "If one prepared food, it has a great taste." The literal meaning of ལག་བཅུད་ seems to have been "nutriment that comes from the hands". For the lack of a better term, I translate ལག་བཅུད་ཆེ་ in this context as "excellent housewife".

119 Lit. "a time of [you] having riches".

120 Lit. "of excellent harvest coming up".

121 མང་རབ་ཏུ་སོང་བ་, lit. "what exceedingly occurred many".

122 One would expect ལས་ instead of ལ་, but all editions consulted by de Jong attest to dative (ML: 33).

123 ནོར་སློངས་བྱེད་པ་, lit. "what functions as wealth-raising".

124 སྟོན་མོ་ "feast" is modified by two determinative phrases: (1) ཆང་དཀར་ཡོལ་གྱི་ "of porcelain cups beer"; and (2) གཡང་ཚེ་དང་བཅས་པའི་ "that accompanies fortune and life".

125 Lit. "for the meaning to be summarised".

126 Lit. "attached in [their] minds the really (ཡང་དག་) taking care of us".

127 Figuratively for "being greed"? Haller adds that "food" is used here metaphorically for "property" (2009: 61).

128 Snapping one's fingers is considered a sign of disregard (J: 575a, s.v. སེ་གོལ་).

129 Lit. "struck with the hit of [his] sleeve".

130 The text reads གྲི་ལོག་ལོག་. གྲི་ seems to be cognate with འགྲི་ "to roll one's self" (J: 100b). Jäschke quotes the phrase འགྲི་ལྡོག་/ལོག་ "to roll one's self, e.g. from pain, despair etc." (ibid., s.v. འགྲི་).

131 Lit. "Do not be a crying man."

132 Lit. "As for the mother, thereafter [her] weeping had no end."

133 Lit. "to console mother's heart".

134 Lit. “through crying [it] is not useful”.

135 Lit. “have to be non-shameful”.

136 སོས་ is a rare case in which a v4-stem is used to express stative passive, lit. “to be raised” (see Bialek 2020a).

137 In this clause the second དོར་ is modified by two independent determinative phrases: རང་གི་དོར་ལ་དབང་རྒྱུ་མ་བྱུང་བའི་ and སྙོང་བྱས་པའི་.

138 The phrase ཛ་གདང་རྒྱུག་ is formed analogously to the following དུད་པ་ལང་རྒྱུག་. Therefore, གདང་ should be understood as a v1-stem of a verb, like ལང་ is. The verb གདང་ is identified here with གདང་ “to open wide” (J: 265a).

139 Lit. “real understanding of theirs will have risen”.

140 ཆུ་སྙོར་, lit. “that what gives substance (སྙོར་) to water”.

141 མི་གཡོག་ . . . བྱས་, lit. “was a servant”.

142 Lit. “were shedding tears due to grief and renunciation”.

143 More correctly: “while [they] were shedding tears, in a moment, all were silent”.

144 Lit. “Being the deed of practising (lit. “taking to heart”) of the victorious truth of suffering, [this] is [Mi-la Ras-pa’s] second [deed].”

145 Bracketed subheadings are added to structure the text for the reader.

146 གཞོན་ནུར་གྱུར་པ་ is an attribute added to the proper name of Mañjuśrī, འཇམ་དཔལ་.

147 With these words the aforementioned Mañjuśrī is most probably meant.

148 Some editions and commentaries read གྲུབ་པའི་རིག་འཛིན་ “accomplished knowledge holders” (see Eimer 1986: 54 and SSP: 77).

149 According to Indian tradition Vyāsa classified the *Vedas* and compiled *Mahābhārata* and the *Purāṇas*, Vālmīki is attributed with the epic *Rāmāyaṇa*, and Akṣapāda composed *Nyāyasūtras*, the foundational text of the Nyāya philosophical school.

150 རིགས་པས་, lit. “with the right method”, ergative of manner.

151 ཡོད་མེད་པའི་ should be read as *ཡོད་པའམ་མེད་པའི་. The second verse can be reconstructed as *སྣང་དོར་ལ་བློ་གྲོས་ལྡན་པ་མཁས།།. མཁས་ requires dative for its second argument: X_{ABS} Y_{DAT} *mkhas* “X is skilled in Y”.

152 བླུན་པོས་དེ་ལྟ་མིན་ stands for *བླུན་པོས་དེ་ལྟ་གོ་བ་མིན་.

153 That is, owls and other nocturnal birds.

154 For བླུན་པོས་མིན་ compare the footnote to 3b.

155 For ཁྭ་ཏས་མིན་ compare the footnote to 3b.

156 Lit. “[He] becomes a one of stronger intellect.”

157 Lit. “is not measured”; v4-stem as stative passive (see fn. 136 on p. 280).

158 The meaning of the last couplet is that as long as one has not played a drum, no difference between the drum and any other drum can be established. At the beginning of verses 6a and 6c one could add *ཅི་ཡི་བར་དུ་ and *ཇི་སྲིད་ to complement དེ་ཡི་བར་དུ་ and དེ་སྲིད་. For relative pronouns see Lesson 14.

159 Lit. “All men gather by themselves even though [nobody] has gathered them.”

160 ཉི་ལྡན་མེ་ཏོག་ stands for ཉི་ལྡན་པའི་མེ་ཏོག་.

161 མཐར་ཕྱིན་, lit. “one who arrived at the end”.

162 ཐམས་ཅད་མཁྱེན་པ་, Skt. *sarvajñaḥ* (Mvy: 14; Ishihama/Fukuda (eds.) 1989: 1), is an attribute of a Buddha. Here the phrase is used figuratively.

163 ཤེས་རབ་ stands for *ཤེས་རབ་ལྡན་པ་, lit. "[one] having wisdom". An alternative translation of the first couplet would be "Achieving happiness in this and the other world is wisdom."

164 The first line is difficult to interpret. I understand it as an ellipsis in which the verb ཤེས་ (paralleling ཤེས་ in the next line) has been omitted: *ཡོན་ཏན་སྐྱོན་གཉིས་སུས་ཀྱང་གསལ་པར་ཤེས།། lit. "Anyone knows that virtue and misdeed are clear."

165 ལོངས་ stands for ལོངས་སྤྱོད་.

166 A possible interpretation of the latter couplet is to see Skt. *ratnadvīpa*, lit. "island of jewels", behind རྒྱ་མཚོའི་གླིང་. According to Buddhist legends, the island abounds in jewels (Hahn 2003c: 38, fn. 9).

167 ཡོན་ཏན་ stands for ཡོན་ཏན་ཅན་. Alternatively, one can translate ཡོན་ཏན་མིན། literally as "[This] is not merit."

168 Lit. "From *A Treasury of Aphoristic Jewels*, wise ones being investigated, [this was] the first chapter."

Linguistic glossary

The Linguistic Glossary only includes terms that have not been defined in the textbook but belong to the basic linguistic vocabulary that should be apprehended by students. The definitions provide explanations relevant to Classical Tibetan grammar.

Adjunct is an optional part of a clause or sentence. Its removal does not affect the remaining part of the sentence. In the clause "Yesterday, I watched a good movie" the word *yesterday* is an adjunct; if one removes it, the clause "I watched a good movie" is still syntactically correct.

Agent is an animate participant of an action who deliberately initiates the action and has control over its course.

Agglutination is a morphological process in which lexical and grammatical morphemes are attached to the base word, each contributing an independent meaning. The morphemes usually do not change their form (or if they do then only moderately) so that each morpheme can be easily discerned from other morphemes.

Aspect is a grammatical category of verbs that expresses internal temporal constituency of events. The most common distinction is between imperfective and perfective aspect. Perfective aspect refers to events as complete and bounded, whereas imperfective aspect is used for events that are seen as not complete, or ongoing, in any temporal frame.

Assertive (evidentiality) expresses certainty about an event that does not require any further evidence to be accepted.

Causative is a grammatical form that indicates that a subject causes someone or something else to do something.

Clitic is a grammatical or lexical morpheme that attaches to a word, phrase, or a clause. On the other hand, it resembles affixes in not being allowed to stand independently in a clause. All clitics of Classical Tibetan are enclitics, i.e. they are postposed to their base.

DOI: 10.4324/9781003224198-28

Direct object is an obligatory argument of transitive verbs that can be made the subject of a passive construction with the same verb. In Classical Tibetan it usually follows the subject and directly precedes the verb.

Egophoric (evidentiality) indicates personal engagement or personal knowledge of events on the part of the speaker.

Evidentiality is a grammatical category that indicates the source of, or access to, information provided by the speech-act participant. In Classical Tibetan evidentiality can have one of the following values: egophoric, assertive, and sensory evidence.

Exclusive pronoun is the 1st person plural pronoun "we" that excludes the addressee.

Inclusive pronoun is the 1st person plural pronoun "we" that includes the addressee.

Indirect object is the second and obligatory object of ditransitive verbs.

Lexicalisation is a process by which newly coined phrases or words are set in the language and their meanings become conventionalised, i.e. independent of their etymological meaning.

Morpheme is the smallest meaningful unit of a language. Some morphemes are allowed to stand independently in a clause, but others are not.

Object, see s.vv. Direct object and Indirect object.

Patient is an animate or inanimate participant of an action that undergoes change as a result of the action.

Predicate is an obligatory element of each clause that serves either to assign a property to a single argument of a clause or to relate two or more arguments of a clause to each other.

Predicative is (besides subject) the second obligatory element of a clause with a copula verb. It expresses a property that is assigned to the subject of the clause.

Sensory evidence (evidentiality) indicates that the event is available to the agent through her personal experience as a witness to the event.

Subject is the only obligatory argument of clauses with intransitive verbs, and one of two obligatory arguments in clauses with transitive verbs. In Classical Tibetan, the subject typically precedes the object in a clause with a transitive verb.

Suffix is a grammatical or lexical morpheme that is placed after the base word to which it refers. In Classical Tibetan a suffix may consist either of one syllable or a single consonant but it has only one word in its scope.

Theme is a participant of a state or event that does not change itself.

Appendices

Appendix A
Writing instructions

The following figures serve to demonstrate the order and manner in which the single strokes of a letter should be written. Although there are no strict rules for writing the letters, in general the vertical strokes are written from top to bottom and the horizontal ones from left to right.

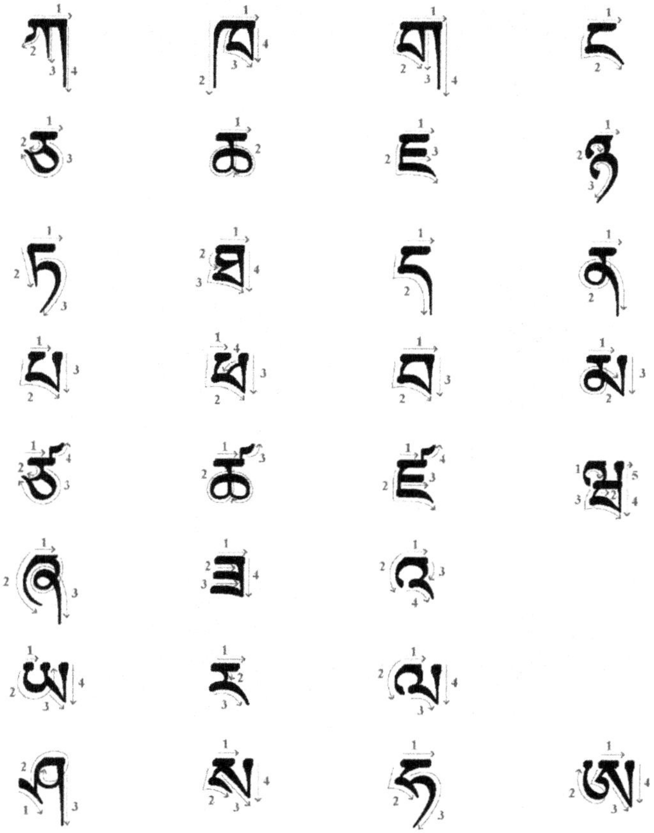

Appendix B

Transliteration systems. A comparative table

The following table juxtaposes letters of the Tibetan དབུ་ཅན་ script with the transliteration system used in the textbook (left) and the so-called Wylie transliteration (right; Wylie 1959). Shadowed fields of the table mark the transliterations that differ.

ཀ	*k*	*k*	ཁ	*kh*	*kh*	ག	*g*	*g*	ང	*ṅ*	*ng*
ཅ	*č*	*c*	ཆ	*čh*	*ch*	ཇ	*ǰ*	*j*	ཉ	*ñ*	*ny*
ཏ	*t*	*t*	ཐ	*th*	*th*	ད	*d*	*d*	ན	*n*	*n*
པ	*p*	*p*	ཕ	*ph*	*ph*	བ	*b*	*b*	མ	*m*	*m*
ཙ	*c*	*ts*	ཚ	*ch*	*tsh*	ཛ	*ȷ*	*dz*	ཝ	*w*	*w*
ཞ	*ź*	*zh*	ཟ	*z*	*z*	འ	*γ*	'			
ཡ	*y*	*y*	ར	*r*	*r*	ལ	*l*	*l*			
ཤ	*ś*	*sh*	ས	*s*	*s*	ཧ	*h*	*h*	ཨ	*q*	

Within the project Tibetan and Himalayan Digital Library, an 'Extended Wylie Transliteration Scheme' (EWTS) has been developed in order to include letters that are needed to transliterate Tibetan renderings of Sanskrit and Chinese words. A detailed description of the system can be found in the online publication *Teaching THDL Extended Wylie* by Alexandru Anton-Luca. Like the Wylie transliteration system, the Extended Wylie Transliteration Scheme avoids using diacritic signs.

Appendix C

Combinations of sub-, pre-, and superscripts with base letters

Subscripts

Subscript ◌ྱ *-y-*

ཀྱ-	ཁྱ-	གྱ-	པྱ-	ཕྱ-	བྱ-	མྱ-
ky-	*khy-*	*gy-*	*py-*	*phy-*	*by-*	*my-*

Subscript ◌ྲ *-r-*

ཀྲ-	ཁྲ-	གྲ-	ཏྲ-	ཐྲ-	དྲ-	ནྲ-	པྲ-	ཕྲ-	བྲ-	མྲ-	ཤྲ-	སྲ-	ཧྲ-
kr-	*khr-*	*gr-*	*tr-*	*thr-*	*dr-*	*nr-*	*pr-*	*phr-*	*br-*	*mr-*	*śr-*	*sr-*	*hr-*

Subscript ◌ླ *-l-*

ཀླ-	གླ-	བླ-	ཟླ-	རླ-	སླ-
kl-	*gl-*	*bl-*	*zl-*	*rl-*	*sl-*

Subscript ◌ྭ *-w-*

ཀྭ-	ཁྭ-	གྭ-	ཅྭ-	ཉྭ-	ཏྭ-	དྭ-	ཙྭ-	ཚྭ-	ཞྭ-	ཟྭ-	རྭ-	ལྭ-	ཤྭ-	སྭ-	ཧྭ-
kw-	*khw-*	*gw-*	*čw-*	*ñw-*	*tw-*	*dw-*	*cw-*	*chw-*	*źw-*	*zw-*	*rw-*	*lw-*	*św-*	*sw-*	*hw-*

Prescripts

Prescript ག *g-*

གཅ-	གཉ-	གཏ-	གད-	གན-	གཙ-	གཞ-	གཟ-	གཡ-	གཤ-	གས-
gč-	*gñ-*	*gt-*	*gd-*	*gn-*	*gc-*	*gź-*	*gz-*	*g.y-*	*gś-*	*gs-*

Prescript ད *d-*

དཀ- དག- དང- དཔ- དབ- དམ-
dk- dg- dṅ- dp- db- dm-

Prescript བ *b-*

བཀ- བག- བཅ- བཏ- བད- བཙ- བཞ- བཟ- བཤ- བས-
bk- bg- bč- bt- bd- bc- bź- bz- bś- bs-

Prescript མ *m-*

མཁ- མག- མང- མཆ- མཇ- མཉ- མཐ- མད- མན- མཚ- མཛ-
mkh- mg- mṅ- mčh- mǰ- mñ- mth- md- mn- mch- mʒ-

Prescript འ *ɣ-*

འཁ- འག- འཆ- འཇ- འཐ- འད- འཕ- འབ- འཚ- འཛ-
ɣkh- ɣg- ɣčh- ɣǰ- ɣth- ɣd- ɣph- ɣb- ɣch- ɣʒ-

Prescripts + subscripts

Prescript ད *d-* + subscript

དཀྱ- དགྱ- དཔྱ- དབྱ- དམྱ- དཀྲ- དགྲ- དཔྲ- དབྲ-
dky- dgy- dpy- dby- dmy- dkr- dgr- dpr- dbr-

Prescript བ *b-* + subscript

བཀྱ- བགྱ- བཀྲ- བགྲ- བཀླ- བཟླ- བརླ- བསླ-
bky- bgy- bkr- bgr- bkl- bzl- brl- bsl-

Prescript མ *m-* + subscript

མཁྱ- མགྱ- མཁྲ- མགྲ-
mkhy- mgy- mkhr- mgr-

Prescript འ *ɣ-* + subscript

འཁྱ- འགྱ- འཕྱ- འབྱ- འཁྲ- འགྲ- འདྲ- འཕྲ- འབྲ-
ɣkhy- ɣgy- ɣphy- ɣby- ɣkhr- ɣgr- ɣdr- ɣphr- ɣbr-

Superscripts

Superscript ར *r-*

རྐ-	རྒ-	རྔ-	རྗ-	རྙ-	རྟ-	རྡ-	རྣ-	རྦ-	རྨ-	རྩ-	རྫ-
rk-	*rg-*	*rṅ-*	*rǰ-*	*rñ-*	*rt-*	*rd-*	*rn-*	*rb-*	*rm-*	*rc-*	*rj-*

Superscript ལ *l-*

ལྐ-	ལྒ-	ལྔ-	ལྕ-	ལྗ-	ལྟ-	ལྡ-	ལྤ-	ལྦ-	ལྷ-
lk-	*lg-*	*lṅ-*	*lč-*	*lǰ-*	*lt-*	*ld-*	*lp-*	*lb-*	*lh-*

Superscript ས *s-*

སྐ-	སྒ-	སྔ-	སྙ-	སྟ-	སྡ-	སྣ-	སྤ-	སྦ-	སྨ-	སྩ-
sk-	*sg-*	*sṅ-*	*sñ-*	*st-*	*sd-*	*sn-*	*sp-*	*sb-*	*sm-*	*sc-*

Superscripts + subscripts

Superscript ར *r-*

རྐྱ-	རྒྱ-	རྨྱ-
rky-	*rgy-*	*rmy-*

Superscript ས *s-*

སྐྱ-	སྒྱ-	སྤྱ-	སྦྱ-	སྨྱ-	སྐྲ-	སྒྲ-	སྣྲ-	སྤྲ-	སྦྲ-	སྨྲ-
sky-	*sgy-*	*spy-*	*sby-*	*smy-*	*skr-*	*sgr-*	*snr-*	*spr-*	*sbr-*	*smr-*

Prescripts + superscripts

Prescript བ *b-* + superscript ར *r-*

བརྐ-	བརྒ-	བརྔ-	བརྗ-	བརྙ-	བརྟ-	བརྡ-	བརྣ-	བརྩ-	བརྫ-
brk-	*brg-*	*brṅ-*	*brǰ-*	*brñ-*	*brt-*	*brd-*	*brn-*	*brc-*	*brj-*

Prescript བ *b-* + superscript ལ *l-* or ས *s-*

བལྟ-	བསྐ-	བསྒ-	བསྔ-	བསྙ-	བསྟ-	བསྡ-	བསྣ-	བསྩ-
blt-	*bsk-*	*bsg-*	*bsṅ-*	*bsñ-*	*bst-*	*bsd-*	*bsn-*	*bsc-*

Prescripts + superscripts + subscripts

Prescript བ *b-* + superscript + subscript

བརྐྱ-	བརྒྱ-	བསྐྱ-	བསྒྱ-	བསྐྲ-	བསྒྲ-
brky-	*brgy-*	*bsky-*	*bsgy-*	*bskr-*	*bsgr-*

Appendix D
Particles

Grammatical particles

Auxiliary	/གྱིན་/
Case	ན་, ལ་, /གྱི་/, /དུ་/, /གྱིས་/, དང་, ནས་, ལས་
Collective	ཕྲག་
Comparative	/བས་/
Converbal	/ཅིང་/, /སྟེ་/, /གྱང་/, ཙ་ན་, དུས་, མ་ཐག་
Final	འོ་
Focus	ནི་
Imperative	/ཅིག་/
Indefinite	/ཅིག་/
Interrogative	འམ་
Negation	མི་, མ་
Number	རྣམས་, དག་, ཚོ་, ཅག་, འོ་ཅོག་
Numerical	ཙ་
Purposive	རྒྱུ་
Quotative	/ཅེས་/

Derivational particles

Diminutive	/བུ་/
Nominal	/པ་/, པ་, /པོ་/, པོ་, མ་, མོ་, /ག་/, གོ་
Possessive	ཅན་

Appendix E

Semantics of converbal particles

		Particle		*Function*	*Translation*	*Lesson*
Converbal particle		Concessive	/ཀྱང་/	Concessive	"although; despite"	10
		Concessive	རུང་	Concessive	"although"	16
		Coordinative	/ཅིང་/	Temporal	"while; during"	8
				Coordinative	"and"	
		Gerundial	/སྟེ་/	Introductory		9
				Gerundial		
		Purposive	རྒྱུ་	Purposive	"to"	16
			ཙ་ན་	Temporal	"as soon as, when"	15
			དུས་	Temporal	"when, after"	15
			མ་ཐག་(ཏུ་)	Temporal	"immediately thereafter"	15

		Particle		*Function*	*Translation*	*Lesson*
Case particle	Verb + particle	Comitative	དང་	Coordinative	"and"	12
		Dative	ལ་	Coordinative	"and"	12
		Elative	ནས་	Resultative		12
				Anteriority	"after"	
		Ergative	/ཀྱིས་/	Causal	"because"	12
		Genitive	/ཀྱི་/	Adversative	"whereas"	12
				Concessive	"although"	
				Contrasting	"but"	
		Locative	ན་	Temporal	"when"	12
				Conditional	"if"	
		Terminative	/དུ་/	Purposive	"to, in order to; lest"	12
	Verb + པ་/བ་ + particle	Comitative	དང་	Coordinative	"and"	12
		Dative	ལ་	Simultaneity	"as"	12
		Delative	ལས་	Anteriority	"upon"	12
		Ergative	-ས	Causal	"because, due to"	12
		Locative	ན་	Temporal	"when"	12
		Terminative	-ར	Complement	"that"	12
				Adverbial		

Appendix F
Analytical verb constructions

Auxiliary	**Construction**	**Grammatical meaning**
འགྱུར་	v1 + པར་/བར་ + འགྱུར་	Future tense
	v2 + པར་/བར་ + གྱུར་	Perfective aspect
	v1 + པར་/བར་ + གྱུར་	Past progressive
ཡིན་/ལགས་	v2 + པ་/བ་ + ཡིན་	Perfective aspect
	V + པ་/བ་ + ཡིན་	Egophoric
	ཡོད་པ་ཡིན་	Emphasis
ཡོད་/མཆིས་/མངའ་	v2 + ཡོད་	Perfect
	v1 (/v3) + པ(ར)་/བ(ར)་ + ཡོད་	Assertive
	v1 + auxiliary particle + ཡོད་	Progressive aspect
བྱེད་/བགྱིད་/མཛད་	V + པར་/བར་+ བྱེད་	Causative
	v3 + པར་/བར་ + བྱ་	Passive
འདུག་	V + (པར་/བར་) + འདུག་	Sensory evidence
	V + (པ(ར)་/བ(ར)་) + འདུག་	Assertive
	V + COORD + འདུག་	Progressive aspect
འབྱུང་	v1/v2 + བྱུང་	Past/egophoric
འོང་/ཡོང་	V + (TERM) + འོང་	Future tense
སོང་	v2 + སོང་	Perfective/sensory evidence
ཟིན་	v2 + (པར་/བར་) + ཟིན་	Perfective

Appendix G
Syntactic structures

In the following, an overview is provided of all syntactic constructions discussed in the textbook. The constructions are divided into phrases, clauses, and sentences (i.e. complex clauses). Excluded are analytical verb constructions to which Appendix F is devoted.

Phrases

1. Order of nominal grammatical categories in noun phrases (Lesson 1)

   [gender] [number] [definiteness] case [focus]

2. Word order in noun phrases (Lesson 1)

   Noun (N) – Adjective (A) – Numeral (NUM) – Determiner (DET)

3. Genitive phrases (Lesson 3)

   $\text{MODIFIER}_{\text{GEN}}$ HEAD "head of modifier"

4. Appositional phrases (Lesson 9)

   NP Appositive "NP which is Appositive"

5. Postpositional phrases (Lesson 10)

   NP+GEN+RN+case particle
   NP_{ABS}+RN+case particle
   NP+Postp

6. Possessive attribute (Lesson 14)

   HEAD + $[\text{N+A}]_{\text{POSSESSIVE ATTRIBUTE}}$

7. Comparative (Lesson 15)

   N བས་/ལས་ A "[more] A than N"

Clauses

1. Clauses with identity copula ཡིན་ (/མིན་) (Lesson 2)

   S_{ABS} P_{ABS} ཡིན་ (/མིན་) "S is (not) P."

2. Locative clauses with existential copula ཡོད་ (/མེད་) (Lesson 3)

   P_{LOC} S_{ABS} ཡོད་ (/མེད་) "S is/exists (is not/does not exist) in P."

3. Possessive clauses with existential copula ཡོད་ (/མེད་) (Lesson 3)

   P_{DAT} S_{ABS} ཡོད་ (/མེད་) "P has/possesses (does not possess) S."

4. Clauses with an intransitive verb (Lesson 4)

   S_{ABS} V_{INTR}-γo_{FNL} "S does V."

5. Clauses with a transitive verb (Lesson 5)

   S_{ERG} O_{ABS} V_{TR}-γo_{FNL} "S does O."

6. Clauses with a ditransitive verb (Lesson 5)

   S_{ERG} $O_{2/DAT}$ $O_{1/ABS}$ V_{TR}-γo_{FNL} "S does O_1 to O_2."

Sentences

1. Complex sentence (Lesson 8)

   $[[\ldots CONV]_{CLAUSE} [\ldots CONV]_{CLAUSE} [\ldots CONV]_{CLAUSE} \ldots V+\gamma o_{FNL}]_{SENTENCE}$

2. Clauses with embedded direct speech (Lesson 13)

   $Speaker_{ERG}$ – Direct $speech_{QUOT}$ – Verb of speaking

Glossary

ཀ

ཀ་ཁ་ alphabet

ཀ་ཁོལ་ pillar-hole

ཀ་ཆིགས་ཆེན་མོ་ *Ka chigs čhen mo*, title of a historiographical work

ཀ་བཞི་གདུང་བརྒྱད་མ་ (PN) Ka-bźi-gduṅ-brgyad-ma

ཀུན་ [I] (N) all, everyone; [II] (A) all

ཀུན་མཁྱེན་ the Omniscient One

ཀུན་དགའ་བོ་ (PN) Kun-dgaɣ-bo (Skt. Ānanda)

ཀུན་དགའ་ར་བ་ copse

ཀུན་ཏུ་ [1]all around; completely; [2]through

ཀུན་ནས་ [1]perfectly; [2]everywhere

ཀུན་ནས་དགའ་བ་ surpassingly lovely

ཀོ་ས་ལ་ (PN) Ko-sa-la (Skt. Kośala)

ཀྭ་ཡེ་ (Intrj) Oh! Alas!

ཀྱི་ཧུད་ (Intrj) Oh!

ཀྱེ་ (Intrj) Oh! Alas!

ཀྱེ་མ་ (Intrj) Oh! Alas!

ཀླད་ཀོར་ zero

ཀླུ་རྒྱལ་ (PN) Klu-rgyal

ཀླུ་བརྒྱད་མཁན་ (PN) Klu-brgyad-mkhan

ཀླུ་དབང་ lord of serpents

ཀླུང་ river valley

ཀློག་ v2 བཀླགས་ v3 བཀླག་ v4 ཀློགས་ (TR) to read

དཀའ་བ་ (to be) difficult

དཀར་ནག་ friendly or unfriendly, lit. "white or black"

དཀར་པོ་ white

དཀར་བ་ (to be) loyal

དཀར་མི་ loyal person

དཀར་མོ་ white

དཀར་ཡོལ་ porcelain cup

དཀྱིལ་འཁོར་ disc

བཀའ་ (HON) order

བཀའ་གྲིམས་ (OT; HON for ཁྲིམས་) sovereign law

བཀའ་ཆེམས་ (HON for ཆེམས་) testament

བཀའ་ཆེམས་ཀ་ཁོལ་མ་ *Bkaɣ čhems ka khol ma*, title of a historiographical work

བཀའ་དྲིན་ (HON for དྲིན་) kindness

བཀུམ་ see འགུམས་

བཀུར་ see འཁུར་

བཀོལ་ see འཁོལ་

བཀྲ་མི་ཤིས་ misfortune, mischief

བཀྲེས་ (to be) hungry

བཀྲོལ་ see འགྲོལ་

བཀླགས་ see ཀློག་

རྐང་པ་ leg, foot

རྐང་མིག་ (PN) Rkaṅ-mig (Skt. Akṣapāda)

རྐུ་ v2 བརྐུས་ v3 བརྐུ་ v4 རྐུས་ (TR) to steal

རྐོ་ v2 བརྐོས་ v3 བརྐོ་ v4 རྐོས་ (TR) to dig (out)

རྐོས་ see རྐོ་

རྐྱང་ single

རྐྱེན་ cause

རྐྱེན་གྱིས་ (Postp) on account of (+ GEN)

སྐྱོག་ལབ་ slander

སྐོག་ལབ་ཏུ་ slanderously

སྐ་རགས་ girdle

སྐད་ ¹voice; ²words

སྐད་ཅིག་ a moment

སྐལ་བ་ fortune

སྐུ་ (HON for ལུས་) body

སྐུ་འཁྲུངས་ v2 འཁྲུངས་ (INTR; HON for འཁྲུང་) to be born

སྐུ་ཐིམ་ (HON for ཐིམ་; INTR) to disappear

སྐུ་ཚེ་ (HON for ཚེ་) lifetime

སྐུར་ v2/v3 བསྐུར་ v4 སྐུར་ (TR) ¹to send; ²to give

སྐུལ་ v2/v3 བསྐུལ་ (TR) to exhort

སྐོང་ཆུ་ལག་ arm(s) of the Skoṅ-čhu river

སྐོང་ཆུ་ལག་ཁ་ mouths [of] the arms [of] the Skoṅ-čhu river

སྐོམ་ ᴵ(to be) thirsty; ᴵᴵ(N) thirst

སྐོམ་ཚུགས་ chin

སྐོར་ v2/v3 བསྐོར་ v4 སྐོར་ (TR) ¹to surround; to besiege, to encircle (+ DAT); ²to turn; ³to set in motion

སྐོལ་ v2/v3 བསྐོལ་ v4 སྐོལ་ (TR) to boil

སྐྱ་ (to be) ¹pale; ²flavourless

སྐྱ་བོ་ pale

སྐྱབས་ protection

སྐྱིད་སྡུག་ happiness and misery

སྐྱིད་པ་ (to be) happy

སྐྱིད་པོ་ happiness

སྐྱེ་ v2 སྐྱེས་ (INTR) ¹to be born; ²to arise; ³to grow

སྐྱེ་བ་ ¹birth; ²life

སྐྱེ་བོ་ man

སྐྱེད་ v2/v3 བསྐྱེད་ (TR) to generate

སྐྱེན་པ་ (A) precipitate

སྐྱེལ་ v2/v3 བསྐྱལ་ v4 སྐྱོལ་ (TR) to bring

སྐྱེས་ see སྐྱེ་

སྐྱེས་པ་ man, male person

སྐྱེས་བུ་ living being, person

སྐྱེས་བུ་ཆེན་པོ་ great person (Skt. *mahāpuruṣa*)

སྐྱོ་ (INTR) to be vexed (with + DAT)

སྐྱོང་ v2 བསྐྱངས་ v3 བསྐྱང་ v4 སྐྱོངས་ (TR) to guard, protect

སྐྱོན་ ¹fault; harm; ²misdeed

སྐྱོབ་ v2 བསྐྱབས་ v3 བསྐྱབ་ v4 སྐྱོབས་ (TR) to guard; to save, to rescue

སྐྲ་ hair

སྐྲག་དངང་ v2 སྐྲག་དངངས་ (INTR) to be terrified, frightened

སྐྲག་དངངས་ see སྐྲག་དངང་

སྐྲི་ v2 བསྐྲིས་ v3 བསྐྲི་ v4 སྐྲིས་ (TR) to charge, to assign

བསྐལ་པ་ aeon

བསྐུར་ see སྐུར་

བསྐུལ་ see སྐུལ་

བསྐོར་ see སྐོར་

བསྐྱང་ see སྐྱོང་

བསྐྱབ་ see སྐྱོབ་

བསྐྱབས་ see སྐྱོབ་

བསྐྱལ་ see སྐྱེལ་

བསྐྱེད་ see སྐྱེད་

བསྐྲི་ see སྐྲི་

ཁ

ཁ་ ¹mouth; ²surface

ཁ་ཆེམས་ testament

ཁ་དོག་ colour

ཁ་མདོག་ complexion

ཁ་ན་ (Postp) on (+ GEN)

ཁ་སྤུ་ beard

ཁ་བ་ snow

ཁ་བ་ཅན་ [I](A) snowy (lit. possessing snow), snow-clad; [II](N) Tibet

ཁ་འཛིན་ assistant

ཁ་ཟས་ food

ཁ་རོག་པ་ silent

ཁང་(པ་) house

ཁང་བུ་ [1]little house; [2]room

ཁབ་ residence

ཁབ་ལེན་རྡོ་ lodestone

ཁམས་ see འཁམས་

ཁམས་པ་ (A) faint

ཁམས་བཟང་ good health

ཁར་ (Postp) [1]on, upon, after; [2]in addition to (+ GEN/ABS)

ཁུང་ hole

ཁུང་བུ་ hole

ཁེ་སྤོགས་ profit

ཁེངས་ see འཁེངས་

ཁོ་ (3SG M) he

ཁོ་ཐག་ see ཆོད་

ཁོ་པ་ (3SG M) he

ཁོ་བོ་ (1SG M) I

ཁོ་མ་ (3SG F) she

ཁོ་མོ་ (1SG F) I

ཁོ་རང་ (3SG M) he, himself

ཁོག་ཆེ་ of great intrinsic power

ཁོང་ (3SG/PL HON) he, she; they

ཁོང་མཛངས་ inner knowledge

ཁོང་སེང་ inner cavern

ཁྭ་ཏ་ crow

ཁྱད་ difference

ཁྱད་པར་ difference

ཁྱད་པར་(དུ་) in particular

ཁྱབ་ (INTR) to be comprised (by + ERG)

ཁྱི་ dog

ཁྱི་མོ་ bitch

ཁྱིམ་ house

ཁྱིམ་ཐབ་ house and hearth

ཁྱིམ་བདག་ householder

ཁྱིམ་མཚེས་ neighbour

ཁྱིམ་སོ་ household

ཁྱུ་ flock

ཁྱུང་ཚ་དཔལ་འདྲེན་ (PN) Khyuṅ-cha Dpal-ɣdren

ཁྱེད་ (2SG/PL; HON) you

ཁྱེད་རང་ (2SG/PL) you

ཁྱེའུ་ boy

ཁྱེར་ see འཁྱེར་

ཁྱོ་ husband, man

ཁྱོ་བཟང་ good husband

ཁྱོད་ (2SG/PL) you

ཁྲ་ falcon

ཁྲག་ blood

ཁྲག་ཁྲུག་ complicate, confused

ཁྲི་ ten thousand

ཁྲིད་ (TR) to lead, conduct

ཁྲིམས་ law

ཁྲི་ལོག་ [I](INTR) to roll one's self; [II](N) a rolling

ཁྲི་ལོག་ལོག་ an incessant rolling

ཁྲོ་ v2 ཁྲོས་ [I](to be) angry/wrathful; [II](N) rage

ཁྲོ་གཉེར་ཅན་ (PN) Khro-gñer-čan (Skt. Bhṛkuṭī)

ཁྲོན་པ་ (N) well

ཁྲོས་ see ཁྲོ་

མཁའ་ལྡིང་ see ནམ་མཁའ་ལྡིང་

མཁས་པ་ [I]skilled (in + DAT), wise; [II]wise one

མཁས་པོ་ a skilled male person; a scholar

མཁྱེན་ (HON for ཤེས་; TR) [1]to recognise, to discern, to realise; [2]to understand, to know

འཁམས་ v2 ཁམས་ (INTR) to faint away

འཁར་བ་ staff

འཁལ་ v2/v3 བཀལ་ v4 ཁོལ་ (TR) to spin

འཁུར་ v2 བཀུར་ (TR) to carry

འཁེངས་ v2 ཁེངས་ (INTR) to be full

འཁོར་ [I](INTR) [1]to turn round; [2]to circle; [3]to roam; [II](N) retinue, attendants

འཁོར་བ་ cycle of existence/rebirth (Skt. *saṃsāra*)

འཁོར་ལོ་ wheel

འཁོར་ལོས་སྒྱུར་ universal emperor

[1]འཁོལ་ v2/v3 བཀོལ་ v4 ཁོལ་ (TR) to appoint

[2]འཁོལ་ v2 ཁོལ་ (INTR) to boil

འཁྱེར་ v2 ཁྱེར་ (TR) to carry, to carry away; to hold, to keep

འཁྲུག་ v2 འཁྲུགས་ (INTR) to be disturbed

འཁྲུགས་ see འཁྲུག་

འཁྲུང་ v2 འཁྲུངས་ (HON for སྐྱེ་; INTR) to be born

ག

ག་རེ་ Where is [he/she/it]?

ག་ལ་ (INT) to/for whom? where?

[1]གང་ (INT) who? what? which?

[2]གང་ (to be) full

གང་དུ་ (INT) where? wither?

གང་ན་ (INT) where?

གང་ན་བ་ whereabouts

གང་ནས་ where from?

གང་བ་ full

གང་ཡང་ any(thing), whatsoever

གངས་ snow-mountain

གངས་ཅན་ Tibet

གད་མོ་ laugh

གར་ (INT) whither? where?

གལ་ཏེ་ if

གལ་ཏེ་ན་ perhaps

གུམ་ see འགུམ་

གུར་ tent

གུས་པ་ reverence

1གོ་ place, spot

2གོ་ (TR) to understand

གོ་ཆོད་ capable

གོ་བ་ understanding

གོང་མ་ previous one

གོན་ (TR) to put on

གོས་ cloth, clothes

གོས་ཐུང་ trousers

གོས་དར་ silk cloth(es)

གོས་སེར་ཅན་ (PN) Gos-ser-čan, lit. dressed in yellow clothes, an epithet of Viṣṇu (Skt. *pītāmbara*)

གོས་ཧྲུལ་ tattered robe

གོས་ལྷམ་ shoes and clothes

གཽ་ཏ་མ་ (PN) Gautama, the name of the Buddha

གྱང་ pisé

གྱིས་ see བགྱིད་

གྱུར་ see འགྱུར་

གྱོན་ (TR) to wear

གྱོས་པོ་ father-in-law

གྲགས་ see འགྲགས་

གྲངས་མེད་(པ་) innumerable

གྲལ་ row

གྲལ་པ་ person sitting in a row

གྲི་གུམ་བཙན་པོ་ (PN) Gri-gum Bcan-po

གྲུ་གསུམ་ triangular

གྲུང་ (to be) wise

གྲུང་ཞན་ weak-minded person

གྲུབ་ see འགྲུབ་

གྲུབ་པ་ accomplished one

གྲོ་ wheat

གྲོག་མཁར་བ་ (PN) Grog-mkhar-ba (Skt. Vālmīki)

གྲོག་མ་ ant

གྲོགས་ friend, companion

གྲོགས་པོ་ a male friend

གྲོང་ཁྱེར་ village, town

གྲོང་ཆོག་ village rituals

གྲོངས་ see འགྲོང་

གྲོས་ཉེས་ bad counsel

གྲྭ་ [1]corner; [2]school

གླ་རྩི་ musk

གླང་ ox

གླང་ཆེན་ elephant

གླང་པོ་ཆེ་ elephant

གླང་བུ་ calf

གླིང་ island

གླེན་པ་ (to be) stupid

དགའ་ (TR) [1]to rejoice in, to be happy/delighted about (+ DAT); [2]to like

དགའ་ལྡན་ (PN) Dgaɣ-ldan heaven (Skt. Tuṣita)

དགའ་བ་ happiness

དགའ་བཤེས་ spiritual advisor, < *དགའ་བའི་བཤེས་གཉེན་ (Skt. *kalyāṇamitra*) friend to virtue, spiritual advisor

དགས་ (INTR) to be cracked

དགུ་ nine

དགུང་ sky

དགུན་ winter

དགུམ་ see འགུམས་

དགེ་བསྙེན་ lay practitioner

དགེ་བ་ [I]virtuous deed, virtue; [II](to be) virtuous

དགེ་ལེགས་ prosperity

དགེ་སློང་ monk

དགོངས་ (HON for སེམས་; TR) to think, to reflect (on + DAT)

དགོད་ (INTR) to laugh; གད་མོ་དགོད་ to laugh

དགོན་པ་ hermitage

དགོན་པ་པ་ hermit

དགོས་ (TR) to need; (MOD) to be necessary, have to, need

དགྲ་(བོ་) enemy

དགྲ་བཅོམ་པ་ Arhat (Skt. *arhant*)

བགེགས་ difficulty

བགོ་ v2 བགོས་ (TR) to put on

བགོ་བ་ clothes

བགོད་ v2/v4 བགོས་ v3 བགོ་ (TR) to divide

[1]བགོས་ see བགོ་

[2]བགོས་ see བགོད་

བགྱི་ see བགྱིད་

བགྱིད་ v2 བགྱིས་ v3 བགྱི་ v4 གྱིས་ (HML for བྱེད་; TR) [1]to do; [2]to say, to ask; སོ་ནམ་བགྱིད་ to cultivate fields

བགྲིས་ see བགྲིད་

བགྲང་ v2 བགྲངས་ v3 བགྲང་ (TR) ¹to count; ²to consider

བགྲེས་པ་ (N) elder man; (A) elder

བགྲོ་ v2 བགྲོས་ (INTR) to confer, to discuss

བགྲོས་ see བགྲོ་

མགུལ་ neck

མགོ་(བོ་) head

མགོན་པོ་ protector

མགོན་མེད་ཟས་སྦྱིན་ (PN) Mgon-med-zas-sbyin (Skt. Anāthapiṇḍada)

མགྱོགས་ (to be) quick

མགྱོགས་པོ་ quick

འགའ་ a few, some

འགལ་ (TR) to contradict (+ COM)

འགུམ་ v2 གུམ་ (INTR) to die

འགུམས་ v2 བཀུམ་ v3 དགུམ་ v4 ཁུམས་ (TR) to kill

འགེམས་ (TR) to rip, to destroy

འགོར་ཏི་ (PN) Ɣgor-ti, place name

འགྱུར་ v2 གྱུར་ (INTR) ¹to change; ²to become; ³to happen

འགྱེལ་ v2 གྱེལ་ (INTR) to collapse, to fall

འགྲགས་ v2 གྲགས་ (INTR) to be called; to be known as (+ TERM)

འགྲན་སེམས་ quarrelsome temper

འགྲུབ་ v2 གྲུབ་ (INTR) to accomplish, to complete

འགྲེ་ (INTR) to roll one's self

འགྲོ་ v2/v4 སོང་ (INTR) ¹to go; ²to pass (of time); ³to become (+ TERM)

འགྲོ་བ་ ¹a being; ²existence

འགྲོགས་ (INTR) to come together, to be accompanied (by + COM)

འགྲོང་ v2 གྲོངས་ (HON for འཆི་; INTR) to die

འགྲོལ་ v2 བགྲོལ་ v3 དགྲོལ་ v4 གྲོལ་ (TR) to untie

རྒན་པོ་ old man

རྒན་མོ་ ᴵold woman; ᴵᴵold

རྒན་གཞོན་ age

རྒལ་ v2/v3 བརྒལ་ v4 རྒོལ་ (TR) to cross (+ DEL)

རྒུད་ (INTR) to grow weak

རྒོད་ vulture

རྒོད་མ་ mare

རྒོལ་ v2/v3 བརྒལ་ v4 རྒོལ་ (TR) to fight (against + DAT)

རྒྱ་ size

རྒྱ་གར་ (PN) India

རྒྱ་གར་སྐད་ Sanskrit, lit. "language of India"

རྒྱ་མཚོ་ ocean

རྒྱགས་ provisions

རྒྱང་(མ་) distance

རྒྱང་ཚད་ (N) a while

[1]རྒྱབ་ (N) the back

[2]རྒྱབ་ v2/v3 བརྒྱབ་ v4 རྒྱོབ་ (TR) to throw

རྒྱལ་ (INTR) to be victorious (over + DEL)

རྒྱལ་ཁམས་ kingdom, realm

རྒྱལ་པོ་ king

རྒྱལ་ཕྲན་ vassal

རྒྱལ་བུ་ prince

རྒྱལ་བྱེད་ (PN) Rgyal-byed (Skt. Jetṛ)

རྒྱལ་བློན་ king and minister

རྒྱལ་མོ་ queen

རྒྱལ་རབས་དཔག་བསམ་ལྗོན་ཤིང་ *Rgyal rabs dpag bsam ljon śiṅ*, title of a historiographical work

རྒྱས་ (INTR) [1]to increase, to grow, to spread; [2]to be full of

རྒྱས་པ་ (PN) Rgyas-pa (Skt. Vyāsa)

རྒྱས་པར་ in detail; extensively

རྒྱུ་སྐར་ lunar mansion

རྒྱུག་ v2 བརྒྱུགས་ (INTR) to run

རྒྱུད་ [1]realm of existence; [2]tantra

རྒྱུན་ flow, stream

རྒྱུན་ཆད་ interruption

རྒྱུན་དུ་ constantly, continually

རྒྱུས་ཡོད་ familiar with; lit. having knowledge (of)

[1]སྒོ་ door

[2]སྒོ་ v2 བསྒོ་ (TR) to say

སྒོ་ཁྱི་ door-guarding dog

སྒོ་ནས་ (Postp) [1]due to; [2]by means of (+ GEN)

སྒོམ་ v2 བསྒོམས་ v3 བསྒོམ་ v4 སྒོམ(ས)་ (TR) to meditate

སྒྱུ་མ་ལྷ་མཛེས་ (PN) Sgyu-ma Lha-mjes (སྒྱུ་མ་ = Skt. *māyā*)

སྒྱུར་ v2/v3 བསྒྱུར་ v4 སྒྱུར་ (TR) to change

སྒྲ་ voice

སྒྲ་ཆེན་པོ་ (PN) Sgra-čhen-po

སྒྲིག་ v2 བསྒྲིགས་ v3 བསྒྲིག་ v4 སྒྲིགས་ (TR) to arrange

སྒྲུབ་ v2 བསྒྲུབས་ v3 བསྒྲུབ་ v4 སྒྲུབས་ (TR) to complete, to accomplish, to achieve

སྒྲོག་ v2 བསྒྲགས་ v3 བསྒྲག་ v4 སྒྲོགས་ (TR) to promulgate

སྒྲོམ་ box, chest

སྒྲོལ་ v2/v3 བསྒྲལ་ v4 སྒྲོལ་ (TR) to rescue

སྒྲོལ་མ་ (PN) Sgrol-ma (Skt. Tārā)

བརྐལ་ see རྐལ་

བརྒྱ་ hundred

བརྒྱད་ eight

བརྒྱལ་ (INTR) to faint away

བརྒྱུད་ lineage

[1]བསྒོ་ see [2]སྒོ་

[2]བསྒོ་ v2 བསྒོས་ (TR) to soil, to stain

བསྒོམ་ see སྒོམ་

བསྒོམས་ see སྒོམ་

བསྒོས་ see ^{2}བསྒོ་

བསྒྲགས་ see སྒྲོག་

བསྒྲིགས་ see སྒྲིག་

བསྒྲུབ་ see སྒྲུབ་

བསྒྲུབས་ see སྒྲུབ་

ང

ང་ (1SG) I

ང་རང་ (1SG) I

ངག་ speech

ངག་ཏུ་ verbally

ངང་རྒྱུད་ forbearance

ངང་པ་ goose

ངན་པ་ (to be) bad, wicked

ངན་བུ་ (1SG) I; humble I

ངར་པ་ leg (of trousers)

^{1}ངལ་ weariness

^{2}ངལ་ (INTR) to be tired; ལུས་ངལ་ to be tired

ངུ་ v2 ངུས་ (INTR) to weep, to cry

ངུར་སྨྲིག་ yellowish red

ངུས་ see ངུ་

ངེད་ (1PL) we

ངེད་རང་ (1SI/PL) I, we

ངེས་ (to be) certain

ངེས་པར་ certainly

ངེས་འབྱུང་ renunciation

ངོ་ face

ངོ་ཚ་ [I]shame; [II]shameful

ངོ་མཚར་ [I]miracle, wonder; [II]wonderful

ངོམ་ v2 ངོམས་ (INTR) to be sated (by + ERG)

ངོམས་ see ངོམ་

ངོས་ (1SG) I

དངུལ་ silver

དངོས་ (1SG) I

དངོས་པོ་ thing

མངའ་ (HON for ཡོད་; COP) to have; to be there

མངོན་པར་ openly, visibly

མངོན་པར་དགའ་ (TR) to be delighted

མངོན་པར་སྟོད་ v2/v3 བསྟོད་ v4 སྟོད་ (TR) to praise

མངོན་པར་སངས་རྒྱ་ v2 རྒྱས་ (INTR) to achieve manifesting enlightenment

མངོན་བློ་ real understanding

[1]རྔ་ drum

[2]རྔ་ v2 བརྔས་ v3 བརྔ་ v4 རྔོས་ (TR) to reap

ལྔ་ five

ལྔ་བརྒྱ་ five hundred

ལྔ་སྟོང་ five thousand

ལྔ་ཚིགས་ third out of five

སྔ་ earlier time

སྔ་དར་ earlier propagation of Buddhism

སྔ་མ་ before

སྔ་རོལ་ past ages, earlier time

སྔག་ v2 བསྔགས་ v3 བསྔག་ v4 སྔོག(ས)་ (TR) to praise

སྔགས་ mantra

སྔར་ [1]earlier; [2]before, ahead

སྔར་ཕན་ until recently

སྔོ་ green

སྔོན་ earlier

བཛ་ see ²ཛ་

བསྡུགས་ see སྡུག་

ཙ

ཙང་ any, any thing, anyone, whatever

ཅི་ (INT) what? (REL) which

ཅི་ལྟར་ (INT) how? (REL) how (also ཇི་ལྟར་)

ཅི་སྟེ་ if

ཅི་འདྲ་ (INT/REL) how; (REL) whatever

ཅི་ཙམ་ (INT) how much?; (REL) so much

ཅིའི་ཕྱིར་ (INT) why?

ཅིའི་སླད་དུ་ (INT) why? on account of what?

ཅུང་ཟད་ a little, a bit

གཅགས་ (INTR) to love

གཅིག་ one

གཅིག་ཏུ་ན་ firstly

གཅིག་པ་ (A) only; the same

གཅིག་པུ་ ¹sole; ²alone, single

གཅིག་པོ་ (A) only

གཅོག་ v2 བཅག་ v3 གཅག་ v4 ཆོག(ས)་ (TR) to break; to knock out

གཅོད་ v2 བཅད་ v3 གཅད་ v4 ཆོད་ (TR) ¹to cut (off); ²to decide; ཞལ་ཆེ་གཅོད་ to pass a judgement

བཅག་ see གཅོག་

བཅད་ see གཅོད་

¹བཅས་ accompanied by, possessed of, together with (+ COM)

²བཅས་ see འཆའ་

བཅིངས་ see འཆིང་

བཅུ་ ten

བཅུག་ see ²འཇུག་

བཅོ་ལྔ་ fifteen

བཅོམ་ see འཇོམས་

བཅོམ་ལྡན་འདས་ the Victorious One (Skt. *bhagavant*), epithet of the Buddha

བཅོལ་ see འཆོལ་

བཅོལ་གཏམས་ trust

བཅོས་ see འཆོས་

ལྕག་ a blow

ལྕགས་ iron

ལྕགས་ཕྱེ་ iron filing

ལྕེ་ tongue

ལྕོགས་ (INTR) to be possible

ཆ

ཆ་ part

ཆ་ལུགས་ appearance

ཆ་ཤས་ portion

ཆག་ see ²འཆག་

¹ཆགས་ (INTR) to be attached to, to yearn for (+ DAT)

²ཆགས་ (INTR) to arise

ཆགས་པ་ I.1love; 2passion; IIpassionate

ཆང་ beer

ཆང་ཚོང་ tavern

ཆང་ཚོང་མ་ beer-seller (F)

ཆད་ see ¹འཆད་

ཆད་པ་ begotten/born from (+ DEL)

ཆར་འདོད་བྱི་ཙུ་ *cātaka*-nestling

ཆས་ garment

ཆིག་རྐྱང་ separate, single

ཆིག་ཤད་ single *śad*

ཆིབས་ (HON for རྟ་) horse

ཆིབས་ཁ་ bridle

ཆུ་ [1]water; [2]river

ཆུ་ཀླུང་ river

ཆུ་ཤྲོར་ meat

ཆུ་བོ་ river

ཆུག་ see [2]འཇུག་

ཆུང་ (to be) small, young

ཆུང་ངུ་ [I](N) [1]the youngest; [2]childhood; [II](A) small

ཆུང་གཉེན་ child-marriage

ཆུང་མ་ wife

ཆུང་ཤོས་ the youngest

ཆུད་གསན་ (TR) to waste

ཆེ་བ་ (to be) great; ཚབས་ཆེ་བ་ very great

ཆེད་དུ་ on account of

ཆེན་པོ་ [I](A) [1]great; [2]big, vast; [II](N) a great one

ཆོ་ངེས་ lamentation

[1]ཆོག་ see གཅོག་

[2]ཆོག་ (MOD) to be allowed, permitted

[1]ཆོད་ (INTR) to be decided; ཁོ་ཐག་ཆོད་ to be certain

[2]ཆོད་ see གཅོད་

ཆོས་ [1]Buddhist teaching, Dharma (Skt. *dharma*), doctrine; religion; [2]religious teaching; [3]thing

ཆོས་གོས་ monk-robe

ཆོས་པ་ follower of Dharma

ཆོས་འབྱུང་ lit. origins of Buddhism; name of a literary genre

[1]མཆི་ (HML; TR) to speak

[2]མཆི་ v2 མཆིས་ (HML for འོང་/འགྲོ་; INTR) [1]to come; [2]to go, to walk

མཆི་མ་ tears

མཆིམས་བཟའ་ lady from the Mčhims family

[1]མཆིས་ see [2]མཆི་

[2]མཆིས་ (HML for ཡོད་) to be there

མཆེད་ (HON) brother

མཆོག་ most excellent one

མཆོང་(ས)་ (INTR) to jump

མཆོད་ (TR) to worship

མཆོད་རྟེན་ shrine (Skt. *stūpa*)

མཆོད་པ་ [1]offering; [2]honours

[1]འཆག་ (INTR) to walk

[2]འཆག་ v2 ཆག་ (INTR) to break

[1]འཆད་ v2 ཆད་ (INTR) [1]to be cut (off; into pieces); [2]to be separated; [3]to descend (from + DEL); [4]to be decided/determined

[2]འཆད་ v2/v3 བཤད་ v4 ཤོད་ (TR) to explain

འཆམ་ (TR) to agree (upon + DAT); ཁ་འཆམ་ to agree

འཆའ་ v2 བཅས་ v3 བཅའ་ v4 ཆོས་ (TR) to place (on + DAT)

འཆར་ v2 ཤར་ (INTR) to rise

འཆར་བྱེད་ (PN) Ɣčhar-byed (Skt. Udayana)

འཆི་ v2 ཤི་ (INTR) to die

འཆིང་ v2 བཅིངས་ v3 བཅིང་ v4 ཆིངས་ (TR) to bind

འཆོར་ v2 ཤོར་ (INTR) to get lost, to perish; མཆི་མ་འཆོར་ (TR/NC) to shed tears

འཆོལ་ v2/v3 བཅོལ་ (TR) [1]to appoint; [2]to entrust (to + DAT)

འཆོས་ v2 བཅོས་ v3 བཅོ་ v4 ཆོས་ (TR) to make, to prepare

ཇ

ཇི་ see ཅི་

ཇི་ལྟར་ see ཅི་ལྟར་

ཇོ་བོ་ lord, master

ཇོ་མོ་ [1]goddess; [2]lady

མཇུག་མ་ tail

འཇང་ (PN) Ɣjaṅ, name of an ancient people

འཇམ་ (to be) soft

འཇམ་པ་ mild

འཇམ་དཔལ་གཞོན་ནུར་གྱུར་པ་ (PN) Ɣǰam-dpal Gźon-nur-gyur-pa, lit. Mañjuśrī who became a youth (Skt. Kumārabhūtamañjuśrī)

འཇའ་ rainbow

འཇལ་ v2 བཅལ་ v3 གཞལ་ v4 འཇོལ་ (TR) to measure out

[1]འཇིག་ v2 ཞིག་ to perish, to collapse

[2]འཇིག་ v2 བཤིག་ v3 གཞིག་ v4 ཤིག་ (TR) to waste; to destroy

འཇིག་རྟེན་ world

འཇིག་རྟེན་པ་ folk, inhabitants of the world

འཇིག་པ་ decay

འཇིགས་ (INTR) to fear

[1]འཇུ་ v2 འཇུས་ (TR) to seize

[2]འཇུ་ v2 བཞུས་ v3 བཞུ་ (TR) to melt

[1]འཇུག་ v2 ཞུགས་ (INTR) to enter

[2]འཇུག་ v2 བཅུག་ v3 གཞུག་ v4 ཆུག་ (TR) [1]to put into; [2]to lead to; [3]to order; (CAUS) to cause, to let

འཇུས་ see [1]འཇུ་

འཇོག་ v2 བཞག་ v3 གཞག་ v4 ཞོག་ (TR) [1]to leave; [2]to lay down

འཇོམས་ v2 བཅོམ་ v3 གཞོམ་ v4 ཆོམ་ (TR) to conquer

རྗེ་ lord

རྗེས་ [I](N) step, trace; [II](Postp) after, behind (+ ABS)

རྗེས་སུ་ (Postp) after, behind (+ GEN)

རྗེས་སུ་ཡི་རང་ v2 རངས་ (INTR) to be very pleased

རྗོད་ v2/v3 བརྗོད་ (TR) to say

བརྗོད་ see རྗོད་

ཉ

ཉག་ lump

ཉན་ v4 ཉོན་ (TR) to listen, to hear

ཉམ་ཆུང་ (to be) weak

ཉམས་ (INTR) to be/get hurt

ཉམས་ཐག་ (INTR) to be exhausted

ཉལ་ (INTR) to lie down

ཉི་དཀྱིལ་ solar disc

ཉི་མ་ sun

ཉི་ཤུ་རྩ་བདུན་ twenty-seven

ཉིད་ [1](DET) the very same; [2]self; [3]alone

ཉིད་དུ་ as such

ཉིན་ day

ཉིན་པར་ during the day

ཉིལ་ལེ་ dangling

ཉིས་ཤད་ double *śad*

ཉུང་ (to be) few

ཉེ་ (INTR) to be near

ཉེ་འཁོར་ kindreds

ཉེ་རིང་ near and distant

ཉེན་ (INTR) to be pained

ཉེས་ (INTR) [1]to be hurt; [2]to be bad; [3]to make a mistake

ཉེས་པ་ [1]moral fault; [2]evil, offence, bad deed; [3]calamity

ཉོ་ v2/v4 ཉོས་ (TR) to buy

ཉོན་ see ཉན་

ཉོན་མོངས་པ་ misery, trouble

ཉོས་ see ཉོ་

གཉའ་(བ་) neck

གཉའ་ཁྲི་བཙན་པོ་ (PN) Gñaɣ-khri Bcan-po

གཉའ་ཤིང་ yoke

གཉིད་ dream

གཉིས་ two

གཉིས་ཀ་ a pair

གཉིས་པ་ second

གཉིས་སུ་ན་ secondly

གཉེན་ (N) relative

གཉེན་ཉེ་འབྲེལ་ (N) relative

གཉེན་ཚན་ relatives

གཉེན་བཤེས་ relatives and friends

གཉེར་ (TR) to take care

གཉེར་ཁ་ attention, care

མཉན་དུ་ཡོད་པ་ (PN) Mñan-du-yod-pa (also Mñan-yod), Indian town Śrāvasti

མཉན་ཡོད་ see མཉན་དུ་ཡོད་པ་

རྙིང་མ་པ་ (PN) Rñiṅ-ma-pa, a school of Tibetan Buddhism

རྙེད་ v2/v3 བརྙེད་/བརྙེས་ (TR) [1]to find; [2]to obtain; དབུ་རྙེད་ to introduce

རྙོག་པ་ whirlpool

སྙད་ v2/v3 བསྙད་ v4 སྙོད་ (TR) to tell

སྙན་ (HON for རྣ་བ་) ear

སྙན་པ་ pleasant, well-sounding; kind; comforting

སྙམ་ [I](TR) to think; [II]thought

སྙིང་རྗེ་ compassion

སྙིང་རྗེ་བ་ compassionate

སྙིང་སྟོབས་ courage

སྙིང་བརྩེ་བ་ loving, kind

སྙུན་ illness

སྙེད་ (DET) about; see also དེ་སྙེད་

སྙོད་ v2/v3 བསྙོད་ (TR) to feed

སྙོལ་ v2 བསྙལ་ (TR) to lay down

བརྙ་ v2 བརྙས་ (TR) to borrow

བརྙས་ see བརྙ་

བརྙེས་ see རྙེད་

བསྙད་ see སྙད་

བསྙལ་ see སྙོལ་

བསྙོད་ see སྙོད་

ཏ

གཏད་ see གཏོད་

གཏམ་ [1]rumour; [2]speech

གཏམ་དཔེ་ proverb

གཏམ་ཚིག་ words

གཏི་མུག་ ignorance

གཏིང་ [1]bottom; [2]depth

གཏུམ་(པ་) (to be) hot-tempered; furious

གཏེར་ [1]treasury; [2]treasure

གཏེར་ཁ་ mine

གཏོག་ v2 གཏོགས་ སེ་གོལ་གཏོག་ to snap one's fingers

གཏོགས་ see གཏོག་

གཏོང་ v2 བཏང་ v3 གཏང་ v4 ཐོང་ (TR) [1]to let go, to send; [2]to give away, to give; [3]to abandon; [4]to let; [5]to set free; མཐུ་གཏོང་ to cast spells; བག་མར་གཏོང་ to give in marriage; གཡར་གཏོང་ to loan; སེམས་གསོ་གཏོང་ to console

གཏོད་ v2/v3 གཏད་ v4 ཐོད་ (TR) [1]to direct, to point (towards + DAT); [2]to deliver up

གཏོར་ (TR) to scatter

གཏོར་མ་ strewing-oblation

བཏགས་ see འདོགས་

བཏང་ see གཏོང་

བཏབ་ see འདེབས་

བཏིང་ see འདིང་

བཏོན་ see འདོན་

རྟ་ horse

རྟ་བདག་ horse-owner

རྟ་པ་ horseman

རྟ་རྫི་ horse-keeper

རྟག་ཏུ་ always

རྟག་པ་ [I]durable; [II]permanence

རྟིང་དུ་ (Adv) later

རྟིང་ལ་ [I](Postp) after (+ GEN); [II](Adv) later

རྟིང་སོར་ (Adv) later

རྟེའུ་ foal

རྟོག་ v2 བརྟགས་ v3 བརྟག་ v4 རྟོག(ས)་ (TR) to consider; to ponder, to examine

རྟོགས་ (TR) to perceive, to apprehend

ལྟ་ v2 བལྟས་ v3 བལྟ་ v4 ལྟོས་ (TR) [1]to look (at/towards + DAT), to watch; [2]to inspect, to examine

ལྟ་ཅི་སྨོས་ how much less, not to mention, to say nothing of (+ ABS)

ལྟ་བུར་ like

ལྟར་ (Postp) like, as (+ ABS)

ལྟུང་ v2 ལྟུང་ (INTR) to fall

ལྟེ་བ་ navel

ལྟོ་ food

ལྟོ་གོས་ food and clothing

ལྟོགས་གྲི་ hunger

ལྟོགས་པ་ hungry

སྟག་ tiger

སྟག་ཕྲུག་ tiger cub

སྟག་མོ་ tigress

སྟན་ mat; seat

སྟེང་ top, surface

སྟེང་ཁང་ upper story

སྟེང་དུ་ [I](Postp) above, on(to) (+ GEN); [II](Adv) up

སྟེང་ནས་ (Postp) from (+ GEN)

སྟེའུ་ axe

སྟེར་ v2/v3 བསྟེར་ (TR) [1]to allow (to + TERM); [2]to give

སྟོང་ thousand

སྟོང་པ་ཉིད་ voidness

སྟོང་རྩན་ (PN) Mgar Stoṅ-rcan Yul-zuṅ

སྟོད་ v2/v3 བསྟོད་ v4 སྟོད་ (TR) to praise; see མངོན་པར་སྟོད་

སྟོན་ v2/v3 བསྟན་ v4 སྟོན་ (TR) [1]to teach, to explain, to instruct; [2]to show, to display; ལུང་སྟོན་ to predict

སྟོན་གྲལ་ feast-row

སྟོན་ཐོག་ harvest

སྟོན་མོ་ feast

སྟོབས་ strength

སྟོབས་ཀྱིས་ (Postp) due to; because of (+ GEN)

སྟོབས་ལྡན་(པ་) strong, powerful

སྟོར་ (INTR) to get lost

བརྟག་པ་ investigation

བརྟགས་ see རྟོག་

བརྟན་པ་ steadfast, firm

བལྟ་ see ལྟ་

བལྟས་ see ལྟ་

བསྟན་ see སྟོན་

བསྟན་བཅོས་ treatise

བསྟན་པ་ (Buddhist) teaching

བསྟོད་ see སྟོད་

ཐ

ཐ་ག་པ་ weaver

ཐ་ཆུངས་ [1](N) the youngest; [2](A) youngest

ཐ་མ་ eventually

ཐག་ཆད་པ་ severed

ཐག་ཆོད་ (INTR) to stop

ཐགས་ texture

ཐང་ plain

ཐད་དུ་ (Postp) to, towards (+ GEN)

ཐབས་ means; stratagem

ཐམ་པ་ (DET) complete, full

ཐམས་ see འཐམ་

ཐམས་ཅད་ [1](N) all; [2](DET) all

ཐར་ (INTR) to become free (from + DEL)

ཐ(ར)་རེ་ཐོ(ར)་རེ་ scatteredly

ཐར་ལམ་ path of release

ཐལ་ལྕག་ a hand-slap

ཐལ་མོ་ palm of the hand

ཐིམ་ (INTR) to disappear (by being absorbed)

ཐུ་ (to be) malicious

ཐུ་བ་ coat-flap

ཐུག་ (INTR) to be about to (+ DAT)

ཐུགས་ (HON for སྙིང་/ཡིད་) mind

ཐུགས་སྐྱོ་ཤས་ (HON for སྐྱོ་ཤས་) grief

ཐུགས་རྗེ་ (HON for སྙིང་རྗེ་) compassion

ཐུགས་རྗེ་ཅན་ compassionate

ཐུགས་ཉམས་ (HON for ཉམས་) mind, heart

ཐུགས་དམ་ (HON for ཡི་དམ་) [1]tutelary deity; [2]meditation; [3]vow

ཐུགས་གདོན་ (HON for གདོན་) demon

ཐུགས་བརྩེ་ (HON for བརྩེ་; INTR) to love, to be kind

ཐུང་ (to be) short

ཐུབ་ (TR) [1]to match; [2]to have the command of; (MOD) to be able, capable; can

ཐེ་ཚོམ་ doubt

ཐེག་ཆེན་ see ཐེག་པ་ཆེན་པོ་

ཐེག་པ་ཆེན་པོ་ Skt. *mahāyana*

ཐོག་ what is uppermost

ཐོག་ཏུ་ (Postp) on (+ ABS)

[1]ཐོགས་ see འཐོགས་

[2]ཐོགས་ (INTR) to get stuck (in + DAT)

ཐོང་ see གཏོང་

ཐོན་ see འཐོན་

ཐོབ་ (TR) [1]to achieve, to attain; [2]to obtain

ཐོས་ (TR) to hear, to listen

མཐའ་ end

མཐར་ [1]in the end; finally; eventually; [2](Postp) at the end of (+ GEN)

མཐུ་ [1]strength; [2]spell

མཐུན་ (INTR) to agree; རྗེས་(སུ་)མཐུན་ to agree

མཐུར་ halter

མཐོ་ (to be) high

མཐོ་རིས་ heaven

མཐོང་ (TR) to see

འཐག་ v2 བཏགས་ v3 བཏག་ v4 ཐོག་ (TR) to weave; ཐགས་འཐག་ (INTR) to weave

འཐབ་ (TR) to fight

འཐབ་ཡ་ adversary

འཐམ་ v2 ཐམས་ (INTR) to shut closely

འཐུང་ v2 བཏུངས་ v3 བཏུང་ v4 འཐུང་ (TR) to drink

འཐོགས་ v2 ཐོགས་ (TR) to carry

འཐོན་ v2/v4 ཐོན་ (INTR) to go out

འཐོར་ (INTR) to be scattered

ད

ད་ now

ད་ལྟ་ now

ད་ལྟར་ now

ད་ལྟེ་ from now on

ད་ལན་ the present

དང་པོ་ [1]first; [2]at first, at the beginning

དང་བ་ (to be) pure

དད་ (INTR) to believe

དད་པ་ faithfulness

དམ་ vow

དམ་པ་ noble

དར་ (INTR) to spread

དར་ཅིག་ a moment

དལ་གྱིས་ gently

དལ་མེད་ without rest

དིར་རེ་བ་ buzzing

དུ་མ་ many

དུག་ poison

དུག་ཅན་ poisonous

དུད་འགྲོ་ animal

དུད་པ་ smoke

དུམ་བུ་ piece

དུར་ grave

དུར་ཁྲོད་ grave

དུས་ time

དུས་སུ་ (Postp) at the time of, when (+ GEN)

དེ་ I(DEM) that; II(DET) the; III(3SG) he/she/it

དེ་སྐད་ those words

དེ་ཉིད་ the very same

དེ་ཉིད་དུ་ at that very moment

དེ་སྐྱིད་ such

དེ་ལྟ་ so

དེ་ལྟ་བུ་ of that kind, such

དེ་ལྟར་ so, that way

དེ་ལྟར་ན་ in that way

དེ་སྟེ་ now

དེ་དུས་ at that time

དེ་ནས་ thereafter, then

དེ་བས་ therefore

དེ་བཞིན་གཤེགས་པ་ Skt. Tathāgata

དེ་ཡང་ see དེའང་

དེ་རིང་ today

དེ་སྲིད་ (COR) so long

དེའང་/དེ་ཡང་ namely

དེར་ [1]there; [2]then

དེས་ན་ for that reason

དོ་སྨད་ consort (?) and [her] children

དོགས་ (INTR) to fear (+ ERG)

དོང་ see འདོང་

དོན་ [1]meaning; [2]goal, purpose; [3]affair, concern; [4]welfare

དོན་འཁོར་མདའ་ (PN) Don-ɣkhor-mdaɣ

དོན་དུ་ for the sake of

དོན་བསྡུ་ briefly

དྭགས་ bright

དྭངས་པ་ pure

དྲག་ expedient

དྲག་ཏུ་ vehemently

དྲག་པ་ noble

དྲག་པོ་ serious; honest

དྲག་ཞན་ high and low

དྲང་སྲོང་ sage

དྲངས་ see འདྲེན་

དྲན་ (TR) [1]to remember, to come to mind; [2]to recall

དྲི་ fragrance

དྲི་མ་ impurities

དྲི་ཞིམ་ nice scent

དྲིལ་ see འདྲིལ་

དྲིས་ see འདྲི་

དྲུག་ six

དྲུག་པོ་ sextet, a group of six

དྲུང་དུ་ (Postp) near to; to (+ GEN)

དྲུང་ན་ (Postp) under, near to (+ GEN/ABS)

དྲུང་ནས་ (Postp) from below (+ ABS)

དྲུང་པོ་ relatives

དྲེས་མ་ (PN) a grass species

དྲོངས་ see འདྲེན་

དྲོན་མོ་ warm

གདང་ (INTR) to open wide

གདན་ mat, carpet

གདའ་ (HML for འདུག་; COP) [1]to be there; [2]to be

གདུང་ v2 གདུངས་ (INTR) [1]to be tormented/pained; [2]to long (for + DAT)

གདུང་རབས་ (HON) generation

གདུངས་ see གདུང་

གདེང་ v2 གདེངས་ (TR) to raise in despair

གདོན་མི་ཟ་བར་ surely

བདག་ (1SG; HML for ང་) I

བདག་(པོ་) master, owner

བདག་ཅག་ (1PL) we

བདུད་ demon

བདུད་མོ་སྟག་འདྲེན་ (PN) Bdud-mo Stag-ɣdren

བདུད་རིགས་ demon-race

བདུན་ seven

བདེ་ (to be) happy/peaceful

བདེ་སྐྱིད་ [I](INTR) to be happy; [II]happiness

བདེ་བ་ happiness

བདེ་བར་ easily

བདེན་ (to be) true

བདེན་པ་ [I]true; [II]truth

མདངས་ brightness

[1]མདའ་ arrow

[2]མདའ་ downland, the lower part of a valley

མདུན་ front

མདུན་དུ་ (Postp) in front of, before; to (+ GEN)

མདུན་སོ་ incisor (lit. front) tooth

མདོ་ Skt. *sūtra*

མདོར་ in short

འདམ་ swamp

འདམ་ v2 བདམ(ས)་ v3 གདམ་ v4 འདོམས་ (TR) to choose

འདམ་ཀ་ choice

འདའ་ v2 འདས་ (INTR) [1]to pass over; [2]to pass away; འདས་པའི་དུས་ the past

འདར་ (INTR) to tremble

འདས་ see འདའ་

འདི་ (DEM) this

འདི་སྐད་(ཅེས་) these words

འདི་ལྟ་སྟེ་ in this way; namely

འདི་ལྟ་བུ་ like this, such as this

འདི་ལྟར་ so, this way

འདི་འདྲ་ like this

འདིང་ v2 བཏིང་ v3 གདིང་ v4 ཐིངས་ (TR) to spread

འདུ་ v2 འདུས་ (INTR) to gather, to come together

འདུ་ཤེས་ཅན་ thinking, lit. having the faculty of thinking

འདུག་ (INTR) [1]to lie (down), to sit (down), to be there; [2]to live; [3]to be

འདུས་ see འདུ་

འདེད་ v2 དེད་ (TR) to drive away

འདེབས་ v2 བཏབ་ v3 གདབ་ v4 ཐོབ་ to cast, to throw, to strike; ཆོ་ངེས་འདེབས་ to lament; ས་བོན་འདེབས་ to sow seeds; སོ་སྒྲ་འདེབས་ to whistle; གསོལ་བ་འདེབས་ to submit a request

འདོགས་ v2 བཏགས་ v3 གདགས་ v4 ཐོགས་ (TR) to bind, to attach; ཕན་འདོགས་ to render service

འདོང་ v2/v4 དོང་ (INTR) to go

འདོད་ (TR) to wish; to desire; (MOD) to wish, want

འདོད་ཆགས་ passion, desire, lust

འདོད་པ་ passion

འདོད་ཡོན་ desired goods

འདོན་ v2 བཏོན་ v3 གདོན་ v4 ཐོན་ (TR) [1]to utter; [2]to obtain; [3]to put, to place out; མགོ་འདོན་ to sustain; to take care; མཆི་མ་འདོན་ to shed tears

འདྲ་ (INTR) to be similar, to be like; to seem (+ COM)

འདྲི་ v2 དྲིས་ (TR) to ask

འདྲིལ་ v2 དྲིལ་ (TR) [1]to wrap up; [2]to summarise; གཅིག་ཏུ་འདྲིལ་ to unite

འདྲེ་ v2 འདྲེས་ (INTR) to be mixed with

འདྲེན་ v2 དྲངས་ v3 དྲང་ v4 དྲོངས་ (TR) [1]to pull; [2]to lead; སྟོན་མོ་འདྲེན་ to offer a feast; གདན་འདྲེན་ to invite

འདྲེས་ see འདྲེ་

འདྲེས་པ་ mixture

རྡིག་ valuables (?)

རྡུགས་ (INTR) to be worn out

རྡུང་ v2 བརྡུངས་ v3 བརྡུང་ v4 རྡུངས་ (TR) to beat

རྡུལ་ dust

རྡེབས་ v2 བརྡབས་ v3 བརྡབ་ (TR) [1]to throw down; [2]to stomp

རྡེའུ་ pebble

རྡོ་ [1]stone; [2]ore

རྡོ་བ་ stone

ལྡག་ v2 བལྡགས་ v3 བལྡག་ v4 ལྡོག་ (TR) to lick

ལྡན་ (to be) possessed of, endowed with (+ COM)

ལྡོག་ v2/v4 ལོག་ (INTR) to come back

སྡར་མ་ coward

སྡིག་པ་ [1]offence; [2]sin

[1]སྡུག་ (to be) pretty, nice

[2]སྡུག་ [I]misery; [II]to be pained

སྡུག་བསྔལ་ [I](to be) afflicted/pained; to suffer; [II]misery, suffering, affliction

སྡུག་པ་ dear

སྡུག་པོ་ misery

སྡུག་མད་ a truly miserable person

སྡུག་སྲན་ hardiness

སྡུད་ v2 བསྡུས་ v3 བསྡུ་ v4 སྡུས་ (TR) [1]to collect; [2]to gather

སྡེ་ class

སྡེབ་ v2 བསྡེབས་ v3 བསྡེབ་ v4 སྡེབས་ (TR) to join

སྡོད་ v2 བསྡད་ v4 སྡོད་ (INTR) [1]to wait; [2]to stay, [3]to live

སྡོམ་ v2 བསྡམས་ v3 བསྡམ་ v4 སྡོམས་ (TR) to fetter

སྡོམ་པ་ vow

བརྡ་ sign

བརྡབས་ see རྡེབས་

བརྡུངས་ see རྡུང་

བལྡག་ see ལྡག་

བསྡད་ see སྡོད་

བསྡམས་ see སྡོམ་

བསྡུས་ see སྡུད་

བསྡེབས་ see སྡེབ་

ན

ན་ (INTR) to be ill

ན་ཆུང་ girl

ནག་པ་ (to be) black

ནག་མོ་ black

ནགས་མ་ forest

ནང་ the inside, interior

ནང་དུ་ (Postp) into, in (+ GEN)

ནང་ན་ (Postp) among (+ GEN/ABS)

ནང་ནས་ (Postp) from (+ GEN)

ནང་པ་ (PN) Naṅ-pa

ནང་པར་ day after tomorrow

ནད་ illness

ནན་ཏར་ very much

ནམ་ (INT/REL) when

ནམ་མཁའ་ sky

ནམ་མཁའ་ལྡིང་ *garuḍa*-bird, lit. one soaring in the sky

ནར་ (INTR) to become long, to lengthen; to get stretched

ནར་ནར་ continuously

ནར་མ་ continuous

ནལ་ incest

ནལ་ལུ་ bastard child

ནས་ barley

ནུ་བོ་ younger brother

ནུབ་ night

ནུབ་མོ་ evening

ནུས་ (MOD) to be able, suitable, capable; can

ནོན་ (INTR) to feel overcome

ནོར་ [1]wealth, goods; [2]cattle

ནོར་ཅན་ [I](A) wealthy; [II](N) wealthy one

ནོར་བདག་ wealthy man

ནོར་བདག་པོ་ wealth's owner

ནོར་ལྡན་ wealthy

ནོར་བུ་ jewel

ནོར་མེད་ impoverished

ནོར་ཡོད་ wealthy

ནོར་སློངས་ source of wealth, possessions, lit. "wealth-raising"

གནག་ yak

གནང་ (HON for སྟེར་; TR) [1]to allow, to permit; [2]to give

གནམ་ the sky

གནས་ I(INTR) 1to last; 2to live; 3to stay; II(N) place

གནོད་པ་ pain

མནའ་མ་ wife

མནར་ (INTR) to suffer, to be pained

མནལ་ (HON; INTR) to sleep

རྣང་ v2 བརྣངས་ (TR) to choke; སྐད་ཀྱིས་རྣང་ to be unable to utter a word, lit. for words to choke

རྣམ་འགྱུར་ facial expression

རྣམ་ཐར་ biography

རྣམ་པ་ (N) kind

རྣམ་པ་སྣ་ཚོགས་ (DET) various kinds (see སྣ་ཚོགས་)

རྣོན་པོ་ sharp

1སྣ་ (N) kind

2སྣ་ nose

སྣ་ཚོགས་ (DET) various kinds (see རྣམ་པ་སྣ་ཚོགས་)

སྣང་ (INTR) to appear

སྣད་ v2/v3 བསྣད་ v4 སྣོད་ (TR) to hurt

སྣམ་བུ་ woollens

སྣུན་ v2/v3 བསྣུན་ (TR) to stick in

སྣོམ་ v2 བསྣམས་ v3 བསྣམ་ v4 སྣོམས་ (TR) to take

བརྣངས་ see རྣང་

བསྣམས་ see སྣོམ་

བསྣུན་ see སྣུན་

པ

པ་གུ་ brick

པད་མ་ lotus

པད་མོ་ lotus

པོ་ཏ་ལ་ (PN) Po-ta-la, name of a mountain

པྲེ་པེ་སྟན་ཆུང་ (PN) Pre-pe-stan-čhuṅ

དཔག་མེད་ countless, innumerable

དཔའ་ (to be) courageous

དཔལ་ glory

དཔེ་ [1]proverb; [2]example

དཔེ་ཆ་ traditional Tibetan print format

དཔོག་ v2 དཔགས་ v3 དཔག་ v4 དཔོགས་ (TR) to measure

དཔོགས་ see དཔོག་

དཔྱད་ see དཔྱོད་

དཔྱོད་ v2/v3 དཔྱད་ (TR) to examine

སྤུ་ hair

སྤོང་ v2 སྤངས་ v3 སྤང་ v4 སྤོངས་ (TR) to abandon

སྤོངས་ see སྤོང་

སྤྱད་ see སྤྱོད་

སྤྱན་ (HON for མིག་) eye

སྤྱན་རས་གཟིགས་ (PN) Spyan-ras-gzigs

སྤྱི་བོ་ top/crown of the head

སྤྱོ་ v2 སྤྱོས་ (INTR) to scold

སྤྱོད་ v2/v3 སྤྱད་ (TR) [1]to do, to practice, to act; [2]to use; [3]to enjoy

སྤྱོད་པ་ behaviour, conduct

སྤྱོད་ཚུལ་ conduct

སྤྱོད་ལམ་ mode of life

སྤྲང་ [I](INTR) to beg; [II](N) beggar

སྤྲང་པོ་ beggar

སྤྲད་ see སྤྲོད་

སྤྲིན་ cloud

སྤྲུག་ v2/v4 སྤྲུགས་ (TR) to shake off

སྤྲུགས་ see སྤྲུག་

སྤྲེ་ monkey

སྤྲེའུ་ monkey

སྤྲེའུ་ཕྲུག་ young of a monkey, monkey-child

སྤྲེལ་ཕྲུག་ see སྤྲེའུ་ཕྲུག་

སྤྲོ་བ་ joy

སྤྲོད་ v2/v3 སྤྲད་ v4 སྤྲོད་ (TR) [1]to give, to return; [2]to make to meet, to introduce

ཕ

ཕ་ father

ཕ་མ་ [1]parents; [2]father and mother

ཕ་མིང་ father and brother(s)

ཕ་རོལ་ (N) [1]the other; [2]the outside; (Postp) beyond (+ GEN)

ཕ་རོལ་ན་ (Postp) beyond (+ GEN)

ཕ་ཤུལ་ patrimony

[1]ཕག་ concealment

[2]ཕག་ swine

ཕག་ཏུ་ secretly

ཕངས་མེད་ abundant

ཕན་ [I]benefit; [II](to be) useful/beneficial

ཕན་བདེ་ happiness

ཕན་པ་ [I]benefit; [II](to be) beneficial

ཕུ་ upland, upper part of a valley

ཕུ་དུང་ sleeve

ཕུ་བོ་ elder brother

ཕུག་ see འབུགས་

ཕུག་རོན་ dove

ཕུང་པོ་ heap

ཕུལ་གང་ a handful

ཕུལ་བྱིན་ victorious

ཕུས་ see འབུད་

ཕེར་ (TR) to be able to bear

ཕོ་ (A) male

ཕོ་ནོར་ man's goods

ཕོ་བྲང་ palace

[1]ཕོག་ see འཕོགས་

[2]ཕོག་ see འཕོག་

ཕྱ་ lot

ཕྱག་ (HON for ལག་པ་) hand

ཕྱི་ after

ཕྱི་མ་ later; next

ཕྱི་བཞིན་ (Postp) after (+ GEN)

ཕྱི་རོལ་ outside

ཕྱིན་ (INTR) to arrive, to come to; to go

ཕྱིན་ཆད་ (Postp) after (+ ABS)

ཕྱིན་ཏེ་ལོ་ཤུ་ཤ་ (PN) Phyin-te-lo-śu-śa, a Tibetan transcription of the Chinese name 賓頭盧埵闍 Bin-tou-lu-duo-she, itself a transcription of Sanskrit Piṇḍoladhvaja (?; Hahn 1996: 318)

ཕྱིར་ [I](Adv) [1]back; [2]again; [3]out, outside; [II](Postp) [1]on account of, due to, because of; for the sake of (+ GEN); [2]in order to (+ ABS); [3]behind (+ GEN)

ཕྱིས་ later

ཕྱུག་ (to be) rich

ཕྱུགས་ cattle

ཕྱུང་ see འབྱིན་

[1]ཕྱེ་ flour

[2]ཕྱེ་ see འབྱེད་

ཕྱེད་ see འབྱེད་

ཕྱེད་ཀ་ half

ཕྱེད་མ་ half

ཕྱོགས་ [1]direction; [2]side

ཕྱོགས་ལ་ (Postp) towards (+ GEN)

ཕྱོགས་སུ་ (Postp) towards (+ GEN)

ཕྲག་(པ་) shoulder

ཕྲག་དོག་ envy

[1]ཕྲད་ particle

[2]ཕྲད་ see འཕྲད་

ཕྲིན་ message

ཕྲུ་གུ་ child

ཕྲོགས་ see འཕྲོག་

འཕགས་རྒྱལ་ (PN) Ɣphags-rgyal, name of an Indian town (Skt. Ujjayinī)

འཕགས་པ་ the Noble One (lit. Surpassing One)

འཕངས་ see འཕེན་

འཕམ་པ་ despondent

འཕུར་ v2 ཕུར་ (INTR) to fly

འཕེན་ v2 འཕངས་ v3 འཕང་ v4 འཕོང་ (TR) to throw

འཕེལ་ v2 ཕེལ་ (INTR) to increase; to thrive

འཕོ་ v2/v4 འཕོས་ (INTR) to change; ཚེ་འཕོ་ to die, to be reborn

འཕོག་ v2 ཕོག་ (TR) to hit

འཕྱ་ v2 འཕྱས་ (INTR) to deride, to laugh

འཕོས་ see འཕོ་

འཕྲད་ v2 ཕྲད་ (TR) to meet with (+ COM)

འཕྲོག་ v2/v4 ཕྲོགས་ v3 དཕྲོག་ (TR) to take away; to deprive of

བ

བ་ cow

བ་ར་བོང་ cow, goat, and ass

བ་ལང་ ox

བ་སུ་མི་ཏྲ་ (PN) Ba-su-mi-tra (Skt. Vasumitra)

བག་མ་ bride

བང་མཛོད་ store-room, magazine; treasury

བད་ས་ལ་ (PN) Bad-sa-la (Skt. Vatsa)

བབ་ see འབབ་

བབས་ see འབབ་

བར་ the middle

བར་འགའ་ sometimes, once

བར་ཆད་ threat

བར་དུ་ (Postp) during, while (+ GEN)

བར་ལ་ (Postp) in the meantime, until (+ ABS/GEN)

བལ་ wool

བལ་པོ་ Nepalese

བལ་ལས་ spinning of wool

བུ་ [1]child; [2]son

བུ་སྟོན་རིན་པོ་ཆེ་ (PN) Bu-ston Rin-po-čhe (1290–1364), a Tibetan Buddhist master

བུ་ཕོ་ son

བུ་མོ་ [1]daughter; [2]girl

བུ་སྨད་ children and [their] mother

བུ་ཚ་ offspring, children

བུག་པ་ hole

བུང་བ་ bee

བུད་མེད་ woman

བོང་བུ་ ass

བོད་ (PN) Tibet

བོད་སྐད་ Tibetan language

བོད་པ་ Tibetan (man)

བོད་མོ་ Tibetan (woman)

བོད་ཡིག་ written Tibetan

བོན་ (PN) Bon, an indigenous Tibetan religion

བོན་པོ་ a male adherent of the Bon religion

བོར་ see འབོར་

བོས་ see འབོད་

¹བྱ་ ¹bird; ²hen

²བྱ་ see བྱེད་

བྱ་བ་ ᴵdeed, act, affairs; ᴵᴵ(so-)called

བྱ་མོ་ hen

བྱ་ཚོགས་ (PN) Bya-chogs, name of a forest

བྱ་རོག་ crow

བྱང་ཆུབ་ enlightenment

བྱང་ཆུབ་སེམས་དཔའ་ Skt. *bodhisattva*

བྱང་སེམས་ see བྱང་ཆུབ་སེམས་དཔའ་

བྱམས་(པ་) ᴵkindness, benevolence, love; ᴵᴵ(TR) to love (+ DAT); ᴵᴵᴵ(PN) Byams-pa (Skt. Maitreya)

བྱམས་མགོན་ protector of benevolence

བྱས་ see བྱེད་

¹བྱི་ rat

²བྱི་ see འབྱི་

¹བྱིན་ blessing

²བྱིན་ see སྦྱིན་

བྱིའུ་/བྱེའུ་ nestling

བྱིས་པ་ child

བྱུང་ see འབྱུང་

བྱེ་ see འབྱེ་

བྱེད་ v2 བྱས་ v3 བྱ་ v4 བྱོས་ (TR) ¹to do, to make, to commit; to prepare; ²to speak, to tell; ³to act as (+ ABS); ཁྱིམ་ཐབ་བྱེད་ to establish a family; བཅོལ་གཏམས་བྱེད་ to entrust; གཏམ་བྱེད་ to make a speech; དབང་བྱེད་ to rule (over + DAT); གཙོ་བྱེད་ to lead, to be most prominent; ཚགས་བྱེད་ to save; ཚེའི་དུས་བྱེད་ to die; ཞེས་བྱ་བ་ called; ལས་བྱེད་ to work; སོ་ནམ་བྱེད་ to cultivate fields

བྱེའུ་ see བྱིའུ་

བྱོན་ see འབྱོན་

བྱོས་ see བྱེད་

བྲ་བོ་ buckwheat

བྲག་ rock

བྲག་སྲིན་མོ་ rock-ogress

བྲན་ servant

བྲན་བཟངས་ (PN) Bran-bzaṅs

བྲམ་ཟེ་ Brahmin

བྲལ་ see འབྲལ་

བྲིན་པ་ [1]in demand; [2]precious

བྲིས་ see འབྲི་

བྲེལ་ (INTR) to be separated from, to be without

བྲེས་ manger

བྲོ་བ་ taste

བྲོས་ see འབྲོས་

[1]བླ་ sign, symbol

[2]བླ་ [I](to be) superior, better; [II]what is above

བླ་མ་ lama, teacher

བླང་དོར་ attracting and repelling

བླངས་ see ལེན་

བླུན་པོ་ (N) fool

བློ་ [1]mind, thought; [2]understanding, intelligence

བློ་གྲོས་ [1]intelligence, intellect; [2]understanding

བློ་ངན་ evil-minded

བློ་ཆུང་ narrow-minded

བློ་འདོད་ greed

བློ་ལྡན་ intelligent, wise

བློན་ཆེ་ great councillor

བློན་པོ་ minister

དབང་ [I]power; [II](TR) to control; to own

དབང་གིས་ (Postp) perforce (+ GEN)

དབང་པོ་ sense

དབུ་ (HON for མགོ་) head

དབུ་སྐྲ་ (HON for སྐྲ་) hair

དབུགས་ breath

དབུལ་ཕོངས་ (to be) poor

དབུས་ (N) middle

དབུས་སུ་ (Postp) in the middle of (+ GEN)

དབྱར་(ཀ་) summer

དབྱིག་པ་ཅན་ (PN) Dbyig-pa-čan (Skt. Daṇḍin)

དབྱུག་ stick

དབྱུ(ག)་གུ་ small staff; stick

འབངས་ subject

འབབ་ v2 བབ་/བབས་ (INTR) to come down (C); to fall (NC); དུས་ལ་འབབ་ for the time to come

འབའ་ཞིག་ (DET) [1]alone, mere, sole; [2]only

འབུགས་ v2 ཕུག་ v3 དབུག་ v4 ཕུག(ས)་ (TR) to bore

འབུད་ v2/v4 ཕུས་ v3 དབུ་ (TR) to blow

འབུམ་ hundred thousand

འབུལ་ v2/v4 ཕུལ་ v3 དབུལ་ (HML for སྦྱིན་/སྟེར་; TR) to offer

འབེབས་ v2 ཕབ་ v3 དབབ་ v4 ཕོབ་ (TR) to throw down

འབོགས་ v2/v4 ཕོག་ v3 དབོག་ (TR) to give

འབོད་ v2/v4 བོས་ (TR) to call, to summon

འབོར་ v2/v4 བོར་ (TR) to abandon; to lose; དསྨོད་འབོར་ to pronounce a prayer

འབྱི་ v2 བྱི་ (INTR) to fall off

འབྱིན་ v2/v4 ཕྱུང་ v3 དབྱུང་ (TR) to cause to come forth/out; to gouge out, to take out

འབྱུང་ v2 བྱུང་ (INTR) [1]to occur, to appear; [2]to happen; [3]to be born (to + DAT); [4]to come out

འབྱུང་པོ་ demon

འབྱེ་ v2 བྱེ་ (INTR) [1]to open; [2]to divide

འབྱེད་ v2 ཕྱེ་/ཕྱེད་/ཕྱེས་ v3 དབྱེ་ v4 ཕྱེས་ (TR) [1]to divide, to separate; [2]to open; ཁྱད་འབྱེད་ to differ

འབྱོན་ v2 བྱོན་ (HON; INTR) [1]to arrive; [2]to appear

འབྱོར་ (INTR) to adhere to

འབྱོར་ལྡན་ rich

འབྱོར་པ་ wealth

འབྲལ་ v2 བྲལ་ (INTR) to be separated/free (from), deprived (of + COM); སྲོག་དང་ འབྲལ་ to die

འབྲི་ v2/v4 བྲིས་ v3 བྲི་ (TR) to write

འབྲིང་པོ་ ^{1}(N) the middle one; ^{2}(A) middle

འབྲུ་ corn

འབྲུག་ dragon

འབྲེལ་ (TR) to unite with, to be associated with (+ COM)

འབྲོང་རུ་ horn of a wild yak

འབྲོས་ v2 བྲོས་ (INTR) to flee

སྦས་ see སྦེད་

སྦེད་ v2 སྦས་ v3 སྦ་ v4 སྦོས་ (TR) to hide

སྦོམ་པོ་ plump

སྦྱར་ see སྦྱོར་

སྦྱིན་ v2/v4 བྱིན་ (TR) to give, to confer

སྦྱོར་ v2/v3 སྦྱར་ v4 སྦྱོར་ (TR) ^{1}to compare (with + COM); ^{2}to join

སྦྲང་རྩི་ honey

སྦྲུལ་ snake

མ།

^{1}མ་ mother

^{2}མ་ (NEG) not

མ་ཐག་(ཏུ་) immediately thereafter, right after (+ v2 or +ABS)

མ་བུ་ mother and children

མ་སྨད་ mother and [her] children

མ་འོངས་པ་ future

མ་རིག་པ་ ignorance

མ་ལུས་པར་ completely

མག་པ་ son-in-law

མང་ v2 མངས་ (INTR) to be many

མང་དུ་ many; a lot

མང་པོ་ many; numerous

མངས་ see མང་

མར་ butter

མར་པ་ (PN) Mar-pa

[1]མི་ (NEG) not

[2]མི་ man, human being

མི་བརྒྱུད་ lineage

མི་ངན་ bad/wicked man

མི་སྙན་པ་ unpleasant

མི་ཐོད་གད་ཁ་ (PN) Mi-thod-gad-kha, a place name

མི་མཐོང་བ་ blind

མི་བདག་ false-master, lit. non-master

མི་ནོར་ man's wealth

མི་ལ་རས་པ་ (PN) Mi-la Ras-pa

མི་ལ་ཤེས་རབ་རྒྱལ་མཚན་ (PN) Mi-la Śes-rab Rgyal-mchan, the father of Mi-la Ras-pa

མི་ལས་ labour

མིག་ eye

མིང་ name

མིང་སྲིང་ brother and sister

མིན་ (NEG COP of ཡིན་) not to be

མིའུ་ dwarf

མེ་ fire

མེ་ཏོག་ flower

མེ་ལོང་ mirror

མེ་ཤིང་ firewood

མེད་ (NEG COP of ཡོད་) [1]not to be, not to exist; [2]not to have

མོ་ [I](3SG F) she; [II](A) female

མོ་ནོར་ woman's goods

མོ་མ་ diviner

མོད་ (INTR) to be abundant, to abound

མོས་ (INTR) to take pleasure in (+ DAT)

མྱ་ངན་ affliction, misery; worry, trouble

མྱ་ངན་ལས་འདས་པ་ Skt. *nirvāṇa*

མྱང་འདས་ see མྱ་ངན་ལས་འདས་པ་

མྱང་ཚ་དཀར་རྒྱན་ (PN) Myaṅ-cha Dkar-rgyan, Mi-la Ras-pa's mother

མྱུར་དུ་ quickly

མྱུར་བ་ quick

མྱུར་བར་ quickly

མྱོང་ v2 མྱངས་ v3 མྱང་ (TR) to experience

དམག་ army

དམག་བརྒྱ་པ་ (PN) Dmag-brgya-pa (Skt. Śātānīka)

དམག་པ་ son-in-law

དམར་པོ་ red

དམོད་ prayer

དམྱལ་བ་ hell

རྨི་ v2 རྨིས་ (TR) to dream; སྙམ་རྨི་ to dream

རྨི་ལམ་ dream

རྨུ་ཐག་ རྨུ་-rope

རྨོ་ v2/v4 རྨོས་ (TR) to sow and plough

རྨོང་ v2 རྨོངས་ (INTR) to get confused

རྨོངས་ see རྨོང་

རྨོངས་པ་ (N) ignorant

རྨོས་ see རྨོ་

སྨད་ children of one mother

སྨན་ medicine, herb

སྨན་པ་ doctor, physician

སྨིན་ ripe

སྨོན་ (TR) to desire (+ DAT)

སྨྱུ་གུ་ reed-pen

སྨྱུག་མ་ reed

སྨྲ་ v2/v3 སྨྲས་ v4 སྨྲོས་ (TR) to speak; to say, to tell

སྨྲས་ see སྨྲ་

སྨྲེ་སྔགས་ lamentation

སྨྲོས་ see སྨྲ་

ཙ

ཙ་ན་ as soon as, when

ཙམ་ (DET) mere, only; as much as, about

ཙམ་དུ་ [1]as if, like; [2]like that

གཙང་མ་ clean

གཙུག་ crown of the head

གཙེ་ v2 གཙེས་ (TR) to harm, to torment

གཙེས་ see གཙེ་

གཙོ་བོ་ [I]the best, eminent one; [II]the chief

བཙན་པོ་ emperor in the Tibetan Empire

བཙའ་ v2 བཙས་ (INTR) to give birth, to bring forth

བཙལ་ see འཚོལ་

བཙས་ see བཙའ་

བཙུན་པ་ respectable, noble

བཙུན་མོ་ queen

བཙོག་པ་ dirty

བཙོན་ prisoner

བཙོན་ར་ prison

བཙོས་ see འཚོད་

[1]རྩ་ [1]foot (of a mountain, etc.); [2]place

[2]རྩ་ (PN) Rca, a place name

རྩར་ (Postp) before, in front of (+ GEN)

རྩལ་ physical skills

རྩིག་ v2 བརྩིགས་ v3 བརྩིག་ v4 རྩིགས་ (TR) to built

རྩིག་པ་ wall

རྩེ་ v2/v4 རྩེས་ (INTR) to play

རྩེ་(མོ་) summit

རྩེའུ་ thorn

རྩོག་པ་ dirty

རྩོག་རྩོག་པ་ completely nasty, messed

རྩོད་ v2 བརྩད་ (TR) to argue, to debate (about + DAT)

རྩོད་པ་ conflict

རྩོམ་ v2 བརྩམས་ v3 བརྩམ་ v4 རྩོམས་ (TR) to set about, to be about; to plan

རྩྭ་ཁ་ grass

སྩལ་ see སྩོལ་

སྩོལ་ v2/v3 སྩལ་ (HON) to give, to bestow; བཀའ་སྩོལ་ (HON) to speak; to order

བརྩད་ see རྩོད་

བརྩམས་ see རྩོམ་

བརྩིགས་ see རྩིག་

བརྩེ་ (INTR) to love

བརྩོན་འགྲུས་ effort; diligence

ཚ

ཚ་ hot

ཚ་ལེ་ alum

ཚགས་ see s.v. ཁྲིད་

ཚང་ den

ཚད་ (N) all

ཚད་མེད་པ་ immeasurable

ཚབས་ very great

ཚར་ see འཚར་

ཚལ་ forest, grove, wood

ཚལ་བ་ splinter

ཚིག་ word

ཚིམ་པ་ satisfied

1ཚུགས་ (TR) to harm

2ཚུགས་ see འཚུགས་

ཚུད་ see འཚུད་

ཚུར་ here, hither

ཚུལ་ way, manner

ཚུལ་དུ་ (Postp) like (+ GEN)

ཚེ་ I.1time; 2lifetime; II(Postp) when (+ GEN)

ཚེ་དང་ལྡན་པ་ elder, venerable (a title)

ཚེ་འཛུགས་ she-goat

ཚེ་སྲོག་ life

ཚེས་ day

1ཚོགས་ crowd, troop

2ཚོགས་ see འཚོགས་

ཚོང་ trade

ཚོད་ the right amount/measure

ཚོན་ paint

ཚོར་ (TR) to recognise, to perceive

ཚོལ་ see འཚོལ་

ཚོལ་བ་ search

མཚན་ 1(HON for མིང་) name; 2characteristic mark, sign

མཚར་བ་ beautiful

མཚུངས་ similar

མཚོ་ lake

འཚང་ v2 སངས་ (INTR) to recover, to wake up

འཚར་ v2 ཚར་ (INTR) to be finished, completed

འཚལ་ (TR) to wish; ཕྱག་འཚལ་ to pay homage; to bow; ཕྱི་ཕྱག་འཚལ་ to say goodbye

འཚུགས་ v2 ཚུགས་ (INTR) to be settled/established

འཚུད་ v2 ཚུད་ (INTR) to enter

འཚེ་ v2 བཙེས་ v3 བཙེ་ (TR) to harm

[1]འཚོ་ v2/v4 སོས་ (INTR) to remain alive; to recover (from illness)

[2]འཚོ་ v2 བསོས་ v3 བསོ་/གསོ་ (TR) to take care; སྲིད་འཚོ་ to rule a dominion

འཚོགས་ v2/v4 ཚོགས་ (INTR) to gather

འཚོད་ v2 བཙོས་ v3 བཙོ་ v4 ཚོས་ (TR) to cook, to brew

འཚོལ་ v2/v3 བཙལ་ v4 ཚོལ་ (TR) [1]to obtain; [2]to search, to look for

ཛ

མཛངས་ wise

མཛད་ v4 མཛོད་ (HON for བྱེད་; TR) to do, to make; to act (as + ABS); སྐྱབས་མཛད་ to protect, to save; གཙོ་མཛད་ to lead; བརྩོན་འགྲུས་མཛད་ to strain oneself

མཛད་པ་ (HON) deed

མཛའ་བོ་ lover

མཛེས་པ་ (PN) Mjes-pa

མཛེས་སེ་ (PN) Mjes-se

མཛོ་ *mjo*, a hybrid between yak and domestic cattle

[1]མཛོད་ repository

[2]མཛོད་ see མཛད་

འཛད་ v2 ཟད་ (INTR) to be consumed; to disappear; མ་ཟད་ not only

འཛམ་བུ་གླིང་ continent (Skt. Jambudvīpa, name of the Indian continent in Buddhist cosmology)

འཛིན་ v2 བཟུང་ v3 གཟུང་ v4 ཟུངས་ (TR) [1]to seize, to hold; to embrace; to take over; [2]to take sth. (DAT) as (TERM); ཡིད་ལ་འཛིན་ to take to [one's] mind

འཛུགས་ v2 བཙུགས་ v3 གཟུགས་ v4 ཟུགས་ (TR) to place

འཛེམ་མེད་ one having no shame

རྫས་ object

རྫི་བོ་ herdsman

རྫུ་འཕྲུལ་ magic tricks, miracles

ཞ

ཞག་ day

ཞང་པོ་ maternal uncle

ཞན་པ་ ordinary

ཞབས་ (HON for རྐང་པ་) foot

ཞལ་ (HON for ཁ་) mouth

ཞལ་ཆེ་ judgement

ཞལ་ཆེ་པ་ judge

ཞལ་ཆེམས་ (HON for ཁ་ཆེམས་) testament

ཞལ་འཛུམ་ (HON) smile

ཞི་ (INTR) to be calm

ཞིང་ field

ཞིང་སྐལ་ field share

ཞིང་ལས་ field-work

ཞུ་ v2/v4 ཞུས་ (HML for ཟེར་/སྨྲ་) [1]to speak; to report; to recount; [2]to ask

[1]ཞུགས་ see [1]འཛུག་

[2]ཞུགས་ (HON for མེ་) fire

ཞུས་ see ཞུ་

ཞེ་སྡང་ hatred

ཞེན་ (INTR) [1]to fix, to penetrate; [2]to long for (+ DAT)

གཞན་ [I](A) other; foreign; [II](N) the other

གཞན་དུ་ differently

གཞི་ cause

གཞུན་པོ་ excellent

གཞོན་ young

གཞོན་ནུ་ [I](N) a youth; [II](A) young

བཞག་ see འཇོག་

བཞམས་ (TR) to calm down, to appease

བཞི་ four

[1]བཞིན་ face

[2]བཞིན་ [I](Postp) according to, in accordance with; like (+ ABS); [II](to be) like

བཞིན་དུ་ (Postp) according to; like (+ ABS)

བཞུགས་ (HON for འདུག་; INTR) [1]to stay, abide; to sit; [2]to be alive

བཞུས་ see [2]འཇུ་

བཞེངས་ (HON; INTR) to rise, get up

བཞེས་ (HON for ལེན་; TR) to take; ཐུགས་ཉམས་སུ་བཞེས་ to experience, to practise

བཞོན་པ་ riding-beast

ཟ

ཟ་ v2 བཟས་/ཟོས་ v3 བཟའ་ v4 ཟོ(ས)་ (TR) to eat; ཟན་ཟ་ (INTR) to eat

ཟངས་ copper

ཟད་ see འཛད་

ཟད་པར་ completely

ཟན་ food

ཟབ་པ་ (to be) deep

ཟབ་པོ་ deep

ཟབ་མོ་ profound

ཟས་ food

ཟས་གཙང་མ་ (PN) Zas-gcaṅ-ma (Skt. Śuddhodana)

ཟིན་ (INTR) to be seized; to be taken over by (+ ERG)

ཟིལ་པ་ dew

ཟུག་རྔུ་ grief

ཟུངས་ see འཛིན་

ཟུར་ནས་ (Adv) for one's part

ཟེར་ (TR) to say, to speak

ཟེར་བ་ saying

ཟོ་ see ཟ་

ཟོ་དང་གོང་པོ་རི་ (PN) Zo-daṅ-goṅ-po-ri

ཟོས་ see ཟ་

ཟླ་བ་ [I]month; [II](PN) Zla-ba

གཟིགས་ (HON for མཐོང་/ལྟ་; TR) to look (at/in + DAT)

གཟེར་ (INTR) to be pained

གཟུག་ quarter share

གཟུགས་ [1]body; [2]shape

གཟུགས་ཅན་སྙིང་པོ་ (PN) Gzugs-čan-sñiṅ-po (Skt. Bimbisāra)

གཟེ་རུ་ small nail

གཟེར་ nail

གཟེར་བུ་ small nail

བཟང་ (to be) good

བཟང་པོ་ excellent, good

བཟའ་བ་ food

བཟའ་མི་ husband and wife

བཟུང་ see འཛིན་

འ

ངེ་ཅག་ (1PL) we

ངེ་བུ་ཅག་ (1PL) we

འོ་སྐོལ་ (1PL) we

འོ་བརྒྱལ་ difficulty, trouble

འོ་ཅག་ (1PL) we

འོ་ན་ (Intrj) well, well then; now then, now

འོ་མ་ milk

འོ་ལགས་སོ་ very well, all right

འོག་ ground floor

འོག་ཏུ་ (Postp) after (+ GEN)

འོག་ན་ [I](Adv) below, underneath; [II](Postp) below (+ GEN)

འོང་ v2 འོངས་ (INTR) [1]to come; [2]to become; [3]to be; ལེགས་པར་འོངས་སོ་ lit. "[You] have arrived well" (an official greeting formula of an admission to the Buddhist order)

འོངས་ see འོང་

འོད་ light

འོད་ཟེར་ ray

འོན་ཏེ་ or if not, or else, or also

འོར་མ་ (PN) Ɣor-ma

འོས་ (INTR) to be suitable

ཡ

ཡང་ (Adv) ^{1}again; ^{2}still, more; ^{3}further

ཡང་དག་(པར་) really

ཡང་ན་ or

ཡང་ཡང་ again and again

ཡན་ (Postp) up to (+ ABS)

ཡན་ལག་ limb

ཡབ་ (HON for ཕ་) father

ཡབ་མེས་ ancestors

ཡར་ up, upward

ཡལ་ (INTR) to disappear

ཡི་ mind; see ཡིད་

ཡི་གེ་ ^{1}(written) text; ^{2}letter

ཡི་དྭགས་ hungry ghost

ཡི་མུག་ (INTR) to despair, to be tormented

ཡིད་ mind

ཡིན་ (COP) to be

ཡུག་ piece of cloth

ཡུང་བ་ turmeric

ཡུན་ time

ཡུན་རིང་དུ་ (Adv) for a long time

ཡུམ་ (HON for མ་) mother

ཡུར་ channel

ཡུལ་ region, country, land

ཡུལ་ཁམས་ country

ཡུལ་མི་ countryman

ཡུས་ blame

ཡོང་ v2 ཡོངས་ (INTR) to come

ཡོངས་སུ་འགྲོལ་ v2 གྲོལ་ (INTR) to become absolutely free

ཡོངས་སུ་ལེན་ (TR) to accept

ཡོད་ (COP) [1]to be, to exist; [2]to have

ཡོན་ཏན་ [1]excellent quality, virtue; [2]good skill

ཡོན་ཏན་ཅན་ excellent

ཡོས་ hare

གཡག་ yak

གཡང་ prosperity, fortune

གཡར་ [I](TR) to borrow; [II]loan

གཡུ་ turquoise

[1]གཡོག་ servant

[2]གཡོག་ v2 གཡོགས་ (TR) to cover

གཡོགས་ see [2]གཡོག་

ར

ར་ goat

ར་མདའ་ help

[1]རང་ [1]self; itself; [2]one's own; [3](1SG) I; [4]merely, only

[2]རང་ v2 རངས་ (INTR) to rejoice; ཡི་རང་ to rejoice, to be happy (about + DAT)

རང་ཉིད་ [1]just; [2]oneself

རང་རེ་ (1PL INCL) we

རང་ལས་ one's own worker

རངས་ see [2]རང་

རན་ (INTR) to be right (to do sth. + v3)

རབ་ [I.1](N) the eldest; [2]the best; [II](A) eldest; utmost

རབ་ཏུ་ very

རབ་ཏུ་བྱེད་པ་ chapter (Skt. *prakaraṇa*)

རབ་ཏུ་འབྱུང་ v2 བྱུང་ (INTR) to join (the religion of the Buddha; Skt. *pra*-√vraj "to go forth, to proceed; to become a monk")

རབ་བྱུང་ a cycle of sixty years

རལ་པ་ lock

རས་ cotton cloth

རས་ཆུང་པ་ (PN) Ras-čhuṅ-pa

རི་ mountain

རི་དྭགས་ animals

རི་བོ་ mountain

རི་བོང་ hare

རི་རབ་ (PN) Ri-rab, a mountain in Indian cosmology (Skt. Sumeru)

རི་ལུ་ globula, pill

རིག་གནས་ science

རིག་པ་ knowledge

རིག་འཛིན་ knowledge holder (Skt. *vidyādhara*)

[1]རིགས་ [1]family, lineage, line; race; state; [2]kind

[2]རིགས་ (INTR) [1]to have the way, manner, to be suitable/right/appropriate (+ GEN/TERM); [2](MOD) must

རིགས་རྒྱུད་ race

རིགས་ངན་ hangman

རིགས་མཐུན་ of one breed, lit. agreeing in kind

རིགས་པ་ method

རིང་ v2 རིངས་ (INTR) [1]to be long; [2]to be far away

རིང་པོ་ [1]long; [2]far away

རིང་པོར་ (Adv) long

རིང་ཞིག་ long time

རིང་ཞིག་ཏུ་ (Adv) for a long time

རིང་ལ་ (Postp) when, during (+ ABS)

རིད་པ་ (to be) meagre, emaciated

རིན་ཆེན་ jewel

རིན་པོ་ཆེ་ (N) jewel, precious stone; (A) precious

རིམ་(པ་) row

རིམ་གྱིས་ successively, in a row

རིམ་པར་ in succession; successively

རིམས་ plague

རིལ་བ་ round

རིལ་བུ་ globula, pill

རུ་ལ་སྐྱེས་ (PN) Ru-la-skyes

རུང་ (INTR) to be suitable

རུས་པ་ bone

རུས་བུ་ small bone

[1]རེ་ (DET) each, every; single

[2]རེ་ (TR) to wish

རེ་རེ་ནས་ individually, each

རེས་ once

རོག་པོ་ black

རོད་ constitution

རྭ་ horn

རློན་པ་ fresh

རློབ་ v2 བརླབས་ v3 བརླབ་ v4 རློབས་ བྱིན་གྱིས་རློབ་ (TR) to bless

བརླབས་ see རློབ་

ལ

ལག་(པ་) hand, arm

ལག་བརྩུད་ཆེ་ excellent housewife

[1]ལགས་ (HON for ཡིན་; COP) to be

[2]ལགས་ (HON address) dear

ལང་ v2 ལངས་ (INTR) to rise, stand up

ལངས་ see ལང་

ལན་ time, turn

ལན་འགའ་ sometimes

ལན་ཅིག་ཕྱིར་མི་ལྡོག་པ་ lit. one who does not come back again (Skt. *anāgāmin*)

ལབ་ gossip

ལམ་ road, way

ལར་ but

ལས་ [1]work; [2](previous) action (Skt. *karman*)

ལས་བསྐོས་ fate

ལིངས་ hunting

ལུག་ sheep

ལུ(ག)་གུ་ lamb

ལུག་ཟླ་ sheep-month

ལུགས་ tradition

ལུང་ prophecy

1ལུས་ [1]body; [2]life

2ལུས་ (INTR) to be remaining, left; to remain

ལུས་སྟོབས་ physical strength

ལུས་མེད་པར་ completely, lit. so that there are no remains

ལུས་སྲོག་ body and life

ལེགས་ (to be) good

ལེགས་པ་ [I]good, correct; [II]good deed

ལེགས་པར་ well

ལེགས་པར་བཤད་པ་ aphorism, lit. well-said-one

ལེགས་པར་བཤད་པ་རིན་པོ་ཆེའི་གཏེར་ (PN) *A Treasury of Aphoristic Jewels*

ལེགས་བཤད་ see ལེགས་པར་བཤད་པ་

ལེན་ v2 བླངས་ v3 བླང་ v4 ལོང(ས)་ (TR) [1]to obtain; to accept; [2]to take; [3]to attract

ལེའུ་ chapter

ལོ་ year

ལོ་རྒྱུས་ account

ལོ་ཏོག་ harvest, crop

ལོ་མ་ leaf

ལོག་ (INTR) to turn

ལོང་ངམ་རྟ་རྫི་ (PN) Loṅ-ṅam-rta-rʒi

ལོང་བ་ blind

ལོངས་སྤྱོད་ v2/v3 སྤྱད་ (TR) to use

ལོན་ (INTR) to pass (of time + ABS)

ཤ

ཤ་ [1]flesh, meat; [2]body

ཤ་ཀོ་ཊ་ཀ་ a tree species (Skt. *śākhoṭaka*)

ཤ་ཁོག་ body of a slaughtered animal

ཤན་ difference

ཤམ་ཐབས་ lower garment

ཤར་ see འཆར་

ཤི་ see འཆི་

ཤིག་སྲོ་ louse and nit

ཤིང་ [1]wood; [2]tree

ཤིང་མཁན་ carpenter

ཤིང་རྟ་ chariot

ཤིང་རྟ་ཆེན་པོ་ (PN) Śiṅ-rta-čhen-po

ཤིང་ཏོག་ fruit (of trees)

ཤིང་ནགས་ forest

ཤིང་ལོ་ tree-leaf

ཤིན་ཏུ་ very

ཤུགས་རིང་ sigh

ཤུལ་ empty place

ཤེས་ (TR) [1]to know, be aware of; [2]to recognise, to realise; (MOD) to be able, capable; can; ངོ་ཤེས་ to recognise

ཤེས་པ་ intelligent

ཤེས་བྱ་ subject matter of knowledge

ཤེས་རབ་ understanding, wisdom

ཤེས་རབ་ལྡན་པ་ sage

ཤེས་རིག་ knowledge

ཤོག་ see གཤེགས་

ཤོམ་ v2 བཤམས་ v3 བཤམ་ v4 ཤོམས་ (TR) to prepare

ཤོས་ the other (of two)

ཤཱཀྱ་ཐུབ་པ་ (PN) Śākyamuni

གཤའ་མ་ righteous

གཤེ་ v2 གཤེས་ (INTR) to inveigh (against + DAT)

གཤེགས་ v4 ཤོག་ (HON for འོང་/འགྲོ་; INTR) to come; to go

གཤེགས་སྐྱོངས་ (HON) farewell ceremony

གཤོལ་ plough

བཤད་ see [2]འཆད་

བཤམ་ see ཤོམ་

བཤིག་ see [2]འཇིག་

བཤེས་གཉེན་ spiritual friend (Skt. *kalyāṇamitra*)

ས

ས་ [1]earth; [2]place; [3]ground

ས་ག་ (PN) name of a lunar mansion (Skt. *vaiśākha*)

ས་རྟ་ Earth-Horse (year)

ས་བོན་ seeds

སངས་ see འཚང་

སངས་རྒྱས་ Skt. Buddha

སད་ (INTR) to wake up; གཉིད་སད་ to wake up

སུ་ (INT) who?

སུ་བྷཱ་ཥི་ཏ་ར་ཏྣ་ནི་དྷི་ནཱ་མ་ཤཱ་སྟྲ་ (PN) *Subhāṣitaratnanidhināmaśāstra*

སུ་ཡང་ anybody, whoever

སུམ་ཅུ་དགུ་པ་ thirty-ninth

སེ་ nugget

སེ་གོལ་ snapping one's fingers

སེ་འུ་ pomegranate

སེང་གེ་ lion

སེང་སེང་ thin

སེམས་ v2 བསམས་ v3 བསམ་ v4 སོམས་ [I](TR) to think (about/of + DAT as + TERM); སྙམ་ སེམས་ to think; [II.1]mind; [2]thought; [3]heart

སེམས་ཅན་ living/sentient being

སེམས་ཅན་ཆེན་པོ་ (PN) Sems-čan-čhen-po

སེམས་ཅན་དམྱལ་བ་ hell; see དམྱལ་བ་

སེམས་ཆུང་ timid

སེམས་གསོ་ consolation

སེར་ག་ crack, fissure

སེར་པོ་ yellow

སེལ་བ་ (TR) to clean away

སོ་ tooth

སོ་སྒྲ་ whistling through the teeth

སོ་ནམ་ agriculture

སོ་བ་ unhusked barley

སོ་མ་ new

སོ་ཚིས་ housekeeping

སོ་སོ་ [1]distinct, separate; [2]everyone

སོ་སོ་ནས་ individually

སོ་སོར་ separately, individually, one after another

སོག་ see གསོག་

སོགས་ and so forth; such as, including, among others (+ DAT/ABS)

སོང་ see འགྲོ་

སོལ་བ་ charcoal

སོས་ see གསོ་

སྲན་མ་ beans

སྲས་ (HON for བུ་) son

སྲིང་མོ་ sister

སྲིད་ I(COP) 1to exist, to be; 2to be possible, to be able; II(N) dominion

སྲིད་པ་ existence

སྲིད་གསུམ་ triple world

སྲིན་པོ་ demon, ogre

སྲིན་མོ་ demoness, ogress

སྲུང་ v2 བསྲུངས་ v3 བསྲུང་ v4 སྲུངས་ (TR) to guard, to protect

སྲོག་ life

སྲོག་ཆགས་ living/animated being, animal

སླ་བ་ easy

སླད་ back part; སླད་བཞིན་པར་ behind

སླད་དུ་ (Postp) in order to (+ GEN)

སླར་ (Adv) back

སླས་ retinue

སླུ་ v2 བསླུས་ v3 བསླུ་ v4 སླུས་ (TR) to deceive, to bewitch, to delude; to conjure up

སློང་ v2 བསླངས་ v3 བསླང་ v4 སློངས་ (TR) 1to order; 2to beg

སློངས་ begging

སློབ་ v2 བསླབས་ v3 བསླབ་ v4 སློབས་ (TR) to learn

སློབ་དཔོན་ teacher

གསད་ see གསོད་

གསན་ (HON for ཉན་; TR) to hear, to listen; སྙན་གསན་ to listen

གསལ་ (INTR) to be clear; to shine

གསལ་རྒྱལ་ (PN) Gsal-rgyal (Skt. Prasenajit)

གསུང་ v2 གསུངས་ (HON for ཟེར་/སྨྲ་; TR) to speak, to say, to proclaim

གསུང་ངག་ (HON for ངག་) wording

གསུངས་ see གསུང་

གསུམ་ three

གསུམ་ཀ་ a trio, the three

གསུམ་པ་ 1third; 2a few

གསུམ་པོ་ a trio, a group of three

གསེར་ gold

གསོ་ v2 གསོས་/བསོས་ v3 བསོ་ v4 སོས་ (TR) [1]to take care; to train; [2]to nourish, to raise; [3]to restore; ངལ་གསོ་ to rest, to take a rest; སེམས་གསོ་ to console

གསོག་ v2 བསགས་ v3 བསག་ v4 སོགས་ (TR) to gather, to collect

གསོད་ v2 བསད་ v3 གསད་ v4 སོད་ (TR) to kill

གསོད་པ་ execution

གསོལ་ (HML; TR) [1]to request, to beg; [2]to speak

གསོལ་བ་ request

གསོས་ see གསོ་

བསགས་ see གསོག་

བསད་ see གསོད་

བསམ་(པ་) thought

བསམས་ see སེམས་

བསྡུ་ v2/v4 བསྡུས་ (TR) to join

བསོ་ see གསོ་

བསོད་སྙོམས་ alms

བསོད་ནམས་ virtue, merit

བསྲུང་ see སྲུང་

བསྲུངས་ see སྲུང་

བསླང་ see སློང་

བསླངས་ see སློང་

བསླབ་ see སློབ་

བསླབས་ see སློབ་

བསླུས་ see སླུ་

ཧ

ཧར་ suddenly

ཧྲུལ་བ་ tattered

ལྷ་ [1]deity; [2]lord

ལྷ་ཆེན་པོ་ (PN) Lha-čhen-po

ལྷ་མ་ཡིན་ semi-god

ལྷ་མོ་ [1]goddess; [2]queen

ལྷག་ the rest, remains

ལྷག་པར་ more

ལྷག་མ་ remnant

ལྷག་ལུས་ the rest, remains

ལྷགས་ (INTR) to come together

ལྷན་ཅིག་ཏུ་ together with

ལྷབ་ལྷུབ་ wide, flowing

ལྷམ་ shoe

ལྷུ་ minor share

ལྷུང་ see ལྷུང་

ལྷུང་བཟེད་ alms-bowl

ལྷུབ་ width

ཨ

ཨ་ཁུ་ paternal uncle

ཨ་ནེ་ aunt

ཨ་མ་ mother

ཨ་ཞང་ maternal uncle

Symbols and Abbreviations

!	incorrect form
*	reconstructed form
√	verb root
>	‘evolved into’
<	‘developed from’
Ø	zero realisation
[. . .]	omitted passage
[so]	added passage
/སྟེ་/	morpheme with changing forms
1st	first person
2nd	second person
3rd	third person
A	adjective
ABS	absolutive
ACC	accusative
Adv	adverb
AT	Amdo Tibetan
AUX	auxiliary
C	controllable
C	Čo-ne edition
CAUS	causative verb
COM	comitative
CONC	concessive
CONV	converb
COORD	coordinative
COP	copula
COR	correlative
CT	Classical Tibetan
D	Sde-dge edition

DAT	dative
DEL	delative
DEM	demonstrative
DET	determiner
DH	Dunhuang edition
DIM	diminutive
DITR	ditransitive
e.g.	for example
EL	elative
Eng.	English
ERG	ergative
EXCL	exclusive
F	feminine
fn.	footnote
FNL	final particle
FOC	focus particle
Fr.	French
GEN	genitive
GER	gerundial
Ger.	German
H	Lha-sa edition
HML	humble
HON	honorific
HT	Hor Tibetan
IMP	imperative
INCL	inclusive
INDF	indefinite
INT	interrogative
INTR	intransitive
Intrj	interjection
IPA	International Phonetic Alphabet
It.	Italian
KT	Kham Tibetan
l.	line
lit.	literal(ly)
LOC	locative
M	masculine
MOD	modal verb
N	[1]noun; [2]Snar-thaṅ edition

NC	non-controllable
NCA	non-controllable/absolutive
NEG	negation
NOM	nominative
NP	noun phrase
NUM	numeral
O	object
O_1	direct object
O_2	indirect object
OT	Old Tibetan
p.	page
P	predicative
pl	plural
PN	proper name
PROH	prohibitive
Pol.	Polish
Postp	postposition
PP	postpositional phrase
PT	Pelliot tibétain
QUOT	quotative
r	recto
REL	relative
RN	relator noun
S	subject
SG	singular
Skt.	Sanskrit
Sp.	Spanish
ST	Southern Tibetan
s.v.	sub voce
TERM	terminative
TR	transitive
U	Urga edition
V	[1]verb; [2]vowel
v	verso
v1, v2, v3, v4	verb stems
vs	versus
WAT	Western Archaic Tibetan
WIT	Western Innovative Tibetan

Abbreviations

BCRD The Buddhist Canons Research Database: http://databases.aibs.columbia.edu/

BDRC Buddhist Digital Resource Center: http://tbrc.org/

BGGB *Biography of Atīśa and His Disciple Ḥbrom-ston.* 1982, reproduced by Lokesh Chandra. New Delhi: Aditya Prakashan.

BS Bu-ston Rin-čhen-grub. 2005. *Buton's History of the Rise of Dharma*, edited by Tony Duff. Kathmandu: Padma Karpo Translation Committee.

BTC Zhang, Yisun. 1993. *Bod rgya chig mȷod čhen mo.* Beijing: Mi-rigs-dpe-skrun-khaṅ.

CDTD Bielmeier, Roland, Felix Haller, Katrin Häsler, Brigitte Huber, and Marianne Volkart, eds. 2013 (draft). *Comparative Dictionary of Tibetan Dialects.*

CDTD.V Bielmeier, Roland, Katrin Häsler, Chungda Haller, Felix Haller, Veronika Hein, Brigitte Huber, Marianne Volkart, Thomas Preiswerk, Ngawang Tsering, Manuel Widmer, and Marius Zemp. 2018. *Comparative Dictionary of Tibetan Dialects (CDTD). Volume 2: Verbs.* Berlin: De Gruyter Mouton.

GLR Bsod-nams Rgyal-mchan. 1750–60 [1368]. *Rgyal rabs gsal bayi me loṅ*, edited by Bla-ma-čhen-po Kun-dgaɣ Ɣphrin-las Rgya-mcho. Sde-dge.

Guru Ñi-sprul-drug-pa Thub-bstan Ɣod-gsal Bstan-paɣi Ñi-ma. 1992. *Rñiṅ ma čhos ɣbyuṅ.* 2 vols. Lhasa.

HJM Haribhaṭṭa, *Seṅ ge źabs ɣbriṅ paɣi skyes pa rabs kyi phreṅ pa źes bya ba* (Skt. *Haribhaṭṭajātakamālā*). D 4152, *skyes rabs*, u 1v1–197r7.

J Jäschke, Heinrich August. 1881. *A Tibetan-English Dictionary.* Reprint, New York: Dover Publications, 2003.

KDDS Herrmann, Silke. 1983. *Die tibetische Version des Papageienbuches.* Sankt Augustin: VGH-Wissenschaftsverlag.

KGBP — Ṅag-dbaṅ Grags-pa. 1972. *Dpal ldan bla ma dam pa grub paɣi khyu mčhog phyogs thams čad las rnam par rgyal baɣi spyod pa čan rǰe bcun kun dgaɣ bzaṅ poɣi rnam par thar pa ris med dad paɣi pu loṅ g.yo byed*. In *Bka' brgyud pa Hagiographies*, edited by Khams-sprul Don-brgyud-ñi-ma, 383–560. Vol. 2. Tashijong.

KhG — Dpaɣ-bo Gcug-lag Ɣphreṅ-ba. 1962. *Čhos ɣbyuṅ mkhas paɣi dgaɣ ston*, edited by Lokesh Chandra. New Delhi: International Academy of Indian Culture.

KR — Koṅ-sprul Yon-tan Rgya-mcho, and Karma Ɣphrin-las. 1997. *Koṅ sprul yon tan rgya mchoɣi rnam thar*. Chengdu.

MB — *Mǰaṅs blun źes bya baɣi mdo*. Sde-dge (D 341 *mdo sde*, a 138r5–140v7); Snar-thaṅ (N 326 *mdo sde*, sa 211r4–215r); Lha-sa (H 347 *mdo sde*, sa 222v3–227r1); Čo-ne (C 980 *mdo maṅ*, a 154v1–157r4); Urga (U 341 mdo sde, a 138r5–140v7); HL = text edition in Hahn (1996).

ML — de Jong, Jan Willem. 1959. *Mi la ras pa'i rnam thar: texte tibétain de la vie de Milarépa*. Hague: Mouton & Co.

Mvy — Ishihama, Yumiko, and Yoichi Fukuda, eds. 1989. *A New Critical Edition of the Mahāvyutpatti: Sanskrit – Tibetan – Mongolian Dictionary of Buddhist Terminology*. Tokyo: The Toyo Bunko.

Nel — Nel-pa Paṇḍita. 1987. *Nel-pa Paṇḍitas Chronik Me-tog phreṅ-ba*, edited by Helga Uebach. München: Bayerische Akademie der Wissenschaften.

Padm — Qo-rgyan Gliṅ-pa. *Gu ru padma ɣbyuṅ gnas kyi skyes rabs rnam par thar pa*. Woodblock (*apud* Schneider 2017).

SBM — Koṅ-sprul Yon-tan Rgya-mcho. 2000. *Śes bya kun khyab mǰod. The Treasury Which Is an Encyclopedia of Knowledge*, edited by Tony Duff. Bauddhanath: Padma Karpo Translation Committee.

SBRG — Ɣphags-pa Blo-gros Rgyal-mchan. 1968. "Śes bya rab tu gsal ba." In *The Complete Works of Čhos-rgyal-ɣphags-pa*, edited by Bsod-nams Rgya-mcho, 1–18. Tokyo.

SSP — Kun-dgaɣ Rgyal-mchan. 2014. *Sa skya legs bshad: die Strophen zur Lebensklugheit von Sa skya Paṇḍita Kun dga' rgyal mtshan (1182–1251)*, edited by Helmut Eimer. Wien: Arbeitskreis für tibetische und buddhistische Studien.

Tār — Tāranātha. 1965. *Dpal gyi ɣbyuṅ gnas dam paɣi čhos rin po čhe ɣphags paɣi yul du ǰi ltar dar baɣi chul gsal bar ston pa dgos ɣdod kun ɣbyuṅ*, edited by A. Schiefner *Târanâthae de doctrinae Buddhisae in India propagatione narratio*. Tōkyō: Suzuki Research Foundation.

TS — Ta-si-tu Byaṅ-čhub Rgyal-mchan. 1989. *Ta si byaṅ čhub rgyal mchan gyi bkaɣ čhems mthoṅ ba don ldan*. Lhasa.

TST	Tāranātha. 1997. "Bčom ldan ɣdas ston pa śākya thub paɣi rnam thar." In *Bčom ldan ɣdas ston pa śākya thub paɣi rnam thar*, 11–203. Xining.
VC	Vibhūticandra. *Byaṅ čhub kyi spyod pa la ɣǰug paɣi dgoṅs paɣi ɣgrel pa khyad par gsal byed.* D 3880, *dbu ma*, śa 192v6–285r7.
VOHD	Schwieger, Peter. 2009. *Tibetische Handschriften und Blockdrucke.* vol. 13. Stuttgart: Franz Steiner Verlag.
WTS	Franke, Herbert, Jens-Uwe Hartmann, and Thomas O. Höllmann, eds. 2005–. *Wörterbuch der tibetischen Schriftsprache.* München: Verlag der Bayerischen Akademie der Wissenschaften.

Bibliography

Andersen, Paul Kent. 1987. "Zero-anaphora and related phenomena in Classical Tibetan." *Studies in Language* 11(2): 279–312.

Bacot, Jacques. 1912. "L'Écriture cursive tibétaine." *Journal Asiatique* 19: 5–78.

Bacot, Jacques. 1946–8. *Grammaire du Tibétain litéraire*. 2 vols. Paris: Libraire d'Amérique et d'Orient.

Beer, Zack. 2019. "Switch-reference in the *Ye shes rgyas pa'i mdo*." *Journal of the Royal Asiatic Society* 29(2): 249–56.

Bentor, Yael. 2013. *A Classical Tibetan Reader: Selections from Renowned Works with Custom Glossaries*. Boston: Wisdom Publications.

Beyer, Stephan V. 1993. *The Classical Tibetan Language*. Delhi: Sri Satguru Publications.

Bialek, Joanna. 2018a. *Compounds and Compounding in Old Tibetan. A Corpus Based Approach*. 2 vols. Marburg: Indica et Tibetica.

Bialek, Joanna. 2018b. "The Proto-Tibetan clusters *s*L- and *s*R- and the periodisation of Old Tibetan." *Himalayan Linguistics* 17(2): 1–50. https://doi.org/10.5070/H917238831.

Bialek, Joanna. 2020a. "Old Tibetan verb morphology and semantics: An attempt at a reconstruction." *Himalayan Linguistics* 19(1): 263–346. https://doi.org/10.5070/H919145017.

Bialek, Joanna. 2020b. "Towards a standardisation of Tibetan transliteration for textual studies." *Revue d'Etudes Tibétaines* 56: 28–46.

Bialek, Joanna. 2021a. "Naming the empire: From *bod* to *Tibet*. A philologico-historical study on the origin of the polity." *Revue d'Etudes Tibétaines* 61: 339–402.

Bialek, Joanna. 2021b. "Social roots of grammar: Old Tibetan perspective on grammaticalization of kinterms." In *Crossing Boundaries. Tibetan Studies Unlimited*, edited by Diana Lange, Jarmila Ptáčková, Marion Wettstein, and Mareike Wulff, 253–88. Prague: Academia Publishing House.

Bialek, Joanna. Forthcoming. *Old Tibetan Annals: A Comprehensive Text Grammar*.

Bielmeier, Roland. 1988. "The reconstruction of the stop series and the verbal system in Tibetan." In *Languages and History in East Asia: Festschrift for Tatsuo Nishida on the Occasion of his 60th Birthday*, 15–27. Kyoto.

Bsod-nams Rgyal-mchan. 1966. *Rgyal rabs gsal ba'i me loṅ: The Clear Mirror of Royal Genealogies; Tibetan Text in Transliteration with an Introduction in English*, edited by Bronislav I. Kuznetsov. Leiden: Brill.

Cabezón, José Ignacio, and Roger R. Jackson, eds. 1996. *Tibetan Literature: Studies in Genre*. Ithaca: Snow Lion.

Csoma, Sándor Kőrösi. 1834. *A Grammar of the Tibetan Language, in English*. Calcutta: The Baptist Mission Press.

Das, Sarat Chandra. 1902. *A Tibetan-English Dictionary with Sanskrit Synonyms*. Reprint. Delhi: Motilal Banarsidass, 2000.

Das, Sarat Chandra. 1915. *An Introduction to the Grammar of the Tibetan Language: With the Texts of Situ Sum-tag, Dag-je Sal-wai Melong, and Situi Shal Lung*. Delhi: Motilal Banarsidass.

DeLancey, Scott. 2003. "Classical Tibetan." In *The Sino-Tibetan Languages*, edited by Graham Thurgood and Randy J. LaPolla, 255–69. London: Routledge.

Dotson, Brandon, and Agnieszka Helman-Ważny. 2016. *Codicology, Paleography, and Orthography of Early Tibetan Documents*. Wien: Arbeitskreis für tibetische und buddhistische Studien, Universität Wien.

Eimer, Helmut. 1986. "dByaṅs-can dga'-ba'i blo-gros' Explanation of Some Expressions from the Sa skya legs bśad." In *Vicitrakusumāñjali. Volume Presented to Richard Othon Meisezahl on the Occasion of his Eightieth Birthday*, edited by Helmut Eimer, 49–60. Bonn: Indica et Tibetica.

Francke, August Hermann, and Walter Simon. 1929. "Addenda to H.A. Jäschke, Tibetan Grammar." In *Tibetan Grammar*, edited by Heinrich August Jäschke. Berlin: Walter de Gruyter.

Garrett, Edward, and Nathan W. Hill. 2015. "Constituent order in the Tibetan noun phrase." *SOAS Working Papers in Linguistics* 17: 35–48.

Goldstein, Melvyn C. 1991. *Essentials of Modern Literary Tibetan: A Reading Course and Reference Grammar*. New Delhi: Munshiram Manoharlal Publishers.

Hackett, Paul G. 2019. *Learning Classical Tibetan: A Reader for Translating Buddhist Texts with Grammatical Annotations and Translations*. Boulder: Snow Lion.

Hahn, Michael. 1996. *Lehrbuch der klassischen tibetischen Schriftsprache*. Swisstal-Odendorf: Indica et Tibetica.

Hahn, Michael. 2003a. "Grundfragen der tibetischen Morphologie." In *Schlüssel zum Lehrbuch der klassischen tibetischen Schirftsprache und Beiträge zur tibetischen Wortkunde (Miscellanea etymologica tibetica I–VI)*, edited by Michael Hahn, 75–94. Marburg: Indica et Tibetica Verlag.

Hahn, Michael. 2003b. "On the origin and function of the particle *dag*." In *Schlüssel zum Lehrbuch der klassischen tibetischen Schriftsprache und Beiträge zur tibetischen Wortkunde (Miscellanea etymologica tibetica I–VI)*, edited by Michael Hahn, 95–104. Marburg: Indica et Tibetica Verlag.

Hahn, Michael. 2003c. *Schlüssel zum Lehrbuch der klassischen tibetischen Schriftsprache und Beiträge zur tibetischen Wortkunde (Miscellanea etymologica tibetica I-VI)*. Marburg: Indica et Tibetica.

Hahn, Michael. 2009. *Podręcznik do nauki klasycznego języka tybetańskiego*. Kraków: Wydawnictwo A.

Haller, Felix. 2009. "Switch-reference in Tibetan." *Linguistics of the Tibeto-Burman Area* 32(2): 45–70.

Harrison, Paul. 1996. "A brief history of the Tibetan bKa' 'gyur." In *Tibetan Literature: Studies in Genre*, edited by José Ignacio Cabezón and Roger R. Jackson, 70–94. Ithaca: Snow Lion.

Hill, Nathan W. 2007. "Personalpronomina in der Lebensbeschreibung des Mi la ras pa, Kapitel III." *Zentralasiatische Studien* 36: 277–87.

Hill, Nathan W. 2010a. *A Lexicon of Tibetan Verb Stems as Reported by the Grammatical Tradition*. München: Bayerische Akademie der Wissenschaften.

Hill, Nathan W. 2010b. "An overview of old Tibetan synchronic phonology." *Transactions of the Philological Society* 108(2): 110–25.

Hoffmann, Helmut. 1950. "Die Gräber der tibetischen Könige im Distrikt 'P'yoṅs-rgyas." *Nachrichten der Akademie der Wissenschaften in Göttingen Philologisch-Historische Klasse*: 1–14.

Hoffmann, Helmut. 1955. "Über ein wenig beachtetes Hilfswort zur Bezeichnung der Zukunft im Tibetischen." In *Corolla Linguistica: Festschrift Ferdinand Sommer zum 80. Geburtstag*, edited by Ferdinand Sommer and Hans Krahe, 73–9. Wiesbaden: Harrassowitz.

Jäschke, Heinrich August. 1883. *Tibetan Grammar*. London: Trübner.

Kolmaš, Josef F. 1967. "In the margin of B.I. Kuznetsov's edition of the Clear Mirror of Royal Genealogies." *Archiv orientální* 35: 467–76.

Lalou, Marcelle. 1950. *Manuel élémentaire de tibétain classique*. Paris: Adrien Maisonneuve.

Laufer, Berthold. 1916. "Loan-words in Tibetan." *T'oung Pao* 17(4/5): 403–552.

Lyovin, Anatole V. 1992. "Nominal honorific compounds in Tibetan." *Mon-Khmer Studies* 20: 45–56.

Nagano, Yasuhiko. 1997. *A Morphological Index of Classical Tibetan*. Tokyo: Seishido.

Potapova, Helen. 1997. "Semantic characteristics of the Tibetan honorific forms." *Mon-Khmer Studies* 27: 215–7.

Ryavec, Karl E. 2015. *A Historical Atlas of Tibet*. Chicago: University of Chicago Press.

Samuels, Jonathan. 2014. *Colloquial Tibetan: The Complete Course for Beginners*. London: Routledge.

Scharlipp, Wolfgang-Ekkehard, and Dieter Back. 1996. *Einführung in die tibetische Schrift*. Hamburg: Buske.

Schiefner, Anton. 1852. "Tibetische Studien I–III." *Mélanges asiatiques tirés Bulletin de l'Académie impériale des sciences des St.-Pétersbourg* 1: 324–94.

Schiefner, Anton. 1859. "Ueber eine eigenthümliche Art tibetischer Composita." *Mélanges asiatiques* 5: 12–16.

Schiefner, Anton. 1868. "Tibetische Studien: IV. Beiträge zur Casuslehre." *Mélanges asiatiques tirés Bulletin de l'Académie impériale des sciences des St.-Pétersbourg* 5: 178–94.

Schiefner, Anton. 1877. "Über Pluralbezeichnungen im Tibetischen." *Mémoires de l'académie impériale des sciences de St.-Pétersbourg* XXV(1): 5–17.

Schmidt, Isaac Jacob. 1839. *Grammatik der tibetischen Sprache*. St. Petersburg: W. Gräff.

Schneider, Johannes. 2017. "Beobachtungen zur Verwendung der tibetischen Partikel *dang*." *Zeitschrift der Deutschen Morgenländischen Gesellschaft* 167(2): 419–51.

Schneider, Johannes. 2019. "Rezepte für Räucherwerk und andere Wohlgerüche aus dem tibetischen Tanjur: Nāgarjunas **Aṣṭāpadīkṛtadhūpayoga*." *Berliner Indologische Studien* 24: 15–61.

Schwieger, Peter. 2006. *Handbuch zur Grammatik der klassischen tibetischen Schriftsprache*. Halle: International Institute for Tibetan and Buddhist Studies.

Schwieger, Peter. 2009. *Tibetische Handschriften und Blockdrucke*. Vol. 13. Stuttgart: Steiner.

Simon, Walter. 1968. "Tibetan *re* in its wider context." *Bulletin of the School of Oriental and African Studies* 31(3): 555–62.

Skal-bzang 'gyur-med. 1994. *Bod kyi brda sprod rig payi khrid rgyun rab gsal ba me loṅ. Le clair miroir: Enseignement de la grammaire tibetaine*, edited by Heather Stoddard and Nicholas Tournadre. Arvillard: Prajñā.

Sommerschuh, Christine. 2008. *Einführung in die tibetische Schriftsprache. Lehrbuch für den Unterricht und das vertiefende Selbststudium*. Norderstedt: Books on Demand.

Sørensen, Per. 1994. *The Mirror Illuminating the Royal Genealogies: Tibetan Buddhist Historiography. An Annotated Translation of the XIVth Century Tibetan Chronicle: rGyal-rabs gsal-ba'i me-long*. Wiesbaden: Harrassowitz.

Takeuchi, Tsuguhito. 2012. "Formation and transformation of old Tibetan." In *Historical Development of the Tibetan Languages*, edited by Tsuguhito Takeuchi and Norihiko Hayashi, 3–17. Kobe: Kobe University of Foreign Studies.

Takeuchi, Tsuguhito. 2015. "The function of auxiliary verbs in Tibetan predicates and their historical development." *Revue d'Etudes Tibétaines* 31: 401–15.

Taube, Manfred. 1970. "Das Suffix *-ma* in tibetischen Buchtiteln." *Mitteilungen des Instituts für Orientforschung, Deutsche Akademie der Wissenschaften zu Berlin* 16(1): 107–17.

Tournadre, Nicholas. 1991. "The rhetorical use of the Tibetan ergative." *Linguistics of the Tibeto-Burman Area* 14(1): 93–107.

Tournadre, Nicolas. 2010. "The Classical Tibetan cases and their transcategoriality: From sacred grammar to modern linguistics." *Himalayan Linguistics* 9(2): 87–125.

Tournadre, Nicolas. 2014. "The Tibetic languages and their classification." In *Trans-Himalayan Linguistics: Historical and Descriptive Linguistics of the Himalayan Area*, edited by Thomas Owen-Smith and Nathan W. Hill, 105–29. Berlin: De Gruyter.

Tournadre, Nicholas, and Sangda Dorje. 1998. *Manuel de Tibétain Standard, langue et civilisation: Bodkyi spyiskad slobdeb*. Paris: Mondes et Langue.

Uray, Géza. 1952. "A Tibetan diminutive suffix." *Acta Orientalia Academiae Scientiarum Hungaricae* 2: 183–220.

Uray, Géza. 1954. "Duplication, gemination and triplication in Tibetan." *Acta Orientalia Academiae Scientiarum Hungaricae* 4: 177–244.

van Driem, George. 2011. "Tibeto-Burman subgroups and historical grammar." *Himalayan Linguistics* 10(1): 31–9. http://escholarship.org/uc/item/2641q8vv.

Vollmann, Ralf. 2001. "Wortstruktur und Wortbildung im Tibetischen." *Grazer Linguistische Studien* 55: 93–127.

Vollmann, Ralf. 2006. "Der Wortbegriff im Tibetischen." *Grazer Linguistische Studien* 66: 75–97.

Wylie, Turrell. 1959. "A standard system of Tibetan transcription." *Harvard Journal of Asiatic Studies* 22: 261–7.

Zeisler, Bettina. 2004. *Relative Tense and Aspectual Values in Tibetan Languages: A Comparative Study*. Berlin: Mouton de Gruyter.

Index